BIOGRAPHICAL SERIES · VOLUME IV

*Bernt Julius Muus*
St. Olaf College Archives

# Bernt Julius Muus

*Founder of St. Olaf College*

## by Joseph M. Shaw

1999
*The Norwegian-American Historical Association*
NORTHFIELD · MINNESOTA

*To my daughter Betsy*

# *Preface*

St. Olaf College in Northfield, Minnesota, will on November 6, 1999, celebrate the 125th anniversary of its founding on November 6, 1874. On that occasion the Association is pleased to publish as volume four in its Biographical Series this authoritative biography, *Bernt Julius Muus: Founder of St. Olaf College*, by Joseph M. Shaw. The Reverend Bernt Julius Muus (1832–1900) arrived in Goodhue county, Minnesota, from his native Snåsa, Norway, in 1859, the same year that he had been ordained as a Lutheran minister in the Church of Norway, and became, as a commentator stated, "the dominant man in Goodhue county" until his return to Norway in 1899, where he died the following year. Muus's entire ministerial career was thus devoted to work among emigrated Norwegians.

His vocation was that of a pioneer pastor. Muus, as presented by Shaw, was an indefatigable servant of the young Norwegian Synod, the Lutheran church body organized in 1853; from his base in the Holden congregation he expanded the Synod's influence by organizing new congregations, by assisting in the erection of church edifices, by promoting the salutary benefits of a Christian education, and by defending the Synod's general mission among Norwegians in America. But Muus was also a man of independent thought and therefore in several instances dissented from the view of the majority of his pastoral colleagues on doctrinal issues; his dissent eventually led to a severance with the Synod. It was these conflicts, in particular the controversy in regard to the doctrine of predestination, that from 1889 led to a transformation of St. Olaf College, or St. Olaf's School as it was called until that year, from an academy to a four-year college. In his family life as well, Muus experienced disharmony, not entirely without personal blame, leading to the scandal of legal separation from Oline Muus, his wife of many years.

It speaks to Shaw's great merit as a scholar that he paints a credible portrait of Muus the man as well as Muus the theologian and church leader. Muus was a strong-willed person, at times even judgmental and self-righteous, and consequently there were differing opinions about him and his achievements. His pastoral concerns and devotion to his duties are obvious as is his obstinacy and unbending confidence in his own convictions.

Joseph M. Shaw is professor emeritus of religion at St. Olaf College, his alma mater, graduating in 1949; he served on the college faculty from 1957 until his retirement in 1991; he continues his service to the college as its historian. In 1974, as a part of the centennial celebrations, he published *History of St. Olaf College 1874–1974*. Shaw's scholarship, however, moves beyond his several works treating aspects of the history of the college. Among his many publications are *Pulpit Under the Sky* (1955), a biography of Hans Nielsen Hauge, *If God Be for Us* (1966), the two volume work *Our New Testament Heritage* (1968–1969), *The Pilgrim People of God* (1990), and two co-authored works on Christian humanism, *Readings in Christian Humanism* (1982) and *The Case for Christian Humanism* (1991). He has also written *Dear Old Hill* (1992) and in 1997 the history of the St. Olaf College choir.

Mary R. Hove, my assistant in the editorial work for nearly twenty years, is responsible for the index and she assisted in preparing the manuscript for publication. Her dedication and expertise remain major resources in the Association's publication program. An accelerated publication schedule required an extra effort. Ruth H. Crane, assistant secretary, did much to move the work forward in an expeditious manner, making it possible to meet set deadlines.

Odd S. Lovoll
*St. Olaf College*
*University of Oslo*

# Acknowledgments

Preparation of the biography of Bernt Julius Muus was supported in part by two summer grants from the Minnesota Private College Research Foundation with funds provided by the Blandin Foundation of Grand Rapids, Minnesota. I thank the foundations for their aid. Sandra Mueller, grant coordinator, and Chandra Mehrotra, program evaluator, gave courteous assistance at every turn in implementing the project. The Blandin funds enabled me to secure the services of student research assistants Kristin Johnson and Liv Zempel of St. Olaf College.

My thanks to the Ella and Kaare Nygaard Foundation for a grant to conduct research on portions of the Bernt Julius Muus biography and for extending the grant an additional six months to allow completion of the project. St. Olaf College President Mark U. Edwards, Jr., who serves as President of the Nygaard Foundation, took personal interest in the project and offered his encouragement.

St. Olaf College through former President Melvin D. George and President Mark U. Edwards, Jr. has provided office space, equipment, and access to library, archives, computer, and secretarial services. Jody Greenslade, at one time secretary for the Department of Religion, assisted me in organizing the early chapters of the book. I thank her and the Department for their assistance. Personnel at the Academic Computing Center have also been generous with their time and skills.

Here I express appreciation for the opportunity to discuss the career of Bernt Julius Muus with his great-grandsons, Bernt Julius "B. J." Muus and Herman "Ham" Muus, and their mother, Mrs. Herman Ingebrigt (Gladys) Muus. In extending greetings to them and to other Muus family members and relatives, I am happy to state that it has been a privilege to study the life and contributions of their worthy ancestor. I am aware that further information about Pastor Bernt Julius Muus is in the possession of family members whom I did not manage to interview.

Special thanks to Professor Odd Lovoll, editor of the Norwegian-American Historical Association, and his capable assistant, Mary Hove, for friendly collegiality in the process of editing the manuscript. I also express appreciation for the linguistic and historical wisdom of Lloyd Hustvedt, professor emeritus of Norwegian and secretary of the Association. It is a pleasure to acknowledge the expertise of Joan Olson and Gary DeKrey, St. Olaf archivists, and of Forrest Brown, archivist for the Norwegian-American Historical Association, who graciously helped me locate needed materials.

Duane Fenstermann, former archivist at Luther College, Decorah, Iowa, gave generously of his time in making available copies of the correspondence between Bernt Julius Muus and Norwegian Synod pastors H. A. Preus, Laur. Larsen, and U. V. Koren. Rachel Vagts, current archivist at Luther College, has also been helpful in responding to requests. In Decorah I had profitable conferences regarding Muus and the Norwegian Synod with Dr. Leigh Jordahl and the Reverend John Victor Halvorson.

Professor Todd W. Nichol of the Luther Seminary faculty, St. Paul, Minnesota, helped me on several historical matters. Director Bruce Eldevik of the Luther Seminary Library, St. Paul, Minnesota, located and sent needed documents. Paul Daniels and Liddy J. Howard of the Evangelical Lutheran Church in

America Region 3 Archives, located at Luther Seminary, provided information about some of Muus's mission churches. My inquiries to the Goodhue County Historical Society always brought useful responses from Heather Craig, Librarian and Archivist. Susan Garwood-DeLong, director of the Northfield Historical Society, assisted in locating illustrations. Thanks to these friends for their assistance.

The problem of reading the handwriting of Muus and his correspondents was solved by Solveig Steendal, who transcribed the letters into readable typescript. My thanks to Ms. Steendal for this vital service. To Elise and Phillip Sanguinetti of Anniston, Alabama, I express the gratitude of myself and my wife for warm hospitality accorded us when we traveled to Alabama to visit Fruithurst and the grave of Oline Muus. Elise, a writer, is the granddaughter of Professor H. T. Ytterboe and daughter of Edel Ytterboe Ayers, whose observations about Mrs. Muus I have cited in this book.

Thanks to Dr. Eugene L. Fevold, professor emeritus of church history at Luther Seminary, St. Paul, Minnesota, for collegial generosity in giving me permission to use his rich collection of notations on the life and work of Bernt Julius Muus. Earlier in his career Dr. Fevold had planned to write a dissertation on Muus, but decided on a different topic for his doctoral studies. Another instance of receiving significant help in research was realized through the courtesy of Lars Kindem of Burnsville, Minnesota, who made it possible for me to obtain copies of Goodhue and Hennepin County court records relative to suits filed by Mrs. Oline Muus against Bernt J. Muus. I thank Mr. Kindem for access to these important documents and for useful conversations about the Muuses' separation.

Here I also express gratitude to Kathryn Ericson of Cannon Falls, Minnesota, author of an excellent article on the Muus vs. Muus case. Ms. Ericson also made available additional information and documents pertinent to the Muus story. My thanks to

Clint Sathrum, architect, who drew the maps that appear in the early chapters.

A number of pastors and lay persons provided information about southern Minnesota churches founded or served by Pastor Muus. The Reverend Michael J. Lockerby, pastor of Holden and Dale congregations, made available the invaluable Holden ministerial books and let me visit the parsonage in which Pastor Muus and his family once lived. The late Reverend Arthur Thorson and his wife Marcella accompanied me on a visit to churches and farms in the Holden area. Thorson had served as pastor at Holden for 24 years. I enjoyed conversations about Holden history with Mrs. Marie Voxland, Holden historian. Lloyd Voxland took me on a tour of churches around Holden once served by Muus. The Reverend Donald L. Berg shared his historical knowledge of Muus's ministry in the area and supplied copies of key periodical articles from Muus's time.

The Reverend Charles Espe of New Richland, Minnesota, provided historical information about Pastor Muus's ministry at Le Sueur River Lutheran Church, and the Reverend Allan Tveite of Waseca, Minnesota, did the same with respect to North Waseca Lutheran Church. In New London, Minnesota, Henry Odland and Orlynn Mankell were my guides to visit Crow River and Norway Lake churches, served by Pastor Muus in the 1860s, and informed me of the histories of these and other congregations. The Reverend Roger Hanson of Madelia, Minnesota, helped me acquire information about Linden Lutheran Church in Brown county and Rosendale Lutheran Church in Watonwan county, both served by Pastor Muus at one time. My thanks to these friends for their assistance.

A study trip to Snåsa, Norway, Muus's birthplace, was facilitated by a travel grant from the Norwegian Royal Ministry of Foreign Affairs. At the university in Trondheim I met with Professor Jørn Sandnes whose personal knowledge of Snåsa history and professional publications about the Snåsa area increased my understanding of the Muus family's history. I am also grateful for his informative comments regarding B. J. Muus's education.

In Snåsa, musicians Marti Kveli and Steinar Dahl put me in touch with Terji Sundli, cultural secretary for the municipality, and Arve Hjelde, school adviser and director, who gave me an informative tour of the historic Snåsa church, its graveyard, and the parsonage in which B. J. Muus was born. Mr. Sundli gave me a valuable book on the cultural history of Snåsa. During the Snåsa visit I enjoyed the hospitality of Per Magne Kippe, his wife Grethe, and their sons, Vegar, Haakon, and Erlend, the oldest. Erlend and Vegar are among many Snåsa young people who have attended St. Olaf College.

Additional Snåsa hospitality was shown me by Joralf Gjerstad, local historian, and Dr. Olgeir Haug, Snåsa physician. In Dr. Haug's car we made two extensive tours of Snåsa and environs, including Krogsgaarden, the Muus family farm, and at a distance east of Snåsa, Megar at Imsdalen where, through Mr. Gjerstad's initiative, a bell tower and outdoor chapel have been built on the site of an ancient church. Each year on July 29 a worship service is held at the place to commemorate the anniversary of the death of St. Olaf. The tour also included a stop at Olaf's spring.

My wife, Mary Virginia, and my daughters, Nancy, Betsy, Margaret, and Mary, have given friendly support to the preparation of this book. A gift of art work by my son-in-law, Paul A. Carew, provided the inspiration for the dust jacket. I am pleased to dedicate this book to my daughter Betsy, Smith College graduate and history major who has followed the progress on the Muus study with interest and encouragement and who traveled to Norway with me the summer I visited Snåsa. When we were in Trondheim, we visited the Nidaros Cathedral and spent some moments at the grave of Bernt Julius Muus.

Joseph M. Shaw
*St. Olaf College*

# Table of Contents

# Bernt Julius Muus

Founder of St. Olaf College

# One

## Bernt Julius Muus from Snåsa

Bernt Julius Muus was born in Snåsa, Norway, on March 15, 1832. According to his own account, his birth took place in the "blue room" on the second floor of Vinje *prestegård*, the parsonage for the Snåsa parish, a large two-story residence with three wings. This imposing house is about a two-minute walk from the historic Snåsa church, standing directly in the line of sight as one leaves the church by the main door.[1] Bernt Julius was baptized in the Snåsa church on April 19, 1832. His baptism is recorded in the Snåsa parish register in the handwriting of his grandfather, the Reverend Jens Rynning, pastor for the Snåsa parish and presumably the one who baptized his grandson.[2]

The parents of Bernt Julius Muus were Ingebrigt Muus and Birgitte Magdalena Rynning. They were then living at Krogs-gaarden, the Muus family farm which lay close to the church and the parsonage. Since Birgitte Magdalena was the daughter of the pastor, it seems probable that, as the time approached when she and Ingebrigt would welcome their first child into the world, the mother-to-be would be brought to the spacious parsonage nearby where she could be under the loving care of her mother, Severine Cathrine Steen Rynning.

Jens Rynning was the son of a public official in the Tromsø area.

3

*Vinje Parsonage, Snåsa, Norway. Birthplace of Bernt Julius Muus*
St. Olaf College Archives

He attended the Latin School in Trondheim, studied theology, was a teacher in Trondheim and a private tutor in the home of a government administrator, served as pastor in Ringsaker for about twenty years, and was appointed pastor in Snåsa in 1824.[3] Rynning's daughter, Birgitte Magdalena, mother of Bernt Julius Muus, was born in 1814.

On his father's side, Bernt Julius as the son of Ingebrigt Muus belonged to an old, widespread family with roots in Denmark and Norway. His ancestors sought careers in many different fields, some in the military and a number of them in the ministry. For several generations the Snåsa parish was served by pastors bearing the Muus name.[4]

"The Muus family can trace its roots back to the year 1642," declared a headline in the Norwegian regional newspaper *Trønder-Avisa* on June 17, 1974. The occasion for a story about the Muus family was a wreath-laying ceremony at the grave of Bernt Julius Muus on the grounds of the Nidaros Cathedral in Trondheim as part of the celebration of the 100th anniversary of the founding of St. Olaf College. In observance of the Centennial an inscription was added to the gravestone identifying Bernt Julius Muus as the

"FOUNDER OF ST. OLAF COLLEGE." Representing St. Olaf at the ceremony was the college president, Sidney A. Rand. Representing the descendants of Pastor Muus and placing the wreath on the grave was Bernt Julius Muus "the younger," the great-grandson of the Reverend B. J. Muus and a graduate of St. Olaf College, Class of 1949.[5]

The reference to 1642 in the newspaper story is explained by the fact that in that year the ancestor was born who first brought the Muus name to Snåsa, Magister Niels Muus. Niels Muus served as the pastor in Snåsa from 1695 until very close to his death at age ninety-five in 1737. He stubbornly insisted on continuing his pastoral service even after his son and grandson had taken over those duties in the Snåsa parish.

On the second Sunday after Epiphany in 1736, the year before Niels Muus died, a memorable worship service took place in the Snåsa church. At the baptism of Petter Johan Muus, great-grandson of Niels Muus, three generations of Muus pastors participated. Niels Muus was a sponsor for the little boy being baptized; Pastor Peder Muus, the grandfather, performed the sacrament of baptism; and the boy's father, Pastor Paul Muus, preached the sermon.[6]

This episode and a number of other colorful stories about Magister Niels Muus appear in an invaluable family history titled *Niels Muus's æt: Muus-slegten i Snaasa 1642–1942* (Niels Muus's descendants: the Muus family in Snåsa). The principal author of this volume is Bernt Julius Muus himself. It can be said that he was the foremost historian of the branch of the family stemming from Niels Muus. The first edition of *Niels Muus's æt* was printed in 1890, then revised and re-issued by B. J. Muus in 1897. A descendant, Alfred Muus of Snåsa, prepared a new edition that extended the family history forward to the year 1942. Bernt Julius also wrote *Jens Rynnings æt*, a book about the family of his maternal grandfather.

Roots of the larger Muus family can be traced farther back

than 1642, the year of Niels Muus's birth. There are signs of the Muus family in Denmark in the sixteenth century. During the Danish-Norwegian union, movement between the two countries was common. In fact, "Muus" is most likely a Danish not a Norwegian name. A certain Laurids Muus was mayor of Varberg, Denmark, in about 1550.[7] Two generations later a second Laurids, Laurids Nielsen Muus, was also mayor in Varberg. His son, Niels Lauridsson Muus (1613–1685), became the parish pastor in Trogstad, Norway, and thus the progenitor of the Trogstad Muus relatives.[8]

The linkage from Denmark to Norway that leads eventually to Bernt Julius Muus was made through a Rasmus Muus, presumably an older brother of Laurids Nielsen Muus. Rasmus married a woman named Bente with whom he had a son, also named Niels. This man, Niels Rasmusson Muus, became a district judge (*sorenskriver*) in Aker and in Hedmark, Norway. It is through him that the Muus family line extends to Magister Niels Muus and the branches of the family found in Snåsa, Hedmark, and Oslo in Norway, and in Denmark, France, Germany, and the United States.

Niels Rasmusson Muus with his first wife, Elisabeth Henriksdatter, had a daughter, Bente Nielsdatter Muus, who married Peder Olufsson (or Olufsen), a farmer's son and deputy to his father-in-law, the district judge. Serving on behalf of and with the authorization of the judge, Peder Olufsson was himself often called *sorenskriver* and, being married into the Muus family, even had the name Muus ascribed to him.[9]

Peder Olufsson and Bente Nielsdatter Muus became the parents of Niels Pedersson Muus, born December 23, 1642, in Vang near Hamar, Norway. This is the renowned Magister Niels Muus whom Bernt Julius Muus regarded as the key Muus ancestor and whose name he placed in the title of his book on the family's history. As did others of that time, Niels took the name of that parent who was of the more cultured background, namely his mother,

*Magister Niels Muus*
From Bernt Julius Muus and Alfred Muus,
*Niels Muus's aet*

Bente Nielsdatter Muus, whose father held the respected position of district judge.[10]

One learns a number of things about Bernt Julius Muus from a somewhat closer look at four important ancestors: Niels Muus, Jens Rynning, B. J. Muus's grandfather on his mother's side, Ole Rynning, his uncle, and Ingebrigt Muus, his father. Certain qualities of strength, independence, and foresight from these four carried over to the young man who left Norway in 1859 to serve his fellow Norwegians in America.

Why was Niels Muus invariably called "Magister Niels Muus" or "Mester Niels"? The first and most obvious answer is that while he was at the university in Copenhagen preparing for his theological examination he also earned the "magistergrad," an advanced university degree. Secondly, it is known that Niels

7

Muus himself always placed the title "Magister" before his name, and thirdly, his descendants consistently employed the designation. Bernt Julius Muus relates how Paul Muus, his grandfather's brother, always spoke of "Mester" Niels, never "the pastor," when he told the young Bernt Julius stories about the ancestor.[11] The practice has continued among Snåsa people and others who become interested in the life of Niels Muus. He is still identified as "Magister Niels."

Stories about the fascinating Niels Muus could easily become a lengthy and entertaining excursus. A few facts and a couple of anecdotes must suffice to show his significance in the Muus family story. Peder Olufsson died in 1660 when his son Niels was eighteen years old. When his mother remarried, Niels left home and made his way to Roskilde, Denmark, where an aunt and her pastor husband lived. There Niels was befriended by a young woman who later become his wife, Maria Johansdatter Duenkircken, and by Maria's aunt, the director of a Protestant nunnery in Roskilde. Maria and her aunt arranged for Niels to enter the Roskilde Latin School where he made excellent progress.[12]

During this stage of his education, Niels worked as an assistant to the regular sexton in Gliim church, not far from Roskilde. An old church record book contains a list of the various assistants who served Gliim church. Among them was Niels Muus, who entered his name as "Nicolaus Musenius Norwegus" followed by the date, 1673.[13]

In 1674 Niels Muus completed the course at the Roskilde Latin School and took up theological studies at Copenhagen's university where, as noted, he also took the "Magister" degree. After two years as an assistant pastor in Bremerholm congregation in Copenhagen, he served as pastor aboard a ship during the war between Denmark-Norway and Sweden.

King Christian V himself was on the same ship, it is told. When a ferocious storm arose, Pastor Niels in the royal presence offered an intensely fervent prayer for deliverance. After the storm had abated, the king expressed his gratitude for the efficacious prayer by offering to fulfill whatever request Niels would make. Niels then asked for an assignment on land, whereupon he became an army chaplain. Another version of the story has Niels explaining to the king that he was tired of the turbulent life on the sea and would like a quiet pastorate. To that the king responded, "Then it must be in Norway."[14]

After further military service during the 1670s, Niels Muus was appointed by King Christian V to the position of chaplain in the cathedral church in Trondheim in the year 1680. The year before taking the new assignment Niels married Maria Johansdatter Duenkircken in Roskilde. Once in his position in Trondheim, he was soon embroiled in a lawsuit involving the dean of the cathedral, Ole Jacobsen Borchman, the bishop, Dr. Peder Krog, and himself. Muus had complained that during a communion service when the wine supply ran out and more wine had been obtained in haste, Dean Borchman had failed to consecrate the additional wine before distributing it. The bishop sided with Muus, but when the case eventually went before the highest court, Borchman won, the Bishop was fined, and Muus lost his position in the cathedral church. One report claims that Muus's dismissal was hastened by the fact that during a heated argument with Borchman, Muus had grabbed the dean's beard. In any event, Niels Muus left the Trondheim position in 1693.[15]

During the thirteen or so years that Muus was chaplain in Trondheim he had already begun the kind of non-pastoral work that was part of his fame, the energetic clearing of land for cultivation. He called one of his properties Roe-Muuslien and another Tempelvolden.[16] This interest in the outdoor life would continue and increase when Niels assumed his next church position. The king appointed him to the Snåsa call in 1695, and thus began Niels Muus's extraordinarily long ministry in Snåsa and vicinity. There he remained, eventually being named pastor emeritus, until his death in 1737.

Writing about Niels Muus on the threshold of his tenure as parish priest in Snåsa, the Norwegian historian Jørn Sandnes states, "At this time he was not a young man, but he was still astonishingly full of vitality and drive. He never thought of settling down to rest in his later years but threw himself into a series of different tasks."[17] Those activities were so frequently related to clearing land, buying property, managing farms, and starting sawmills that reports began to circulate, not surprisingly, that Muus was neglecting the clerical duties expected of a pastor.

Indeed, so the story goes, the bishop himself became suspicious that the Snåsa pastor was not tending to the spiritual needs of his flock. To find out for himself, the bishop showed up unannounced at the Snåsa parsonage late one Saturday night. Sure enough, Magister Niels was nowhere to be seen; he was up at one of his favorite sites in the country, Hylla, which he had cleared for farming. During the night his wife Maria sent a message to Niels about the situation; Maria also had the foresight to send Muus's clerical vestments with the messenger.

The next morning the bishop went to the Snåsa church, and seeing no pastor on hand, allowed the worship service to commence. When the time came for the liturgical part of the service, which the pastor was expected to lead, suddenly Magister Niels stepped up before the altar in full vestments and calmly intoned the liturgy, ignoring the presence of the bishop. Then he mounted the pulpit and delivered a very good sermon during which he managed to slip in the comment: "It takes a good cat to catch an old mouse."[18]

The time came, unfortunately, when someone *did* catch the old mouse. During the Great Nordic War the Swedish military forces near the border to the east of Snåsa surmised that information about their movements was being forwarded to Norwegian authorities by the wily old priest in Snåsa, and they were right. One autumn morning in 1718 a Swedish patrol came to Hylla and took the seventy-six-year-old Magister Niels captive and transferred him to Salaberget, eighteen miles from Stockholm, where he was held prisoner until April 1719. Then he was given travel money and allowed to return to Snåsa.[19]

In addition to having to endure the hardships connected with his capture and imprisonment, Niels suffered heavy financial losses owing to the plundering of his possessions by the Swedes during his absence. But those circumstances only fired Niels's determination to take up his labors again with renewed zeal, busying himself with his sawmills and farms.[20]

In his book *Niels Muus's æt*, B. J. Muus presents materials about his ancestor assembled from various sources, but refrains from offering his own thoughts about the colorful Magister Niels. Still, one gets the impression that Bernt Julius Muus admired Niels and enjoyed passing along the entertaining stories about him. In his own pastoral ministry Bernt Julius would focus much more seriously on the spiritual and theological duties of a pastor, but like Niels, he would also display an independent spirit in standing up to ecclesiastical authorities, expending great physical energy in carrying out his pastoral calling, and gaining a reputation for fearless determination in achieving his goals. Along with the energy and boldness, Bernt Julius, like his ancestor Niels, also applied occasional humor to his tasks.

The line of descent from Niels Muus to Bernt Julius Muus goes through two pastors, Peder Johan Muus (1682–1750) and his son Paul Muus (1708–1766), two military officers, Lieutenant Petter Johan Muus (1763–1813) and Lieutenant Broder Nicolai Muus (1776–1819), and a successful country merchant, Ingebrigt Muus (1805–1882), the father of Bernt Julius Muus. Through his mother Bernt Julius Muus was a descendant of the Rynning family. In 1831 Ingebrigt married Birgitte Magdalena Rynning (1814–1833), the daughter of the Snåsa pastor Jens Rynning (1778–1857).

Jens Rynning is significant in the story of Bernt Julius Muus for two obvious reasons: he was an important figure in the succession of pastors who served the Snåsa parish, and he was Muus's grandfather. The latter fact looms especially important because Muus's mother, Birgitte, died in November of 1833, twenty months after Bernt Julius was born, and thereafter Bernt lived

11

*Jens Rynning*
From Kaare Granøyen Rogstad, *Fest-skrift til Snåsa*

with his grandparents, Pastor Jens Rynning and his wife, Severine Cathrine Steen.[21]

Bernt Julius characterized the Rynnings as "my dear grandparents," implying that with them he knew the security of a close family circle. His relationship with the grandfather seems to have been a healthy and affectionate one even though Pastor Rynning was known as an austere, formal man. Historians tell of Jens Rynning's several abilities, his efforts to improve agricultural practices in the Snåsa area, his recognized scholarship, his service as the first mayor of Snåsa, his interest in new roads, broader schooling opportunities, and a better organized postal service, but they also report that in personality he was aloof and unyielding. He was an aristocrat who, apart from matters related to agriculture, had little to do with the people of Snåsa even though he was their pastor.

Nevertheless, in his own way he worked to raise living standards through his close knowledge of farming techniques. He was literally what was called in the eighteenth century a "potato priest." He actually gave expert advice, sometimes from the pulpit, about effective methods for increasing potato production and showed the way by his own example. He taught the farmers about crop rotation and how to drain soil that had too much acidity.[22] He did a great deal of writing, winning a prize for one of his articles, holding membership in the Royal Norwegian Scholars' Society, to which he contributed a manuscript on Snåsa history, and writing for the newspaper *Morgenbladet*.[23]

Jens Rynning's many talents did not exactly burnish his role as pastor, however. He was said to have little gift for preaching. He had an eccentric way of making entries in the official pastoral record books, filling the available space with gratuitous notations. He was criticized for being slipshod in handling the accounts for the schools and the needy. Bishop Peter Olivarius Bugge complained of Rynning's "habitual obstinacy" and laid a hefty fine on him, though it was considerably reduced the following year by a royal resolution.[24]

Like many other pastors of his time, Jens Rynning was opposed to emigration, but history has magnified his attitude because his son Ole Rynning not only went to America but became a famous figure in the cause of Norwegian emigration. Ole Rynning's story, including his writing of the book that he sent back to Norway, will be summarized later.

Examples of Pastor Rynning's anti-emigration views may be gleaned from a letter he published in the Norwegian newspaper *Morgenbladet* in the fall of 1839, a year after his son had perished in America. He had received a curious letter from one Hans Barlien, writing from Missouri, who sent a few vague lines about "your son's fate" but devoted the rest of the letter to instructions for traveling to America and acquiring land in Missouri. Pastor Rynning had read enough about America not to be taken in by Barlien's overstated claims. In fact, Rynning referred to "my son's book" to correct misinformation in the Barlien letter. He was skeptical about the picture of contentment and peace to be found in America, being well aware that the slave traffic and human rights were on a collision course. "It seems as if a struggle of life and death awaits those regions," he wrote. For these and several other reasons he appealed to his readers: "Therefore, dear country-men, do not let yourselves be charmed by sweet expectations of leisure in America. Working under the hot sun tires one more than it does in our cold air, and yet you have to exert yourselves more over there than here."[25]

If Illinois was unhealthy for Norwegians, Missouri and its low swamps would be even more dangerous, he wrote. It is best to obey God and remain in the land where God gave us life. The only advantage for Norwegians in America, Rynning noted dryly, is that over there they can eat wheat bread while at home it is flat bread.[26] In one part of the letter Rynning compares conditions in Norway and North America. The items included are serious but a few are unintentionally amusing. To take a few examples, Norway has freedom from land taxes, better quality of air, no snakes, the essential human rights, easier access to the sea, an abundance of building materials, civil peace, and a normal ratio between the sexes. By contrast, in North America one must pay land taxes, breathe unhealthy air, put up with a great number of snakes, en-dure conditions of slavery in many states, go long distances to a river or the sea, have difficulty obtaining logs and stones for building, live in uncertainty regarding peaceful relations with others, and accept a life of single blessedness since most of the 150,000 [sic] people who immigrate each year are males.[27]

It was in the household headed by this gifted, unconventional, anti-emigration minister that Bernt Julius Muus lived from 1833 until 1842 when he was enrolled in the Latin School in Trondheim. What Bernt Julius would have seen in his grandfather was the model of a scholarly, versatile pastor, though not one whose inter-ests centered in the Bible, preaching, and pastoral care. Rather, he would have seen in action a parish pastor whose concept of ministerial service embraced a wide range of practical and secular matters affecting the community's welfare. Although only a small boy at the time, Bernt Julius would have heard adults talking about the lure and dangers of America, and would have been aware to some extent of the comings and goings of the oldest son in the Rynning family, his uncle Ole Rynning.

Born in 1809, Ole Rynning had a short but immensely meaningful career. He traveled to America in 1837 on the Norwegian ship *Ægir*, being one of only two persons aboard who did not belong to the peasant class.[28] Ole became the leader of a group of immigrants trying to establish a settlement at Beaver Creek in Illinois. The site was a poor choice because of the swampy quality of the land. Most of the settlers became sick with malaria and died. Ole did his best to help and encourage them but he too became seriously ill. During the winter of 1837–1838, despite illness, he managed to write a small book with detailed information about America. His friend Ansten Nattestad took the manuscript of the book with him back to Norway in the spring of 1838 and had it published in Christiania (now Oslo) that same year.

The book, a slim volume of fewer than forty pages, was titled *True Account of America for the Information and Help of Peasant and Commoner*.[29] Meanwhile, Ole's health had improved for a short time so that he was able to work on the Illinois Canal, but he became sick again and died in the fall of 1838, unaware of the fame that would gather about his name, principally because of the remarkable influence of this book.

Ole Rynning showed much promise as a young man. He attended the university in Oslo, where he pursued theological studies. During his student years a vigorous literary conflict was raging between Henrik Wergeland, the famous poet and champion of the common people who agitated vigorously for full Norwegian independence, and another well-known poet, Johan Sebastian Welhaven, who with his followers formed a group called the Intelligence Party. Their taste in poetry as well as in politics

15

was more refined and aristocratic than that of Wergeland's Patriots, with a less bombastic sort of patriotism.[30] "In that conflict there can be no doubt that Rynning stood on Wergeland's side, because Rynning was a friend of the people, a spokesman for the poor and downtrodden just as much as Wergeland was."[31]

Whether Rynning and Wergeland were personal friends is not known, but it is clear that Rynning belonged to the student circle dominated by the fiery and popular Wergeland. In keeping with his insistence that Norwegians should take pride in their native cultural values, Wergeland became "the Father of the Day," that is, the man who initiated the first celebrations of Norway's Constitution Day, May 17, "Syttende Mai."[32] On that festive day Norwegian patriotism expresses itself in bursts of flags, parades, parties, and speeches.

In addition to sharing Wergeland's patriotic zeal for Norway, Ole Rynning also espoused the cause of the ordinary people, especially the poor and the oppressed. Ansten Nattestad, the friend who was with Ole at the ill-fated settlement in Illinois and who brought the manuscript of *True Account of America* back to Norway, said this about Rynning's view of emigration: "Nothing could shake his belief that America would become a place of refuge for the masses of people in Europe who toiled under the burdens of poverty."[33]

But the two university contemporaries, Rynning and Wergeland, had different attitudes toward emigration. Such Norwegian romantics as Wergeland and Bjørnson were cool about the rush to America. In their view, the best course was for people to stay in Norway and participate in the nation's rebirth.[34] Nevertheless, Ole Rynning not only went to America himself but strongly influenced subsequent emigration by his book.

As to Ole's personal decision to leave for America in 1837, various factors are known but there is not full certainty as to how they are to be weighed. Bernt Julius Muus shed some light on the matter in a communication to Rasmus B. Anderson, the author of *First Chapter of Norwegian Immigration, 1821–1840*, first published in 1895. In the book Anderson quotes the following from Muus about the cause of Ole Rynning's emigration: "I do not know it [the cause] positively, but what I have been able to learn from the family is that his parents, and particularly his mother, desired that Ole should study theology. He had no taste for it. On the other hand he had made a contract with my father, who lived on the farm joining the parsonage, to buy from him a large marsh, which he was going to cultivate. He was to have this marsh and two small farms belonging to the cottagers for 400 dollars (Norwegian money). As he was unable to raise this money he went to America."[35]

The lack of money to buy the marsh seems credible as a factor in influencing Rynning to leave for America. Snåsa's local history points to another possible reason, a break with his father over Ole's engagement to the daughter of a "husmann," a landless peasant. According to this account Ole's conservative father, the clergyman Rynning, was displeased by the fact that in 1835 Ole and a group of patriotic young people had raised a large memorial stone near the parsonage and inscribed on it the legend "17de mai." After that, and the engagement to a young woman of a lower class, "father and son no longer walked together."[36]

There would be a certain romantic satisfaction in holding that Ole Rynning's zeal for America was what stirred Bernt Julius Muus to emigrate, but such a claim cannot be demonstrated. The fact remains, nonetheless, that Ole Rynning's book was avidly read and digested in many parts of Norway, including the Snåsa parish. There is a first-person account of how the book was received in Snåsa before the news arrived of Ole's tragic death. An eyewitness is quoted as saying: "For a time I believed that half of the population of Snåsa had lost their senses. Nothing else was spoken of than the land which flows with milk and honey. Our minister, Ole Rynning's father, tried to stop the fever. Even from the pulpit he urged the people to be discreet and described the hardships of the voyage and the cruelty of the American savage in most forbidding colors."[37]

It is not unlikely that Bernt Julius Muus, age six, was present in the Snåsa church when the pastor, his grandfather, spoke out against emigration. One can imagine that a bright and observant boy living in the parsonage would have been caught up in the stir created in Snåsa, first by the enthusiastic reception of Ole Rynning's book and then by the mournful news that the pastor's son had met his death in Illinois in the fall of 1838.

On the other hand, it seems prudent not to speculate too much on the impact of Ole Rynning's emigration on Bernt Julius Muus, since the information Muus sent to Rasmus B. Anderson seems to indicate gaps in what he knew of his uncle's story. Bernt Julius was not certain about the cause of Ole's emigration, nor did he know the date of Ole's death.[38] Still, he did grow up in a household and a community where the name of Ole Rynning was known and respected.

In the few years before he left for America in 1837, Ole Rynning became known and loved in Snåsa as a warmhearted and gifted man of the people, a champion of justice and friend of the poor. He established a school for talented youth in the Vinje parsonage and served as its first teacher. The same observer who had told of how Ole's America book was received in Snåsa and how stunned the community was to learn of his death characterized Ole as "their favorite, 'han Ola,' who had not an enemy, but a multitude of friends who looked up to him as to a higher being, equipped with all those accomplishments that call forth the high esteem and trust of his fellow citizens."[39]

The idea of traveling to America to be of service to his countrymen was a concept familiar to the mind of the young Bernt Julius Muus, whether inspired directly by Ole Rynning's example or not. As events unfolded, just as Ole Rynning had been zealous for the enlightenment and well-being of the common people, so Bernt Julius Muus offered his services to the church to serve the ordinary folk who made up the immigrant constituency in America. Moreover, just as Ole tutored promising young persons in Snåsa, so in time Bernt Julius would establish a school in

*Ingebrigt Muus*
From Bernt Julius Muus and Alfred Muus,
*Niels Muus's aet*

Minnesota designed to offer a higher education to the children of immigrant farmers and other working people.

The father of Bernt Julius Muus was Ingebrigt Brodersen Muus (1805–1882), successful merchant and owner of the prosperous family farm, Krogsgaarden, originally called Krossgaarden. With his first wife, Birgitte Magdalena Rynning (1814–1833), whom he married in 1831, Ingebrigt Muus had two children, Bernt Julius, born March 15, 1832, and a daughter, given her mother's name, Birgitte Magdalena, born October 31, 1833. Ingebrigt's first wife died November 9, 1833, only nineteen years of age. He married again October 5, 1840, taking as his wife Kirsten Elisabeth Moe (1817–1913). From the second marriage were born seven children, four girls and three boys, Bernt Julius's half-sisters and half-brothers.[40]

19

As a young man starting out in business Ingebrigt would travel northward to sell goods from Snåsa, especially homespun cloth and butter, and buy herring. In 1831 he secured a trading license and became the leading merchant in the entire township, for several years without any competition. When the pastor and the sheriff made their two yearly trips up to a rural region called Li, Ingebrigt Muus went along, bought goods there and sold them in Trondheim.

Ingebrigt also ran a country store at his farm where he sold the usual sort of merchandise that people needed. Though not much of a drinking man himself, he sold liquor from his store. It is said that many of the women in the district operated secret stills and sold their brandy to merchant Muus to make a little spending money. Unknowing, their husbands would drop by Krogsgaarden to buy the liquor at a much higher price.[41]

Ingebrigt Muus assumed his share of community leadership by serving as vice-mayor on the first town council in 1837 and as a member of the council for a total of twelve years. Bernt Julius tells that his father usually went about in homespun clothing, with a flat blue cap on his head. Only when he went to Trondheim or on special occasions did he wear a broadcloth suit and a hat. Once a certain Peer Kong was challenging all comers to "pull fingers" with him as a show of strength, offering to put up his beautiful brown horse against a sum of money, winner take all. Finally Ingebrigt took him on, won the contest, and took the brown horse home to Krogsgaarden where it remained the rest of its life.

In the process of adding new buildings to Krogsgaarden Ingebrigt sent orders for the necessary furnishings to his business connection in Trondheim. One order was for some chamber pots, a common household item in the days before indoor plumbing. The Trondheim merchant decided to play a practical joke by sending a huge shipment of chamber pots, far beyond the number needed. Ingebrigt's solution was not to send them back but to serve porridge in them to the country people from Li. The latter regarded the pots as very practical, so before long they had bought out the whole supply. Travelers in the Li region subsequently reported their amazement at being served cream porridge (*rømmegrøt*) in chamber pots.[42]

In the book *Niels Muus's æt* Bernt Julius Muus relates these stories about his father with detached, quiet amusement. When he gives one little glimpse into his father's religious life, he does so without editorializing: "It does not appear that he has been zealous in making use of the sacrament of the altar. He has preserved two letters, dated 1841, from his minister, Pastor Rynning, which on closely written pages crammed with Bible verses and admonitions give him a powerful dressing down because he has neglected to go to communion for eight whole years."[43]

In thinking about the kind of model Ingebrigt Muus placed before his eldest son, one cannot recite the conventional marks of piety that some young men entering the holy ministry can ascribe to their fathers, though it appears that Ingebrigt did urge Bernt to study theology. What Bernt Julius learned from his father was not so much piety but something of how to deal with different kinds of people and how to transact business. One of the ways in which Pastor Muus ministered to his congregations in Holden and vicinity was to help parishioners with legal and financial advice. He was so effective in such matters that the oral tradition in and around Holden was that Pastor Muus was in effect, though of course not officially, a lawyer. It may be added that Ingebrigt's droll, understated humor reappears in the adult life of his son.

The important persons in Bernt Julius Muus's background included lively and colorful women as well as such men as the four discussed above. His grandmother, Severine Cathrine Steen Rynning, occupied a very important place in his life since he lived in the home of his "dear grandparents" from the fall of 1833 after his mother's death until 1842 when he left to attend school in Trondheim.[44] One wishes more were known about the relationship between grandson and grandmother. In letters to his father from the university Bernt always lists his grandmother among those to whom he sends greetings.[45] Most likely he means Grandmother Rynning.

An especially memorable woman was his other grandmother, Beret Ingebrigtsdatter Vestre Sjem, the wife of Bernt Julius's grandfather, Broder Nicolai Muus. Beret's parents did not want her to marry Broder Nicolai because they believed that "at Krogsgaarden there was nothing but poverty," an assessment that carried some truth at the time. They wanted her to marry Christian Kleiv because he was well-off. They got Beret to go to work for Kleiv for a few weeks. She returned and announced her refusal to go back. She had decided to marry Broder Muus, and so they were married.

Bernt Julius remembered with fondness this fat, feisty grandmother who went barefoot in the summer, worked with prodigious energy in the hay field, and once intervened with physical force when her husband was about to have at his brother Paul with a sword after both had been drinking heavily. Her husband, Broder Nicolai Muus, paid off the debt on the farm and made many improvements at Krogsgaarden. After he died Beret managed the estate alone for a time, often laughing at the small size of the hay bundles handled by the young men.[46]

In a scholarly study of Magister Niels Muus, engineer Rolf Falch-Muus drew together the main features he had discovered in members of the Muus family. They were tall, robust, of sturdy physical build, and often very long-lived. Second, and possibly the strongest characteristic, was the love they all felt for the soil and its cultivation. This affection for the land was seen as a manifestation of a deeper quality, the need to create something, to see tangible results of their labors, and to leave something behind for those who were to follow them, especially their own children. Finally, suggests Falch-Muus, in the Muus family there ran a pronounced sense of justice and a powerful drive to see that justice was done.[47]

Most of these characteristics may be applied to Bernt Julius Muus. He did not happen to be tall, but he has been described by a contemporary as "handsome, well-proportioned, robust in health." The same writer adds: "There have been different opinions about this man, but that witness must be given him, that he was a *man*. . . . He was a man, a diligent soul, for whom no sacrifice was too great, no difficulty so mighty, that it could deter him from doing what he saw to be his duty."[48] Surely the element of wanting to build for the future was prominent in Muus's work. This characteristic was in evidence in the address Pastor Muus gave when he dedicated St. Olaf's School on a January day in 1875: "Generation succeeding generation will perhaps receive its training in this school which today begins its work in a very humble manner. Here will be sown many a seed which will subsequently bear rich fruit. Many a seed may possibly be planted here which will develop into a large tree whose delightful shade will afford comfort to family, church, and state."[49]

After reporting in *Niels Muus's æt* that he went to live with his grandparents after his mother's death in the fall of 1833, Bernt Julius Muus writes, "There I was brought up until I was ten years old when, in 1842, I was sent to Trondheim's Latin School to see if I could amount to something in the world. During my childhood I heard from all directions many stories about my ancestors, especially about 'Master' Niels."From that point on in the book Muus presents an account of his ancestors, beginning with Niels Muus, but offers next to nothing about his childhood in Snåsa. He does say that his interest in the family was awakened at an early stage and that it was stimulated further when relatives told him that if he became a pastor he would be entitled by inheritance to the Snåsa call.[50]

Little is known about Bernt Julius Muus during the years between his birth in 1832 and 1842 when he entered the Latin School in Trondheim. He was only one-and-one-half years old when he was taken to live with his grandparents, the Rynnings. In 1833 his uncle, Ole Rynning, returned to Snåsa from the university and established a private higher school for advanced pupils which he continued until he left for America in 1837.[51] Bernt Julius of course was much too young to be a part of that school. Certainly one would expect the scholarly Pastor Rynning to take a direct hand in the education of his grandson even as Ingebrigt Muus, the father, would also exert some influence.

Jens Rynning in fact was a leader in promoting education in the parish. In 1828, the year after a law was passed providing that there should be at least one permanent school in each parish, Rynning secured approval for a plan whereby the Snåsa parish, including the Li area, would have three teachers moving from place to place to give instruction, each within a given district. Each district consisted of two subdivisions, which received twelve weeks of instruction each. More teachers were added during the next years and the number of weeks of instruction increased both in the country districts and in Snåsa. By 1843 the combined weeks of instruction by all the teachers numbered thirty-two in the Li districts (Nordli and Sørli) and fifty-eight in Snåsa.[52]

While opportunities for schooling in the Snåsa area were improving during the childhood years of Bernt Julius Muus, there is no data available to indicate that he was taught in any of the ambulatory schools. Information on his elementary education prior to 1842 is fragmentary. His grandfather's zeal for education assured that he would be provided with an appropriate early schooling. Pastor Rynning might have wanted to teach the young boy himself but it is more likely that he secured tutors for him. Without further evidence to consider, one is disposed to accept as credible the reports that while being raised by his mother's parents Bernt Julius had the benefit of instruction from a private teacher.[53]

The Reverend Jens Rynning and his wife had to provide the major parental influences for Bernt Julius. One can well believe that the boy received tender and affectionate care in the home of the grandparents and that the grandfather "looked after the gifted lad with fatherly love,"[54] even though, as suggested earlier, Pastor

Rynning was not known in the community for the warmth of his personality. Ingebrigt Muus, Bernt's father, remained a guiding presence in his life. Judging from the stories Bernt Julius tells of his father and the affectionate tone of the letters he wrote to him from Oslo some years later, it is evident that Bernt and his father had a close, understanding relationship.[55]

As a boy growing up in Snåsa, Bernt Julius had access, with his father and with companions his own age, to the inviting features of the out-of-doors in and around the small rural community. Sooner or later he would have experienced fishing and boating on the beautiful Snåsavatnet (Lake Snåsa). The hills and forests around Snåsa would encourage youthful explorers in all seasons. "Through his boyhood years and early youth he was a lover of nature who loved to wander in the woods and mountains," states one writer, adding that Muus's boyhood experiences of skiing and covering long distances were to his advantage years later when, as a prairie pastor in America, he had to travel many miles to establish personal contacts with countrymen and women.[56] It follows that young Bernt Julius grew up with a good opportunity to develop a strong and healthy physique, a prospect confirmed by the adult Muus's vigor and stamina as a pastor in rural Minnesota.

One would prefer to hear from B. J. Muus himself about his childhood activities in Snåsa, his own accounts of skiing, hiking, fishing, and the like, or recollections of indoor life, such as reading and browsing through his grandfather's impressive library. Especially interesting would be recollections of conversations with his grandparents and with his father and stepmother. But such source material is not available. Among Muus's letters that have survived is one written to his brother, presumably his half-brother Martinus, in which he movingly expresses his fondness for Snåsa and the pleasure of recalling his parents, his home, his relatives, and his childhood days. "My childhood home is and will always remain unforgettable for me. I have roamed about a good deal in the world, and in many places I have met with good

25

will, but nothing is like 'that spot of earth where the voice of life for the first time rose up from the tiny chest,' and nothing is like parents and family. I have always loved dreaming back to my childhood days, and, if God lets me live, my thoughts in many a quiet moment will return to the unforgettable Snåsa with its memories."

The letter just mentioned was written from Oslo in 1870 shortly after Muus had visited his relatives in Snåsa and before he left Norway to return to America. He was still aglow with the pleasure of getting to see his parents and his siblings. Looking back at the privilege of being with them in Snåsa he wrote, "It is a sunlit place on my journey through life."[57]

Another expression of his affection for Snåsa is some lines in his book *Niels Muus's æt*. In the foreword to that book he wrote: "Circumstances have brought it about that I have left my dear Snåsa and my dear fatherland. It is not lack of love for them which has brought me to place the great ocean between me and them."[58]

Snåsa, the home community of Bernt Julius Muus, lies in the middle of Norway, as a glance at a map confirms. It is located in the North-Trøndelag district, some 180 kilometers (108 miles) and about a three-hour train ride north and east from Trondheim. The population of Snåsa municipality has decreased in recent decades. In 1982 it stood at about 2,600. Main sources of livelihood for the residents are forestry and farming.

The Norwegian term for the administrative entity that includes the town of Snåsa and the surrounding area is "kommune," meaning municipality. According to figures from recent times, the "kommune" encompasses an area of 2,332 square kilometers (900 square miles), most of which consists of forest, mountains, and lakes. Lake Snåsa is the sixth largest freshwater lake in all of Norway. It is 42 kilometers (25 miles) in length and 118 square kilometers (45 square miles) in area. It has been a vital part of Snåsa life over the years both for fishing and for travel by boat. There is also good hunting and berry picking in the vicinity.

26

*Snåsa Church*
Gift from Joralf Gjerstad

The town of Snåsa lies at the north end of the lake; at the opposite end, toward the southwest and in the general direction of Trondheim, are Sunnan and Steinkjer. On a higher elevation in the town lies the Snåsa church, a noble building which for centuries has been at the heart of the cultural life of Snåsa. Constructed of a beautiful gray stone, it is surrounded by lovely trees and a well-kept cemetery where B. J. Muus's parents and his Rynning grandparents are buried. Its oldest section, now the chancel and sacristy, dates from about the year 1200.[59] The church was restored in 1869.

Attached to the east end of the Snåsa church is a small chapel that is usually not open to the public. In the book *Niels Muus's æt*, this little addition to the church is called "Muus'ernes Gravkapel," meaning the Muuses' burial chapel. It was built at the direction of

27

the renowned Magister Niels Muus in 1703 as a burial place for himself and his descendants. On the east side of the chapel is a small window and directly above it a marble plaque with an intriguing set of inscriptions. At the very top are some runic letters that presumably mean "Muus." Next is a brief inscription in Greek that says, "To the one who understands." Then follows, in Latin, the main message of the tablet:

THE SEPULCHERS ERECTED IN STONE WHICH YOU SEE PRESERVE THE BONES OF MUUS, CONSECRATED TO GOD. DO NOT TOUCH THE BONES CONSECRATED TO GOD WITH VIOLENT FINGERS, FOR I WISH THE TOMB TO BE LEFT UNDISTURBED. GO AWAY AND BE MINDFUL OF DEATH.[60]

The use of Greek and Latin, the blunt warning to the reader, and the strong if somewhat eccentric pride of family are all characteristic of Magister Niels. On a visit to Snåsa in 1894, Bernt Julius Muus, then as earlier keenly interested in his family's history, investigated the interior of the burial chapel and drew up a list of the coffins and the inscriptions identifying the deceased. Perhaps at his instigation and as part of the examination of the site, twenty-eight coffins were taken from the Muus Chapel and interred a few feet away from its walls. On the same 1894 visit Muus also gathered oral history from several persons, went through the old Snåsa ministerial books in the archives in Trondheim, and did further investigation of his family's history.[61]

Among the many interesting furnishings inside the church is the ornate pulpit, which was reconditioned in 1936. On the side facing the congregation is the one-word inscription in gold letters: LOGOS, the Greek word for "Word," that is, the Word of God. On the canopy over the pulpit is another Greek inscription that means, "Fear not, but speak." On the pastor's side, written on the slanting wooden surface of the lectern, where a preacher normally places the Bible or sermon manuscript, are the Norwegian words for the same admonition: "Fear not, but speak." Those who came to know Pastor Muus as a preacher and leader certified that he did not fear to speak his mind. John Nathan Kildahl, second president of St. Olaf College, knew Muus personally as fellow pastor, adviser, and colleague. He said of Pastor Muus: "I believe I have never known any man of whom it could be said with greater truthfulness that he feared God and no man."[62]

What his home surroundings meant to Bernt Julius Muus has been suggested in references to the men and women representing his family history, in his letters, and in his visits to Snåsa in 1870 and 1894. From the legendary Magister Niels to Ingebrigt Muus, one can say with confidence that place and land, farms and crops, forests and lakes, mountains and streams, were integral to the interests and livelihood of his forebears.

Had Bernt Julius not chosen to emigrate to America, he could have expected eventually to take over the ownership and management of Krogsgaarden. As the oldest son, he could have exercised his right of inheritance (odelsrett), which would mean paying the stipulated inheritance tax. In 1882, when his father died, Bernt made an attempt to acquire the family farm but failed to exercise his right in time, though he was also put off by the high amount of the tax.[63] Some years later, in 1894, he inquired about the value of Krogsgaarden on behalf of his son Nils, who had some interest in buying it.[64] Evidently nothing came of the effort.

Bernt Julius Muus was ten years old when he was sent from Snåsa to the Cathedral School in Trondheim. There he grew from childhood to young manhood and there he received the first part of the education that prepared him for a life of service as a pastor.

# Two

# Education in Norway

The education of Bernt Julius Muus began in the Snåsa parsonage where he lived with his grandparents, the Reverend Jens Rynning, his mother's father and the pastor of the Snåsa parish, and his grandmother, Severine Cathrine Steen Rynning. The schooling in this setting was of unusual quality, affording the grandson the chance to observe firsthand what went on in a parsonage, the company of his learned grandfather, and the private tutoring the grandparents provided for him. Pastor Rynning was known for promoting education in the parish. He also tutored at least one local teacher.[1] As noted earlier, he would have had a special interest in the education of his grandson.

Young Bernt, born in 1832, was too young to be included in the private school for advanced students that Ole Rynning conducted in Snåsa from 1833 when he returned home from the university until 1837 when he left for America.[2] In Snåsa, as in other rural places, the only kind of education available to most children was provided by teachers who went from place to place instructing the young, the so-called ambulatory schools. In 1828 Pastor Jens Rynning had drawn up a plan for three such schools in the Snåsa parish and a permanent school at Forberg. In 1848 the Norwegian Parliament passed a law requiring common schools in the towns.[3] Secondary schools were not organized in rural districts until after 1877.[4]

At the age of 10, in 1842, Bernt Julius Muus was sent to the Trondheim Cathedral School. The journey from Snåsa to Trondheim would have taken at least a full day. Perhaps the first part of it was made by boat on the lake, Snåsavatnet, with stops at Jorstad and Valøy. Part of the journey surely would have been by horse and carriage. One is curious as to who made the trip with the young boy. His father, Ingebrigt Muus, accustomed to traveling to Trondheim, most probably took his son to the Cathedral School and made the necessary arrangements there as part of a business trip to the city.

Bernt Julius attended the Trondheim Cathedral School from 1842 until 1849. There he was regarded as one of the most capable students. His studies included work in languages, Latin, Greek, Norwegian, French, and German. A mid-year report card dated December 20, 1844, indicates grades of "excellent" in Arithmetic and German, "very good" in Religion, Latin, Greek, History, Geography, and French. His overall mark at that stage of his studies at the Cathedral School was "very good," corresponding to a high B or B+ average in the American letter system of grading.[5]

The rector of the school in B. J. Muus's time was the philologist Frederick Moltke Bugge, known as a defender of the classical gymnasium and the classical spirit over against "realism" with its utilitarian emphasis and "fanaticism."[6] He is also remembered for the support he gave to the brilliant self-taught linguist and student of Norwegian dialects, Ivar Aasen, by securing a stipend for him.[7] As to the young man from Snåsa, Muus recalled that Bugge expected much from him and would say, "You are always a middle-of-the-road man, Muus." In telling this, Muus would add, "The truest word he ever spoke."[8]

While studying in Trondheim Bernt Julius Muus was at the age to be preparing for confirmation. After a prescribed period of instruction, which typically included Bible and Catechism, he was

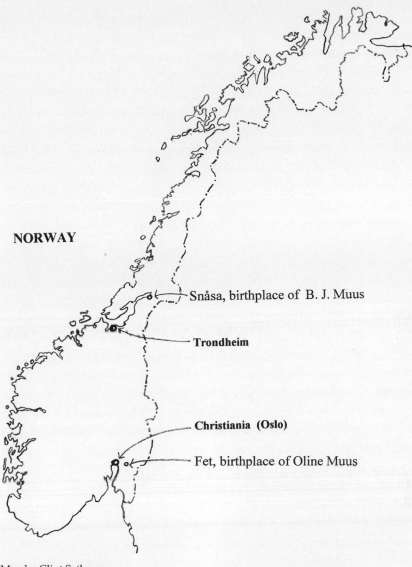

NORWAY

Snåsa, birthplace of B. J. Muus

**Trondheim**

**Christiania (Oslo)**

Fet, birthplace of Oline Muus

Map by Clint Sathrum

confirmed by the Reverend Christian Petersen in Vår Frue church (the Church of Our Lady) in Trondheim on April 11, 1847.[9]

By 1849 Muus had completed the gymnasium course in Trondheim and was deemed qualified to take the *eksamen artium* that came at the completion of Latin School or *gymnas*. Students would not take the *eksamen artium* at the school they had been attending but in the capital city, Oslo. If they passed, they would then be qualified to enter the university.

Muus's teachers attested that he was ready for the arts examination. A formal document in Latin addressed "To the most learned and distinguished Senate of the Royal Frederick University" in Oslo, signed by Rector F. M. Bugge and another official and dated July 7, 1849, recommends that "the young man Berntius Julius Muus" be admitted to the arts examination. The document records that Muus was born in the Snåsa parish in 1832 and was enrolled in the Nidaros Gymnasium in 1842. It states further that he appeared worthy of "academic citizenship" and continues: "In ability he seemed to us sufficiently qualified. He displayed while under our tutelage in every instance diligence and industry which was by no means unpraiseworthy and has always won the favor of his teachers by his modest character."[10] Later in 1849 Bernt Julius Muus passed the *eksamen artium* with honors, receiving the grade of *laudabilis* or "praiseworthy."[11] He received the same standing in the remaining steps of his education: the *eksamen philosophicum* in 1850, the *teologisk embedseksamen* in 1854, and the *praktisk teologisk eksamen* in August of 1858.

As one would expect, the Norwegian system of education differs considerably from the one known in the United States, though a few general comparisons can be made. By the time Bernt Julius Muus had finished the Cathedral School in Trondheim, he was seventeen years old, a typical age for a young person completing Latin School or *gymnas*, where specialization began much earlier than in American schools. The *eksamen philosophicum* would then have been a more extensive study of the liberal arts, including further language study beyond the Latin, Greek, German, and French he had pursued in Trondheim.

As to Muus's theological education, the first of the two examinations, the *teologisk embedseksamen*, constituted the academic study of theology, covering biblical, historical, and doctrinal courses. The second, as the term *praktisk* indicates, consisted of the practical subjects the candidate needed for work in a parish. A theological student would not be ready for ordination into the ministry until he had taken the practical theological examination.

For many young persons entering the church's ministry, there is some memorable point at which a conscious decision is made to pursue such a career. In Bernt Julius Muus's case, there is no firsthand evidence of such a decisive moment. It is reported that within the Muus family there was an expectation that he would become a pastor, and that his mother on her deathbed expressed such a wish. His early encounters with the study of theology convinced him that he was unworthy of the holy ministry, so he began to consider mathematics and other subjects suitable to the field of civil engineering. But when his father wrote that he should continue with theology, Bernt Julius acquiesced as a matter of obedience to the Fourth Commandment, "Honor thy father and thy mother."[12]

Among likely influences one naturally thinks of the long succession of Muuses in the holy ministry, going back to the redoubtable Magister Niels. An interesting autobiographical item is Bernt Julius's comment in the foreword to *Niels Muus's æt* that his grandfather's brother, Paul, often pointed out to him that, in the event he became a pastor, he would be entitled by inheritance to be pastor in Snåsa.[13]

There is of course the fact that Bernt Julius was brought up in a parsonage under the daily influence of his grandfather Jens Rynning, the local pastor. His uncle, Ole Rynning, had also been a student of theology, though apparently an unwilling one. Muus himself wrote years later that Ole had "no taste" for the study of theology. It is also known that Ole had included in his book, *A*

35

*True Account of America*, an anti-clerical chapter that had been removed by a prominent Norwegian clergyman, Dean Kragh, before the book was published.[14]

Despite the evidence that seems to pit Ole Rynning against the
church and its servants, to which may be added his strained relationship with his pastor father, the Reverend Jens Rynning, there
was a great deal in the character and example of Ole Rynning that
could have made a strong impact on Bernt Julius Muus. Like his
nephew, Ole also had an excellent record as a university student
and like his nephew took action to provide educational opportunity for his people. It was when he returned to Snåsa in 1833, fired
with patriotism and eagerness to lift the lot of the rural people
around him, that he became a private tutor to a small group of especially promising young men.[15]

One cannot take for granted that Ole Rynning's influence was a
factor in Bernt Julius Muus's eventual decision to become a minister. But the possibility may be considered that, however uncon-
sciously, he was following in his uncle's footsteps when he went
to the university, studied theology, and emigrated to America to
be a minister to his fellow Norwegians out on the prairie where
Ole Rynning gave his life. In his career as a pastor in America,
Muus carried out a calling parallel to the one that his uncle Ole
had begun so courageously and sacrificially.

As an "academic citizen" of the relatively new Royal Frederick
University in Oslo and a student in the theological faculty in the
capital city of Norway at the middle of the nineteenth century, B. J.
Muus was directly in the path of important national and cultural
developments that were creating a new nation. Norway had established its own university in 1811 and had written its own constitution in 1814. The long period of dominance by Denmark gave
way to the union with Sweden in 1814, but the desire for full political and cultural independence grew in intensity each decade.

The Norwegian Parliament elected Karl XIII, the king of Sweden,
as the king of Norway, and Karl Johan as crown prince, thus sig-

nifying that it was by her own choice and as an independent state that Norway entered into the union. On November 9, 1814, Karl Johan came to Oslo where he pledged to uphold the constitution of Norway.[16]

Times of disillusionment, political growing pains, and economic distress followed the excitement of the signing of the constitution. But gradually conditions improved and enthusiasm for a better future returned. The constitution had stipulated that no more than two-thirds of the representatives in the Storting could be from country districts. A rural leader, Ole Gabriel Ueland from western Norway, worked with some success to arouse the farmers to participate more fully in political life. In the realm of the arts, painters such as Johan Christian Dahl and poets such as Henrik Wergeland inspired all Norwegians to patriotism and a new pride in their country.[17]

In 1821 Norway received its own distinctive flag, and in 1824, led by the fiery Wergeland, the people won the right to celebrate May 17, Constitution Day. An important law of 1837 provided local communities with the right to govern themselves. The old Conventicle Act of 1741, which had forbidden people to assemble for religious meetings apart from the clergy's supervision, was repealed in 1842; religious liberties were guaranteed three years later. In 1848 the Storting passed a law placing a common school in every town and the same year the first modern road was begun. It was also in 1848 that Marcus Thrane, pioneer labor leader who later emigrated to America, organized a labor society in Drammen, the first of some three hundred such groups.[18]

A unique intellectual battle raged in the 1820s and 1830s between two conceptions of Norway's new identity. On one side were those who, with Henrik Wergeland, would sever all ties with Denmark and recast Norway's present history as continuous with the Old Norse saga times. On the other side were those who followed another great poet, Johan Sebastian Welhaven. These members of the intelligentsia respected the long-standing connection with Copenhagen and welcomed influences from other countries without being any less enamored of Norway's own culture. In time, the two ideas would merge, but it was Wergeland's nationalistic view that captured a place in the nation's memory.[19]

Norway's national rebirth that began early in the nineteenth century gained new momentum in the 1840s and 1850s, a period that has been described as the Age of National Romanticism. In politics the drive for democracy and social justice was led by Gabriel Ueland, Marcus Thrane, Johan Sverdrup, and Søren Jaabæck, among others. These liberals and reformers were stimulated by the French Revolution of 1848 while conservatives among the official classes were alarmed at the prospect of radical politics in Norway.[20]

An important feature of the cultural renaissance of the period was the effort to recover the history and art of Norway's past. "To recapture the folk culture, to reveal the 'hidden Norway,' and to make the treasures concealed among the people the common property of all was one of the great achievements of national romanticism."[21]

P. A. Munch studied Old Norse and produced an eight-volume history of Norway. Magnus Brostrup Landstad, with help from Olea Crøger and Ludvig Lindeman, issued a volume of folk songs. Jørgen Moe and Peter Christen Asbjørnsen gathered and retold the folk tales and legends that had lived for centuries among the people. The leading figure in shaping an authentic "Norwegian" language, *landsmaal*, was the linguist and poet Ivar Aasen. Also writing poems in *landsmaal* was Aasmund Vinje. Prominent painters of the period were Hans Gude and Adolph Tidemand.

The famous names in music included Ole Bull, the violinist, and the composers Halfdan Kjerulf, Ludvig Lindeman, and Rikard Nordraak. It was Nordraak who set to music the poem by Bjørnstjerne Bjørnson, "Ja vi elsker dette landet," which became the national anthem.[22]

A movement to establish a national theater was led by Bjørnson,

Ole Bull, and Henrik Ibsen in the early 1850s. Bjørnson was to enjoy growing fame as poet and man of the people. His peasant stories, including *Synnøve Solbakken*, published in 1857, received great popular acclaim during the decade. Henrik Ibsen published his first drama, *Catalina*, in 1850.[23] But romanticism was even then on the wane, and greater realism was appearing both in literature and in society itself. Artistic interest was also shifting from the idyllic countryside to the city. The plays of Henrik Ibsen moved from the romanticism of his historical dramas to the later realistic treatment of social themes.[24]

The extent to which these cultural and political movements made an impact on the mind of Bernt Julius Muus, university student and theological candidate in the capital city in the 1850s, is difficult to judge. Only a handful of his letters are available. From them it appears that he kept himself informed about the events of the day. Writing to his father in April of 1854, Bernt Julius in a passing reference shows acquaintance with the work of Eilert Sundt, a contemporary scholar who studied gypsies and other groups of poor people in the country.[25] Thanking his father for sending him fifty *speciedalers*, Muus playfully notes that the bills he is happy to have in his pocket do not seem to thrive there for more than a day or two before they wander off again, like those described in "Sundt's gypsy book." He tells his father that he has nothing amusing to write beyond what is in the Norwegian newspapers, but one item he has picked up from the foreign press is the king's recent ruling that no more than four foreign ships at a time can be in a harbor where there is a fortress. Muus thinks it is a silly decision. The Storting has held three secret meetings about it, on one occasion debating for six hours. In the same letter Bernt cautions his father against working too hard, having heard from a friend at home that his father had not been well.[26]

In June of 1854, writing again to his father, Bernt expresses delighted surprise that his sister Birgitta will be coming to Oslo. He hopes that the trip will be good for her, granting that in the city one can be led astray on many paths unknown in the quiet country. "Besides, I believe that people will be more satisfied to be at home if they have been out and looked around." Bernt states that he is out of money and requests some more. He writes about an industrial exhibit that would interest his father and also mentions an agricultural meeting at which there will be delegates from Sweden and Denmark. The letter reports speculation that Norway's neutrality might be in danger. Foreign newspapers are taken up with the question whether a pact between France and England will be concluded. In Muus's view the king, Oscar I, is a man of solid character who is striving with all his ability to be honest and upright.[27]

On October 26, 1854 Bernt writes to thank his father for a letter with fifty *speciedalers* enclosed. He notes that Birgitta earlier had written for money and records the sums she has received. At the moment, Birgitta is going around with a stuffy nose, seeming to catch one cold after another. Bernt is sorry to hear about the poor fall weather that hinders the drying out of the grain. A cousin has been appointed judge in Størdalen and Verdalen. As to Bernt's personal affairs, he was very busy getting ready for the decisive examination over his theological studies, *teologisk embedseksamen*, which was to begin November 20 and conclude by the middle of December.[28]

Having received his academic theological degree, Muus took the next step of meeting the requirement in practical theology, the *praktisk theologisk eksamen*, which he completed with honors in August of 1858. As a theological student in Norway in the 1850s, he inherited a half-century of religious developments that were as remarkable in their contexts as were the political and cultural movements since 1814.

In religion as in politics and art, Norway was moving toward greater independence. Hans Nielsen Hauge, the lay preacher who revived religious life in the late eighteenth and early nineteenth centuries, died at his farm north of Oslo in 1824 but his influence lived on. According to Norwegian church historian Einar

Molland, "It was he who set in motion the laymen's activity so characteristic of Norwegian church history in the nineteenth and twentieth centuries, the work which has given Norwegian church life its mark of distinction today."[29] In his university life and in America Bernt Julius Muus would acquire knowledge and sympathetic understanding of the pietistic, low-church brand of Lutheranism that is traced back to Hauge.

The Haugean teaching, biblical, pietistic, and loyal to Luther's Small Catechism, came into conflict with the rationalism that many Norwegian pastors had absorbed while studying theology in Denmark. When Norway established its own university in 1811, beginning its operation in 1813, the two young theologians appointed to the theological faculty represented a reaction against rationalism. Svend Borchmann Hersleb and Stener Johannes Stenersen, who began their teaching in 1813 and 1814 respectively, had been influenced directly in Copenhagen by the famous Danish poet and hymnist, N. F. S. Grundtvig. With his encouragement they embraced traditional biblical Christianity and the Lutheran confessional heritage. Molland writes of the influence they exerted on their students:

"During the time these men lectured, there arose a generation of theologians who were Biblicists and mildly orthodox Lutherans. These pastors viewed the Haugeaners somewhat sympathetically, although there was indeed a gulf between them and the farmers, who belonged to a different class in a sharply stratified society. They had been taught by their professors that preaching was a matter for the official clergy."[30]

For a brief time it appeared that the ideas of Grundtvig would prevail in the theological faculty in Oslo through Hersleb and Stenersen. In fact, Grundtvigianism had an attractive proponent in the able Oslo pastor W. A. Wexels, who wielded much influence. But when Grundtvig in 1825 announced the "matchless discovery" that the Apostles' Creed took precedence over Scripture in the life of the church, Hersleb and Stenersen could no longer agree with him.[31]

Thus before Bernt Julius Muus arrived in Oslo in 1849 and pursued his studies there in the early 1850s, the theological climate had been formed by the biblical, orthodox Lutheranism of Hersleb and Stenersen. Their theology for the most past rejected continental rationalism, responded at first to Grundtvig's joyful Christianity, but later backed away from Grundtvig's "churchly view" with its stress on the antiquity and authority of the Apostles' Creed.[32]

Within the wider church, the lay movement continued with the founding in Stavanger of the Norwegian Missionary Society in 1842. With Hans Palludan Smith Schreuder as its able representative, the church also revealed its interest in missionary work. Schreuder was a "new type" of missionary, at home among the laity and the regional missionary societies, but eager to receive the endorsement of the Norwegian church. With a strong sense of being called to become a missionary, he had taken studies in medicine alongside his theological course. Schreuder was ordained by Bishop Chr. Sørenssen in May of 1843 and left for South Africa a few weeks later.

Schreuder had written that the "often judgmental emotionalism" that seemed to mark many missionaries did not appeal to him, because it was in complete contrast to the confidence and steadiness that he valued in the Christian view of the world.[33] Schreuder and his South African mission represent one kind of stirring in Norwegian religious life in the 1840s. His name is also significant because two future leaders among the Norwegians in America gave serious consideration to joining the Schreuder mission before deciding on America as their place of service.

One of these was Claus L. Clausen, a Danish layman and teacher who emigrated to America where he joined the Norwegians and, as an ordained pastor among them, exerted important leadership in the first decades of organized church life in Wisconsin, Iowa, and Minnesota. Prior to leaving Denmark and Norway for America, where he was called to be a teacher in the Muskego settlement, Clausen had conferred with Schreuder and others about going to Africa as a missionary.[34]

The other was Bernt Julius Muus. Before deciding on the call to Goodhue county in Minnesota, he too weighed the possibility of going to Africa to work among the Zulus as part of the Schreuder mission. In a candid letter to Laur. Larsen written from Oslo April 5, 1859, Muus wrote that even before he had taken up the study of theology he had thought of missionary work and in particular of Schreuder's work among the Zulus, but that he shrank away from what he perceived as conditions too difficult for him to endure.[35]

Foreign mission interest and thriving lay activity were healthy signs in Norwegian religious life in the 1840s but not everything was tranquil. Extreme religious groups appeared within and outside of the church, some of them moved at times to fanaticism. The publication of a revised catechism aroused much ire among the lay people. They protested the removal of some familiar pietistic strictures against worldly diversions and the insertion of teachings associated with Grundtvig.[36]

By entering the university in 1849 and pursuing his philosophical and theological studies in the 1850s, Bernt Julius Muus sat under two of Norway's most influential theologians of the nineteenth century while they were in their prime. They were Carl Paul Caspari and Gisle Johnson. Caspari was a German orientalist and Old Testament scholar appointed to the Oslo theology faculty in 1847. His initial acquaintance with Norway came through Gisle Johnson, whom he met while the latter was studying in Germany. Johnson urged him to apply for the vacant position in the Oslo faculty. Johnson himself was appointed a lecturer in theology in 1849. From 1849 through the next twenty-five years, Caspari and Johnson dominated the theological faculty and exerted a powerful, lifelong influence on their students[37].

Of the two Oslo theologians, Caspari was the more scholarly

but Johnson was the one who had a broader impact on the spiritual life of the times. Early in his career Caspari published reputable works on the Old Testament but in the 1850s he shifted his research to church history. He investigated the history of the Apostles' Creed and succeeded in disproving the Grundtvigian claim that the Creed spoken at baptism went all the way back to Jesus himself and had been preserved unchanged through the entire history of the church.[38]

Caspari refuted the Grundtvigians on historical grounds, and Johnson opposed them on the basis of Lutheran dogmatics. As confessional Lutherans they were united in their determination to oppose Grundtvig's influence, but the overall result of their work went far beyond such polemics. Johnson in particular became the leader of a revival movement in Norway that Einar Molland regards as of more significance and with broader consequences for Norwegian church and society than the Hauge movement[39].

The reason that the Johnsonian revival had such an impact was that it combined the rather precise tenets of orthodox Lutheran theology with the ardor and pietism that lay preaching and mission organizations had kept alive since Hauge's day. Moreover, in a striking way it brought together awakened lay people of scant education with persons of university training, especially the young pastors taught by Caspari and Johnson who carried the revival further. Writes Molland, "Thanks to this zealous generation of pastors, Norwegian church life became thoroughly colored by Johnsonian orthodoxy and pietism."[40]

In the decade of the 1840s, an awakening was already under way brought about in large part by the establishment of the Norwegian Missionary Society and subsequent mission meetings in different parts of Norway. Lyder Brun in Bergen and Gustav Adolph Lammers in Skien were powerful preachers who led vital spiritual movements in their parishes and beyond. The revival reached the capital city and there Gisle Johnson emerged as the unexpected leader. It began inauspiciously in 1851 when Johnson, then a young lecturer in theology not ordained to the ministry, accepted the invitation of Sven Brun, an Oslo pastor, to lead some Bible studies.[41] Johnson's powerful meditations gripped his listeners. Large crowds of people streamed to hear him. The spiritual atmosphere was changed throughout the city. The revival was felt among all the social classes, including the educated and, not least, the theological students.[42]

Gisle Johnson's effectiveness as teacher and preacher was most unusual. The very idea of a theology professor conducting devotional meetings was in itself something wholly unexpected. And so was the overwhelming impact of this quiet, modest man with the thin, quavering voice as he delivered what one hearer described as an "almost meticulous lecture." Johnson preached law and gospel, and the law laid bare all pseudo-Christianity and sin. The assembly trembled, it was reported, when Johnson in his soft voice quietly quoted the words of the prophet, "There is no peace for the ungodly, says my God."[43] He was totally unlike those speakers who hope to convince their listeners by the overwhelming force of their delivery. Yet there was such astonishing power in his steady, unpretentious speech that the hearts of his listeners were opened to recognize their true condition and to long for the experience of new life in God.[44]

Gisle Johnson was a master in being able to analyze the human soul and its needs. As an admirer of the work of Søren Kierkegaard, the Danish philosopher, he did not hesitate to make use of Kierkegaard's "stages on life's way" in his lectures on doctrine and faith. The first stage, as Johnson applied it in describing the genesis of faith, was the natural human being's impulse to look out for the self, an aesthetic-rationalistic egoism. This stage is marked by pain, dissatisfaction, unrest, anguish, and doubt. By a leap the person moves to the second stage, that of being under the law. The conscience is awakened, the person confesses sin, has an awareness of God, and experiences fear and remorse. The third stage is also reached by a leap, bringing the person finally to "the Christian faith," characterized by Johnson as "a uniquely

45

new form of the human being's personal existence." Such termi-
nology is suggestive of the modern existentialism that owes a
debt to Kierkegaard.[45]

Bernt Julius Muus was in Oslo during the height of the
Johnsonian awakening. He may be counted among the many
theological candidates on whom Gisle Johnson and Carl Paul
Caspari left their mark. He heard them lecture in the university
classroom, and it is highly likely that he was among those who
heard Johnson's Bible studies given at Our Savior's church, the
cathedral in Oslo.[46]

The impact of Caspari and Johnson on Muus was the subject of
conversations between Muus and S. O. Simundson, a younger
pastor who worked closely with Muus in the Holden area during

*Bernt Julius Muus*
From *Niels Muus's æt*

46

*Oline Christine Kathrine Muus*
From *Niels Muus's æt*

Muus's final years. Simundson wrote, "He had as a student come under the powerful influence of Caspari and Johnson. . . . Under their guidance he had come to a spiritual awakening."[47]

Writing from Norway, Muus himself commented about the Johnsonian awakening in a letter to Laur. Larsen in the spring of 1859: "In our churchly situation there is very little new. The religious movement that has prevailed in recent years has not stopped, but it has a much calmer character than it had a couple of years ago. May it not sink down into the quiet of death."[48]

The revival included house meetings where men and women gathered to read the Bible, sing, pray, and encourage one another in leading Christian lives. At one of these meetings in Oslo Bernt Julius Muus met the young woman whom he would marry in 1859, Oline Christine Kathrine Pind. "Both Muus and Oline Christine belonged to the group of 'the awakened,'" wrote

47

William C. Benson.[49] Both of them thus had firsthand exposure to the winds of revival, and their knowledge of a Bible-centered, pietistic, Christian outlook on life went with them to America.

Not only Muus but many other pastors who emigrated to America took the Caspari-Johnson theology with them. From Johnson more than Caspari, who was not a pietist, they absorbed a strict Lutheran orthodoxy that made room for the pietistic mode of life favored by the awakened lay people. Thanks to Johnson this theology also embraced a greater concentration on the inner, psychological experience of faith than was normally true of the older confessional Lutheranism.

A student who later became a bishop, Johan Christian Heuch, tells of the impression Johnson made on him and others. "His lectures often gripped me so that the pen involuntarily slipped from my hand, so occupied was I with what I had heard. To doubt the rightness of his statements never entered the hearts of his genuine disciples . . . . He was certain in his cause. With him there was not the slightest doubt that the Lutheran church doctrine, as he presented it, was congruent with the truth."[50]

Much as they were admired by most of their disciples, Caspari and Johnson were not without their critics then and later. One student attended a Johnson lecture and decided then and there never to hear another one. As he left the auditorium he asked himself, "Is this scholarship? Where in this is there any place for independent thought? The result is already decided on beforehand."[51]

Caspari had a good reputation as an Old Testament scholar and was impressive in the classroom as he dramatically quoted Old Testament texts in Hebrew. When he switched to studies of the ancient church, his researches into the history of the Apostles' Creed and the three-volume work in German that resulted served notice to the scholarly world that Norway had a theological faculty where research was taking place. But Caspari too had his shortcomings. In his Old Testament lectures the students heard nothing of the new biblical research. Caspari chose to view the contemporary literary-critical treatment of the Old

Testament as an attempt to revive the old rationalism, deserving only of a few comments to warn against it. In dealing with the creation stories in Genesis, he held to a literal interpretation of the six days.[52]

The theological graduates of the Caspari-Johnson era went out into the church with a strong theological foundation and a personal zeal to preach the message they had been taught. What they had missed in their training, however, was preparation for dealing with the modern world and its problems. A deep chasm separated theology and the rest of intellectual life in Norway around the middle of the nineteenth century. Johnson had circumscribed his students' spiritual horizon, writes Molland, outside of which lay the modern cultural movements and the new scholarship. "On one of the church's fronts the Johnsonian candidates came up miserably short: over against the cultural life."[53]

Norway's poets and novelists were quick to portray how ill-suited Johnson's disciples were to cope with situations and new ideas beyond the protected circle of pious believers. Novelist Alexander Kielland contrasted the older type of pastor with the Johnsonians, largely to the detriment of the latter. In the older generation one meets the aristocratic priest, happy to be a royal official in the state church, open to the joys of social life and the good things of culture, and keeping his distance from the common folk and their awakenings. On the other side is the Johnsonian curate with his uneasy conscience, unhappy in his role as state church pastor when called upon to pray for the military forces, a man who sees himself as a missionary in the dead congregations where the awakened people are his comfort.[54]

Similarly, Bjørnstjerne Bjørnson, who would eventually storm into the American Midwest to attack B. J. Muus along with the rest of the Norwegian Synod clergy, wrote a scene in which a theology student was unable to hold his own when thrown into an argument with a medical student. Of the theology student Bjørnson writes, "His persistent studies had been strictly theological; he had no time for anything more, and his faith was that of the old peasant heritage, all too secure in itself to take notice of scholarly doubt."[55]

From the standpoint of the late twentieth century one more readily tends to side with the critics of the Caspari-Johnson school than with the young pastors of that orientation. Theology students and pastors trained narrowly within a particular tradition and out of touch with their culture can be limited in their effectiveness and are easily caricatured. On the other hand, the pastors who emigrated to America discovered that the Lutheran doctrine and personal piety absorbed from Johnson found an eager reception among their fellow Norwegians out on the prairie.

These emigrating pastors, many with good minds and familiarity with an intellectual culture outside of the theological realm, deliberately gave first priority to the basic preaching and teaching tasks as the kind of ministry most needed in the difficult pioneer situation. They looked ahead to the time when they could address the educational and cultural needs of their people, but their Lutheran training in Norway moved them to start with preaching, catechising, and forming congregations. In the ensuing decades, the Norwegian-American community repeatedly would experience the tension between Lutheran church piety on the one hand and new forms of social, cultural, and intellectual life on the other.

For a few years Bernt Julius Muus remained in Oslo. He finished his theoretical studies in theology December 15, 1854, when he took the *teologisk embedseksamen*.[56] It was close to four years later, in August of 1858, that he completed the study that qualified him to take and pass the *praktisk teologisk eksamen*, the practical theological examination.

Since the practical examination required only one year of preparation, Muus had time for other pursuits prior to his departure for America in the fall of 1859. From 1854 on he was a private tutor in the employ of a clergyman, Archdeacon Frederik Rode, and also in the home of C. A. Dybwad, the editor of *Christiania*

*Posten.*[57] During the same period he also taught at the Christiania Borgerskole, an institution whose students would have been from fourteen to sixteen years of age. A little handbook for the school, printed in 1828, announces that it offered the general knowledge necessary "for every enlightened member of civil society."[58] Subjects to be studied were reading, writing, religion, Norwegian grammar and style, geography, history, arithmetic, and the beginning elements of geometry, natural history, Latin, German, and French.

The information about this school where young Bernt Julius Muus taught before being ordained and emigrating is of interest because the description of its offerings resembles that of St. Olaf's School in Northfield, founded by Muus and others in 1874. Moreover, the experience Muus gained as a teacher in such a school added to his lifelong interest in education.

Perhaps the most significant of Muus's roles during the Oslo interim was that of co-founder and co-editor of a church paper, *Norsk Kirketidende* (Norwegian Church Times). His partner in this enterprise from 1856 to 1859 was a fellow student of theology, Theodor C. Bernhoft.[59] Writing in the first issue of *Norsk Kirketidende* in 1856, Muus explained the task of the paper as one of discussing the church's situation, shedding light on many questions "which are stirring with renewed strength in our time," and offering its columns for anyone who would wish to elucidate a doctrinal point or a particular church practice, or bring up a topic for further discussion in a brotherly spirit of love.[60] Some of the topics Muus himself discussed in the paper included the validity of infant baptism, missionary work at the North Pole, the Catholic Mission, minutes from a laymen's meeting in Sarpsborg, deaconess work in the church, and the tenth German Evangelical *Kirchentag* in Hamburg. In the early 1860s, soon after he got settled in the Goodhue parish, Muus submitted articles to the paper from America.[61]

Quite unexpected among Muus's achievements before he left for America was the translating of a small book from English to

Norwegian. The book in question was *Parables from Nature* by Margaret Gatty. Muus's translation was published in Oslo in 1857.[62] The stories in Gatty's book, inspired in part by Hans Christian Andersen's *Fairy Tales*, use creatures of nature to dramatize the truth of a biblical text. For example, in "A Lesson of Faith," the Caterpillar, with the cheerful encouragement of the Lark, learns to *believe* that she will become a Butterfly. The biblical text for the story is Job 14:14, "If a man die, shall he live again? All the days of my appointed time will I wait, till my change come." A story about a Sedge Warbler singing of "The Unknown Land" illustrates the point of Hebrews 11:16, "But now they desire a better country." In the tale, the Magpie assumes the role of the skeptic who plants in the young bird's mind the question of whether there even exists an Unknown Land. All in all, the stories offered an attractive apology for Christianity suitable for young people who were hearing and asking questions about the faith in which they had been raised.

The surprising aspect in Muus's having translated this book from English is that little or nothing is known about his having had any opportunity to learn the English language. A report of the subjects studied and grades earned at the Trondheim Latin School dated December 20, 1844, indicates that he was instructed in Latin, Greek, Norwegian, French, and German, but there is no mention of English. His grades in Latin, Greek, and French were "very good" and in German "excellent."[63]

One may surmise that Muus learned English while preparing for the *eksamen philosophicum* at the University in Oslo. The idea of translating Mrs. Gatty's little book might have come up in connection with his work as a private tutor in a home where language skills were encouraged or possibly in relation to his teaching at the Borgerskole.

While he certainly had a working knowledge of English that he put to good use after his arrival in America, Muus, like other early Norwegian pastors in America, quite consistently used the Norwegian language in his sermons and public addresses. He also used Norwegian in letters to fellow pastors but from time to time inserted an English word or phrase. More important in Muus's attitude toward the English language is the fact that when he founded St. Olaf's School in Northfield, Minnesota, in 1874, he and his associates agreed at the outset that English would be the language of the school.

# Three

## The Call to America

On May 10, 1859, Bernt Julius Muus took pen in hand and addressed a letter to King Oscar, king of Norway and Sweden, requesting ordination. The letter, which is preserved in the National Archives in Oslo, reads as follows:

"To the King!

The undersigned, who was born March 15, 1832, has undergone the theoretical part of the theological degree examination in the fall of 1854 and the practical part in the fall of 1858 and has been called to be pastor for the Norwegian Evangelical Lutheran congregations in Goodhue County, Minnesota Territory in North America, petitions Your Majesty to be ordained, with those modifications which his position as pastor in that foreign land might make necessary.

Enclosed are the undersigned's baptismal certificate as well as evidence of having undergone the last part of the theological degree examination.

Christiania the 10th of May 1859

Most obediently
Bernt Julius Muus"[1]

Subsequent correspondence went from His Royal Highness the Crown Prince (King Oscar died July 8, 1859) to the Church Department, from the Church Department to the Bishop, J. L. Arup, and from Bishop Arup back to the Church Department, regarding Candidate Muus's impending ordination. The issue was whether Muus, called to serve in America, would have to take the same pastoral oath as the candidates serving in Norway, which Muus was not willing to do. The outcome was that he would not have to do so, but in the event that he returned to serve as a pastor in Norway, he would be required to take the regular oath.[2]

The substance of the oath is indicated in Muus's letter to the Reverend A. C. Preus of July 5, 1859, where he quotes part of the Latin text. After stating that he could not subscribe to what he calls "the civil assertion" in its present form, he writes, "Therefore I petitioned the Christiania bishop to be released from the expressions, 'Let the ceremonies accepted in the church be observed nor let anything be allowed against the ecclesiastical constitutions.'"[3] The likely reason Muus declined to take the oath was his practical instinct that conditions for doing pastoral work in America would require flexibility and a measure of freedom from some of the "ceremonies."

Muus tells Preus that he had also requested from the bishop an interpretation of the section of the oath that appeared to say that everyone who did not keep the oath inviolably in all its parts was renouncing his salvation. After conferring with the church department, continues Muus, the bishop excused him from making the assertion, taking the view that it was only for those who would be serving in the church in Norway.[4] Muus's view is confirmed by a communication from the Church Department to Bishop Arup which states: "The Department assumes as correct that candidates who are ordained to accept appointment as pastors in America are released from taking the oath."[5]

The ordination of Bernt Julius Muus took place in Oslo on July 8, 1859. The minister conducting the ordination service was the bishop of the Christiania Diocese, Jens Laurits Arup. The place of the ordination is not on record, but very likely it was Our Savior's, the church where Muus's contemporary Laur. Larsen had been ordained shortly before he left for America two years earlier.[6] The text used for the ordination sermon was 2 Corinthians 12:8–10: "And he said to me, 'My grace is sufficient for thee, for my strength is made perfect in weakness. Most gladly therefore will I rather glory in my infirmities, that the power of Christ may rest upon me. Therefore I take pleasure in infirmities, in reproaches, in necessities, in persecutions, in distresses for Christ's sake, for when I am weak, then I am strong.'"

Late in his life, Muus asked his younger colleague, Pastor S. O. Simundson, to preach on this text at his funeral.[7] As it happened, however, the request could not be fulfilled, since Pastor Muus ended his days in Norway and was buried in Trondheim rather than at Holden.

Bernt Julius Muus had met Oline Christine Kathrine Pind during the Johnsonian awakening in Oslo. The time of their first meeting is not known, but Muus refers to her by name in a brief letter dated May 20, 1857. Writing to "Student Otto Lundh" Muus says, "Oline has asked me to inform you that she is coming to the city on Saturday together with her mother and will be at a hotel. Where, she doesn't say, but presumably at Skandinaven."[8]

Bernt and Oline were engaged by that time, having decided in the early part of 1857 to commit themselves to marriage.[9] Certainly the tone of the short message suggests such a relationship, Bernt having been entrusted with the role of setting up this meeting in the city. There is no clue as to the purpose of the meeting, but one senses an easy friendship among the three young people. Muus stayed in touch with Otto Lundh, writing to him from America many years later urging him to act without delay in getting Muus's genealogy printed.[10]

Bernt Julius Muus had been thinking about going to America to serve in Goodhue county, Minnesota, as early as 1857. Therefore his fiancée was well aware that in marrying Muus she herself had to be prepared to accept emigration and the challenges of establishing a new way of life in America. In his April 5, 1859, letter to Laur. Larsen, Muus states that it is possible that he will come to America as a married man, and that his prospective in-laws have been asking him many questions that he has been unable to answer. There were questions about finding servants, about the climate, about a place to live, "and I can't remember all of them," writes Muus, sounding a bit harried but full of curiosity concerning the situation he might soon be facing in America.[11]

On July 12, 1859, four days after his ordination, Bernt Julius Muus married Oline Christine Kathrine Pind. The bride was the daughter of Johan Christian Pind, *lensmann* (sheriff or bailiff), an administrative official, in Fet township, east of Oslo. The bride's mother was Hanna Lovise Poulsen. Oline's father served in the position of *lensmann* in Fet from 1825 until his death in 1863. Through a series of purchases, he became the owner of considerable property, including a grist mill and an important farm that was the site of a local court. The Fet township history, in listing the children in the Pind family, records the name of a daughter who died at age four, Oline Katrine Kierstine (1829–1833). The name of the young woman who married Bernt Julius Muus is given as Katrine Christine.[12] At some point, apparently, Muus's bride added to her name the "Oline" from the deceased sister.

The marriage of Bernt Julius Muus and Oline Christine Kathrine Pind took place in Fet Church in Oline's home community on July 12, 1859. Writing briefly about the occasion many years later, Oline Muus stated that the ceremony was conducted by Pastor Landmark. She added a detail about the unfavorable weather. "There was a furious storm that day so we scarcely could get across the Glommen River to the church. A bad omen."[13]

It is not known whether Bernt or the newlywed couple made a trip from Oslo to Snåsa in North Trøndelag and back. In his July 5, 1859, letter to A. C. Preus, Muus had written, "I will be ordained the 8th of July in Christiania, whereupon I will take a trip home to Snåsa to take leave of my family, and hope to reach America by the end of September." Muus could not have made the long trip to Snåsa and back in the four days between his ordination on July 8th and his marriage July 12th. It is more likely that he would have made the trip after his marriage, taking his bride with him to meet his family in Snåsa. But there is no firm evidence that such a trip was made, either by the newly married couple or by Muus traveling to Snåsa alone. All that is certain is that he planned to visit Snåsa right after his ordination and that he would be going to America with his wife and a servant girl.[14]

"There are no shepherds and a hundred wolves," wrote Pastor Ulrich Vilhelm Koren to Laur. Larsen after both had settled in America, graphically stating the urgent need for more pastors to serve the growing number of Norwegians coming to America.[15] Larsen was in touch with Muus before the latter emigrated and remained an important person in Muus's career in America. A year younger than Muus, Larsen had emigrated to America in 1857, responding to the need for pastors among the Norwegian immigrants in the American Midwest. He was pastor for the Rush River congregation in St. Croix county, Wisconsin, but also conducted an itinerant ministry among many other Norwegian settlements, including several in Minnesota.

Larsen emerged as one of the leading figures in the Norwegian Lutheran Church in America, commonly called the Norwegian Synod. In 1859 he left the Rush River parish to assume the position of professor of theology for Norwegian candidates studying at the Missouri Synod's Concordia College, St. Louis, Missouri. The following year Larsen was chosen by his Norwegian Synod colleagues to make a trip to Norway for the purpose of enlisting more pastors to come to America to help serve the immigrants. Larsen was among the Norwegian Synod pastors who founded Luther College, which began in 1861 in a parsonage in Halfway Creek, Wisconsin, and was moved to Decorah, Iowa, the next summer. And it was Larsen who was chosen as the first president of the new institution.[16]

As the letter referred to indicates, Bernt Julius Muus had confi-

*Pastor Laur. Larsen*
Courtesy Luther College Archives

dence in and respect for Larsen and looked to him for advice regarding the forthcoming journey to America, where Muus would take his place among the other pioneering Norwegian immigrant pastors. At the beginning of the letter Muus thanks Larsen both for the latter's contributions to *Norsk Kirketidende* and for "your private letter to me."[17]

From its first year of existence, Muus and Bernhoft's church paper, *Norsk Kirketdende*, carried in its columns appeals from pastors in America for help from the mother country. In issue No. 14, early spring of 1856, it advertised a specific pastoral call in America and in issue No. 20, dated May 18, 1856, reported that the call was still not filled. The congregation had been trying to get a pastor since 1854. With other similar congregations this one had tried appointing a layman from their midst or receiving the services of one of the wandering unordained preachers, but the results had not been satisfactory. "The congregations here want to have pastors who have studied—they have seen enough of the unlearned and uncalled to appreciate the difference."[18]

In one issue after another *Norsk Kirketidende* published letters from pastors in America underscoring the great need among their fellow Norwegians who had settled in America, the "hunger" for the Word and the Sacraments, the far-flung settlements, and the impossibility of the few pastors available visiting these distant outposts more than once or twice a year. "A Norwegian Pastor in America" submits a letter that is published in the issue of February 6, 1859. He writes: "We are now 12 Norwegian pastors here and have as a minimum 3 or 4 permanent congregations, but besides that, as we calculated at our last pastors' conference, nearly 80 different settlements of Norwegians which we serve as so-called mission districts from 2 to 6 times a year. Of these, some can be from 1 to 200 miles from the nearest pastor, so one can easily see how impossible it is for so few pastors to be able to undertake so much."[19]

The writer goes on to point out that the sects have their preachers going about, especially in the more distant districts, taking advantage of the fact that the pastors cannot be there very often. By "sects" the early Norwegian Lutheran pastors in America usually meant other denominational groups. The latter posed a problem for them only when they tried to proselytize in the Norwegian settlements.

In the light of the frequent contributions to *Norsk Kirketidende* submitted by pastors in America, including Laur. Larsen, A. C. Preus, H. A. Preus, Jacob Aall Ottesen, and others, and the personal acquaintance developing between Larsen and Muus, it is obvious that Muus was confronted personally with the pastoral needs of Norwegians in America. In September of 1858, *Norsk Kirketidende* published Larsen's article, "Pastoral calls in America," which again appealed for Norwegian theology candidates to come to America. The article also included a description of Larsen's parish in Wisconsin plus an explicit mention of Goodhue county in Minnesota and other places where pastors were needed. In October of 1858 the paper carried an article by A. C. Preus titled "Vacant pastorates in America."[20]

In June of 1860, *Norsk Kirketidende* made public a list of eleven vacancies in America. By that time, Muus had already left for America and was at work in the Holden parish in Minnesota, but the article merits mention for interesting details about the Rush River call in Wisconsin that became vacant when Pastor Larsen moved to St. Louis. The salary announced would be 300 dollars plus a travel sum of 150 dollars and the usual incidental income. The pastor's farm (*prestegaard*) in Rush River was 80 acres in size, of which 23 acres could be cultivated. There were about 100 families in the congregation.[21]

The promise of travel money is to be noted. Before Muus arrived at Holden, members of the congregation gathered a sum of money to assist him in the travel expenses he incurred when he and his wife made their journey to America in the fall of 1859.[22] Incidentally, the fare for one adult from Europe to Quebec during the 1850s would probably have been between fifteen and thirty dollars.[23] Halle Steensland, who emigrated in 1854, wrote that the cost from Norway to Quebec or New York by sailing ship in his time was from sixteen to twenty dollars.[24]

The rural Holden congregation in Goodhue county, southern Minnesota, was founded in 1856. The name "Holden" was inspired by a community in Telemark from which many of the first settlers in the area had come.[25] In the summer of 1855 the Reverend Nils Brandt, from Oconomowoc, Wisconsin, was the first Norwegian pastor to preach and conduct baptisms in the Holden area. On his way to this part of Minnesota he came first to Red Wing and from there walked along the Zumbro River, sleeping on a pile of hay the first night and finding shelter in Henrik Talla's cabin the second night. The Reverend P. A. Rasmussen visited the area and preached in several places in 1856.[26]

In the summer of 1856, a group of interested persons held a meeting in a field about 150 yards west of the site of the present Holden parsonage and decided to form a congregation. The official founding date was September 12, 1856, when the Reverend H. A. Stub, who had been making a pastoral visit to the settlement, presided over a meeting at which the congregation was duly organized and a constitution was adopted. Action was also taken to authorize the Council of the Norwegian Evangelical Lutheran Church in America to issue a letter of call on their behalf to secure the services of a regular pastor.[27] Trustees who signed the authorization to the church council were Knut K. Finseth, Kjostøl Gundersen Naeseth, Halvor Olsen Huset, and Christopher Lockrem.[28]

According to this procedure, the church council of the parent church body would act as an agent for the Holden congregation in finding a pastor. Therefore it was the church council of the Norwegian Synod that actually extended the call to Muus. Thus Pastor Muus himself, writing a sketch of the Holden congregation's first twenty-five years, after summarizing the visits to Holden by other pastors between 1857 and 1859, wrote of his call as follows: "In the meantime the church council had called Candidate in Theology from Christiania University B. J. Muus to [be] the congregation's pastor."[29]

The role of the university in transmitting the call to Muus is made clear in Muus's letter to A. C. Preus on July 5, 1859. He states that the letter of call from the Norwegian Evangelical Lutheran congregation in Goodhue county, Minnesota, was issued to him by Pastor S. Brun and a certain *lektor* whose name is illegible but who very likely was Gisle Johnson. The theology faculty at the university performed the service of transmitting to the candidate the letter of call that had come from a congregation in America through the church council of the Norwegian Synod and from that committee to Norway. Thus Muus recalled that the church council called him "from Christiania University." Similarly, Laur. Larsen's call two years earlier was mediated through the theology faculty. His biography states that Larsen saw advertised six calls in America "which the two distinguished theologians, Gisle Johnson and Sven Brun, were authorized to fill."[30]

It is not known exactly how and when the Holden congregation established direct communication with Candidate Muus in Norway, who at the time was in the midst of getting the journal *Norsk Kirketidende* launched. The people in Holden could have learned of Muus through such Norwegian-American churchmen as A. C. Preus, H. A. Preus, J. A. Ottesen, and Laur. Larsen, who had come to know of him and his ability through their correspondence with *Norsk Kirketidende*. These leaders in the Norwegian Synod had used the pages of that journal to urge theology candidates in Norway to come over and join their ranks to minister to the many Norwegian immigrants who were without pastoral care. In particular, A. C. Preus and Laur. Larsen had direct knowledge of the situation in the Holden area since both had done itinerant pastoral work in that community.

Pastor Larsen had visited Goodhue county in June of 1858 and again in June of 1859. "As soon as he [Larsen] heard that Bernt Julius Muus was considering a call from Goodhue County, he opened a correspondence with him and encouraged him to come," writes Larsen's biographer.[31] In an important letter that was part of that correspondence, from Muus to Laur. Larsen, April 5, 1859, it appears that Muus's struggle to come to a decision had to do primarily with the commitment to go to America, not with whether he should accept the call to Holden. In fact, he discusses the matter with Larsen without mentioning a "call" as such.

Having informed Larsen that he has now decided to come to America, he goes on to discuss the place of his future service in somewhat informal terms. He states that since the "Goodhue and Fillmore congregations" have expressed a desire to have him come there and since it appears that the president of the Synod also would like to have him located there, he has pictured this place as his sphere of work. Then he adds that he intends to arrive in America in late September or in October of that year, 1859.

Evidently Muus had needed time to arrive at his decision. One infers that the call from the church council had been in his hands for quite some time before he decided in 1859 to accept it. The delay in answering Larsen's private letter to him, for which he is apologetic, is clearly tied to the soul-searching he had done regarding the invitation to serve the church in America. He explains to Larsen that he had put off answering because he did not want his reply to carry any suggestion of pretense, but now he could not postpone answering any longer. "It is therefore my decision," he writes, adopting a more formal tone, "if the Lord will vouchsafe to use me for that purpose, to go over to America and to place those talents and energies that I might have at the disposition of my former countrymen."[32]

This letter and the later one to A. C. Preus in July of 1859 shed important light on Muus's decision to take up work in America, but they do not provide all the information one would like to have. There must have been other communications between Pastor Muus and the church council of the Norwegian Evangelical Lutheran Church in America, and at some point perhaps some direct correspondence between the Holden congregation and Pastor Muus.

One sidelight on Muus's call appears in the reminiscences of P. O. Floan, a member of Holden congregation from a later generation. Floan tells of an old letter left in the Holden parsonage for safekeeping by Pastor Muus that, in Floan's view, could have been a factor in Muus's coming to Holden. The letter was a personal one, not an official letter of call, sent not to Muus but to a certain Pastor Færgestad in Meranger, Norway, urging him to accept the call to Holden. The letter was written by Saave Aaker, secretary of the congregation, and signed by Peter Olson Floan and Ole Peterson Floan, P. O. Floan's grandfather and father respectively.

The older Floans had been members of Færgestad's congregation in Norway before emigrating; they hoped he would come to be their pastor in Holden. The sending of this personal letter implies that Pastor Færgestad had already received an official letter of call. According to Floan, Fægerstad had nearly decided to come to America, but changed his mind and sent the letter to *Norsk Kirketidende*, the paper co-edited by Muus. Muus published the letter, but no one responded. It is reasonable, Floan suggests, that the letter signed by his grandfather and father had much to do with Muus's decision to accept the call from Holden.[33]

Another source of information about Muus's original decision to come to America is the foreword to the book he compiled about his family's history, *Niels Muus's æt: Muus-slegten i Snaasa*. There he writes: "I believe that it was God's will that I should come here to summon, in my Lord's name, my emigrating countrymen to the bridal feast of the King's Son. When I journeyed over here in 1859, there was a great shortage of preachers of the Word; in Norway there was an abundance."[34] The latter point is corroborated by Laur. Larsen's finding that in 1857 there had been 300 candidates in Norway who were without a pastoral call.[35]

The view has been expressed that Muus came to America because he lacked confidence that he would qualify for a position in Norway. Clearly there was keen competition for clerical appointments. Pastor S. O. Simundson, a younger contemporary and colleague who knew Muus in his declining years, after mentioning Muus's brief consideration of missionary work, stated: "He did not apply for the ministry in Norway, he told me, for fear he might stand in the way of some one who was abler than he."[36] Similarly Pastor N. J. Ellestad in a memorial piece published in 1900 after Muus's death wrote: "Convinced of his own uselessness and unworthiness, he always held back from seeking any call in his native land. He knew that as a rule others would also be seeking the same call, and he was afraid that he would get in the way of better men than himself."[37] After deciding against going to South Africa, he felt free to accept the call to Holden since there would be no danger there of standing in the way of someone better qualified.[38]

In the light of Muus's subsequent reputation in America as a determined leader and man of vision who forged ahead to carry out his plans with or without the cooperation and consent of others, the notion of his being too unsure of his abilities to seek a call in Norway seems difficult to accept. Nevertheless, Muus could well have harbored such feelings of unworthiness at that stage of his life. Later events proved him to be a man of high ability and iron will, but he could also be introspective and diffident. His exposure to pietism during his Oslo years would have encouraged a self-effacing attitude as would the Lutheran theology of sin and grace, especially as mediated by Gisle Johnson, for whom the consciousness of sin was a central ingredient in the content of faith.[39]

Something of Muus's lack of self-confidence is in evidence in the letter to Laur. Larsen. Muus reveals that the thought of a ministry in America had been on his mind for some time before 1859. He feels that he ought to explain to Larsen the series of conflicting decisions he had been struggling with for some time. His first impulse as soon as he became a theology candidate, and indeed before then, was to become a missionary. The Schreuder mission among the Zulus in Africa was one possibility that had been on his mind, but he felt that he lacked the strength of body and soul that would be required on the mission field. As he writes to Larsen regarding the mission possibility, "My faith was weak and my flesh even worse, so that to a high degree I dreaded it; I did not see it as reasonable that I could endure in a work for example such as Schreuder's in Zulu."[40]

Where he found himself turning away from the idea of joining the Schreuder mission, he could face with more equanimity the prospect of working among the Norwegian congregations in America. Yet he held back. It was partly a matter of feeling incompetent, partly a matter of his youth—he was not yet twenty-five years old—and partly also the founding of *Norsk Kirketidende* that kept him from taking the final step. But the thought of America continued to ferment within him, as it had done for about five years. It was in about 1857 that he decided to go to America if the church leaders there wanted him, but he was reluctant to leave *Kirketidende*, which, he thought, was also doing some good.[41]

That, in brief, is the whole story, he tells Larsen. The only thing that would stand in the way would be the chance that the bishop would not ordain him because he would not take the usual pastor's oath.[42] As it turned out, his refusal to take the oath did not stand in the way, so his ordination took place on July 8, 1859, and on July 12th he and Oline Christine Kathrine Pind were married.

Whether or not he made the planned "trip home to Snåsa," either alone or with Oline after their marriage, Muus and his young wife must in any case have had some very busy weeks of preparation before they embarked for the new world that fall.

On the fifth of September, 1859, Pastor and Mrs. Bernt Julius Muus and a servant girl by the name of Karen registered with the Oslo police office, giving their destination as "Amerika."[43] It would be of considerable interest to know more about the events of the summer and the circumstances of the journey. Where did the young couple spend their time between the July wedding and the September departure? What did they pack to take with them? Who assisted them in getting ready for the long voyage? Who saw them off? What ship did they travel on? How long did the voyage take? Where did they arrive in North America, New York or Quebec? What kind of a crossing was it? What kind of journey to reach Minnesota?

Information is incomplete on these questions. Because Oline's home was so much closer to Oslo than Snåsa, it is probable that members of her family had much to do with the preparations and the send-off. One would expect that Muus's friend and co-editor of *Norsk Kirketidende*, Theodor C. Bernhoft, would have been among those who waved an emotional farewell to Muus and his wife. The name of the ship they boarded in Oslo is not known. In all probability they sailed from Oslo to England and from England to North America. The total journey from Oslo, Norway

*Coon Prairie Church*
From H. Halvorsen, *Festskrift til Den norske Synodes Jubilaeum*

to Wisconsin took a little more than one month, from September 5 to about October 12, 1859. Muus had asked Larsen how much the trip from Liverpool to America would cost, and "how much from Quebec to Goodhue?" Thus one surmises that Quebec was the port of entry into North America and that Bernt and Oline and the servant girl then made their way, probably by boat and rail, from Quebec to Wisconsin and Minnesota.[44]

The time of arrival in the Midwest was in the first part of October. Muus had written Larsen that he expected to reach America by the latter part of September or in October. The Norwegian Synod's paper, *Kirkelig Maanedstidende*, reported that Pastor Muus attended the meeting of the Norwegian Lutheran Synod at Coon Prairie, near LaCrosse, Wisconsin, which began October 14, 1859. The notice says that Muus had just arrived in LaCrosse from Norway a couple of days before, and that the Synod expressed its pleasure in having "this servant of the Word in its midst." Muus and five other pastors requested that they be made members of the Synod and their request was granted unanimously.[45]

About three weeks later, Pastor and Mrs. Muus arrived at the rural community of Holden in Goodhue county. The congregation, established in September of 1856, had been awaiting a pastor for three years.

# Four

# The Holden Settlement

Goodhue county, Minnesota, was established by action of the Minnesota Territorial legislature on March 5, 1853. It was named for James M. Goodhue, native of Hebron, New Hampshire, graduate of Amherst College, lawyer, and pioneer Minnesota journalist. Goodhue published and edited *The Minnesota Pioneer* with vigor and vivid style from his arrival in St. Paul in 1849 until his untimely death in 1852.[1]

This serene county in southern Minnesota proved to be an exceptionally favorable place for white settlers to establish homes and farms. They soon learned to value its water, woods, fertile soil, and other desirable features such as excellent drainage, stone quarries, and a natural beauty that inspired one writer to describe the area in glowing words: "On its splendid course from Itasca to the Gulf, the mighty Mississippi passes no fairer land than that which it touches from Prairie Island to Central Point, where, guarded on the north by towering bluffs and broken here and there by picturesque valleys, Goodhue county stretches to the southward in undulating prairies. Unusually blessed by nature with deep soil and abundant natural resources, and endowed with a wealth of prehistoric and historic lore, it is a fitting home for the sturdy people who have here made their dwelling place."[2]

71

Goodhue county with its 784 square miles of land lies on the west side of the Mississippi River about forty-five miles southeast of St. Paul. Its northeastern boundary, a stretch of about thirty miles, is formed by the Mississippi River and part of Lake Pepin. The county seat is Red Wing, situated on the west side of the great river, an important stop for river boats and a natural market town. To the north of Goodhue is Dakota county and to the south are Wabasha, Olmsted, and Dodge counties. On the west is Rice county and a corner of Dakota county.[3]

The topography of Goodhue county is chiefly that of rolling prairie, particularly in the central and southeastern parts, which is where the Norwegians established themselves. Somewhat hilly terrain is found in the north and northwestern parts of the county. The highest spot in Goodhue is Kenyon township in the southwestern corner of the county, 1,250 feet above sea level. Similar elevations are found in Cherry Grove, Roscoe, Leon, and Belle Creek townships, as well as in two of the "Norwegian" townships, Holden and Wanamingo. The descent to Lake Pepin takes one to an elevation of 665 feet.[4]

The Cannon River flows eastward into the Mississippi in the northern part of the county; the Zumbro River, north and middle branches, in the southern part of the county, also empties into the Mississippi. In addition to the two rivers are several creeks which are also significant as water sources and for drainage.[5] Given the preference of the early Norwegian immigrants to the Midwest for sites with trees and water as well as tillable land, it is no surprise to find them living in the vicinity of the Little Cannon River in Warsaw and Holden townships, and of the north branch of the Zumbro River in Wanamingo and Minneola townships. Regarding the land his grandfather bought in Wanamingo township and where his parents also lived, P. O. Floan wrote, "It was a good farm with plenty of good timber and water on it. They made no mistake in locating in Goodhue County."[6]

Some settlers, however, did make mistakes in their choice of land. It has been observed that at first the Norwegians generally

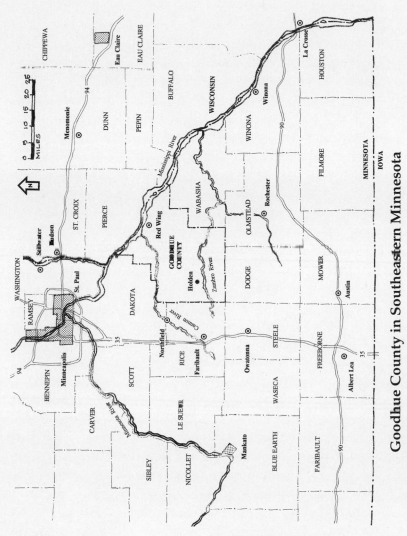

**Goodhue County in Southeastern Minnesota**

*Goodhue and neighboring counties Southeastern Minnesota*
Map by Clint Sathrum

preferred wooded lands to prairie, but later sought out the plains.[7] So it was with some of the Norwegians in Goodhue who eagerly chose wooded land in the western part of the county, only to learn from hard experience how difficult it was to remove the stumps of large oaks in the process of clearing the land.[8]

Goodhue county was part of the coveted "Suland" west of the Mississippi and south of the Minnesota rivers. This area was opened for settlement following the treaty with the lower Sioux at Mendota on August 5, 1851, and its ratification by the Senate in 1852.[9] President Millard Fillmore proclaimed the Sioux treaties on February 24, 1853.[10] Surveying of public lands west of the Mississippi began that year. Congress granted the privilege of preemption of unsurveyed public lands in 1854.[11] Not until 1855 was the first installment of land in the southeastern corner of the state offered for sale. "The pioneers of the day, however," writes William Watts Folwell, "had no troublesome scruples, and they continued to swarm over the thirteen counties west of the Mississippi River in the region of the lower Minnesota."[12]

As early as 1852 promoters were laying out townsites in such places as Winona, Belle Plaine, and Mankato. At that time about 5,000 trespassers reportedly were in the area between the lower Minnesota and the Mississippi.[13]

That the rush for land in 1854–1857 would be strong in the southeastern corner of Minnesota is seen in the fact that three of the six Minnesota land offices in existence in 1855, Brownsville, Winona, and Red Wing, were along the Mississippi River in that part of the territory.[14] Goodhue county with its desirable features lay directly in the path of the land-seekers. Norwegians were among the pioneers who, even before 1855, displayed a determined interest in acquiring land in Goodhue county.

Pastor Muus came to America to offer pastoral leadership among fellow Norwegian immigrants, being called specifically to serve the Norwegians in Goodhue county. His call and his coming belong to the remarkable population movement whereby

74

thousands of persons left their homes in Europe to make a new life in America in the nineteenth and early twentieth centuries.

The story of Norwegian migration to America has been told many times in both scholarly and popular fashion, but its magnitude and human drama continue to fascinate all who reflect upon it. When historians and analysts of the phenomenon submit the figure of nearly 800,000 persons leaving Norway for America between 1836 and 1930,[15] one realizes that it was a movement of prodigious scale and historic import.

By making their way to America in 1859, Pastor and Mrs. Muus were actually coming slightly before the three great waves of Norwegian emigration began to roll. In fact, the year of their journey falls within a brief period of decline in emigration, from 1855 to 1860, when "only" 11.5 per cent of Norway's increase in population emigrated.[16]

The beginning of the great migration story goes back to the dramatic voyage of the "Sloopers," the fifty-three emigrants who came to New York on the vessel *Restauration* that left Stavanger July 4, 1825.[17] From 1836, emigration from Norway was an annual event expected each spring when ships would sail directly to America from Norway.

One expert on emigration places the first of the three largest waves of emigration from Norway in the period from 1866 to 1874, the second in the 1880s and early 1890s, and the third in the first years of the twentieth century.[18] The first two waves, according to this scheme, coincide with the time of B. J. Muus's ministry among Norwegians coming into Minnesota.

Another way of describing emigration from Norway is to outline it, as Einar Haugen has done, as a phenomenon unfolding according to five acts. The first was the period of beginnings, from 1836 to the Civil War. The second, lasting through the 1860s and into the 1870s, gained its momentum from the Homestead Act of 1862, which made free land available to settlers. Word of this law spread quickly to Norway. "Now the Norwegians were really ready to come," writes Haugen. A third great wave of migration began in 1879, a fourth started in 1899, and a final but smaller surge took place after World War I.[19]

Immigrants like the Muuses who reached America during the period of beginnings indeed were ahead of the most spectacular movements from Norway to America. Nevertheless, they too belonged to an already significant migration in that 78,000 Norwegians had left Norway between 1825, the voyage of the *Restauration*, and the end of the Civil War, 1865.[20] To some extent the Muuses were non-typical emigrants in that they came from Oslo, not initially a locus of much enthusiasm for emigration. To one traveler who left from that city, however, the spring of 1853 was a "great season for emigration from the port of Christiania."[21]

It was from the inner fjord country of western Norway and such districts in eastern Norway as Telemark and Numedal that the early emigrants set out, but interest was spreading rapidly into all districts during the forty-year "founding phase of Norwegian emigration," from 1825 to 1865.[22] Many members of the congregations Muus would serve came from Telemark, as did the name Holden (now Holla) itself.[23]

To speak of the Holden settlement is to refer to that part of Goodhue county in which Norwegian immigrants staked their claims in the decade of the 1850s. Four townships in particular define the settlement. Holden township together with Wanamingo township, writes Theodore Nydahl, "is the center of the Norwegian colony in Goodhue." Warsaw to the north of Holden and Minneola to the east of Wanamingo were the other two townships most heavily populated by Norwegian settlers.[24]

The population of Goodhue county rose rapidly in the decades of the 1850s and 1860s. United States Census records indicate a population of 8,977 in the county in 1860. By 1870 the figure was 22,618. In 1860 there were 1,152 persons in Goodhue county who were born in Norway. In addition were those who, while not born in the old country, were born of Norwegians who came to Goodhue county after staying for a time in some other settlement.

Ten years later, in 1870, the number of Norwegians in the county was 4,099.[25]

The Telemark name "Holden" has become associated primarily with the rural Lutheran church that was Pastor Muus's home base throughout his forty-year ministry. It was also given to the township on the western border of Goodhue county and to a post office in the northern part of the township. Holden Lutheran church is not actually in Holden township but is located to the east in Wanamingo township.

In her book *Norway to America*, Ingrid Semmingsen refers to the Holden region to illustrate how the immigrants' place of origin in Norway is reflected in the names of congregations. She writes: "In Minnesota Vang Prairie was settled by people from Valdres with its Vang parish, Holden by people from Telemark with a parish of the same name. There are still places here called by Norwegian names like Eidsvold, Gol, Toten; Dovre and Oslo are close together in Goodhue County, Minnesota."[26]

Norwegian settlement in Minnesota began in the southeastern corner of the state in Goodhue county.[27] Theodore Nydahl points out that Goodhue county has the distinction "of being the most prominent of the Norwegian settlements in Minnesota." Nydahl quotes a statement by Hjalmar Rued Holand, author of a history of Norwegian settlements: "Wisconsin has its Koshkonong, Minnesota its Goodhue county, and Iowa its Winneshiek."[28]

The first Norwegian to make an appearance in Goodhue county was Matthias Petersen Ringdahl from Hadeland. He came to Red Wing in 1851 and later took up farming near Zumbrota.[29] Ringdahl built a shack in Pine Island township in the southeastern corner of the county that quickly became a stopping place for early settlers.

In the fall of 1854, Ringdahl and a Swede, Nels Nelson, ventured into the southwestern part of Goodhue county where they had heard there were some other white people. There they found two brothers, Henrik Nilsen and Toge Nilsen Talla, originally from the Sogn district of Norway, their sisters Mrs. Jens Ottum and Mrs. Nils K. Fenne, William Ronningen and Nils Gulbrandsen from Telemark, and the family of Tosten A. Aabye from Sigdal. This company had just arrived in the county from Dodgeville, Wisconsin.[30]

When Bernt and Oline Muus eventually reached the Holden community in Goodhue county in 1859, they would come to know these Norwegians from various districts in the homeland who had come to the area before them. The arrival of the party of Norwegians from Dodgeville, Wisconsin, in Goodhue county in Minnesota is one example of immigrants living in one settlement for a time and then moving on. Another is the following incident from the Holden Church's Centennial History. "Mrs. Tosten Aabye was awakened one morning by the sound of a strange cow bell. She prepared breakfast and fed the family as quickly as possible. Taking the children with her, she waded through the tall wet grass to find the strange cow and its owner. Soon she came upon a group camped on a hillside. They had come from Koshkonong and in the party were Ole and Amund Oakland, Andreas Bonhus, Hans Ovaldsen and Gunder Hestemyr, all Telemarkings. Others were Haldor Johnson, John Stromme, Andreas Hessedalen and Kolbein Ektveidt, all from Bergen."[31]

It was a familiar pattern; many Norwegian immigrants moved from one settlement to another, "always seeking better land to the west," as Odd Lovoll writes.[32] Koshkonong in southern Wisconsin was one of several early, prosperous Norwegian settlements in that state that functioned as way stations for immigrants pushing on to cheaper land. Similarly, immigrants would stop for a time in Winneshiek county in northern Iowa before moving west or north into Minnesota.

While the Norwegian Ringdahl had entered Goodhue county in 1851, an early account focused on a later arrival: "It was in 1854 that the Norwegians occupied Goodhue County; they took it so to speak by storm and settled down in two townships at once—in Holden and Wanamingo; indeed, they also took part of Leon and Minneola townships."[33] The image of taking the county by storm leads to a couple of stories about Goodhue Norwegians and Native Americans, but the language could also apply to some of the conflicts between the settlers.

One of the stories involving brushes with Indians was about a native woman attempting to steal a child from a Norwegian home. Mrs. Ole Bakke had left her child in its bed when she stepped out to fetch some water. It was gone when she returned but she heard it crying in a nearby grove of trees. She raced to the spot and saw the Indian woman with her child. When she saw Mrs. Bakke coming, she set the child down and ran away.[34]

The incident brings out the fact that for a few years after the treaties with the Sioux at Traverse des Sioux and at Mendota in 1851, Indians continued to be seen in the area and settlers were accustomed to their presence. "Very rarely did they do any harm," writes Theodore Nydahl. "Now and then one of them might frighten a household by putting his face against a windowpane and peering inside, but as a rule this was merely the preliminary to a request for food or the purchase of ammunition."[35] After the outbreak of the Dakota Conflict of 1862 there were rumors in Goodhue county of hostile activity and frightened reactions, but the rumors proved false.[36]

The arrival of Matthias Petersen Ringdahl in 1851 and the entry into Wanamingo township of the Talla Nilsen (or Nelson) brothers and their party in 1854 place the Norwegians among the earliest settlers of Goodhue county. Intensive land-seeking took place in the years from 1853 to 1855 with the result that by 1855 "practically all the desirable land was taken."[37] During the early 1850s the laws for the fair and equitable acquisition of land were not clearly determined and known, so some of the settlers competing for the fertile tracts devised their own rules.

In any community where vigorous characters contend with difficulties and dangers, and often with one another, colorful stories with a basis in fact in time become legends that may stretch credibility. Pastor Muus himself became the subject of many stories, and he found himself among a host of robust personalities whose brash exploits were bound to be told by one generation to the next. The clash between the Talla brothers and Big Sven Nordgaarden is a clear example of local history taking on a legendary cast.

The meeting between Matthias Petersen Ringdahl and the Talla brothers and their party has already been mentioned. Tøge Nilsen Talla and his brother, Henrik Nilsen Talla, were from Luster in the Sogn district of Norway. They had had some experience of the wider world before staking out homesteads in Goodhue county in 1854. Tøge had been a gold miner in Australia and his brother Henrik had been working in California, where he had managed to accumulate a fair amount of money. They and two married sisters joined a group of Norwegians in Dodgeville, Wisconsin, and from there traveled in six prairie schooners to Wanamingo township in the spring of 1854. The site they arrived at was so promising and appealing that Tøge was moved to a burst of pioneer eloquence: "I have lived, I have roamed about through many countries, but never have I seen a more beautiful sight than this. Farewell to foreign yokes and tiresome wandering without home and comfort. Here is where I want to live and here I will die."[38]

It happened of course that others besides the Talla brothers and their immediate friends also wanted to live amid the rich fields and pleasant groves of Goodhue county, but Tøge and Henrik were determined to grab as much of this desirable land as they could. Hjalmar Rued Holand explains their procedure: "As discoverers of this beautiful district, they were not satisfied with selecting the best plots of land for themselves, but they also roamed about and put their names on all the surveyor's posts over a wide area. Their idea in doing this was to give a semblance of priority to the land, so that later landseekers would be induced to buy the rights to the land from them."[39]

With some other settlers from Sogn and with some from Stril, a somewhat derogatory name given to an area north and west of Bergen, the Talla brothers and their immediate circle worked out an agreement to stand united in a plan to prevent other people

80

from staking claims on the lands they had illegally appropriated. They would tell land-seekers that Minnesota law allowed them to hold land for relatives coming later. Henrik Talla even dictated, as a sweating Andreas Bonhus did the writing, a formal document filled with high-sounding resolutions and sprinkled with borrowed legal phrases that would lend it an air of authority.[40]

The point of the plan and the pretentious document was that its signers would stand together in driving off anyone who dared encroach upon "their" land. Brother Tøge produced an awesome oak club on which they all solemnly pledged to uphold the Law of the Club (*Klubbeloven*), and indeed to use the club when necessary against any intruders. Whereupon the signers soon took possession of and controlled nearly two townships of land, with the Talla brothers taking the lion's share. For more than a year the Law of the Club worked very satisfactorily in keeping new arrivals out of the territory claimed by its authors.

The confrontation that was sure to come took place with the appearance of a fearless immigrant from Telemark known as Big Sven Nordgaarden, the champion who would end the reign of the Club. This man was always called Big Sven (*Storesvend*) because of his huge size and broad shoulders. He was part of a large group of immigrants in thirty covered wagons who had left Stoughton, Wisconsin, to seek land farther west. The caravan was wending its way on a broiling hot summer's day in 1855 across a wide plain south of where the Tallas had their farms. After the hard day's trek under the hot sun the travelers welcomed the sight of two farms, some trees, water, and a chance to meet some white people again.

But when Tøge and Henrik Talla came out to meet them, the new arrivals quickly sensed that they were not welcome. The Tallas gruffly advised them to move on, saying that all the land there was already taken. But Sven, speaking for his company, announced that they would not wander about in the dark for any man, and that was that. He turned to unyoke the oxen while Henrik and Tøge mumbled something to one another and left.

The next day, Big Sven and his party found wonderful land as they proceeded northward, but every section marker bore the name "Nelson," the Talla brothers' patronymic (sometimes spelled "Nilsen"). The truth of the situation was becoming clear to Sven and his companions as the day wore on. Around noon they approached a pretty cluster of trees. Said Sven, "Well, it doesn't matter to me if the next piece bears the name of Nelson or of Jørgen What's-his-name. I am going no farther than to that grove over there." The place in question was about half a mile south of where the Holden parsonage would be built a few years later.

The rest of that day passed without incident as the new immigrants led by Sven examined the area on foot. The next day, however, brought the showdown. Big Sven and some others were cutting down trees to build a house when they saw a group of seven or eight men plus some women and children approaching. Tøge Talla with a club on his shoulder led the procession and the others carried cudgels. Sven's reaction was to remark, "Well, look at that. Now the fun is about to begin." One of Sven's friends had a loaded gun which he offered to Sven as the other party was drawing closer. Sven declined. "No, we mustn't be too hard on them," he said, and grabbing an oak branch from the ground he added, "Oak against oak is enough." Then Sven instructed the man with the gun to slip into the woods and work his way around behind the Talla party. He was not to shoot at anyone but to fire the gun into the air at the right moment.

As Holand describes the next events, the Club Law group was emphatic in ordering Big Sven and his friends to get out at once, threatening sure and sudden death. But Sven was not about to back down. Tøge raised his club and Sven lifted his at the same time. Holand continues the story: "Then suddenly a gunshot resounded. Tøge turned his head to see what it was. At that exact moment, Sven landed a powerful blow on his neck. Tøge dropped, and his club executed a dance over the ground. Then Sven turned to Henrik and beat him so hard that he broke his oaken stick." Henrik's sisters rushed into the fray and the Strils attacked Sven with their sticks. "The action was hot and violent. The women wailed and the boys howled, but to little avail. With a sudden jerk, Sven freed himself, grabbed the club from a woman's hands, and now went on a Telemarkian berserk. All by himself, he took on the whole bunch with amazing effectiveness. Those who still had the power to use their legs fled pell-mell over the plain."[41]

While such episodes add color to the immigrant experience and provide entertainment for later generations, it must be kept in mind that the people involved were not fictional characters but real persons whose names and activities belong to the history of Goodhue county. More specifically, the leading figures in the story just related, the two Talla brothers and Sven Nordgaarden, became members of the Holden Lutheran parish. In Holden's parish record book Sven is recorded as member No. 177; Tøge Nilsen Talla is No. 183 and Henrik Nilsen Talla No. 184.[42] Pastor Muus's first Christmas service in the Holden area was held at the home of Tøge, and Henrik's home was also used for church-related meetings.[43]

More stories have been told about Sven. He slipped from his role as champion of justice to become a land-grabber himself. He also sank into heavy drinking and brawling, but eventually moved on to other parts of Minnesota and into North Dakota where he reformed and won new fame as a lawyer, defending newcomers from the wiles of land stealers.[44]

Henrik Talla also became a changed person and a reliable citizen after his clash with Sven Nordgaarden. He gave up his land claims and settled down as a productive blacksmith. By the time his farmer friends were heading for their fields, it was said, Henrik already would have put in hours swinging his hammer. "With hard work and intelligent handling of his excellent farm," writes Holand, "he eventually became one of the richest men in Goodhue County." He carried his wealth without ostentation, becoming more open and friendly as the years went by. By the time he died Henrik Talla was one of the most respected citizens in the county.[45]

Once when Pastor Muus was collecting money to get St. Olaf's School launched, he asked Henrik Talla for a donation. Muus's regular practice was to ask parishioners for specific amounts, depending on their wealth. "Of you, Henrik, we want $500.00," he said. "No, indeed not," Henrik answered, "but I will give you $50.00." Muus refused to accept the smaller sum and Henrik refused to raise it, but later his grandchildren established a scholarship fund at St. Olaf.[46]

His brother Tøge Nilsen Talla, unhappily, gained a reputation as a greedy money-lender. One of his clients was Ole Bakko (or Bakke), the husband of the woman who rescued her child from the Indians. Tøge pressed Ole relentlessly for repayment of a loan, forcing Ole to take his oxen into town and sell them. A heavy snowstorm delayed his return home. In the meantime, Tøge was at the Bakko farm harassing Ole's wife in a crude effort to collect his money. Shortly thereafter, when Ole heard about this, he became enraged to the point of potential violence. Having sold his oxen, he went to Tøge, still seething, delivered the money, and left. But just outside the door lay a big grindstone. In his burning anger, the powerful Ole picked up the grindstone and hurled it through the stout door into the room where Tøge was sitting. The heavy grindstone ripped the door off its hinges and in its momentum slammed against Tøge, knocking him against the stove, which fell over in the crash. Tøge lay sprawled on the floor clutching the money. The stove, the kitchen utensils, the door, and the grindstone were scattered about on the floor. Surveying the scene, Ole delivered a volley of choice threats and left.[47]

Ole Bakko was the brother-in-law of Anders K. Finseth, and had arrived in Goodhue county in 1855 in company with the Finseth brothers Knut, Anders, and Herbrand. Anders K. Finseth gained prominence as county commissioner, state senator, presidential elector, and member of the church council for the Norwegian Synod.[48] His brother Knut K. Finseth also served as county commissioner and in 1868 represented Goodhue county in the Tenth Legislature.[49] After Knut died in September of 1869,

Pastor Muus wrote a warm memorial piece about him in the church journal, *Kirkelige Maanedstidende*. In describing the spiritual growth of this layman, Muus at the same time revealed some of the difficulties he himself had faced when he began his ministry at Holden. When many in the parish seemed not to care whether the pastor lived or starved to death, Finseth time after time had extended a friendly helping hand to Muus. The young pastor also treasured the fact that Finseth was one with whom he could discuss spiritual matters, getting beyond the usual topics of "wind and weather, horses and trade."[50]

Another Finseth, Ole K., would become one of the signers of the Articles of Incorporation at the founding of St. Olaf's School in 1874. These men were Hallings, from Hemsedal in the Hallingdal district of central Norway. Among Muus's parishioners were also immigrants from Sogn and Telemark, and from Land and Valdres.[51]

Norwegians and Swedes made up the largest part of the population of Goodhue county, the Swedes in the northern part of the county in the vicinity of Vasa and the Norwegians in the south and southwest.[52] The first requirement on arriving at one's claim was to build a shanty, "at least twelve feet square, with a door and a window." One also had to make such improvements as plowing some furrows or fencing in at least half an acre.[53] Gaining title to the land called for a trip to the land office in Red Wing, where the settler paid two hundred dollars to purchase 160 acres of land at $1.25 per acre. Most settlers had to borrow the money at an interest rate of twenty-five per cent.[54] The price for unimproved land soon rose to $15 per acre.[55]

Since the Goodhue inhabitants came with the intention of farming, they had to break the land and plow it, for which heavy labor they used teams of oxen to pull the plows. Oxen were also hitched to the wagons that hauled the grain to the markets in Red Wing or Hastings and took families to church. They were the usual working animal during the 1850s and until about 1865, when horses replaced them.[56]

"Wheat was the great cash crop" that became important commercially in Minnesota in 1858, and Goodhue was one of the leading wheat counties in 1860 and 1870.[57] At first the grain was sown by hand in the ancient broadcasting manner and harvested with a sickle or cradle.[58] Threshing was done by flailing or by having the oxen tread the grain. Machines came into use in 1859 and 1860. During the first wheat-growing years the price per bushel received in Red Wing was from thirty-five to fifty cents. Hauling the grain to Red Wing in ox-drawn wagons provided a welcome opportunity for friendly socializing among the drivers. Harvest hands received sixty-five cents a day in the period before the Civil War.[59]

The pioneer farmers did not neglect such livestock as cattle, sheep, and hogs, even though wheat raising was growing in importance. A shipment of cattle from the Rochester area to Boston took place in 1859. In 1866 Fillmore, Olmsted, Goodhue, and Dakota were among "banner" livestock counties. Interest in sheep production was fairly strong in the early 1860s but declined after 1866. Neighbors would hold hog-killing bees after the first freeze in the autumn. Pork to be sold could be sent to LaCrosse and from there shipped by rail to Chicago.[60]

Modern readers have heard about the log houses of the pioneers, but at an earlier stage the dwellings were even more rudimentary. For some, their first shelter was the covered wagon that brought them.[61] One settler who arrived in the Vang area in 1855 tells of building a crude shelter framed with poles from the woods and covered with hay for the roof.[62] There were those who made houses of sod and some who had dugouts in a hillside. But the log house was the standard for a time, usually about ten by twelve feet, but sometimes much larger. These modest dwellings were always open to take in those who came along later, wrote one pioneer, and would often house two or three families.[63]

Theodore Blegen tells of the farmer in Goodhue county who built his log dwelling on a larger scale, 16 x 26 feet, divided by a log partition, to accommodate both people and domestic animals. "On one side of this cabin lived the farmer and his family, on the other, pigs, calves, and chickens; and on one occasion a church service was held in the building to the accompaniment of a barn-yard choir."[64]

The pioneers had to be resourceful in providing themselves with food and clothing. They subsisted on simple fare, milk, cheese, eggs, bread, corn, potatoes, a few other vegetables, and pork. The "prodigal use of pork," in the opinion of a frontier observer, caused much sickness among the settlers, making them "susceptible to the dangerous bilious fever." Oline Muus, Pastor Muus's wife, found that the limited diet in the summer of "bread, butter, and almost always pork" did not agree with her.[65] One pioneer recalled that they traded butter and eggs in order to get sugar and coffee. To make the coffee last longer they added bits of bread crust to it.[66]

Severe winters with deep snow in 1855 and 1856 brought a shortage of flour but the settlers shared the last barrel of it equally among themselves. Fortunately, game was plentiful, including deer.[67] A damaging hailstorm in the fall of 1858 right before harvest wiped out most of the wheat crop, bringing on another harsh winter. P. M. Langemo and his neighbors scraped together what little wheat they could salvage and sent it to the mill in Northfield to be ground into flour. "Mothers would bake bread, ration it out by slices and pray that the flour in the barrel would last until the next crop."[68]

The early settlers wore homemade clothing. There is even a report that Pastor Muus, usually fastidious in dress, appeared at the 1867 synodical conference in homespun clothes.[69] The women carded wool, spun the yarn, wove cloth, and sewed the garments.[70] If a farmer's cow or ox died, neighbors would ask for a piece of the hide, from which they fashioned leather foot coverings.[71] Whiskey was cheap, seventy-five cents for a gallon, reports P. O. Floan. It helped to relieve the tedium on the long grain hauls to Red Wing and was also used to treat a friend or neighbor who stopped in. There was excessive drinking by some, but for the most part the old-timers were moderate in their consumption.[72]

The pioneers were quick to provide for the education of their children. Before any schoolhouses were built, the Norwegians held their parochial schools in farmhouses during the three summer months. The children would sit on benches around a table in the middle of the room. The teacher was often a graduate of a teachers' seminary in Norway. For the Norwegians it was only natural to have schools for religious instruction taught in their own language. The subjects were usually Catechism, Luther's Explanation of the Catechism, and Bible History. Teachers customarily received 50 cents per day as their wage.[73]

Ole Solberg was a highly respected pioneer lay religion teacher. As the group of children became too large to be accommodated in a given log house, he simply led his flock to a larger house. The first Norwegian schoolhouse was built when members of the Holden congregation each brought a log and the men worked together to set it up. The dimensions were 16 by 20 feet, but Solberg managed to find room for seventy children in the building.[74]

An early English or common school in District No. 61 was held in Henrik Talla's barn with the large doors thrown open for light. The students sat on long benches without any backrests. The teacher at times had to discourage ducks, chickens, and pigs from entering the hall of learning.[75] More schoolhouses were built during the 1860s and the county school system was organized with a Presbyterian minister, the Reverend J. W. Hancock, appointed as the first county superintendent in 1864. His report at the end of the year told of 87 districts organized and 56 school buildings owned by the districts, 34 of them frame and 22 log.[76] The increase of public schools did not mean the end of the parochial system of religious schooling for the Norwegians and their children. It continued during the three summer months in each district, often meeting in the same school buildings that were public schools the rest of the year.[77] In the 1860s and 1870s, the use of the public schools by Norwegian immigrant families became a hotly debated issue.

Theodore Nydahl has pointed out that the Norwegians were in

no hurry to learn English since in such a homogeneous community there was little need to do so. Few in the first generation spoke any English and their children were more at home with Norwegian than with English, in part because of their attendance at the "Norwegian school," as they called the summer parochial school. Nydahl observes that not until the third generation will one find the use of English preferred over the Norwegian language.[78]

The early attention to religious instruction in Norwegian went hand in hand with the eagerness to find a pastor and establish a church. While visiting pastors did vital work in stimulating the settlers to seek the blessing of God on their new existence, at Holden the decisive initiative to provide preaching and church life came from the laity within the first two years of the settlement's beginning.[79] It was taken for granted that a pastoral leader would have to be sought from Norway, since in the 1850s the Norwegians in America had not as yet established their own theological seminary.

*Five*

## Pastor at Holden

Norwegian emigrants brought with them to America varied experience of the two main kinds of religious life in their homeland. First, they would have been familiar with the state church of Norway with its Lutheran theology, educated pastors, and orderly services of worship. Second, many emigrants would have been exposed to a more informal, pietistic, personalistic, and laity-based kind of Christianity that traced its origins to the renewal movement headed by Hans Nielsen Hauge in the late eighteenth and early nineteenth centuries. The famous ship *Restauration* that left Stavanger for America in 1825 had a number of Haugeans on board along with its contingent of Quakers.

In the American Midwest it was a rough, vigorous lay leader by the name of Elling Eielsen who promoted the Haugean view of Christianity. Eielsen had emigrated in 1839 and, by preaching to fellow Norwegians in Chicago on his arrival there, may have been the first to preach a Norwegian sermon in America.[1] Ironically, this crusty opponent of the clergy decided for practical reasons to become a pastor himself and was ordained October 3, 1843, thus becoming the first ordained pastor among the Norwegian Lutherans in America.[2] Eielsen did missionary work among the Norwegian immigrants in and around the Fox River

91

*Pastor B. J. Muus*
St. Olaf College Archives

settlement in Illinois, and in Wisconsin. Neither gifted as an orga-
nizer nor inclined to be one, Eielsen consented when two younger
associates, Ole Andrewson and Paul Andersen, aspired to organize groups of Eielsen followers. The result was a church meeting
in Jefferson Prairie, Wisconsin, in the spring of 1846, at which
the Evangelical Lutheran Church in America was brought into
being.[3]

In 1875 this church group changed its name to Hauge's
Norwegian Evangelical Lutheran Synod in America, but a small
minority continued as Eielsen's Synod with Elling Eielsen himself
as president. The man who served as president of Hauge's Synod
its first year was Østen Hanson, a pastor whose parish in Goodhue
county was located a very short distance east of the Holden parsonage and church. Over the years Hanson and Muus, while serving in "rival" synods, became trusted friends and colleagues.

The principles fostered by the Eielsen Synod and Hauge's Synod have been summarized as follows: "Christianity is something to be *experienced*, which experience involves a spiritual awakening, conversion, and a separated life; worship is simple and informal, in contrast to ritualism and formalism; lay activity, the practice of Christian testimony in public as well as in private, is to be encouraged."[4]

The church group to which Holden Lutheran Church belonged and into which Pastor Bernt Julius Muus was received as a member in October 1859, even before he arrived at the Holden community, was The Synod for the Norwegian Evangelical Lutheran Church, commonly called the Norwegian Synod. In retrospect it seems natural that Muus would join this particular church, but one of his professors in Norway, C. P. Caspari, expressed surprise when he heard it. Since Caspari regarded Muus as a pietist because of his participation in the Johnsonian awakening of the 1850s in Oslo, he concluded that Muus had joined the Norwegian Synod because the free church situation in America had led him to change his viewpoint.[5] No doubt Caspari and Johnson would have experienced further astonishment if they were made aware that Muus chose to remain in the Norwegian Synod even when he had strong reasons to leave.

The Norwegian Synod was organized in 1853 in a community in Rock county, southern Wisconsin, first known as Rock Prairie but later named Luther Valley. The Reverend Adolph Carl Preus was its first president.[6] He was succeeded in that position in 1862 by another Preus, his cousin, the Reverend Herman Amberg Preus, who continued as president of the Synod until his death in 1894. Muus was acquainted personally with both men and corresponded with them, especially with H. A.Preus, during most of his ministry.

The hallmarks of the Norwegian Synod were its university-trained clergy, respect for form and tradition in all phases of church life including worship, strict adherence to the Bible, fierce loyalty to Lutheran confessional teachings, and a disposition to emphasize the divine initiative in salvation more than the human response of faith. Muus remained a member of the Norwegian Synod through most of the years of his ministry. When Holden Lutheran Church, because of theological differences, voted to leave the Synod in 1887, Muus himself chose to continue as a member.

Over many years of vigorous theological debate, Muus became more and more out of step with the Missouri influenced theology of the Norwegian Synod, but continued to regard himself as a member until he was ousted at a meeting of the Minnesota District of the Synod in 1898.[7] Pastor L. M. Biørn, one of Muus's contemporaries, said of this event: "Muus grieved more over this action than many realized who saw him calmly smoking his pipe outside the church where the judgment had been passed on him."[8] Biørn also stated that Muus never felt at home in the United Norwegian Lutheran Church, the body formed in 1890 that the Holden congregation joined.

There were other Norwegian Lutheran church groups wielding influence in the complex growth of the church among Norwegian immigrants in the nineteenth century. The church situation can be pictured in terms of a spectrum with Eielsen's Synod and Hauge's Synod on the left, the Norwegian Synod on the right, and in the middle not one but two Norwegian church groups, the Norwegian-Augustana Synod and the Conference for the Norwegian-Danish Evangelical Lutheran Church in America. In 1890, the latter two groups joined dissidents from the Norwegian Synod, the so-called Anti-Missourian Brotherhood, to form the United Norwegian Lutheran Church.

B. J. Muus was an important figure in the changes leading to the formation of the United Norwegian Lutheran Church. He saw himself as a loyal supporter of the Norwegian Synod even as he played a conscientious gadfly role in its meetings. Muus was clearly a leader in arranging for the Anti-Missourian Brotherhood to establish its own theological seminary in Northfield at St. Olaf's School in 1886, an action that enabled the school founded by Muus to become a college.

These changes could not have been foreseen when Muus first arrived at Holden, the rural parish northeast of Kenyon, Minnesota. Muus would become a controversial figure and a key church leader, but his first sphere of responsibility and the role he steadily pursued was that of parish pastor.

The influx of Norwegians into Goodhue county began with Matthias Petersen Ringdahl, who came to Red Wing in 1851 and settled on a farm near Zumbrota, a few miles south and east of where the Holden Lutheran church would be located. The Holden area received a good many Norwegians from such Wisconsin colonies as Dodgeville, Koshkonong, and Stoughton. Tosten Anderson Aabye and the Talla brothers, for example, were among those who had heard about good land in Minnesota and made their way to Goodhue county from Dodgeville.[9]

It was also from neighboring Wisconsin that the first pastor arrived to minister to the settlers. He was the Reverend Nils O. Brandt from Oconomowoc, Wisconsin, the first Norwegian pastor to minister west of the Mississippi River, coming into the area in 1855.[10] Brandt had graduated from the University in Oslo in 1849, received ordination at the hands of Bishop J. L. Arup, and arrived in Wisconsin in 1851, where he was called to serve churches at Rock River and Pine Lake near Watertown, Wisconsin, east and north of Madison. He began visiting distant settlements of Norwegians immediately after his arrival, traveling to western Wisconsin, eastern Minnesota, and northeastern Iowa.[11]

Brandt belonged to the group of six Norwegian Lutheran immigrant pastors who founded the Norwegian Synod in 1853. At the request of this body, Brandt and Pastor J. A. Ottesen in June of 1857 traveled to investigate Lutheran theological schools in Columbus, Buffalo, and St. Louis. On the basis of these visits, they recommended that the Norwegians establish a professorship at Concordia College in St. Louis for the training of candidates for the ministry. Brandt later became a pastor in Decorah, Iowa, where he was also a professor of languages and religion at

Luther College.[12] While the Brandts lived in Decorah there were visits and friendly letter exchanges between the Brandt and Muus families.

Brandt made his first visit to Goodhue county in June of 1855 when he stopped to see Matthias Petersen Ringdahl and his wife at their house in Pine Lake township. He had come from Wisconsin into Minnesota territory to visit the Talla group in Wanamingo, but in Red Wing he had heard of the Pine Island Norwegians and decided to visit them as well. Word was sent out to other Norwegians in the vicinity and a Lutheran service of worship was held, perhaps the first such service held among Scandinavians in the county.[13]

Presumably this is the same 1855 visit described in the Holden Centennial History, which gives further particulars. According to this account, Pastor Brandt came on foot along the Zumbro River, sleeping on a pile of hay under the stars the first night and finding shelter in Henrik Talla's cabin the second night. On this 1855 visit to Holden, Brandt conducted the first baptism and officiated at the first wedding registered in the church's record books. Baptized on June 26, 1855 was Anders, son of Tosten Anderson Aabye and Oline Christensdatter. On June 27, 1855, Tøge Nilsen (Talla) and Oline Olsdatter were married.[14] The Reverend P. A. Rasmussen was another traveling pastor who did some preaching in the Holden vicinity in 1856.[15]

The all-important work of organizing the church at Holden was done in the fall of 1856 by the Reverend H. A. Stub, another immigrant pastor from Wisconsin and another founder of the Norwegian Synod. Stub visited the area and baptized twenty-five children on September 11, 1856. The next day he presided at the organizational meeting at which a constitution was adopted and a request was sent to the church council of the Norwegian state church to secure a resident pastor.

During the previous summer future members of the Holden church had already met to begin organizing and to secure a deed for 100 acres of land where the church and parsonage were to be built. This historic meeting had taken place at a site west of the present parsonage where the Grønvold house once stood and where, in more recent times, the Lloyd Voxland house was built. It should be noted that one woman, Ingeborg Iversdatter, was among the signers of the constitution. Other signers included Saave Aaker, Ole Huset, Sven Nordgaarden, Ole Solberg, P. N. Langemo, Christen Westermoe, and Erik G. Gunhus.[16]

Pastoral work at Holden continued through 1857, 1858, and 1859 up to Pastor Muus's arrival in the fall of 1859. Pastor J. S. Munch came from Wiota, Wisconsin, to preach in September of 1857. From Rush River, Wisconsin, in 1858 came another pastor traveling on foot, the Reverend Laur. Larsen, a young immigrant minister who in a few years would become the first president of Luther College. During his visit in June 1858 Larsen conducted several services and baptized 100 children, thirty-three of them under an oak tree near the site of the Valley Grove church. The following year Larsen returned to the Holden area on pastoral visits in June and September, again conducting many worship services and baptizing eighty children. During his September visit he dedicated the Holden cemetery. The Reverend A. C. Preus was another of the visiting pastors, coming from Koshkonong, Wisconsin, in July of 1859.

That was the month when Muus wrote to A. C. Preus stating that he had received a call from the Norwegian Evangelical Lutheran congregation in Goodhue county, Minnesota. He told Preus that he hoped to reach America by the end of September but the Muuses did not arrive in Wisconsin until the middle of October of 1859.

The date of the Muuses' departure from Norway is known, as is the approximate time of their arrival in the near vicinity of LaCrosse, Wisconsin. Otherwise, no particulars have come to light regarding the Muuses' journey across the Atlantic, nor the port and exact date of their arrival. Police office records in Oslo show that they registered to travel to America on September 5, 1859,[17] and the church journal reports their attendance at a synod meeting in Wisconsin October 14, 1859. Thus their entire journey took only about five and one-half weeks, quite a swift voyage for those days. Sailing ships could take from eight to fourteen weeks to make the trip. In his book *The Promise of America*, Odd Lovoll reproduces a published "list of provisions" that advises emigrants bound for America to take along enough food to last them for ten weeks.[18]

Glimpses into the experience of others crossing the Atlantic during the same period can be of interest. Elisabeth Hysing Koren and her husband, the Reverend Ulrik Vilhelm Koren, came to America by way of Germany. They sailed from Hamburg September 15, 1853, and arrived in New York November 20, a crossing that had taken nine and one-half weeks. Halle Steensland, traveling to America on the brig *Niord* in the spring of 1854, reported that the journey from Stavanger to Quebec took six weeks. In the summer of the same year the *Laurvig*, commanded by Captain H. Cock-Jensen, was at sea for a total of twelve weeks in crossing from Helgerå, in southern Norway, to Quebec.[19]

The conditions experienced by the Muuses aboard ship can only be guessed at since information is lacking. Because Muus was a minister, it is possible that he and his wife occupied first-class quarters, as the Korens did, and thus enjoyed a measure of comfort. In one of her diary entries Elisabeth Koren wrote, "It was stormy and cold yesterday. We spent the morning in our little cabin—it is always best there—until it was time to go in and enjoy our 'Kirschen mit Klöse' [cherries with dumplings] which tasted very good and warmed us up well, and was followed by fricasseed chicken with raisins and almonds."[20] Mrs. Koren, who made daily visits to the sick women aboard the ship, noted that "The lowest deck is full of steerage passengers, who look weak and exhausted."[21] Cholera took the lives of fourteen persons during that voyage.[22]

Accounts of emigration journeys across the Atlantic frequently describe the appalling conditions suffered by those emigrants, the majority, who were in steerage on the sailing vessels taking them to America. Captain Cock-Jensen describes the primitive arrangements on his own ship: "Two rows of bunks of rough boards were built up, one above the other, the whole length of the ship from fore to aft. . . . Light was admitted through open hatchways and partly through skylights in the deck. There was canvas in the hatchways, but during storms and rough seas these often had to be covered, and if this continued for any length of time the air in the room below occupied by the emigrants became frightfully bad. There was no first or second cabin. Each passenger paid twenty-five dollars for his passage, but had to supply himself with bedding and food for the voyage. The board consisted chiefly of smoked and salted meat, *fladbröd*, and casks of sour milk."[23]

Even if the Muus party had better accommodations, which seems probable, the fact remains that a great many of the immigrants they came to know in Minnesota would have traveled to America under the kind of shipboard conditions described here. Emigrant literature provides moving accounts of illness and death aboard the vessels, and burials at sea. Captain Cock-Jensen tells of the spread of dysentery among his passengers until thirteen had been lowered into the sea. The outbreak of the illness was directly related to the confinement of the emigrants below decks during severe storms. He writes: "One can imagine the sufferings of the wretched creatures who were shut up in the dark room night and day, for the hatches were battened as the waves went over the decks continually. The room of the emigrants was lighted by two or three lamps that were burning night and day down there in the poisoned air and amid all the filth. As a result of this wretchedness an unfortunate contagious disease broke out, namely dysentery."[24]

Naturally there were also pleasant experiences aboard an emigrant ship that could offset somewhat the miseries of foul quarters, illness, and bad food. When the weather was favorable there would be a hum of activities on deck. Many occupied themselves with reading. Women sewed, knitted, and chatted. Men smoked their pipes and watched the sky and the sea. The younger people quickly organized games and competitions. Often there would be dancing to the music of an accordion or some other instrument.[25]

Beginning in the 1860s, steamships began to replace sailing ships, and by the 1870s only steamships carried the Atlantic traffic. The faster steam-powered vessels reduced the time of passage in the 1880s to about two weeks. But the Muuses presumably traveled on a sailing vessel, as did the Korens a few years earlier. Even with sailing ships the time of crossing was becoming shorter through the 1850s, as Halle Steensland's experience indicates. With bigger ships and favorable wind conditions the average length for the trip across the Atlantic had been lowered to thirty-nine days by 1860.[26] Interestingly enough, that is almost exactly the presumed length of time expended by Bernt Julius Muus and his wife Oline in traveling from Oslo all the way to Wisconsin.

It has been suggested that their landing port in North America was most likely Quebec. Muus specifically had asked Laur. Larsen about the cost of a journey from Liverpool to Quebec. The repeal of the British Navigation Acts in 1849 allowed Norwegian ships to bring emigrants to Quebec and return to Great Britain with a cargo of lumber. Between 1854 and 1865, states Ingrid Semmingsen, more than ninety percent of some 44,000 Norwegian emigrants came by sailing ship to Quebec. This increased volume of travel reduced the price of a ticket to Quebec to the range of about $12 to $15.[27]

To proceed from Quebec to southern Minnesota entailed a further journey of about seven days. One might travel by boat through the Welland Canal into the Great Lakes and on to Milwaukee or Chicago, where one took the train to one's destination. When the Canadian railroad was built in the latter part of the 1850s, it became possible to journey by train directly from Quebec to Toronto, and in 1859 the train connection was extended to Port Huron and Detroit. Once it was available, many emigrants understandably preferred that faster mode of transport to the agonizingly slow and costly series of transfers from boat to train and train to boat that formerly was endured between Quebec and Milwaukee or Chicago. In 1854 Halle Steensland had journeyed by train from Quebec to Montreal, from Montreal by canal boat to Lake Ontario, across this lake on a steamboat to Hamilton, Canada, from there by train to Windsor, then across the river to Detroit, and finally by train, sitting on planks in a freight car, to Chicago.[28]

The Muuses could have traveled from Quebec to either Milwaukee or Chicago when they arrived in the Midwest in October of 1859. One surmises that it was Milwaukee, since the first record of their presence is at a church meeting near La Crosse, Wisconsin.

The journal of the Norwegian Synod, *Kirkelig Maanedstidende*, had reported the presence of Bernt Julius Muus as newly arrived from Norway at its synod meeting at the Coon Prairie Church, southeast of LaCrosse in Vernon county, Wisconsin, on October 14, 1859. There is no information on where the Muuses spent the rest of October. It must have been somewhere in the vicinity of Rochester, Minnesota, given the following account of their coming to Holden as described in the Centennial History of Holden Lutheran Church: "Finally the big day arrived that the settlers were to have a resident pastor. Rev. B. J. Muus and his bride arrived from Snaasen, in Trondhjem, Norway. Family records tell us that Mr. Saave Aaker was sent to Rochester to meet the pastor and brought them here by ox-team. Perhaps this slow locomotion gave them a good chance to become acquainted. Saave Aaker became the precentor (*klokker*) and was a warm personal friend of the young pastor until his untimely death by a bolt of lightning in 1862. Rev. Muus preached his first sermon on Nov. 6, 1859, at Ole O. Huset's place, using the text for All Saints' Day."[29]

The above reference to Pastor Muus and his bride arriving "from Snaasen" serves to identify Muus's home community in

101

*Ole Huset farm home*
Photo by Joseph M. Shaw

Norway, but is in error in assuming that the Muuses left Norway from Trondheim, which is some distance from "Snaasen" or Snåsa. It was in Oslo, not Trondheim, that Pastor and Mrs. Muus and a servant girl boarded a ship for the new country. Muus had written about visiting his home after his ordination, but it is not known whether he alone or in company with his bride managed to make a trip to Snåsa after their marriage July 12, 1859, and before their departure from Oslo for America in early September.[30]

As the Holden congregation's history reports, Muus delivered his first sermon on November 6, 1859, at Ole Huset's place. The farmhouse in which that first service was held is still standing, though enlarged and renovated. The farm was occupied until 1991 by Howard Loren Voxland, son of Halvor L. Voxland and grandson of Lars Voxland (1861–1926), who was married to Christine Aabye. These two lived on a farm that had been homesteaded by Tosten Anderson Aabye who, with his wife Oline, donated the land on which Holden Lutheran church was built.[31]

102

Thus the coming of the Muuses to Holden and the development of Muus's ministry in that community are bound up with various Holden families, most of whom were recent immigrants. Saave Knudson Groven Aaker, the man who drove the ox-team to bring the Muuses to Holden, was born in Upper Telemark from where he emigrated to America in 1852. Aaker's name soon appears as one of the "fathers," that is, sponsors or godparents, in the Holden ministerial record book where the baptism of his granddaughter Marie Aaker is recorded. Another of Marie's sponsors was Oline C. K. Muus.[32] This little girl's name is of particular interest, not simply because one of her sponsors was her grandfather and the other the pastor's wife, but also because she would become the very first person to register at St. Olaf's School fifteen years later, in 1875. Marie Aaker had the distinction of being student No. 1 among all who have attended the institution which became St. Olaf College. In her later years Marie Aaker (Mrs. Theodore Bordsen) would receive annual visits from the president of the college on or near Founders' Day, November sixth.

The name of Saave Knudson Aaker is the first to appear in the list of members of the Holden congregation. Opposite his name is the date of his death, June 22, 1862.[33] The second member in the list is his wife, Anne Andreasdatter. Some other notable Holden parishioners among the earliest members are Ole Olson Huset and Peder Nilson Langemo, the man who was the last to bid Muus goodbye in July of 1899 when the veteran pastor, by then aged and worn, was assisted aboard the train in Kenyon, Minnesota, to leave for Norway.[34]

The pastors who came to Holden from other places to preach and perform other ministerial duties did not confine their labors to Holden alone but moved about to various other places where Norwegian settlers were to be found. Thus even before Muus reached Holden in the late fall of 1859, pastoral services had been extended eastward from Holden to Zumbrota, encompassing stations at Minneola, Dale, Hegre, and Lands, south to Gol and

103

Moland, west to Tyske (i.e. German) Grove, later called Valley Grove, and north to Vang and Urland. All of these became very familiar sites for Pastor Muus as he carried out his forty-year ministry in and around Holden.

Muus preached his first sermon in the Holden area on November 6, 1859, at the Ole O. Huset farm, which is less than a mile from the site where Holden Lutheran church would be built. From their arrival in the fall of 1859 until they could move into the parsonage in March of 1860, Muus and his wife stayed with the Knut Pedersen Haugen family on its farm one mile south of the present Vang Lutheran church. Of that pleasant stay Muus would later write: "Here he [Muus] lived at no cost to the congregation and in addition enjoyed an extraordinary amount of help and friendliness from the family."[35]

Many entries in the Holden Ministerial Record show that numerous church functions, including Sunday services, marriages, and confirmation classes, took place at the home of Knut P. Haugen. Muus also made use of many other parishioners' homes for such meetings. It is interesting that the very first Christmas service conducted by Pastor Muus that first year, 1859, at which there was also holy baptism, was held at the home of the former Club Law chieftain, Tøge Nilsen Talla.[36]

The new pastor and his wife moved into the parsonage, begun in 1859, when it was partially ready for occupancy in the spring of 1860. "The first floor is in fine shape," wrote Muus in a letter to Laur. Larsen dated March 12, 1860. An entry in the Holden Ministerial Book for March 5, 1860, indicates that he is holding confirmation instruction there and on March 22 the same year the congregation met at the parsonage to discuss building a church.[37]

As soon as the Holden congregation was organized in 1856, the members talked of building a church, each to contribute two timbers.[38] In his review of Holden's early history Muus refers to the decision in 1860 to go ahead with the building. In 1861 the bare essentials of a church were erected. Under the supervision of contractors whom Muus identifies as "the American Hill and

104

the Norwegian Ole K. Simmons of Red Wing," the church was framed up, enclosed, and the floor laid. In the cornerstone of this first Holden church was placed a two-foot piece of wood, 4" x 4", on which the following information about the building was written in pencil: "This house was commenced in 1861 by D. C. Mill [*sic*] and Simmons and the outside and floor finished the same for 1700 dollars. The inside was finished in 1865 by A. J. Grover and N. Mulliken under a contract to do the work for $550.00 and will be finished by the 1st day of July and will then be dedicated."[39]

Except for the misspelling of the name of the American builder, Hill, this unusual wooden document accords with Muus's history of Holden's first twenty-five years, which states that work on the interior began in 1864 and was completed the next year.[40] But the dedication, anticipated in 1865, did not take place until November of 1871 because it was so difficult at that time to procure tools, equipment, and materials.[41]

In the meantime, Pastor Muus was using the parsonage and parishioners' homes for his crowded schedule of worship services, confirmation classes, Bible classes, weddings, and other pastoral acts that he recorded meticulously in the Holden congregation's record books. Here, for example, are the ministerial activities Muus carried out in November of 1859, his first month in the Holden area:

"Nov 6    All Saints' Service and Baptism at the Ole Huset farm

Nov 7    Marriage ceremony at Knut Pedersen Haugen's home [where Muus and his wife were staying]

Nov 9    Bible reading with Infant Baptism at Anders Otternæs home

Nov 13    Worship Service with Infant Baptism in German Grove at the Jan Hansen home

Nov 16    Bible reading at the Halvor Odegaarden home

Nov 20    Worship Service with Infant Baptism at Ole Huset farm

*The first Holden Church, begun in 1861*
St. Olaf College Archives

Nov 24    Bible reading and Infant Baptism at the Gudbrand
          Nilsen Haugen home in Valdres Settlement
Nov 27    Worship Service with Infant Baptism in German
          Grove at the Eilif Trulsen home
Nov 30    Worship Service with Infant Baptism in Zumbrota at
          the Knud Klemmesen home."[42]

In January of 1860 the pace of activity increased, with Muus hurrying about the vicinity to carry out at least twenty separate ministerial actions, including twelve worship services, at least two confirmation classes, two weddings, and two confirmation rites. The congregational records list the families in whose houses these functions took place and also the various localities, such as Zumbrota Falls, German Grove, and Red Wing. Like other pioneer pastors, Muus quickly responded to requests for ministerial services beyond his immediate community.

A particularly interesting letter from Muus to his colleague, Laur. Larsen, dated February 8, 1860, reveals how Muus is adjusting to his new surroundings and the varied challenges he faced three months after his arrival in the Holden community. At the same time Larsen, too, was in the very first phase of a new and difficult experience. In October of 1859 the Norwegian Synod had appointed him to serve as professor to the Norwegian students then studying at Concordia College in St. Louis. At the time of their correspondence in early 1860 Larsen was 27 years old and Muus 28.[43]

Muus tells Larsen of the many good friends the latter has in the area who would gladly hear from him and would dearly like to have him come back for a visit. Muus's host, Knut P. Haugen, says that Larsen had promised to come in the summer and stay with the Haugens. Muus reports that he is soon to move into the parsonage. He has yet to receive the travel stipend he was promised, nor has he heard anything about his regular salary. Nevertheless, he is not suffering want because he has received sums from baptisms and offerings and because Knut Haugen has been so helpful in every way. "I have acquired a good horse and a good cow, so already I have become a man of property," writes Muus.

As to the congregation, Muus doesn't quite know what to say. "Many come to listen to me, and many also drink themselves drunk and get into fights, so the fruit of sin is obvious, but the fruits of faith are of the microscopic sort." Muus says that he has not undertaken any missionary trips other than to a place called Halfbreedsland, which later became known as Hoff. He is being urged to travel about, but is not yet able to do so. "I have no salary and no means of driving across the open fields."

Apparently Larsen had written to ask for some books. Muus mentions a couple of language books his wife has and promises to send them. She also has a German grammar and a book on Norwegian history which can be sent if Larsen wants them.

The last item in the letter has to do with Muus's efforts to collect $20.00 for the fund for Norwegian students at Concordia Seminary. So far he has had no success. He found it reasonable when advised to hold off, since the congregation had many expenses. One man had promised to subscribe $100, but when Muus asked him to put it in writing, he said he would wait "to see what the others did."[44] As time went on, Muus not only became bolder and more effective in collecting money, but achieved a legendary reputation in that regard.

Just as B. J. Muus provided historical information about his family in the form of a written history,[45] so he also laid the groundwork for the history of Holden Church by writing a summary of its first twenty-five years. This document, written in 1880 or 1881, bears the title, "Brief Overview of Holden Congregation's External History in the First 25 Years." When the congregation celebrated its fiftieth anniversary in 1906 it asked L. M. Biørn, longtime colleague of Muus and a neighboring pastor, to compile the sermons and speeches of the occasion into an anniversary book or "Festskrift." In doing so, Biørn decided to include in its pages the "Brief Overview" written by Muus 25 years earlier.[46]

108

This document reveals what Muus himself regarded as the main outward developments in the parish from the organization of the Holden congregation in 1856 until about 1880. From the summary one obtains a condensed view of the first decade or so of Pastor Muus's service in the Holden community.

First Muus reviews the work of his predecessors, then reports his own arrival and the first service on November 6, 1859. He explains that work began on the parsonage in 1859 and that he lived with Knut P. Haugen until he could move into the parsonage in 1860. He tells of the 1860 decision to build a church and the initial construction that took place in 1861.

The Norwegian Synod held an extraordinary session at Holden in 1862 at which time the Holden congregation was admitted to the Synod. In October of that year the congregation, which embraced a number of sub-communities, was divided into four parishes: 1) Zumbrota, later divided into Land and Minneola, 2) Østre Sogn (the eastern parish, the old local name for what is usually known as Holden), 3) Valders, which came to be called Vang, and 4) Tyske Grove, which was later known as Valley Grove. A church building for Tyske Grove was begun the same year, 1862.

In 1863 some members of Pastor P. A. Rasmussen's congregations who were living within the boundaries of the Valders parish affiliated with Holden. Another part of Rasmussen's charge, in the South Prairie or Dale area, called Muus to be their pastor and he accepted. The work of furnishing the Holden (Østre Sogn) church began in 1864, Muus reports, while the Valders parish was divided in two, Valders and the Halling Settlement, later called Gol.

In his overview Muus then skips to 1866, when Tyske Grove joined some other groups to form its own parish. That year a decision was made to enlarge the Holden parsonage. The last year of the decade mentioned by Muus was 1868, when Urland was permitted to organize as a separate parish, and when Land and Minneola combined with Red Wing and Hoff to establish their own parish, calling as pastor N. Th. Ylvisaker.[47]

The correspondence Muus maintained with fellow pastors provides additional insight into his life as a young immigrant pastor in the decade of the 1860s. Of the available Muus letters, the preponderance are to Laur. Larsen and H. A. Preus. The February 1860 letter to Laur. Larsen cited earlier gave glimpses of Muus and his family settling into their new surroundings. Another letter to Larsen in March shows more new experiences being tasted. Muus wonders if there is a peculiar postal practice in this country since he did not receive Larsen's February 25th letter until March 10th. Now the Muuses have moved into the parsonage. He has also secured the services of a reliable man who will take care of the farming for a year, although only a tract of 12 acres has been broken. As to progress in his ministerial work, Muus tells Larsen that up to that point he had met with nothing but good will from all the people even though on a couple of occasions he had had to be "rather sharp" with them.

Larsen's latest letter was most gratefully received because Muus had been troubled by a severely critical letter from the president of the Synod, A. C. Preus. Preus had complained about Muus's conduct at the latest Synod meeting, contending that Muus had offended against brotherly love and had manifested impudent behavior. Muus chooses not to go into the nature of the matter, but he is relieved that Larsen had not seen his conduct as offensive. Muus is thankful for Larsen's good will and the continuing correspondence.[48]

In his letters to Larsen and to H. A. Preus, Muus often furnishes brief reports on domestic doings and sends greetings from his family and others. Since Larsen had ministered in the area before Muus arrived, there are occasions for Muus to convey personal greetings as he remits modest cash contributions to the Norwegian students in St. Louis from lay people who fondly remembered Larsen's labors among them. One such person was Mrs. Ole Knutsen Trondkleven, who sent Larsen $1.25 with her warm greetings. She regrets that she is unable to send him a cheese, since he is so far away, "but since I was in the vicinity," Muus explains with droll satisfaction, "I got it."[49]

The two young pastors, Larsen and Muus, exchanged personal and family news as they carried out their respective duties. The Synod leaders selected Pastor Larsen to make a trip to Norway in 1860 to persuade Norwegian pastors to come over to America to help minister to the increasing number of immigrants. When he reached New York on his return shortly before Christmas, his mail informed him that a daughter had been born into the family while he was still at sea.[50] Arriving in St. Louis in January, he received a letter from Muus with $5.00 enclosed, $2 of which Muus owed Larsen. The other $3 was for the students in St. Louis. On the personal level Muus also had some family news: "We live well. We now have a little daughter called Birgitte Magdalena."[51] Birgitte was born November 24, 1860. The name also belonged to Bernt Julius Muus's mother, Birgitte Magdalena Rynning, and to his sister.

Muus has bad news for Larsen in April of 1861. A certain teacher who had come to America with Larsen has turned out to be "not only a Grundtvigian but also a fornicator." He had made one of his pupils pregnant but then married another young lady. As to the "Grundtvigian" charge, Muus and other pastors in the Norwegian Synod were wary of the influence of the renowned Danish churchman, N. F. S. Grundtvig, in large part because they perceived the Dane's emphasis on the importance of the Apostles' Creed as a threat to the primacy of Scripture.[52] In the same letter Muus mentions a visit to Rush River in Wisconsin, Larsen's former call, and reports that he is about to leave for another trip there.[53]

In November of 1861 Muus explained in a letter to the Norwegian Synod church council that he had missed a pastors' conference in Decorah because at the time he was still out on his "fall visitation," where he had assisted in establishing two new congregations in Meeker and Monongalia counties.[54] Early in 1862 Muus informed the church council that a pastors' conference had asked him to write to the council requesting that one J. Midbo be called as a traveling preacher to help him because, with his many congregations to serve, he could not visit them more than twice a year and in some cases only once a year. With the influx of immigrants, Muus writes, new settlements are being formed. He did not know how he could reach them because in the summertime he ought to spend some time at home in his main congregation.[55]

In the spring of 1862 Pastor Muus issued an invitation to Laur. Larsen to preach at a place he identifies as "Halfbreedlandet about 20 miles from here."[56] This preaching place, where Muus established a congregation known as Hoff, was located within a strip of land along the Mississippi known in Minnesota history as the Half-Breed Tract.[57]

Concern for the welfare of nearby and more distant congregations is frequently expressed by Muus in his letters of the 1860s. Writing in January of 1863 to H. A. Preus, now president of the Norwegian Synod, Muus states that he has forwarded Preus's letter from the church council to Pastor Thomas Johnson with its request to call Johnson to serve the congregation in Nicollet county. He hopes that the church council has received a reply. Closer to home it looks as if the Valders settlement will join with Holden. At the end of the letter Muus adds, "If it should be of interest to you, I can report that my wife has given birth to a son. Everything is fine."[58]

The newcomer to the Muus family was Nils, born January 6, 1863. A month after the birth, as Muus wrote to Laur. Larsen, he was more expansive about the new baby, describing him as "a big boy who ardently makes music both at opportune and inopportune times." Muus continues, "My wife is healthy and spry and everything is going well."[59]

Writing to H. A. Preus in August of 1864 Muus can say that "we have had an excellent year." Specifically, he has in mind raising money for the university cause, which means Luther College. Muus has received pledges for about $1,000 and hopes to get all the cash in the fall. Much more could be done and more help would be much appreciated. Muus suggests to Preus that if he attends the meeting in Clausen's congregation (St. Ansgar, Iowa) on September 9th, he ought to make a trip up to the congregations around Holden to promote the university cause.[60]

Muus has borrowed $210.00 for the university fund, which he sends to Larsen toward the end of 1864 as a loan to the fund, asking that receipts be sent to him whenever payments are made until the amount of the loan has been met. Muus is perturbed by a letter sent out by Pastor Ottesen demanding $15,000 from the congregations in November for the university fund. Since Muus had raised around $1,000 during the year he thought he had done his part. On the personal side, Muus remarks that they are getting along as usual, "though even more isolated from the world than usual since we seldom get mail."[61]

In letters to Larsen and Preus Muus regularly apprises them of the "western" congregations he is serving. He informs Larsen in April of 1865 that Christiania, North Waseca, Le Sueur River (also called St. Olaf's Lake), and "Tyske Grove" were in the process of organizing themselves into a new parish and intended to call their own pastor.[62] By the time a letter of call was transmitted to Chairman Preus and the church council, however, only the first three of these congregations had joined in the request. Despite Muus's efforts to persuade Tyske Grove to join the others in calling a pastor, it has declined. At that time Tyske Grove was still a sub-unit annexed to the Holden congregation.[63]

Writing to Preus in October of 1865, Muus thanks the Synod president for his friendly letter of 18 September, which he received on his arrival home after a journey "in the west." On that trip he had installed N. Quammen as pastor "in his new congregations," namely, Christiania, Fox Lake, North Waseca, and Le Sueur River. Earlier Muus had recommended as pastor of these congregations a promising student, Knut Thorstensen, who had been serving them temporarily. Now he expresses his reservations about removing this man and putting Quammen in his place. The argument had been that Thorstensen had too many youthful acquaintances in these places, but now it appears that Quammen too has many acquaintances there. The only difference, comments Muus, is that those who knew Quammen were not fond of him while Thorstensen's acquaintances loved him as a Christian. Bowing to higher authority, Muus tosses off a Latin phrase to the effect that what's done is done.[64]

The same letter to Preus reveals Muus as at once ready for controversy and critical of himself. He asks Preus if he should publish his speech given at a recent conference with leaders of the Augustana Synod and brings up other possibilities of articles to be written. It seems that their lot is to be in the thick of controversy, which is not necessarily a bad thing. "Woe to you when all people speak well of you," Muus quotes from the gospel of Luke. Muus then confesses that he has a desire to throw himself into this polemical writing, "but I am a rather sluggish person who has difficulty in getting moving, and when I get going there are many interruptions related to official business, so the good intentions remain where they are."[65]

More often than not, Muus's letters to Laur. Larsen in Decorah include a careful accounting of sums of money that have been gathered in his churches for housekeeping expenses, professors' salaries, and needy students at Luther College. In many cases the names of individual donors are listed, with the exact amount given by each, even if it was as little as twenty-five or fifty cents. He mentions that he had sent $10.00 to Professor F. A. Schmidt for the students, but had not received a receipt.[66]

As Muus was meticulous in handling the sums he was constantly transmitting to Luther, so he also expected equally careful record-keeping in Decorah. Larsen had written that a young man from Holden, Andreas Aaker (or Scott), owed $20.00 to the housekeeping treasury. After the money was sent, Larsen wrote that he only owed $8.00. Muus replied with some irritation, "If he did not owe more than $8.00, then send the rest back. His mother is poor." Muus adds that he is afraid nothing can be expected for the University Fund from his area this year. The wheat harvest was poor and money cannot be borrowed for less than a 24 percent interest rate.[67]

Yet cordial relations between Muus and Larsen continued. Writing to Larsen in December of 1867 as he sends $35.45 from the Reformation Day offering at Land congregation, Muus is happy to hear that the financial situation at Luther has eased up somewhat. He reports that he has moved into the expanded parsonage, now a large house with eight rooms of which only three are ready. Under the whole house is a basement. Muus closes with the prayer that God will give Larsen and his family a happy Christmas and will bless Larsen's work.[68]

As a rural pioneer pastor Muus could scarcely predict what the next issue in the community might be. In all innocence he had agreed to give a talk at a concert in Red Wing arranged by some Norwegians and Swedes. There would be some tableaux with people in national costumes and some singing. Proceeds were to go to the needy in the vicinity. All of a sudden a laymen's commission met and delivered a letter to Muus criticizing the "display" as being based on the principle of "the end justifies the means," characterizing it as "highly insulting to the Norwegian nation and the cause of God's kingdom," and asking Muus to do what he could to prevent it from taking place. He replied that he could not prevent the concert from being held, but he could refrain from taking part in it. Two congregational meetings were held, at both of which all those present denied having made the accusations against the concert. At a third meeting they admitted making the allegations but absolutely refused to make amends for spreading untruths. Muus proposed that he invite Preus or a member of the Church Council to come to Holden but the congregation would not agree. "Remember us in your prayers!" writes Muus in closing.[69]

The above was reported to Preus in May of 1868. A month later Muus could tell the president of the Synod that things had calmed down somewhat. "Most of my opponents have acknowledged their wrongdoing and have asked for forgiveness from

115

God, the congregation, and me." At a recent congregational meeting nearly all had accepted the teaching Muus had set forth and summarized in three statements: 1) Nothing in God's creation is evil in itself nor anything produced by God's creation; 2) the use of these things is not in itself evil; 3) but misuse is evil. After reporting some other local problems Muus writes, "Times have been hard up here, but I have my hope in the living God, and one is not ashamed of hope."[70]

The task of ministering to the growing number of Norwegians in the Holden area called for changes in how the congregations were to be organized. The realignment of 1862 divided the Holden congregation into four parishes: Zumbrota, Østre Sogn, Valders (Vang), and German Grove. Zumbrota later was divided into Land and Minneola. By 1868 a different arrangement was in effect. Holden consisted of three sub-units, Østre Sogn, Valders, and the Halling Settlement, all served by Muus. N. Th. Ylvisaker was now the pastor of Land, Minneola, Red Wing, and Hoff.[71]

The frontier situation posed various problems of morality, some more serious than others. Writing to Larsen in late 1868 Muus passes along a warning received from Norway concerning "a nasty lay preacher" with the reputation of an adulterer and drunkard who had disappeared from Norway a couple of years earlier. Larsen should be advised of such a person lest he try to gain admittance to one of the Scandinavian schools.[72]

It was a different matter with lighter issues that unduly agitated congregations and claimed a disproportionate share of a pastor's time and patience. In May of 1868, three congregational meetings had been called to wrangle over the entertainment in Red Wing, provoking Muus to deliver his statement on the goodness of God's creation. In December Muus could tell Larsen that the trouble seemed to be dying down, but a new issue had made its appearance, arousing Muus to further annoyance. "The next dispute to shake the church perhaps will be about dancing," he writes. According to what he had read in the Norwegian Synod's publication, *Kirkelig Maanedstidende*, the editors had fabricated a new dogma, namely, that it is a sin—and here Muus quotes the church paper—"that a man take a strange woman by the waist and thus spin around with her in a dance." Indignantly Muus asks, "Where is this written in God's Word? Nowhere. Is this what healthy common sense teaches? It teaches us that such claims are stupidities." But what we learn from such assertions, he continues, is that even God-fearing people let themselves abandon the ground of God's Word in order to drive out on the thin ice of human teaching. Switching the metaphor, Muus likens this folly to building with hay and straw which will be burned up. May God grant that more will not be burned at the same time.[73]

A pastor's discouragement in getting the message across was reflected in the tribute Muus wrote after Knut K. Finseth died in September of 1869. Finseth had exemplified the high value of "childhood instruction," that is, the church's catechetical training, in leading a person toward Christian maturity. But not everyone was responsive to God's Word. Muus remembered from his first years at Holden as "an inexperienced beginner" how his most earnest preaching efforts seemed to make no impact whatsoever. He wrote, "It seemed to me I was preaching in such a way, so I thought, that every person either must be ashamed before God and repent, or that they must drive me out of the settlement." But neither happened. People were used to getting a verbal thrashing from the pastor. They shook it off, chatted with their friends, and had a clear conscience before they had gone half a mile down the road toward home. As things gradually improved, Knut Finseth was a good influence within the congregation and a steady friend to the pastor.[74]

Two of Pastor Muus's chief concerns for the future well-being of the settlers are expressed in a letter to H. A. Preus written late in 1869. One was to raise the level of available education. Muus began the operation of an academy in the Holden parsonage in 1869, describing it as "a high school in which the youth of the congregations could acquire a better education than could be

*Present Holden Church*
Photo by Joseph M. Shaw

obtained in our parochial and common schools."[75] Muus sends to Preus, as promised, a copy of the schedule to be followed "at my academy." The experiment with Holden Academy prepared the way for the founding of St. Olaf's School in Northfield in 1874.

The second concern on Muus's mind in December of 1869 was that with the prospect of building another church in the vicinity the question of more pastors naturally had to be faced.[76] One help-ful step forward had been taken in 1868 when N. Th. Ylvisaker came to serve Land, Minneola, Red Wing, and Hoff. Two more pastors would arrive in the 1870s to assist Muus with pastoral responsibilities among the daughter congregations of Holden.

# Six

# The Daughter Congregations

From the beginning of his ministry in Minnesota, Pastor Muus's frontier missionary situation gave him no choice but to leave the Holden parsonage and church from time to time to do pastoral work in surrounding and more distant communities. It had been the same in Wisconsin with such early pastors as C. L. Clausen at Luther Valley, H. A. Preus at Spring Prairie, N. O. Brandt at Pine Lake, and Laur. Larsen at Rush River. Larsen once stated the basic missionary strategy of the Norwegian immigrant pastors: "It was our aim to visit all the Norwegians we heard of, if they were not served by any other pastor, and if we could possibly reach them."[1]

In Muus's case, pastoral efforts were divided between more local and more distant spheres of labor, that is, between Holden and its daughter congregations on the one hand and the more distant mission congregations on the other. The present chapter is devoted to the daughter congregations, and the following chapter will take up Muus's missionary travels to preaching stations and congregations farther removed from the Holden base.

Within a relatively few miles of Holden were clusters of Norwegians who were soon gathered into sub-congregations of Holden. Muus himself used the term *menighet* (congregation), for

Holden as the "mother church" or "main congregation." He employed the term *sogn* (parish) for the nearby units that had a large measure of independence and the right to order their own affairs, but would also take part in meetings that concerned "the entire congregation."[2]

The names of several of these nearby "parishes," which appear repeatedly in Muus's letters, in the Holden record books, and in the various local histories, have already been mentioned. On an imposing monument to Pastor Muus and the pioneers that stands outside the present Holden church appears a list of "daughter congregations" of Holden, with the following names: Dale, Gol, Hegre, Land, Minneola, Moland, Vang, Valley Grove, and Urland. The designation of "daughter" is applicable in light of the initiatives of Muus, whose work radiated out from Holden. "Holden Lutheran Church of Kenyon, Minnesota, is the Mother Church of most of the Lutheran Churches in Goodhue County." So begins the Holden 90th anniversary history. When Muus wrote to H. A. Preus in 1871 inviting him to come to dedicate the Holden Church, he referred to it as "our old church up here which is the mother of all the others."[3] Considering the fact that pastoral services had reached these places at an early stage and that these several churches close to Holden grew up together, one could find good reason to use the "sister" metaphor, but the "daughter" idea is established firmly enough to be retained.

Holden deserves recognition as the congregation that issued the call that brought Muus to Goodhue county from Norway. At the same time it must be acknowledged that his field was Goodhue county. The first time Muus is listed as one of the Church's pastors in the pages of the Norwegian Synod's journal, *Kirkelig Maanedstidende*, he is identified as "B. Muus, Goodhue Co." The same issue, reporting Muus's arrival from Norway, refers to him as "Pastor Muus, who is called as pastor in Goodhue Co. Minnesota."[4]

As shown earlier, before Muus arrived on the scene a number

120

of pastors had done ministerial work in the area among several groups of Norwegian Lutherans in addition to the one that founded Holden. Furthermore, Muus himself did not confine his first efforts to Holden but within his first month, November of 1859, he was holding worship services, baptisms, and Bible readings with people in Valley Grove, Valders or Vang, and Zumbrota.[5]

In its early history "Holden" actually embraced several preaching places within an area of 32 square miles, extending from east of Zumbrota to west of Kenyon, north to the village of Nerstrand and south to the community of Moland.[6] As time went on, various combinations or separations occurred. A significant change was the division of "the congregation" on October 13, 1862, into the following parishes: 1. Zumbrota (later divided into Land and Minneola), 2. Østre Sogn (i.e. Holden), 3. Valders (which came to be called Vang), 4. German Grove (later called Valley Grove). In 1864 the Valders parish was divided into two: Valders and the Halling settlement (later called Gol).[7]

A few years later, in 1868, when Muus wrote to Laur. Larsen to clarify how the congregations he was then serving ought to be listed, he explained that "there is no such separate parish called Holden, but Holden is the name for a collection of three parishes," which he then named as Østre Sogn, Valders, and the Halling settlement. He also pointed out that at that time three other congregations with which he had been associated, Land, Minneola, and Hoff, were being served by Pastor Ylvisaker.[8] On October 18, 1868, a month before this letter to Larsen was written, N. Th. Ylvisaker had been ordained to serve Red Wing as well as the three congregations just named.[9] While Muus was directly involved in the founding of the Synod congregation in Red Wing, he regarded it and Hoff as mission congregations rather than as offspring of Holden.[10] The information above illustrates how the alignments changed among and between some of the daughter congregations. In response to the need and to Muus's repeated requests for help, additional pastors came into the area who served as assistants to Muus and soon

121

became the resident pastors for one or more of the daughter congregations.

To the nine "daughter congregations" listed on the monument at Holden church may be added Hoff and Red Wing, making a total of eleven congregations to be named and characterized briefly in the present chapter. In all cases there is a connection with Holden and with Muus even if, in some instances, Muus himself was not the founder and first pastor. Nor do the stories of these churches present themselves along a neat chronological line. For some of them 1859, the year of Muus's arrival, is the key date marking the beginning of Muus's labors in their midst. Other dates will require noting, such as the organization of a congregation, the beginning or end of a relationship with another parish, the securing of their own pastor, the construction of a church building, or some other milestone.

Vang Lutheran church is located two miles east and two and one-half miles south of Dennison, Minnesota. In Muus's day it was first called Valders since the Norwegians in that vicinity were from the district of Valdres, as the name is now spelled, a valley in south-central Norway that had a Vang parish.

Vang shared the same early history prior to Muus's coming that Holden had known, having been included in pastoral visits from 1856 to 1858 by Nils Brandt, H. A. Stub, Johan S. Munch, A. C. Preus, and Laur. Larsen. The Valders community was also served by another notable personage of that era, the Reverend P. A. Rasmussen, then affiliated with the Elling Eielsen group, who carried out pastoral work in 1856 and 1858. When Muus first arrived, he refrained from taking up work among the "Valdrises" since he regarded them as belonging to Rasmussen's field of labor. After Rasmussen joined the Norwegian Synod in 1862, Muus felt free to conduct an active ministry in Valders. In 1863, that part of Rasmussen's congregations that lived within the borders of the

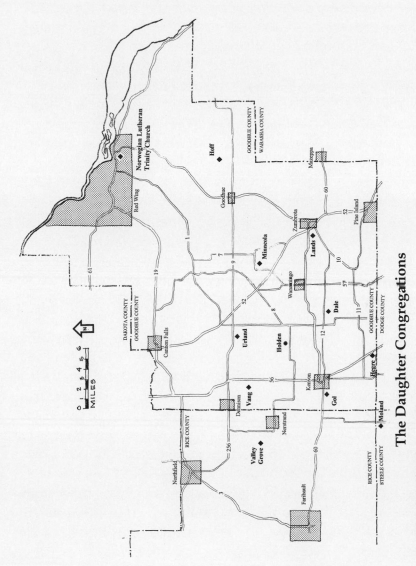

**The Daughter Congregations**

*Locations of Daughter Congregations*
Map by Clint Sathrum

Valders parish joined the Vang congregation. The first church building was started the same year.

Pastor Muus expressed his opinion that the proposed location of the church was too far south, away from the center of the Valders settlement. He predicted, correctly, that in a short time the people in the Halling settlement, then part of the Valders parish, would be strong enough to form their own congregation, and that sooner or later, as people from the northern part of the Vang parish joined the Vang church, there would be conflict because of the church lying so far to the south. In 1864 the Hallings did indeed organize themselves as the Gol congregation.[11]

But the Vang church was built on the proposed site in 1863. It was dedicated on October 18, 1868. Taking part in the dedication ceremony were pastors Th. Johnson, J. B. Frich, Laur. Larsen, Even Homme, and Abraham Jacobson. Larsen preached the dedicatory sermon. Muus himself was not present for the occasion because on that day he was dedicating a church in Red Wing and participating in the ordination of its pastor, N. Th. Ylvisaker. At the Vang dedication an offering of $89 was received for the housekeeping fund at "the educational institution," which was Luther College.[12]

Muus had a personal connection with the Vang community that he remembered with appreciation. About one-half mile south of the site of the first Vang church and cemetery was the farm of the Knut P. Haugen family with whom Muus and his wife had spent their first winter in America, from November of 1859 until they could move into the new Holden parsonage in March of 1860. Recalling the hospitality of the Haugens Muus wrote, "Here he [Muus] lived at no cost to the congregation and in addition enjoyed an extraordinary amount of help and friendliness from the family."[13]

The original Vang church was located one mile south of the present church on a site immediately to the west of the cemetery. Muus reports in his clergy journal that Christmas Day services

*Old Vang Church*
Felland collection; St. Olaf College Archives

were held "in Valders Church" December 25, 1863. In an entry the next month, on January 21, 1864, Muus notes the holding of worship services in the relatively new church, now referring to it as "Vang."[14]

While Muus himself was absent on the occasion of the dedication in 1868, he wrote up the event for the journal *Kirkelig Maanedstidende*, where he described the church as a frame structure 30' x 40' with a 20' x 20' sacristy on the east. Later a portico with steeple and a 1200-pound bell was added on the west. "We dearly wanted a bell to call us to God's house," Muus wrote, "and besides, at times it was rather unpleasant to have the prairie wind coming directly in through the church door."[15]

In his article for the journal Muus identifies the church as "Vang's Church in Valders parish of Holden congregation." Both "Vang" and "Valders" remained in use for a time but in the long run "Vang" was the name that passed down to recent times. As reported, Valders became two parishes in 1864: Valders (or Vang) and the Halling settlement, later called Gol.[16]

Eventful times for the Vang congregation lay ahead, even

125

within Muus's lifetime. Having shared a pastor with Gol in the 1870s, Vang in 1882 decided to join Urland in calling John Nathan Kildahl as the pastor for the two congregations, an action that led to considerable uproar regarding the location of the parsonage. As Muus had feared, there was also difficulty within the congregation in the 1890s when the building of a new church one mile north of the old church was proposed. A minority expressed their dissatisfaction by forming their own congregation, Little Cannon Lutheran Church, and building their own church south and east of the old Vang church. The latter was used for weddings and other events until 1902 when it was torn down.[17]

The new Vang church was completed in 1897. It was designed by a Swedish immigrant, Olof Hanson, whose deafness had brought him to the Minnesota School for the Deaf in Faribault, to which he returned to teach temporarily after completing his education and traveling in Europe. Hanson designed the sanctuary of the Vang church with large areas of glass to invite the light from outdoors in on the congregation. He also created an open seating area unbroken by pillars and side aisles that would enhance the communal nature of the church, the worshippers assembling under a ceiling that was in the form of a Greek cross.[18]

During the latter part of the nineteenth century Vang Lutheran Church was served by a number of outstanding pastors in addition to Muus, three of whom became well-known leaders in church and education. Pastor M. O. Bøckman, who served from 1875 to 1880, taught at the Divinity School in Northfield founded by the Anti-Missourian Brotherhood from 1886 to 1890, then at Augsburg Seminary, and finally at the theological seminary of the United Norwegian Evangelical Lutheran Church. There he taught New Testament and led the institution as its president.

John Nathan Kildahl, who was Vang and Urland's pastor from 1882 to 1889, spent a year as president of the Hauge Synod's Red Wing Seminary and was elected president of St. Olaf College in 1899. Carl A. Mellby, Vang's pastor from 1892 to 1898, took a leave

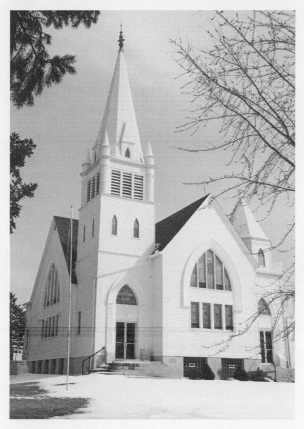

*Present Vang Church*
Photo by John Gorder

from his pastoral duties to study in Leipzig, Germany. In 1901 he joined the faculty at St. Olaf College.[19]

Another church that began as part of Holden and later became a separate parish was Urland Lutheran Church. It is in Leon township, nine miles south of Cannon Falls, Minnesota. The church building sits close to Goodhue county road #9, which runs between highways 52 and 56. Leon township has rich soil and "is one of the most desirable farming sections in the county, containing uplands, creeks and wooded tracts."[20]

127

*Urland Lutheran Church*
Photo by John Gorder

The Urland congregation organized itself as a separate parish in 1868, though still maintaining a connection with Holden, but in 1872 it became an independent congregation and built its own church at a cost of $8,842. A beautiful frame structure measuring 50 x 35 in the nave and 20 x 22 in the sanctuary, the Urland church was large enough for 500 people. It was dedicated in 1874, Pastor Ole Juul from New York preaching the dedication sermon. In writing up the event for the church journal, Muus devoted equal space to summarizing the sermon and to describing the practical, inexpensive heating apparatus that had been devised for sending heat from the basement up into the nave of the church. "The furnace, without the pipe, cost about $30," wrote Muus.[21]

Pastor Muus served the congregation as pastor from 1859, the year of his arrival, until 1879, when Thorvald August Hansen-Berger began a short period of service as pastor of Urland and Vang before returning to Norway in 1881. Other early pastors whose service at Urland took place while Muus was still active at

128

Holden were J. N. Kildahl, 1882–1889, N. A. Ofstedal, 1889–1892, C. A. Mellby, 1892–1898, and Anders E. Hauge, who began in 1898.[22]

A list of the officers of the Urland congregation as of 1872 has the names of Lars A. Flom, William Olson, Thorsten A. Melhus, Rognald J. Ohnstad, Ole A. Melhus, Johannes Ingebrigtson, and I. D. Hustvedt.[23] The mention of I. D. Hustvedt presents an opportunity to underscore the important role of lay teachers in Muus's congregations and throughout the Norwegian-American parishes. Iver D. Hustvedt belonged to that generation's remarkable cadre of lay religious instructors who gave decades of service to local congregations. For example, Ole J. Solberg at Holden taught for thirty years, and Iver Hustvedt is credited with teaching in the Urland vicinity for over forty years, from 1868 to 1910. Of such lay persons Gustav B. Odegaard has written, "Many of these teachers had a tremendous fund of knowledge, and gave instruction in Norwegian reading and orthography, in hymnology, Bible history, New Testament, and Catechism. Since in the early days the public school term in the country schools was only five months long, there was much opportunity for religious instruction. The teacher moved around in the congregation, spending a month or so in each district, using the public school building, which was granted by the district."[24]

From 1879 Urland was used to sharing a pastor with nearby Vang. This working relationship brought with it a squabble regarding the location of the parsonage. In 1881 Urland agreed to share a call with Vang and the next year the two congregations agreed to call John N. Kildahl as their pastor. A parsonage, to be owned jointly, was needed. After several efforts to arrive at an agreement, the decision finally was to place the parsonage near the Vang church with Urland being responsible for 40 percent of the initial cost and future upkeep.[25] The parsonage was built in 1884 at a cost of $4,780, of which Urland paid $1,912.[26]

In the record book in which Muus kept track of his day-to-day pastoral activities, the third entry, for November 13, 1859, indicates

129

that on the 20th Sunday after Trinity he held a worship service and conducted a baptism at the home of Jan Hansen in "Tyske Grove" or "German Grove."[27] Some Germans were among those who had settled in the western part of Holden township and in Rice county. Muus was known to deliver sermons in German when it was appropriate to do so. As early as 1852 two Norwegian families from Hallingdal in Norway had arrived and two years later several more families from the same district came to the area.[28] The rural congregation organized there later used the name Valley Grove.

Valley Grove is about three miles northwest of the village of Nerstrand. It is within three miles, south and west, of Vang church. The first Norwegian Lutheran pastor to visit Valley Grove was Nils O. Brandt, in 1855. The congregation was organized in 1856, the year when Pastor H. A. Stub came to the Holden-Goodhue settlement that included members from Valley Grove in the west to Zumbrota in the east. The number of Norwegians increased rapidly. When Pastor Laur. Larsen came to conduct services in the area during the summer of 1858, he baptized 100 children. Thirty-three of them were baptized under an oak tree near the site of the future Valley Grove church on June 18, 1858.[29]

After his arrival at Holden in 1859, Muus made frequent pastoral visits to Valley Grove as he did to other locales, meeting in homes as was the custom before churches were built. A week after the service at the Jan Hansen place, Muus was back to lead a worship service and baptize at the home of Eilif Trulsen. He was present in the community on January 8, 1860, and again on January 22.[30]

The Valley Grove group belonged to the Holden congregation from 1856 until 1862 when it became one of the four parishes into which Holden was divided. The building of a limestone church began that year. Its dimensions were 55' by 35' and 20' in height and its cost was $1,200. The altar was on the east wall. Along the west wall was a gallery that extended forward to about the middle of the side walls.

*Valley Grove Church, built in 1862*
Photo by Joseph M. Shaw

At the dedication on Sunday, October 18, 1868, the main address was given by Nils O. Brandt, the first pastor to visit the settlement in 1855. Brandt also read a written greeting sent by Pastor Muus who regretted that he was not able to be present, being in Red Wing that day. Muus had served the congregation as its pastor from 1859 until 1866 when Nils A. Quammen became the pastor. Muus's greeting reads in part: "God help you to be built up more and more on the foundation of the apostles and the prophets, to free yourselves from the devil's seduction by false doctrine or other ungodliness, and to grant you one day to enter your Father's great house above! God bless you and your pastor!"[31]

The congregation outgrew the stone church. In 1894 it built a frame church at a cost of $3,100,[32] but left the first church intact where it was used for many years for educational and other

131

*Valley Grove Church, 1894*
Photo by Joseph M. Shaw

purposes. In fact, both church buildings are standing and are being cared for to the present day, although regular worship services were discontinued in 1973.[33]

Nils Quammen served as the pastor for Valley Grove from 1867 until 1908. Quammen was one of Muus's first co-laborers, both in pastoral work and in the cause of higher education. When other neighboring pastors were cool toward Muus's efforts to raise money for an academy in Northfield, Quammen was willing to share in the risky venture and solicit money among his parishioners at Christiania, north of Northfield, and in the Valley Grove parish. Later, as a member of St. Olaf's Board of Trustees, Quammen joined those who were determined to keep the school alive, promising in 1876 to raise $2,500 among his people.[34]

Dale Lutheran church is located six miles east of Kenyon, Minnesota. The first members were Norwegians living in the South Prairie area south of Holden. Earliest worship services

132

were held in a log meeting house on Peter Holman's land near the joining of Spring Creek and the Zumbro River.[35] P. A. Rasmussen of Lisbon, Illinois, was called to serve the congregation in 1857 and continued as pastor until 1863. Wishing to continue his travels to many preaching places, Rasmussen did not become a resident pastor but advised the congregation to call Pastor Muus. The call was extended on September 23, 1863, and Muus accepted.[36] Muus's journal reveals regular visits to "South Prairie," for example, the Third Christmas Day service, December 27, 1866, and a service at the home of Jens Ottum on March 8, 1867.[37]

The name "Dale" was chosen by the parishioners after the church they and their ancestors had known in Sogn, Norway. The Dale church in Norway is a magnificent stone edifice with a 900-year history and is still in use. It is said that because of the location on a steep mountainside, the stones for the Norwegian church had to be carried down to the site "by sure-footed workers."[38]

The first church for the Goodhue county Dale congregation was a wooden frame structure, built in 1877 at a cost of $7,000. Pastor Muus laid the cornerstone July 15, 1877, perhaps recalling the congregational meeting of January 8, 1874, when a discussion had been held about the materials to be used in the church. Muus had recommended stone. Wood buildings are unsteady against the prairie winds and always need repair, he argued, while a stone church will stand for generations without needing repair. When the vote was taken, 44 were in favor of a wooden church and 3 opposed.[39] The incident belies the claims by some that Muus exercised total control over his parishioners.

Dedication of the Dale church took place on November 22, 1877. Officiating minister was Jørgen A. Thorsen. He was assisted by pastors Quammen and Ylvisaker, "and by the congregation's pastors Muus and Boeckman." Marcus Olaus Bøckman came from Norway in 1875 to be an assistant to Muus. Another assistant from Norway, Th. A. Hansen-Berger, who served at Urland as well as Vang, came in 1878. The 1877 church was destroyed by fire in 1947. It was replaced by a stone church in 1949.[40]

Another pastor in Dale's early history (1880–1883) was Ludvig Marinus Biørn, who served the neighboring Land and Minneola congregations and was also a leader in the wider church. He was secretary of the Norwegian Synod 1879–1887, chairman of the Anti-Missourian Brotherhood 1887 to 1890, and vice president of the United Norwegian Evangelical Lutheran Church from 1890 to 1894. Biørn also wrote a biography of P. A. Rasmussen and key sections of the Holden Fiftieth Anniversary booklet.[41]

Muus, continuing his work at Holden and his missionary travels, served as the pastor of Dale Lutheran Church from 1863 until 1880 when the congregation chose to sever its connection with Holden and become a separate parish. In the late nineties Muus stepped in to serve Dale again for a two-year period shortly before he returned to Norway in 1899. Since then, Dale and Holden have resumed and maintained their old partnership, having joint call committees and being served by the same pastors.[42]

Just one mile west of Kenyon, Minnesota, is an attractive stone church, the cornerstone of which was laid by Pastor Muus in 1870. This building was dedicated by the congregation of Gol Lutheran Church on June 21, 1874, the Third Sunday after Trinity, with the Reverend Ulrik Vilhelm Koren, vice president of the Norwegian Synod, performing the appropriate rites.[43] On the same day Urland Lutheran church, north of Holden and four miles east of Dennison, was also dedicated.

Pastor Koren was available for the important dedication ceremony at Gol church because he and other pastors of the Norwegian Synod were in attendance at the annual meeting of the church body at the Holden church from June 13 to 21 that summer of 1874. At that Synod meeting an action was taken that belongs to the beginnings of St. Olaf's School in Northfield. The June 1874 Synod meeting heard an offer from merchant Harald Thorson of Northfield of a five-acre property and $500 in cash if the Synod would begin and operate an academy in that town. The Synod expressed mild and approving interest, thanked

Thorson for his offer, but took no further action that would have provided monetary support for the Northfield academy.[44]

Subsequently, Muus, Thorson, N. A. Quammen, and various members of Muus's churches, including Knut P. Haugen, O. K. Finseth, and O. Osmundson, took independent action to secure enough money to begin St. Olaf's School. In his characteristically terse and economical way, Muus expended exactly one sentence on this historic moment in his review of Holden's first twenty-five years: "In 1874 people began to work for the construction of St. Olaf's School."[45] For him it was natural that a new educational venture was only one of many items considered by the church body as it held its synod meeting and dedicated new churches.

The name "Gol" comes from Hallingdal in the mountain country of south central Norway. For some time, as Muus visited this community and recorded his ministerial services there, he referred to it as the "Halling settlement." Since the Halling settlement for a time was part of the Holden congregation, one finds names of some of its residents among the original signers of the constitution of the Holden Church: Halvor H. Odegaarden, Erick and Ole Gunhus, Herbrand and Knut Finseth, Sr., Ole K. and Knut Finseth, Jr., Ole J. Bakke (or Bakko) and Kjetel Finnesgaard.

The Gol church had the same dimensions as Urland, 50 x 35 in the nave and 20 x 22 in the sanctuary. Over the 16 x 16 entrance was a tower, a spire, and a bell weighing 600 pounds.[46] The church was built of stone at a cost of $8,200. The stone was quarried from a location close to the Zumbro River and hauled to the building site by members. Remembering features of the church in Gol, Norway, they made the stone walls three feet thick at the base.[47]

The procuring of the stone uncovers another local story about Pastor Muus, one in which the authoritarian pastor again failed to get the upper hand. At the time Pastor Muus was collecting money for building the Gol church, a group of Haugeans west of Kenyon was also starting preparations to put up a church

*Gol Lutheran Church*
Photo by John Gorder

structure, and they too planned to build with stone, though they did not complete their church until 1888. Some time around 1870 Muus was out collecting money for Gol's building program. By then his reputation for telling parishioners exactly how much each should contribute was well established. He approached a Gol member by the name of Ole Erickson to ask for $200 in cash and a certain amount of stone for the Gol church. Ole objected that he was not able to give the $200 but was willing to donate some stone for the church. Pastor Muus would not

136

accept the stone without the cash, so he left. Later he returned and told Ole that he was willing to settle for the donation of the stone without insisting on the money. Said Ole, "You're too late. I have already promised the Hauge congregation the stone for its church."[48]

Pastor Muus served the Gol church until 1881, but before that time his two assistants from Norway, Bøckman and Hansen-Berger, also provided some of the pastoral services. A parsonage was built across the road from the church in 1881, first occupied by Bøckman, Gol's first resident pastor, who served until 1886. Bøckman, Hansen-Berger, and their successors would also serve at Moland Lutheran Church, a congregation located about 10 miles south and west of Kenyon, Minnesota.[49]

Pastor Bøckman left in 1886, being called to teach at the Anti-Missourian Brotherhood's theological seminary established that year in Northfield at St. Olaf's School. He was succeeded at Gol and Moland by Pastor Mads O. Andenæs who, with Candidate Thorleif Homme, served from 1886 to 1889. The next pastor called to serve Gol and Moland was Knut O. Lundeberg. He added First Evangelical Lutheran Church in Kenyon to his charge when that congregation was organized in 1891. Lundeberg left in 1895 to become the founder and first president of a new synod, the Lutheran Brethren. The Reverend Simund O. Simundson arrived in 1896 to serve Gol, Moland, and First Lutheran of Kenyon.[50]

By the time Pastor Simundson came on the scene, Muus was in the final years of his ministry. Simundson told several anecdotes about his dealings with Muus in a talk given at St. Olaf in 1931, one of them with the Gol parsonage as its setting. On May 4, 1899, the day after resigning from his congregation at Holden because of his failing health, Pastor Muus came to ask for Simundson's help in teaching the confirmands and holding Pentecost services. He was much relieved when Simundson quickly agreed to take over these duties. As the two pastors stood in the hallway of the parsonage, Muus looked around and said, "Her kommer jeg aldrig mer" ("I will never come here again"). Then Muus had lunch with the Ladies Aid, meeting that day in the parsonage, said goodbye to the ladies and to Simundson, and left.[51]

Moland Lutheran Church, on the county line ten miles southwest of Kenyon, draws its members from four counties: Steele, Dodge, Rice, and Goodhue. The Norwegians in the community had developed a congregational identity by the year 1878, meeting in homes and in schoolhouses. The congregation's history acknowledges in a general way the organizing work of "B. J. Muus and his assistants" in the area but mentions specifically Pastor Th. Aug. Hansen-Berger as in attendance at their business meetings in 1878–1879. A more formal organization of a congregation, including the adoption of a constitution, took place in 1880, when M. O. Bøckman was called to serve as pastor. His salary was to be paid by having each landowner give six dollars, each confirmed boy one dollar, and each confirmed girl fifty cents annually. The Moland congregation contributed $700 to the cost of the parsonage.[52]

By 1883 plans were underway to build a church, but in the meantime worship services were held in the Strandemo and Underdahl parochial schoolhouses. The church, built by the members in 1884 at a cost of $3,400, was to be 44' x 32' x 16'. According to local folklore, the large cottonwood tree on the north side of the church grew from a whip that one of the members had used in guiding his horses during the landscaping of the church grounds. When the job was finished, the man jabbed the cottonwood stick into the ground and said, "Now we are done." The stick took root and grew into a stately cottonwood tree. In 1893 the congregation purchased a thousand pound bell for $242.80 and added to the church a bell tower with stairway.[53]

With Moland being paired with Gol for much of its history, the pastors mentioned above are also counted among Moland's pastors: Hansen-Berger (1879–1880), Bøckman (1880–1886), Andenaes and Homme (1886–1889), K. O. Lundeberg (1889–1895), and Simundson (1895–1923).[54] Pastor Simundson was the first to

*Moland Lutheran Church*
Photo by Joseph M. Shaw

keep a separate record book for the Moland congregation and the first to use an automobile.[55]

When the widespread Holden congregation was divided in 1862 into four parishes, one of them was Zumbrota. Later Zumbrota itself was divided into Land and Minneola.[56] As time passed, the congregations related to Holden seemed to be linked to one another in pairs, Vang and Urland, Gol and Moland, and Lands and Minneola. Holden and Dale had long been together in one charge. In the early 1880s Holden and Hegre constituted a call served by Pastor Muus.[57]

The name "Land" was taken from a district in Norway from which early members of the congregation had emigrated. As the use of Norwegian gradually was replaced by English, the congregation decided to clear up the confusion as to how the name should be written—"Land," "Land's," or "Lands"—and settled on "Lands" without the apostrophe.[58]

139

The first Norwegian service of worship in Goodhue county was held Sunday morning, June 25, 1855, by the Reverend Nils O. Brandt on the farm of Mathias and Ingeborg Ringdahl, charter members of the Lands congregation. Ringdahl, it has been noted, was the first Norwegian settler in Goodhue county. In 1859, after Pastor Muus had arrived at Holden, Ringdahl, Knud Klemmesen Juveli, and Andrew Nerhaugen were the committee members who invited Muus to hold occasional services in their community. One of Muus's early visits among the settlers who would constitute the Lands congregation took place on November 30, 1859, when he conducted a worship service and baptized two children under an oak tree at the home of Knud Klemmesen Juveli.[59] Muus's clergy journal shows repeated visits to Zumbrota or Zumbrota Falls where he conducted services at the homes of Andreas Erstad, Chr. Pedersen Lunde, and others.[60]

Having begun under Pastor Muus, Lands belonged to the Zumbrota parish from 1862 to 1868. In the latter year, Lands and Minneola combined with Red Wing and Hoff to form their own parish, calling as pastor N. Th. Ylvisaker from Norway. Letters from Muus to Pastor H. A. Preus, president of the Norwegian Synod, reveal how eagerly Ylvisaker's arrival was awaited. Ylvisaker was ordained in Red Wing, Minnesota, on October 18, 1868, the same day the Norwegian Lutheran church in that city was dedicated.[61]

According to the Lands congregation history, Pastor Muus is credited with selecting a site on the top of a hill, one and a half miles west of Zumbrota, as the place where the church should be built. The land was purchased from Andreas and Olina Erstad for $20. The decision to build was made in March of 1866 and construction started in 1867. The congregation had agreed on a building 50' by 33' with a 16' by 18' addition if funds were voted for it. It would be a frame structure with a steeple. There was no basement under the church. It was heated by two stoves at the rear. Since the chimney was at the other end of the building, stove pipes on either side ran the length of the sanctuary. The lumber was purchased in Red Wing and hauled in by wagons. Total cost of the church was between $4,000 and $4,500. It was dedicated November 8, 1871, by the Reverend H. A. Preus. Also present were Muus, Kr. Magelssen, Quammen, and Lands' own Pastor Ylvisaker.[62]

The church remained in use until 1911 when the congregation voted to build a new, larger church of brick that could seat 800. The new church was dedicated in 1913.

Newly arrived from Norway with his wife and five children, and newly ordained, Ylvisaker assumed the call that included four congregations: Lands, Minneola, Hoff, and First Norwegian Evangelical Lutheran of Red Wing. He and his family lived in Red Wing from 1868 until the Lands parsonage was built in 1872. In part because of the pastor's failing health, his responsibility was limited to Lands and Minneola. On April 16, 1877, Pastor Ylvisaker died at the age of 45.[63]

The two congregations, Lands and Minneola, then called the deceased pastor's brother, Johannes B. Ylvisaker, who accepted the call and was ordained by Pastor Muus on July 18, 1877, in the Lands church. This pastor served for two years, after which he took a position as professor of theology at the Synod's seminary in Madison, Wisconsin. The next pastor was L. M. Biørn, who came to Lands and Minneola from Manitowoc, Wisconsin, arriving in the fall of 1879. Biørn, mentioned earlier in relation to Dale, served as pastor for the two congregations from 1879 until his death in 1908.

The Lands church and its surroundings form a visually appealing scene. The present brick church, dedicated in 1913, replaced the old one which lay some 200 feet farther to the west. A stone marker shows where the old church stood. The parsonage burned in 1899 and a new one was built a few rods west of the site of the original one. Between the parsonage and the church is an attractive wooded park with a covered shelter.

As a unique reminder of the ministry of Pastor Muus the congregation prizes the oil painting done by artist Arne Berger.[64] The

141

*Oil painting in Lands Church. Gunner Johnson and B. J. Muus*
Photo by John Gorder

painting depicts Pastor Muus and a driver in a wooden cart drawn by two oxen. The driver has been identified as Gunder (or Gunner) Johnson, a pioneer member of the Monongalia congregation, later called Crow River, which Muus founded in 1861.[65] The Crow River church is approximately four miles south of Belgrade, Minnesota, in what is now Kandiyohi county.

The Minneola community is located five miles northeast of Wanamingo, Minnesota. It is said that the word "Minneola," also the name of the township in which the Lutheran church is located, is a composite of the two Indian words "minnie" and "ola" that together mean "much water." The north branch of the Zumbro River runs east and west across the township. Springs and rivulets also add to the abundance of water in the township.[66]

142

The Minneola Lutheran Church, in common with Lands, was originally a part of the Holden congregation and served by Pastor Muus. Minneola and Lands were assigned to Zumbrota when the Holden congregation was divided into four parishes in 1862. The first worship services were held in a new barn on the John Vollan farm in the mid-1860s. Minneola organized as a congregation on July 1, 1867, with sixteen charter members and Muus continuing to serve as pastor.[67] In 1868 Minneola and Lands ended the tie with Holden and joined Hoff and Red Wing to form an independent parish, calling N. Th. Ylvisaker to be its pastor. After 1872 Ylvisaker, whose physical strength was declining, was able to serve only Minneola and Lands. When he died in 1877, the two congregations called his brother, Johannes B. Ylvisaker, and after him L. M. Biørn who began his ministry at Minneola in 1879.[68] In the long-standing partnership between Lands and Minneola, the pastor serving the two congregations has resided in the parsonage located near the Lands church.

The Minneola congregation built a church in 1870, the members hauling the lumber to the site from Red Wing. Cornerstone laying took place October 30, 1870. The church was dedicated June 21, 1874, by the Reverend P. A. Rasmussen, assisted by the Reverend Johannes B. Frich. The absence of Pastor Muus is explained by the fact that from June 13 to 21, 1874, he and the Holden congregation were hosts to a meeting of the Synod. A minor note of interest has to do with the pulpit for the church, constructed in a carpenter's shop in Wanamingo. When it was completed, it was too large to be taken through the shop door and transported to the church, so it became necessary to cut an opening in the wall of the shop to remove the pulpit.[69]

Hoff Lutheran church, no longer in existence, was situated six miles northeast of the town of Goodhue, Minnesota, in section 18 of Belvidere township, Goodhue county.[70] In early references to this place Muus calls it "Halfbreedland," as in the record of a pastoral visit on January 17, 1860, when he conducted services at

143

*Minneola Lutheran Church*
Photo by John Gorder

the home of Ole Knutsen. Two days later he was there to hold another service.[71] In a letter to Laur. Larsen in February of 1860 Muus states that he has not made any mission journeys "except to Halfbreedland."[72] In April of 1862 Muus writes to Laur. Larsen inviting him to preach at Halfbreedland, which he describes as "about 20 miles" from Holden. At about this time references to Halfbreedland give way to the township name, "Belvidere." For example, in June of 1862, when the Norwegian Synod held an extraordinary meeting at Holden, Muus's journal indicates which of the visiting clergymen were scheduled to be at the various nearby places of worship. On June 15th, Pastor Kristian Magelssen was to be at Belvidere and on June 23rd Pastor Jacob Aal Ottesen would be there. On March 1, 1866, Muus, continuing his practice of forwarding to President Laur. Larsen sums of money from his congregations and members "for professors' salaries and housekeeping expenses" at Luther College, transmits $1.15 from "H. Olsen, Belvidere Congregation."[73]

When the congregation was organized in 1867, the members chose the name "Hoff," after a church in Toten, Norway, where most of them had come from. The first organizational meeting was held at the home of K. L. Anderson with eighteen men present. Under the guidance of Pastor Muus, the Articles of Incorporation were registered on June 18, 1867. Apparently the adoption of the name "Hoff" was simultaneous with the building of a church. Muus's journal indicates a visit to "Belvedere" on January 9, 1867. An entry for August 1st of that year records a worship service in Hoff, and the entry for October 16th states, "Divine worship in the Hoff church."[74] The church structure itself has been described as "a large building 30 feet by 60 feet, built on top of a hill with the cemetery to the south and east side of the building."[75]

Muus served as the pastor of Hoff Church until 1868 when Hoff, together with Lands, Minneola, and First Evangelical Lutheran in Red Wing separated from Holden and formed a separate parish, calling as their pastor the Reverend N. Th. Ylvisaker. As Pastor Ylvisaker's health declined, it was decided that he should serve only Lands and Minneola. Thus in 1875 Hoff and Red Wing called Reier Larsen as their pastor. He served only one year, being followed by Kristen S. Berven, who served until 1887 when a theological controversy over the doctrine of election caused Hoff and the Red Wing congregation to separate from one another. Pastor Berven continued as Hoff's pastor for another year. Hoff was without a permanent pastor until 1890 when L. M. Biørn, pastor of Lands and Minneola, stepped in to serve until 1893. Then Hoff secured the services of Nils Halvorsen, who was also serving Hegre and a church in Wanamingo.[76]

With membership declining for various reasons in the first decades of the twentieth century, the congregation voted to close

145

the church in 1938. The church building was sold and the proceeds given to the St. Olaf College radio station and to the centennial appeal of the Norwegian Lutheran Church.[77]

The contemporary descendant of the congregation in Red Wing, Minnesota, with whose early history B. J. Muus was associated is United Lutheran Church. First known as Norwegian Lutheran Trinity Church, it took the name Evangelical Lutheran Trinity Church of Red Wing in 1897 and became United Lutheran Church in 1930 when it merged with St. Peter's Evangelical Lutheran Church. The congregation places the beginning of its history at the year 1858 when the Reverend Laur. Larsen, then of Rush River in Pierce county, Wisconsin, was called by eight Norwegian families to hold services in Red Wing.[78]

On January 18, 1860, during a very busy month for Pastor Muus, who had just arrived at Holden a little over two months earlier, he led worship services in Red Wing at the home of Thor Simonsen. His clergy journal indicates subsequent visits to Red Wing in May and September of 1860, and regularly though not frequently thereafter. A November 1861 service was held at the home of Paal Berg.[79] At times Red Wing, lying farther from Holden than such places as Urland, Vang, and Dale, was included in some of the missionary trips that took Muus to more distant congregations. For example, a service in Red Wing followed immediately upon a short mission visit into Wisconsin to the Coon Prairie congregation.

Muus established a congregation consisting of eight families in Red Wing in 1864. At first the little group met in the basement of the German Lutheran church. But with many Norwegians in the town and in the light of Red Wing's importance as the main market for the sizeable Norwegian settlement in Goodhue county, Muus's group soon aspired to build a church. They bought a lot for $300 and proceeded to raise money, at first going counter to Muus's stiff warning against the shame of "begging" money from the townspeople. In Muus's account of the steps by which

146

his Red Wing flock eventually built a church, there is a mixture of droll humor and annoyance at the tactics of a rival group of Norwegians, the followers of Elling Eielsen. Describing the 1866 cornerstone laying in the synod monthly, *Kirkelig Maanedstidende*, Muus charges that the Elling people first caused trouble by bidding up the price on the first lot the congregation tried to buy, and second, by cashing in deceitfully on the efforts of Muus's congregation to raise funds. When the Ellings learned that the Synod people, though contrary to Muus's advice, were soliciting money in the town, they "used the opportunity to go around the city gathering gifts of Christian love from Christians, Turks, and Heathen for *their* church." The townspeople, not realizing that there were two groups of Norwegians at work, thought they were giving toward the cause of the Synod congregation Muus had organized. "So," concludes Muus, "we received only shame from this begging."[80]

Nevertheless, the church was built at a cost of about $2,200. The basement and superstructure were already in place when the cornerstone was laid by Muus on October 10, 1866. The congregation first met for the sermon in the nave, which measured 42 by 30 feet, then went to the basement where Muus placed a steel cylinder in a hollowed-out stone in the wall. Into the cylinder went a description of the ceremony, written in Norwegian and Latin, and some American and Norwegian coins. Another stone was placed over the opening and Muus struck three blows in the name of the Holy Trinity, declaring the cornerstone of the church to be laid. Then the assembly went back upstairs to the nave of the church where a child was baptized, an offering was received, and the Collect of Thanksgiving was chanted by Pastor Quammen. Muus concludes his account of the cornerstone-laying occasion with a prayer that God would soon send them a zealous resident pastor.[81]

Two years later, the church was dedicated and a pastor was ordained. On Sunday, October 18, 1868, the church was dedicated in the morning and Ylvisaker, recently arrived from Norway, was ordained by Synod president H. A. Preus in the afternoon. His

*Norwegian Lutheran Trinity Church*
Courtesy of the Goodhue County Historical Society,
Red Wing, Minnesota

call, as noted previously, included Lands, Minneola, and Hoff as well as the Red Wing church.

Pastor Muus also submitted an account of the dedication and ordination to *Kirkelig Maanedstidende*. It reflects the joy of the festive occasion, his own satisfaction in the events of the day, and the warm response of the guests to the hospitality they had received in Red Wing. By this time the church was complete in all essentials and the members were glad to know that it was paid for.

148

Muus writes, "And perhaps some felt a smidgen of pride in the fact that it had been paid for by Norwegian Lutherans, and not by Sects, Turks, or Heathen."[82]

Because a conference of Synod pastors was being held in Red Wing at the same time, several of the visiting clergy participated in the dedication and ordination and were given lodging in the homes of the church members. The hospitality and friendship they experienced prompted Muus to observe, playfully and with obvious pleasure, that "these Norwegian pastors, who always do what is bad, in return took with them the hearts of some of the parishioners." He adds that he had just received a letter from one of the pastors with a friendly greeting to the dear Red Wing people and the comment that the recent pastors' conference was the most pleasant one he had attended in America.[83]

Six miles south of Kenyon and one mile south of Skyburg in Goodhue county is Hegre Lutheran church, organized November 11, 1878, by Norwegian immigrant farmers. Before this date services had been held in private homes and in the Clark schoolhouse. In his history of Holden's first twenty-five years B. J. Muus states that in 1878 "a new parish, Hegre, was established," implying a connection to Holden.[84] By that time the two pastors from Norway who had come to be Muus's assistants, Bøckman and Hansen-Berger, both, with Muus, provided ministerial services for Hegre.

The name "Hegre" was chosen by members who came from a Hegre parish in Norway. The congregation became independent of Holden in 1880, but because of a crop failure was not able to pay a pastor's salary for about two years. During that time lay members led services and Muus was called to serve as temporary pastor until 1884.[85] Land for a church was acquired in 1877 and a church was built in 1880 at a cost of $2,000. A chancel was added in 1884 and a steeple soon after that.[86]

Other pastors serving Hegre during the nineteenth century were Anton Winter, Nils Ofstedahl, Nils J. Lockrem, and Nils

149

*Hegre Lutheran Church*
Photo by John Gorder

Halvorsen. The first deacons, elected in 1896, were A. W. Hegseth, J. P. Hegseth, and T. Jarstad. The first janitor, Lars Erickson, was to receive a salary of $25 per year from which he was expected to supply wood for the heating of the church.[87]

Pastor Muus distinguished between the "external" and "inner" history of Holden and its daughter congregations when he wrote a brief review of the first twenty-five years. To a large extent the present chapter has dealt with the external history. It was certainly not in Muus's spirit to disparage names, dates, organizations, meetings, funds, buildings, and the like as if such externals were unimportant. The impact of Muus's work in southern Minnesota has lasted well over a century because he and his associates early recognized that the church can have a future only when men and women in their local communities accept the need to organize congregations, call pastors, raise money, and build churches. Muus himself wrote about this external history in summarizing developments at Holden.

But he also set forth some of the themes that constitute the inner history of the congregation, by which he meant Holden and its several parishes. "There the work is devoted to securing everything on Christ the Rock," he wrote. "One achieves this by a clearer realization of truth unto godliness, by turning away doctrinal errors, preventing sinful schisms, caring for the instruction of the young in the Christian faith, supporting the weak, raising the fallen, standing by the troubled, strengthening the dying in their final struggle, excluding the obstinate and unrepentant."[88] Actions of this kind, belonging to the "inner history" of a congregation, are indicative of the aims Muus pursued as pastor of Holden and its daughter congregations.

# Seven

## Mission Travels

"A good share of the work of our pastors is like that of missionaries," said the Reverend H. A. Preus in a lecture given in Oslo in the spring of 1867. As examples he mentioned that pastors B. J. Muus and Thomas Johnson served from thirteen to sixteen congregations. Preus was in Norway to give firsthand information about the Norwegian-American church and to recruit Norwegian pastors to come to America to minister to the growing number of Norwegians who had emigrated.[1] Muus's friend and colleague Laur. Larsen had visited Norway in 1860 with the same purpose of persuading theology candidates to join the pastoral forces in America. He reported that Pastor Muus was then serving his old parish, Rush River in Wisconsin, and added that Muus was caring for an enormous district approximately 200 miles in length with at least twenty-five preaching places or congregations. A later count was twenty-eight preaching stations.[2]

Muus's mission travels took him to at least fourteen counties in southern Minnesota and three or four western Wisconsin counties. The area he covered in his travels was said to be the size of the entire country of Denmark, or around 15,000 square miles.[3] The preaching sites and communities visited by Muus lay in an arc that curved west and northwest from Goodhue county in

153

southeastern Minnesota up through the south-central part of the state past Willmar as far north as New London and St. Cloud. In addition, Muus made preaching visits to Minneapolis, St. Paul, and the counties in western Wisconsin that lay close to the St. Croix and Mississippi rivers and hence relatively close to his home base in Goodhue county.

Muus was indefatigable in his efforts to reach the scattered settlements, employing every mode of transportation available. He traveled by horse and buggy or by ox team, walked, rode horseback, skied in the winter, took the train when it was available, and even swam rivers when circumstances required it. Reviewing Muus's ministry some fifty years later, one historian estimated that by that time there were more than 150 congregations in the regions Muus had visited as he pursued his wide-ranging pastoral duties.[4]

For the most part, the mission journeys took place in the early part of the 1860s, during Muus's first decade in America. Immigration continued apace but the process of securing pastors for the budding congregations out on the prairie was very slow. The efforts of Larsen and Preus to recruit pastors from Norway produced few candidates.[5] Muus himself went to Norway in 1870 in another attempt to stimulate interest in the pastoral needs in North America.

In about 1881, writing a short review of the Holden congregation's "external history," as he called it, Muus used the final paragraph to indicate the mission work that had been launched from that congregation. He gave a compact summary of this aspect of his ministry in these words: "From Holden congregation mission work has been done in Hoff and Red Wing congregations, Goodhue Co.; in Northfield, Fox Lake and Faribault, Rice Co.; in Christiania, Dakota Co.; in North Waseca and Le Sueur River congregations, Waseca Co.; at Jackson Lake and in South Bend, Blue Earth Co.; in Madelia and southwest [Rosendale] and northwest [Linden] from there in Watonwan and Brown Co[unties]; in St. Peter, in Swan Lake, and Nicollet congregations, Nicollet Co.; in

154

Carver congregation, Carver Co.; and Bergen congregation, McLeod Co.; in Naes congregation, Meeker Co.; at Crow River and Norway Lake, Kandiyohi Co.; in St. Paul and Minneapolis; at St. Francis River, 18 miles northeast of St. Cloud; in Hudson and Rush River congregations, St. Croix and Pierce Co., Wis.; in Menomonie and east of there in Dunn Co., Wis."[6]

Hoff and Red Wing, listed here by Muus as mission stations, were included among the daughter congregations in the previous chapter for two reasons. First, they are located in Goodhue county, relatively close to Holden. Second, at an early date they joined Land and Minneola, two daughter congregations, to comprise a single pastoral call served by the same pastor, N. Th. Ylvisaker.

In the present discussion, the order in which Muus himself listed the mission places will be followed in geographical rather than chronological sequence. With close to thirty locations or congregations to be discussed, it is necessary to limit the treatment to Pastor Muus's role in the early life of each congregation and a few added points of interest. If Muus was not always the founder of these more distant congregations, he was influential in seeing them through their first years. In most cases, a church still exists that traces its beginnings to Muus's mission travels.

Rice county lies immediately west of Goodhue county; Dakota county is north of both Goodhue and Rice. Visits to Rice county took Muus to Northfield, Fox Lake, and Faribault. In Dakota county he preached at Christiania and installed N. A. Quammen as the first regular pastor there.

The first Norwegians arrived in Northfield, in the northeast corner of Rice county, in 1855, the year that John Wesley North founded the town. Pastor Muus held a worship service in a home "north of Northfield" as early as June of 1860. On October 1, 1861, he held an "evening service in Northfield," and on December 1, 1865, a worship service at the home of one Mikkel Andersen.[7] St. John's Lutheran Church, which names Muus as its founder, traces its beginning to March of 1869, when Muus held a service at

155

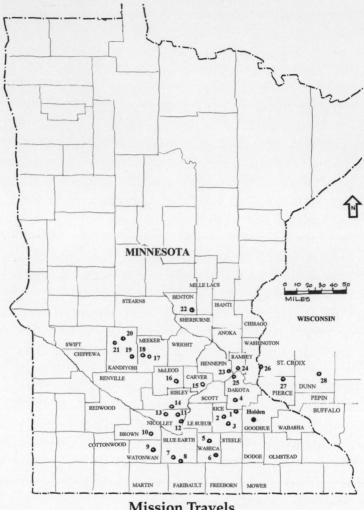

## Mission Travels

| | | | |
|---|---|---|---|
| 1. St. John's | 8. Delavan | 15. Carver | 22. St. Francis |
| 2. Fox Lake | 9. Rosendale | 16. Bergen | 23. Immanuel |
| 3. Zion | 10. Linden | 17. Ness | 24. Christ Lutheran |
| 4. Christiania | 11. Norseland | 18. Arndahl | 25. Fort Snelling |
| 5. North Waseca | 12. St. Peter | 19. Throndhjem | 26. Ebenezer, St. Croix County, WI |
| 6. Le Sueur River | 13. Swan Lake | 20. Crow River | 27. Rush River, Pierce County, WI |
| 7. Jackson Lake | 14. Norwegian Grove | 21. Norway Lake | 28. First Norwegian, Dunn County, WI |

*Mission Travels of B. J. Muus*
Map by Clint Sathrum

the home of Knute Thorson and installed the Reverend N. A. Quammen as the pastor. The name first used was the First Norwegian Evangelical Lutheran Congregation of Northfield.[8] After six years Quammen resigned. In 1875 the Reverend Thorbjorn Nelson Mohn, principal of the St. Olaf's School established in Northfield in 1874, became the pastor. Before the congregation was able to build its own church, worship services were held at St. Olaf's School, then located near the Northfield business district, in the German Methodist church, and in the Moravian church. In 1880, when it incorporated under a new constitution, it took the name St. Johannes Lutheran Church at Northfield, Minnesota.[9]

Setting out to build a church, the congregation collected money, appointed a building committee, and secured a site. According to the fiftieth anniversary history, "The work progressed rapidly enough to enable the congregation to assemble for dedication services Nov. 13, 1881. Rev. Muus preached the sermon and performed the dedication ceremony." The church was a frame building located on the corner of Fourth and Washington Streets in Northfield.[10]

With Pastor Muus as the founder of both, St. John's congregation and St. Olaf's School had close ties from the very beginning. That Northfield had a Norwegian congregation, as well as railroad connections, influenced Muus and Northfield merchant Harald Thorson in placing the school there. A long and rich history of collaboration developed between the educational institution Muus founded in Northfield and the congregation resulting from his mission visitations there in the 1860s.[11]

The Fox Lake church was located seven miles north of Faribault, where the first Norwegians settled in 1855. Pastoral services were first sought from the Valley Grove congregation, where children were taken to be baptized by H. A. Stub in 1856 and Laur. Larsen in 1858. After Muus came on the scene, he baptized children brought to Holden from Fox Lake and taught confirmation pupils at Valley Grove. Invited repeatedly to visit the Fox Lake settlement and conduct services, he had to decline. "I was traveling

*Old St. John's Lutheran Church. Washington Street, Northfield, Minnesota*
Courtesy Northfield Historical Society

four or five weeks without interruption in order to preach just one time for all of my congregations," he wrote.[12]

Once he found time to visit Fox Lake, Muus was astonished to learn on his arrival that the settlers already had a pastor, Nils Olsen from the Christiania settlement and a pastor of the Northern Illinois Synod. Under such circumstances Muus would not serve them, but he was told that Olsen was hired to preach for only a year.

In 1864 Muus was called as the pastor and accepted. That same year he organized the Fox Lake Norwegian Evangelical congregation, beginning with six families, and promised to come every other month, six times a year. He preached his first sermon at the home of Ole Hansen Korsdalen. On November 7, 1864, Muus conducted worship services at the home of Elling Olsen Strand.

He served the Fox Lake congregation as its regular pastor for two years, succeeded by N. A. Quammen, whom he installed in September of 1866. That month Muus also installed Quammen as pastor of Christiania Lutheran Church in Dakota county and of the congregations at North Waseca and Le Sueur River in Waseca county. Quammen continued as pastor at Fox Lake until 1911, a period of 45 years.[13]

The first Fox Lake church was built in 1874. It burned to the ground in 1896 after being struck by lightning. A second church was built and dedicated in the fall of 1897. The last worship services held by the congregation took place in 1961. The church building was dismantled and the materials and furnishings sold in 1961 and 1962. Wrote a local historian, "Seven miles north of Faribault a cemetery and a grassy spot to the west is all that is left to indicate where for over ninety years a Norwegian Lutheran congregation existed."[14]

Zion Norwegian Lutheran Church in Faribault was one of four Norwegian Lutheran congregations whose histories lie behind the present First English Lutheran Church there. B. J. Muus did not organize the Zion congregation, but he made pastoral visits to the Norwegians in the community before Zion Lutheran was founded in 1869. The first to do pastoral work among the Norwegians in Faribault was the Reverend Laur. Larsen. In June of 1859 Larsen stopped in Faribault on his way from St. Paul to southern Minnesota. His biography states: "He was told that a little Norwegian group in Faribault wished services, and stopped there for an evening before proceeding to Goodhue County."[15]

There were other Norwegian Lutheran groups in Faribault, including a congregation established in 1861 that eventually joined the Conference for the Norwegian-Danish Evangelical Lutheran Church. Another was Markers Norwegian Evangelical Lutheran Church, organized by the Haugeans in 1869. The group Muus began to visit in 1865, however it was related to the one earlier associated with Larsen, would soon be organized as Zion Norwegian Lutheran Church.

Muus's journal indicates that he held a worship service on January 16, 1865, "in Faribault city." He was there again on March 8 and 9, and on May 10, 1865. Those are the only entries related to Faribault, as distinct from Fox Lake, north of Faribault. Muus's brief labors were followed by those of Pastor N. A. Quammen, who organized Zion Norwegian Evangelical Lutheran Congregation in 1869 and became its first pastor. There were 136 members at the beginning. Apparently Zion never joined the Norwegian Synod officially even though it was generally in sympathy with most Synod views. But in 1889 members of Zion who disagreed with the Norwegian Synod position on election left Quammen's church to form Immanuel Lutheran Church, a congregation that became a member of the United Norwegian Lutheran Church in 1890.[16]

At the present time, Christiania Lutheran church, in Dakota county, is located at the intersection of County Road 46 and 267th Street West in Eureka township, five miles south of Lakeville. It is to be distinguished from a nearby church and local landmark, Highview Christiania Lutheran church. The two shared some turbulent early history, but Highview became a congregation of the Scandinavian Augustana Lutheran Synod, and in time became affiliated with the Lutheran Free Church. At present both churches belong to the Evangelical Lutheran Church in America.[17] As with Fox Lake and Faribault, the story of Christiania Lutheran Church tells of early work by Laur. Larsen, pastoral visits by B. J. Muus, and the coming of N. A. Quammen as permanent pastor. Before Muus installed Quammen in the fall of 1866, however, he was embroiled in the strife that issued in the emergence of two Christiania churches.[18]

The first Norwegian settlers came to Christiania from Koshkonong, Wisconsin, in 1854; another group came from Muskego the following year. The first attempt at pastoral ministry was carried out by Daniel Brown, a Swedish evangelist who had to leave when it became evident that he was an alcoholic. Laur. Larsen from Rush River visited the settlement in July of 1859 and advised the people to secure the services of Pastor B. J. Muus, scheduled to arrive in Goodhue county in the fall. Before Muus was called, the Christiania community was visited by Ole Paulson, a Norwegian evangelist and colporteur from Carver county, whose prayer meetings produced a religious revival. Through Paulson, the community invited Pastor Peter Carlson from Carver county to come to Christiania. Carlson, a member of the Northern Illinois Synod, served as pastor in Christiania from 1859 to 1861, when he resigned. At an early stage the congregation had 223 members. According to Muus's account in *Kirkelig Maanedstidende*, "When he [Carlson] thought that he could no longer take charge of this congregation, it decided to call the undersigned [Muus]."[19] Before the congregation could carry out this intention, wrote Muus, Nils Olsen of the Northern Illinois Synod appeared and offered to be its pastor. A small portion of the congregation called Olsen, preferring him as Carlson's successor and likely regarding him as more sympathetic to the revival than Muus.[20] This faction continued as a separate congregation that in time became Highview Christiania Lutheran Church.

The disagreements regarding pastoral leadership probably explain why Muus first received a call in 1861 and a second one in 1862. The majority followed through on its initial decision to call Muus and during his pastorate, in 1862, became a congregation of the Norwegian Synod. It was registered in the Dakota county courthouse February 12, 1864.[21] Muus continued to serve until September 25, 1866, when he installed N. A. Quammen as pastor of the Synod Christiania congregation and three other congregations in southern Minnesota.[22] A church building was constructed in 1867. Its dimensions were 34 x 48 feet plus an addition measuring 22 x 24 feet. Cost was $3,000. A parsonage, on eighty acres of land, was built in 1879. Through the influx of more immigrants, membership reached 430 by 1881.[23]

"From the 25th to the 30th of September of this year I had the pleasure of installing Pastor N. A. Quammen in his new congregations. These are: Christiania congregation in Dakota Co., Minn., North Waseca and Le Sueur River congregations, both in Waseca Co., Minn., as well as a little congregation consisting of approximately six families by Fox Lake, seven miles north of the city of Faribault." So began Pastor Muus's report about these congregations published in *Kirkelig Maanedstidende* in February of 1867.[24] Waseca county is located southwest of Goodhue county, between Steele and Blue Earth counties. Two of its larger towns are New Richland and Waseca.

North Waseca Lutheran church, in Waseca county, is about thirty-six miles from Holden and about five and one-half miles northwest of the town of Waseca. The congregation traces its beginnings to Sunday, October 17, 1858, when twenty-three men assembled for an organizational meeting at the home of Aslak Herlaugson, one and one-half miles north of the present church. The Reverend Laur. Larsen was on hand for the meeting, also conducting a service at which twelve children were baptized, six young people catechized and confirmed, and a marriage solemnized. Larsen drafted a constitution, which was adopted, and accepted the call of the congregation to visit the North Waseca rural community twice a year. He returned for a second visit June 19, 1859, but could not continue his services because the Norwegian Synod called him to teach the Norwegian students at Concordia Seminary in St. Louis.[25]

B. J. Muus was called to serve the North Waseca congregation on the same twice-yearly basis, beginning April 17, 1860, and continuing for the next six years. On that April day in 1860, according to his clergy journal, he was present for a "Sermon with Baptism and Communion." His next visit to North Waseca was September 18 and 19, 1860, when he conducted a "Worship Service with Baptism and Communion." A congregational history describes the visits by Muus: "Records show that he spent two days at work in the congregation on each visit, preaching both days and conducting a business meeting one afternoon. A

162

Sunday service always included preaching, catechization, baptism and communion, lasting for three hours or more."[26]

The North Waseca congregation joined the Norwegian Synod in May of 1863 and during that same year began building a 24 by 30 foot church that was first used for worship services in 1864, though it was not finished until 1874. Muus installed N. A. Quammen as the pastor on September 28, 1866. Quammen was succeeded by the Reverend O. A. Mellby, who was called in 1871 to be in charge of a parish that combined North Waseca and Le Sueur River. Pastor and Mrs. Mellby's daughter Agnes and their son Carl became important personages in the history of St. Olaf College. From his personal acquaintance with the founder of St. Olaf Carl Mellby wrote the following about Muus as itinerant pastor: "As a travelling missionary, covering a large part of Minnesota and parts of adjoining states, he came into intimate contact with all kinds of people, learned to know their needs and capacities, lived with them in their sod huts and log cabins and won their respect and confidence as few other men have done."[27]

In the summer of 1856 Norwegian immigrants from Rock county, Wisconsin, came over into Minnesota and settled along the Le Sueur River, in the vicinity of St. Olaf Lake in the eastern part of New Richland township, Waseca county, and in the western part of Berlin township, Steele county. The first Norwegian Lutheran minister to preach, baptize, administer communion, and perform other pastoral services in the settlement was one "Rev. Frederickson," as named in congregation histories. It is likely that this person was Anders Emil Friedrichsen, a pastor known to have served in southern Minnesota in the middle of the 1850s. The Reverend A. C. Preus was another early visitor to the Le Sueur-St. Olaf Lake settlement, followed in 1858 by Laur. Larsen who is said to have organized a "Lutheran Society" that met in homes.[28]

B. J. Muus organized the Le Sueur River Norwegian Evangelical Lutheran Congregation in 1861 but did not become its pastor until 1863. His journal notes that he visited St. Olaf Lake in May of 1862 after being at North Waseca. The first journal entry naming Le Sueur River indicates a congregational meeting there May 18, 1863.[29] That is probably when the bylaws were drawn up that served as the constitution for the congregation for some time. The first church building was constructed in 1861 on land donated by Hans Sunde. It was "built from oak logs, hewn, grooved, and fitted into place." All the labor was donated by members of the congregation. When this church was outgrown, it was removed and the congregation built a larger church on the same site in 1875. The second church was 36x80x20 with a tower and a 95-foot steeple, later raised to 125 feet. Its cost was approximately $1,100.00.[30]

The Le Sueur River congregation sent three delegates to a meeting in Faribault in 1865 to call another pastor, since Muus was finding it too strenuous to look after his many congregations. The result was that N. A. Quammen was called to serve Le Sueur River, North Waseca, Christiania, and German Grove. Quammen was Le Sueur River's pastor from 1866 to 1872. He was succeeded by O. A. Mellby. Like Muus and Quammen, Mellby was also a missionary pastor, at one time ministering to ten outlying stations.[31]

Jackson Lake Lutheran church today is in the town of Amboy, Blue Earth county. The first church stood on a knoll on the south edge of Jackson Lake in Faribault county, seven miles northwest of Delavan. Situated on or close to the border, the church has been described as "the oldest Lutheran church in Blue Earth county" and also has been said to be in Faribault county.[32]

Services were conducted in Bent Pederson's cabin as early as 1859 by a "Rev. Frederickson," presumably the same A. E. Friedrichsen who made an early pastoral visit to the Le Sueur River community and who is said to have ministered in Jackson and Delavan in 1859. B. J. Muus first went to preach and administer the sacraments to the settlers around Jackson Lake in 1860. L. M. Biørn preached there in 1861. On a second visit in 1862, Muus left the draft of a constitution he had drawn up. On May 25, 1862, ten settlers and their families met in the home of Knud

164

*Le Sueur River Lutheran Church*
Courtesy of Le Sueur River Lutheran Church and Pastor Charles Espe

Thompson, adopted the constitution, and organized the congregation. Thomas Johnson served as pastor of Jackson Lake from the spring of 1863 to the fall of 1867. The first resident pastor was T. H. Dahl, 1867 to 1876.[33]

A story fondly told at Jackson Lake had to do with Muus's faithful horse. After it was sold, it was taken to North Dakota, but it wandered back to Holden in southeastern Minnesota, the home of its former master.[34]

165

In 1870, after Muus's ministerial work in the area, Jackson Lake was divided into two parishes, Jackson Lake in the west and Delavan in the east. Delavan Lutheran church was located five miles north of the town of Delavan. Today Faith Lutheran Church of Delavan traces its descent from churches once related to Jackson Lake Lutheran Church.

Linden Lutheran church is five miles northwest of Madelia and five miles southeast of Hanska, in Brown county. The congregation began on the morning of July 6, 1859, when thirteen families met at the home of Jens Harbo with Pastor Friedrichsen present to assist in the organizing process. This group elected officers and adopted a constitution.[35] In the summer of 1860 the Linden congregation called B. J. Muus from Goodhue county to serve "when possible and convenient for him to do so." Muus spent May 10 and 12, 1861, in the Linden community, confirming eight young people and baptizing several children. Writing to Laur. Larsen while on this mission tour, Muus said that the congregations in Brown and Watonwan counties, that is, Linden and Rosendale, formerly served by Friedrichsen, had come under his care. Given this added responsibility, he hoped that he could transmit a letter of call from the small congregations west of the Minnesota River to the Synod's church council in order to secure more pastoral help. He returned to Linden in 1862 and 1863, conducting services and baptizing children. Late in 1863 the congregation called the Reverend Thomas Johnson from Nicollet county, who served as pastor until 1870. A church was built in 1870 and the interior finished in 1874.[36]

Rosendale Congregation, in Watonwan county about six miles southwest of Madelia, was organized in the afternoon of the same day that Pastor Friedrichsen had helped organize the Linden congregation. Rosendale histories give the date as July 2, 1859; the Linden history has July 6. The group first chose the name "Our Savior's." Later it became "South Branch," the name used until 1877 when "Rosendale" was adopted. Beginning with forty mem-

*Linden Lutheran Church*
Photo by Joseph M. Shaw

bers, the congregation worshiped in the homes of members until the district schoolhouse was built in 1873. It used the schoolhouse for services until the church was built in 1909.

Following Friedrichsen, Pastor Muus was one of four pastors serving Rosendale in its first dozen years. Others were Thomas Johnson, Laur. Larsen, and J. B. Frich. Muus's journal indicates pastoral visits to Watonwan county May 13, 1861, May 20, 1862, and May 17, 1863. The Rosendale congregation disbanded in 1975 but the church building still stands.[37]

167

Norseland Lutheran Church identifies a church that began as the Norwegian Evangelical Lutheran Congregation in Nicollet county, often called simply the Nicollet county congregation. Its location is ten miles northwest of St. Peter. Laur. Larsen did early pastoral work there in 1858 and 1859. He was present when the congregation was organized October 24, 1858, and accepted the call to be its pastor, promising to come at least twice yearly. In July of 1859 Larsen had to resign to assume his new position as Norwegian professor at Concordia Seminary in St. Louis, Missouri. Larsen informed the congregation that a pastor from Norway might be coming to Goodhue county and hoped that this man would also visit Nicollet county.[38]

Pastor B. J. Muus from Goodhue county indeed visited the congregation in April of 1860, holding services in the schoolhouse in Section 29, Lake Prairie township. The schoolhouse is mentioned frequently as the site of congregational meetings and worship services before the church was built in 1866. On the 1860 visit Muus also held services in St. Peter, at Swan Lake, and at Northern Grove, later called Norwegian Grove, in Sibley county.

At a congregational meeting on September 24, 1860, Muus was present and accepted the call to be temporary pastor. The congregation expressed the hope that Norwegian groups in Carver county, near Crow River, and in Brown county would join in calling him. The following spring the congregation decided to join with the congregations of Watonwan and Carver counties and Crow River in calling a permanent pastor. Eventually a call was extended to Thomas Johnson, then a student at Concordia Seminary. He accepted May 13, 1863, and was installed later that year.[39] In the meantime, Pastor Muus made additional visits to the area, in May 1861, October 1861, May 1862, September 1862, May 1863, and August 6, 1863, when Johnson was installed. One important feature of his work was the establishment of a parochial school in 1861. To provide sixty-six days of teaching, ten men promised to subsidize six days each, with Sven Svenson as the teacher.[40]

It should be pointed out that the Nicollet county congregation, later Norseland Lutheran Church, was the center of a parish that embraced Norwegian groups in St. Peter, Swan Lake, and Northern Grove. The parsonage for Thomas Johnson, the first resident pastor, was at Norseland. When Johnson was installed "in Nicollet Congregation," it was understood that he also became the pastor for the other three groups.

Clearly Muus was able to reduce the extent of his mission travels when the younger Thomas Johnson came on the scene and took over not just the Nicollet and related congregations but several other mission stations. A parochial report for 1863 names Muus as pastor of Holden, Belvidere, Christiania, North Waseca, and Le Sueur River; it states further that Johnson was pastor of Nicollet, Linden, Watonwan, Jackson Lake, South Bend, Carver, Camden, and Ness.[41] All of these were places visited regularly by Muus during his mission trips between 1860 and 1863.

While one may associate St. Peter, Minnesota, with Swedes, Pastor Laur. Larsen formed a congregation of Norwegian Lutherans there in 1858. The St. Peter group belonged to Nicollet but often held its own services. After Larsen's brief ministry, B. J. Muus included regular stops in St. Peter whenever he traveled the sixty miles or more from Holden out to Nicollet county, making spring and fall visits from 1860 to 1863. Thomas Johnson became the first regular pastor in 1863. The congregation joined the Norwegian Synod in 1867 and built a church that was dedicated July 18, 1869.[42]

Swan Lake Norwegian Evangelical Lutheran church was in Brighton township, Nicollet county, 10 miles northeast of New Ulm. Illustrating the close ties between Swan Lake and Norseland, the main church in the parish, was the request that Andreas Anderson of Swan Lake, two men from "the larger settlement," and two from Northern Grove "on Sundays call together the children in order to instruct them in the Confirmation knowledge."[43] Pastor Muus was at Swan Lake in April and September of 1860, May of 1861, when "worship services were held in the morning and afternoon in Johannes Anderson's house," October of 1861,

169

and May of 1862 and 1863. In August of 1862 Swan Lake and Norwegian Grove were terrorized by Indian attacks that resulted in loss of lives and homes in the vicinity. In the fall of 1863 Thomas Johnson assumed pastoral responsibility for Swan Lake as part of his call to Nicollet or Norseland.[44]

Northern Grove or Norwegian Grove Congregation, in Sibley county south of Gaylord, still belonged to the group of preaching places that centered in the Norseland congregation. With the others, Northern Grove joined in establishing a Norwegian religious school. On May 17, 1861, Pastor Muus conducted morning and afternoon services at Northern Grove. Subsequent visits were made in October of 1861, May of 1862, when he catechized the children at Gunnar Nerison's home, and May of 1863.[45]

The Carver settlement in Carver county was another of the several communities that received an early pastoral visit from Laur. Larsen, who was there in 1858 to begin the organization of a Scandinavian congregation. Pastor Muus visited the Carver settlement on his first missionary trip, in April of 1860, only five months after his arrival in Goodhue county. In September of that year he held services on two occasions at the home of Haagen Christensen in Carver, before and after a trip up to Crow River. The church was organized in 1860. Muus returned to Carver in May and October of 1861, in May of 1862 and May of 1863.[46]

In 1860 Norseland wanted Carver to join it and congregations near Crow River and in Brown county to call a pastor. On May 26, 1862, Norseland collected the sum of $1.80, "which was paid to Johan Tollefson to give Pastor Muus a ride to Carver." In May of 1863 Muus "journeyed to Carver" after holding services at four sites in Nicollet county. When Thomas Johnson was installed as pastor of the Nicollet county congregation, his call included Carver.[47]

Bergen congregation, five miles northwest of Plato, in McLeod county, was organized in 1860 and joined the Norwegian Synod that year. This congregation is named in Muus's overview of mission work launched from the Holden parish.[48]

170

Ness Lutheran Church was founded by Muus in 1861 and was originally called "The Norwegian Evangelical St. Johannes Congregation in Meeker and surrounding counties." At an organizational meeting on October 28, 1861, a constitution was adopted, the name was changed to Ness Congregation, and Pastor Muus, who was present, was called to serve as his time and circumstances permitted. It may be noted that the Ness settlement was 150 miles from Muus's home base at Holden. Muus accepted, trustees were elected, and Nils Pederson agreed to conduct religious school on Sundays.[49]

The Ness congregation was located five and one-half miles southwest of Litchfield. Norwegian immigrants first arrived in the area in 1856. Since they were from Ness in Hallingdal, they chose that name for their congregation. In fact, Ness was once the name of the township and of the city that was later called Litchfield. O. M. Norlie, in the congregation's 50th anniversary history, argues that the name Ness "should not have been rejected by the Americans."[50]

Muus served the Ness congregation for two years, 1861–1862. Services were held in Ole Ness's granary. Muus conducted the first confirmation service in 1861. While the congregation was seeking a permanent pastor, it was served by Thomas Johnson from 1863 to 1867. In 1868, at the same time as the congregation decided to call the Reverend T. H. Dahl as permanent pastor, it joined the Augustana Synod, to which Dahl belonged. The congregation took this action after hearing a debate in Henrik Thoen's home between Dahl and Pastor Abraham Jacobson on the topic of absolution, the latter giving the position of the Norwegian Synod. When written ballots were taken, the result was a unanimous vote for Dahl and the Augustana Synod.[51]

Where to build the church was difficult to decide because members lived far apart. In the fall of 1868 a reorganization took place whereby the original congregation was divided into three separate churches, Ness, Arndahl, and Throndhjem. Ness built its church in 1874. In 1878 the state of Minnesota placed a monument in the Ness church's cemetery to honor five persons buried there who were the first victims of the Dakota Conflict of 1862. Ness Lutheran Church was dissolved in 1968.[52]

Arndahl Lutheran Church, organized in 1861 as a part of Ness, was first served by Muus, Thomas Johnson, and Abraham Jacobson. After becoming a separate congregation, it was served by T. H. Dahl from 1868 to 1873. It built its own church in 1873, having then a membership of 225 persons.[53]

Throndhjem Lutheran church was located west from Ness and Arndahl, in Kandiyohi county. It was served by Muus and the other pastors associated with Arndahl up to 1868 and, like Arndahl, became a separate congregation in the reorganization. From 1868 to 1873 Throndhjem was part of a Norwegian Lutheran congregation in Meeker county called Swede Grove. It built a church in 1871 at a cost of $2,500.[54]

Crow River Lutheran Church, four miles south of Belgrade, was organized by B. J. Muus on November 1, 1861, All Saints' Day, under the name of the Monongalia congregation. Between 1858 and 1870, the northern half of the present Kandiyohi county constituted Monongalia county, from which the congregation took its original name. In 1871 the congregation incorporated as Crow River Norwegian Evangelical Lutheran Congregation.[55]

When Pastor Muus made his visits to Monongalia county, he was 180 miles from Holden. On his journeys toward the Crow River congregation, Muus would sometimes travel in company with young Gunder (or Gunner) Johnson, a member of the congregation who carried the mail between St. Peter and St. Cloud, usually on horseback. Muus's friendly contacts with Gunder Johnson provided the circumstance for the well-known oil painting by Arne Berger that hangs in Lands Lutheran church west of Zumbrota. Often reproduced, the painting shows Gunder as the driver of a cart drawn by a team of oxen with Pastor Muus beside him as his passenger. The date of the painting is 1861. Gunder Johnson (who took the name George) was nineteen at the time and Muus was twenty-nine years of age.[56]

*Crow River Lutheran Church*
Photo by Joseph M. Shaw

For all his youth, Gunder Johnson was a charter member of the Monongalia congregation. The first Norwegians arrived in the district in 1859. Gunder came to America in 1857 and found his way from Wisconsin to Burbank township in 1860. A document signed by B. J. Muus records the organization of the congregation in 1861 in the log house of Postmaster Thor Postmyr. It gives the names of the three trustees and lists Gunder among those who participated in the service of Holy Communion on that All Saints Day.[57]

The first known visit of Pastor Muus to the Crow River region was September 28, 1860, when he held services at the home of Anders Saetren. He was there again May 21, 1861, and returned to establish the congregation in the fall of 1861. In the summer of 1862, on July 15 and 16, he held services at the Monongalia con-

173

gregation and on July 17 ministered at a Norwegian settlement near Norway Lake.[58]

The Crow River congregation's history tells of the "Indian Outbreak" of August 20, 1862, and the "Great Exodus," when many families fled eastward to Waupaca county, Wisconsin, Houston county, Minnesota, and St. Francis River, eighteen miles northeast of St. Cloud. The Dakota tribe of the Sioux Indians had been friendly to the settlers at first, but rose up against them when the government failed to pay a promised sum of money. Pioneers were killed in the areas of Norway Lake, West Lake, Solomon Lake, and Foot Lake. Guri Endresen Rosseland, whose husband and one son were killed, became the heroine of Kandiyohi county when she saved several of the wounded by driving them in her wagon to safety through hostile country.[59]

The families who had gone to St. Francis, totaling around fifty persons, received ministerial services from Pastor Muus when he visited them several times between 1862 and 1864. On October 23, 1864, meeting with the group at St. Francis, Muus recognized two baptisms that had been performed by laymen in his absence and baptized four children born at St. Francis. One of the children was Johan Peter, son of Gunder Johnson and his wife Asbjor. A few days later, on October 26th, Muus held services at the Monongalia congregation, where several families had returned from Wisconsin. Those from St. Francis returned to their homes in early 1865.[60]

Muus's pastoral visits to Crow River apparently ended in 1864. Thomas Johnson next provided ministerial services for a few years. In 1870 the congregation built a unique octagonal log church on land donated by Mathias Johnson, who also supervised the construction. A replica of the old eight-sided log church is kept in the present Crow River Lutheran church.

Norway Lake as settlement and lake was named by Even and Anders Railson, Norwegian brothers who first came to the area west of New London and staked their claims in 1858. Other

Norwegians, some from Wisconsin, joined them in the next few years. First pastoral services were given in 1861 by Andrew Jackson, Swedish pastor from New London. Pastor Muus came to conduct services at the Christopher Engen home in the Norway Lake settlement on July 17, 1862.[61]

A month later Norway Lake was threatened by attacks from the Dakota who, on August 20, 1862, first struck the Swedish settlement at Monson Lake, about six miles to the west, killing thirteen persons. When word reached Norway Lake, Even Railson and Christopher Engen sent their families out to an island in the lake for safety. Others also came out to the "Indian Island," later called the "Isle of Refuge," where they spent a night of fear, compounded by a drenching rainstorm. Three days later the group of fifty refugees left the island and traveled in a caravan to Paynesville. Some from Norway Lake joined the settlers who had fled to St. Francis.[62]

While the Norway Lake congregation dates its beginning from Pastor Muus's visit in 1862, it was not organized formally at that time. After Muus, pastors T. A. Torgerson and Thomas Johnson ministered at Norway Lake, holding services and baptizing children. Some organizing was done on November 19, 1865, when Thomas Johnson baptized two children at Norway Lake, but articles of incorporation were not drawn up until 1868. The congregation took the name the Norwegian Evangelical Lutheran Church of Norway Lake.[63]

B. J. Muus's work at Norway Lake extended at best to 1865, but the Norway Lake congregation was the mother of several other congregations. In 1876 it divided into two separate congregations, East Norway Lake and West Norway Lake. Other divisions took place over the years, producing more than one West Norway Lake congregation north and east of Kerkhoven.[64] Today the Norway Lake parish includes First Lutheran Church of Norway Lake, with a modern brick building, and East Norway Lake Lutheran Church, which worships in a white frame church constructed in 1875. It was from East Norway Lake church that

*East Norway Lake Lutheran Church*
Photo by Joseph M. Shaw

Pastor Lars Johnson Markhus was removed bodily on July 24, 1885, the result of siding with the minority when the congregation was split over the doctrine of election.[65]

St. Francis River was an important preaching place for the people involved and for Pastor Muus even though it was not a congregation as such. After the Dakota uprising in August of 1862, Norwegian settlers from Norway Lake and Crow River fled to St. Francis River, northeast of St. Cloud, although the exact location in Benton county is not described. All that one learns about the two-year stay at St. Francis is that three of the families lived in three rooms and the men had work cutting hay for the logging companies. Muus's journal records a visit to St. Francis on October 23, 1864.[66]

Immanuel Norwegian Lutheran Church, Minneapolis, went by the name St. Anthony congregation when visited by Pastor Muus in February of 1869. The name came from St. Anthony church, the building purchased from a group of Congregationalists for the sum of $2,100. In a unique action, pastors B. J. Muus and N. Th. Ylvisaker lent money to Our Savior's Lutheran Church, the mother congregation, to enable a contingent of its younger members who had settled in Minneapolis east of the Mississippi to buy their own place of worship. Ylvisaker was the first pastor of Our Savior's, which was founded in 1869, and Muus was one of the Norwegian Synod pastors who served the daughter group that became Immanuel.

It was fitting that Muus was present on March 22, 1874, when the St. Anthony group dedicated its church. Muus preached one of the sermons, using 1 Peter 2:4–5 as his text. Other participants in the service were the local pastor, H. G. Stub, and a Pastor Borge. With evident satisfaction, Muus described the church in the Synod's paper as 50 feet long and 30 feet wide, with a large basement suitable for schoolrooms, a tower, and a bell weighing 500 pounds.[67] The original site of Immanuel has been described more closely as near the old bridge and 4th St. S. E. Eventually, Immanuel became a part of Holy Triune Church in Minneapolis. Pastor Muus's contacts with Immanuel Lutheran Church apparently were not frequent, but they were significant enough for him to include Minneapolis among the places where mission work was done from Holden.[68]

Fort Snelling was not mentioned in Muus's list of mission stations, but he was there on February 7, 1861, toward the end of a journey that took him to Waseca, Nicollet, Kandiyohi

(Monongalia), Meeker, and Carver counties. After Fort Snelling Muus went to St. Paul, concluding that particular mission.[69]

Christ Lutheran Church on Capitol Hill, in St. Paul, Ramsey county, began as the Norwegian Evangelical Lutheran Congregation. When the church was dedicated in 1870, the Norwegian Synod monthly, *Kirkelig Maanedstidende,* reported: "This congregation was established as early as 1858, but has always had many difficulties to struggle with."[70] The difficulties stemmed from doctrinal differences between the Norwegian Synod and the Northern Illinois Synod. Pastor Erland Carlsson organized a Scandinavian Lutheran congregation on May 6, 1854. It included Swedes, Danes, and Norwegians, and was affiliated with the Evangelical Lutheran Synod of Northern Illinois, which in turn was associated with the General Synod of the Evangelical Lutheran Church.[71]

Laur. Larsen, one of the pastors who came to assist the congregation in its early years, was wholly in favor of church cooperation among the three nationalities, but could not accept the doctrinal stance of the General Synod. Larsen's complaint against the General Synod was that it required of its pastors and members only that they agree with the "fundamental doctrines" and "main truths" of the church's teaching. In his view and that of other Norwegian Lutherans, such a position was far too lax. "A Lutheran believes that his confessional writings in all their parts teach God's word purely and completely, as it is revealed in the Bible." Moreover, who is to decide which are the "main truths?" According to Larsen, the General Synod did not regard baptism, the Lord's Supper, and absolution as among them, allowing its pastors to believe and teach whatever they wished. Wrote Larsen, "Here the door is wide open for all kinds of doctrinal weather."[72]

A separation occurred in May of 1858 when those favoring continued affiliation with the Synod of Northern Illinois gained control of the congregation. But a minority declined to be associated with this synod and preferred to join the Norwegian Synod. On May 28, 1858, Larsen organized these dissidents into a congregation that still aimed to be Scandinavian. To keep the door open for Swedes and Danes but also to solidify the congregation's confessional identity, making explicit its adherence to the Apostles', Nicene, and Athanasian creeds, the Unaltered Augsburg Confession, and Luther's Small Catechism, Larsen re-worked the constitution, secured the approval of the Synod's church council, and returned on July 5, 1858, to have it adopted. On October 31, 1858, he was called to be the pastor and accepted, though realizing he would not be able to come very often.[73]

When Larsen left his Rush River, Wisconsin, congregation in 1859 to accept the call to Concordia Seminary in St. Louis, other pastors had to step in to serve the new Norwegian Synod congregation in St. Paul. Not surprisingly, B. J. Muus began to serve the St. Paul congregation as part of his mission travels. His journal shows three visits to St. Paul in 1861, one in 1862, one in 1864, and three in 1869, culminating in the installation September 26, 1869, of Olaus Normann as resident pastor.[74]

Adopting a new constitution in 1869, the congregation changed its name to Norwegian Evangelical Lutheran Congregation of Saint Paul, Minnesota. The church dedicated in 1870 was at the corner of L'Orient and Mt. Airy Streets. The next church, built in Romanesque style, was located at University and Park in St. Paul and dedicated December 5, 1915. In 1918 the congregation changed its name to Christ Lutheran Church.[75]

How B. J. Muus's mission activities frequently followed prior work by Laur. Larsen has been a familiar theme throughout this chapter. While Muus's base was Holden in Goodhue county, Larsen's was Rush River, eleven miles east of River Falls, Wisconsin, in Pierce county. The Rush River Lutheran parish was founded in 1855 with the help of the Reverend Nils Brandt, who had held services for Norwegian families the year before. Laur. Larsen came to America in 1857 on a call from Fillmore county, in southern Minnesota, but since that settlement was not yet ready for a resident pastor, the president of the Norwegian Synod, the

Reverend A. C. Preus, recommended that Larsen take the Rush River parish instead. The congregation agreed, and Larsen was installed as pastor on November 8, 1857.[76]

During his two years at Rush River, Larsen made missionary trips to various points in Wisconsin, such as Hudson and Menomonie. His more extensive travels were into Minnesota. In addition to trips to Stillwater and St. Paul, he traveled hundreds of miles through southern Minnesota, founding and serving congregations in Carver, Goodhue, McLeod, Watonwan, Steele, and Waseca counties. Once called to St. Louis in 1859, Larsen could no longer serve the far-flung groups of Norwegians, so he often recommended B. J. Muus, his friend and colleague whose base in Goodhue county was directly across the Mississippi from Pierce county.

Hudson, Wisconsin, in St. Croix county on the St. Croix River, was the first place Larsen visited from his home at Rush River. On February 10, 1858, he organized a congregation there that was known as Ebenezer Norwegian Evangelical Lutheran Church. Thirty years later a split on account of the election controversy brought Bethel Lutheran Church into being. Muus's first visit to Hudson was on April 29, 1860. He was there again November 20, 1861, according to his journal.[77]

Pierce county was the home not only of the Rush River parish but of several other preaching places. To reach all members of the Rush River congregation, Larsen preached at "North Prairie" and "South in the Woods," and in district schoolhouses. In 1858 he organized Little Elk Creek, five miles east of Menomonie and later a congregation at Big Elk Creek.

For a few months after Larsen left Rush River for St. Louis, there were no services in the congregation, although Larsen returned during summer vacations in 1860, 1861, and 1862 to conduct services. When Muus came to the area in the spring of 1860, he preached sixteen sermons in the period between April 30 and May 8. Writing to Larsen about the visit after returning to Holden, Muus said the people were appropriately contrite, which was good to hear, but it was also disturbing to see how much uncertainty and lukewarmness there was toward the Word of God.[78]

On his visit of February 16–20, 1861, he held ten services in the Rush River congregation, clearly implying a ministry to outlying places as well as the main church. Another letter to Larsen reported on the latest trip to Rush River and anticipated the next one. On a Wisconsin mission journey in the fall of 1862, Muus held services in a schoolhouse in Rush River, in another schoolhouse near the home of Ole Moen, at North Prairie, and in Ole Thoresen's home in Menomonie, in Dunn county.[79]

Little Elk Creek Lutheran Church, later known as the Froen congregation, was the first Lutheran congregation in Dunn county, Wisconsin. It was organized by Pastor Laur. Larsen on February 23, 1858, after he had walked more than thirty miles through dense forests to Elk Creek. The group met in the log house built by M. P. Mork and Ole Evenson. The three charter members were Tore Hendrickson, Erik Gunderson, and Ole Evenson. The first complete service was held in the log house on August 9, 1858. On this visit Larsen also established a pastoral ministry at Cranberry Creek.

When Larsen was unable to continue his summer visits to Little Elk Creek and Cranberry Creek congregations, he advised them to call B. J. Muus, which they did. Muus did not accept the call but made a pastoral visit in November of 1862, baptizing Karen Oline Sampson Ove. It seems likely that Muus's journal entry of a visit to Menomonie November 16, 1862, is related to one of these congregations. Elk Creek became the center of a widespread parish and the mother of other congregations.[80]

Apart from an occasional piece in the Synod's paper about a church dedication or an installation, Muus confined his reports about his mission travels to the summary noted at the beginning of this chapter and to entries in the Holden Ministerial Book with its "Geistligt Dagregister," the day-to-day record or journal of ministerial activities. While this journal is invaluable for the information Muus so meticulously recorded, it is strictly a church

181

document, listing only dates, places visited, and ministerial services provided. It cannot begin to reveal the wealth of dramatic episodes, joyous occasions, disappointments, personal contacts, local problems, and comical events Muus experienced as he made the long mission journeys each spring and fall in the early years of his ministry.

The significance of the mission travels may be suggested in two observations. First, Muus's strenuous missionary work attests to his desire and determination to bring the Gospel of Christ and the Holy Sacraments to his fellow Norwegians in distant places. To him, to Laur. Larsen, to Thomas Johnson, and to many other pioneer pastors, such travels were simply part of the call to the ministry of Word and Sacrament, and not special deeds of heroism.

Second, the missionary work of Pastor Muus and like-minded colleagues had lasting effects because they directed their efforts toward the creation of organizational structures. It is one thing to ride the circuit and preach. It is quite another, and more beneficial for the community, when the visiting preacher not only promises to return, but accepts the congregation's call to be its pastor, as Muus did in place after place. In addition to conducting services, baptizing the children, instructing and confirming the young, performing marriages, and burying the dead, Muus and other missionary pastors formed congregations, wrote constitutions, urged the election of trustees, assisted in plans for building a church, and carefully recorded these acts. In short, they established worshipping communities that would continue their service to coming generations.

In that pioneer era, members of a Norwegian settlement were impressed and grateful that a clergyman from a distant point would face the rigors of travel to visit them. They immediately felt an affinity for the church body that had sent the pastor, which in Muus's case was the Norwegian Synod. And when the time came that the congregation decided to join the Synod, the sense of participation in the larger church became stronger.

# Eight

## Church Issues in the 1860s

The Norwegian Synod, to which Pastor Muus and his congregations belonged, conducted its business and discussed theological issues at its regular annual meetings. The pastors of the Synod also had their own meetings. A key part of an immigrant pastor's working life was to attend these assemblies. With relatively few pastors and congregations in the early years, separated by long distances, the regular gatherings were vital for morale and for the advancement of pastoral work. The Synod began with seven pastors and thirty-six congregations in 1853; by 1862 it had grown to twenty pastors and more than 100 congregations.[1]

With such modest numbers, all of the pastors were able to participate directly and freely in the discussion of church matters, and in the process they would soon get to know one another very well, as colleagues and often as personal friends. The practice of holding the meetings at various congregations throughout the Synod also gave both pastors and lay people a firsthand acquaintance with the churches of the Synod in their local settings.

Offsetting the picture of pleasant collegiality at synodical and pastoral conferences was the fact that dissension often arose within the Norwegian Synod. Muus for one welcomed the full and careful discussions at the pastors' meetings, regarding them as a strengthening of the brethren. If disagreement arises, he wrote, there is nothing better than bringing it into the open.[2] When Muus was in Norway in 1870 to urge theological candidates to consider accepting calls to America, he faced the criticism that the Norwegian Synod was "too quarrelsome." His explanation in defense was that since in America there is no state church to hold the congregations together, all must rely on the Word of God to do so, and hence the emphasis upon maintaining the purity of the Word in the immigrant community. The "curse of dissension" continued to mark the life of the Synod through the seventies and eighties.[3]

From June 12 to 20, 1862, a meeting of the Synod took place at Holden, Muus's church. "Welcome to the Synod" wrote Muus to Laur. Larsen in May. Holden's new church building, begun in 1861, was still in a raw, unfinished state, but it had more space than any other church for miles around and thus was known as "Stor Kjerka," the Big Church.[4] The Holden congregation was admitted into the Norwegian Synod at its 1862 meeting. A change of leadership took place at the same meeting. The first president, the Reverend A. C. Preus, resigned, and the Synod elected his cousin, the Reverend Herman Amberg Preus, to succeed him. H. A. Preus continued to serve as president of the Norwegian Synod until 1894.[5]

In addition, three other matters of importance for the future of the Synod also came to the fore. The issues, which would engender considerable debate and acrimony during the 1860s, were lay activity, the doctrine of absolution, and the question of slavery. In each case, the position adopted by the Norwegian Synod was strongly influenced by interpretations received from the Missouri Synod and its theology faculty in St. Louis. These three issues provide the subject matter for the present chapter.

It so happened that the first of these, the issue of lay activity, was brought to a resolution when the Synod met at Holden church in 1862, but absolution and slavery were to require additional years of debate. As these questions were addressed by the

*H. A. Preus*
From Gerhard Belgum dissertation, "The Old Norwegian Synod
in America 1853–1890"

Synod, Pastor Bernt Julius Muus was an avid participant. On lay
activity and absolution, he dissented from the majority view; on
slavery, he began as a moderate and ended as a defender of the
Synod's rigid teaching.

Before they left the old country, religiously informed Norwegian
emigrants were quite familiar with the tensions between clerical
authority on the one side and lay freedom to pray and preach on
the other. In the new land, where no state church existed, where

185

ordained pastors were few, and where lay persons stepped in to provide needed spiritual services, the issue had greater immediacy. As churches were organized, the proper scope of lay ministry became the first issue to settle.[6]

The question of lay activity had already been under discussion since the late 1850s when the Reverend P. A. Rasmussen, a pastor previously associated with the Eielsen Synod, which heartily approved of lay preaching, had discussed lay activity with a group of Synod pastors. Opposing Rasmussen from the Synod side was the Reverend Jacob Aall Ottesen, who in 1858 had received a long letter on the topic from the esteemed teacher of Lutheran theology in St. Louis, C. F. W. Walther. In 1859 Ottesen published articles on lay activity in *Kirkelig Maanedstidende*, concluding "that laymen's prayer and speech in public meetings of edification are contrary to God's Word."[7]

The topic was aired further at a conference at Our Savior's church in Chicago in August of 1860 when the interpretation of Article XIV of the Augsburg Confession was at issue. This article states: "Of Ecclesiastical Order, they teach, that no one should publicly teach in the Church or administer the Sacraments, unless he be regularly called." Did this article totally exclude the participation of lay people in public gatherings of Christians? Was there not a place for lay testimony and prayer?[8] Pastor Rasmussen set forth three grounds in defense of a lay person's right to teach and pray publicly: the doctrine of the universal priesthood of believers, the demands of Christian love, and the practice of the early church.[9] The Synod pastors could accept lay activity in the form of mutual edification, but they were opposed to lay persons doing any teaching on behalf of the whole assembly, which only a properly ordained pastor could do. Moreover, if a lay person were to stand up and say, "Let us all pray," that would also be a form of "teaching" and hence unacceptable.[10] Rasmussen was not able to agree that prayer was teaching in another form, nor did he share the notion that a lay person praying in public was doing something wrong. He asked, "Is the gift of prayer given by God or is it the fruit of study? If it is a gift from God, then anyone possessing it could pray, both to please God and to edify others."[11]

The Synod pastors, uneasy at the prospect of untutored, self-appointed lay preachers sowing confusion among immigrants on the frontier, interpreted Article XIV as restricting teaching, preaching, administering of Sacraments, and praying in public to the ordained ministers. Any utterance by a lay person in a public gathering was acceptable only if done for mutual edification, speaking as an equal to equals, with opportunity for dissent, but not as teaching "in behalf of all."[12] Pastor Rasmussen had no objection to the Augsburg Confession's teaching that public preaching of the Word and administration of the Sacraments should be carried out by a person called to that task, but in addition to the public ministry there was the spiritual priesthood, according to which all Christians have the right and duty to admonish and edify one another. One of Rasmussen's supporters, Pastor John Fjeld, found it astonishing that some would deny lay people the right to pray aloud in their own words in public assemblies.[13]

Siding with Rasmussen and Fjeld, Muus stated that he did not agree with the previous speakers from his synod. Their tendency was much too formalistic. He admitted that their approach was logical and orderly but, in his view, it went against the Word of God. After long and careful study of the 14th Article of the Augsburg Confession, he said, he had never been able to locate the exact boundary between the public teaching office with its rights and the sphere of the laity. Scripture teaches that every Christian is obliged to serve himself and others with such grace and faithfulness as God has given. Every Christian is consecrated and installed to do the work of the universal priesthood, which is to sacrifice and teach. This right cannot be transferred to others; it is one's duty to exercise it when the edification of others demands it. When a called pastor has been appointed, he is entrusted with the public exercise of the right, but when the pastor cannot or will not carry out this duty, the Christian himself must do it. The pur-

187

pose of Article 14 of the Augsburg Confession is to make sure that God's Word actually and amply is preached in the congregation. One must not stress the pastor's right so strictly that the word is not preached richly, or stress the lay person's right to the extent that the pastor's work is restricted. As to the claim that it was wrong or a sin against God's order when a layman prayed in his own words in public meetings, Muus said this was something he had never heard before in his life.[14]

This speech was significant in bringing out Muus's sympathy with lay activity. Unlike many of his fellow Norwegian Synod pastors, Muus had gained firsthand experience in Norway of gathering with devout lay people for prayers, testimonials, and Bible reading. Muus even welcomed the fact that feelings were often stirred among those not fully awakened when a lay person prayed in his or her own words.[15] Muus's remarks on lay activity also singled him out as an independent voice who spoke his mind even when his views did not conform to the thinking of Synod leaders. Toward the close of the Chicago conference, Muus voted with the slim majority of 7 to 5 in supporting a statement written by Rasmussen about lay people edifying one another whereas Ottesen, Koren, Larsen, Brandt, and Magelssen opposed it.[16] It was not the last time Muus would take issue with the views of the leading Synod pastors.

The close vote meant that the issue was not fully resolved. It was on the agenda for the 1861 Synod meeting at Luther Valley church in Rock Prairie, Wisconsin, but long discussions of absolution and slavery left no time for the matter of lay preaching. Writing to a Norwegian church paper, Muus commented that the public expected the 1861 Synod to settle the question of lay activity, but instead they got nothing. He added wryly that "one group" in the Norwegian Synod "which has a fine sense for discovering heresies" had decided that below the discussion of lay activity might be buried other heresies, which could explain why they had agreed, in order to reach clarity on the topic of lay activity, to proceed from the ground up, starting with absolution.[17]

188

*Bernt Julius Muus in 1860s*
St. Olaf College Archives

Lay activity required further attention, in part to clear the way for Rasmussen and other pastors to join the Norwegian Synod. An important step toward a resolution was taken at a conference of Synod pastors at Spring Prairie, Wisconsin, in July of 1861. Muus was among those present, along with such well-known Synod pastors as A. C. Preus, Brandt, H. A. Preus, Ottesen, Koren, Larsen, and Clausen. C. F. W. Walther was there as a guest and later made a presentation.

In the meantime, the Synod pastors covered essentially the same ground that Walther would summarize the next day. The pastoral office is the order established by God for the proclaiming of God's Word and making available the Holy Sacraments in the church.

189

Only one who is regularly called has the right to exercise this office in public gatherings of Christian people. When lay people in the pastor's absence hold other public meetings at which one or several act as teachers for the others, such conventicles or edifying assemblies go counter to God's order. There is a legitimate place for house gatherings where Christian friends read God's word and pray, but when a group assembles publicly with the definite object of common edification by the Word of God with one or more acting as teachers of the others, then only a regularly called pastor should be the teacher. So much is clear from Article 14 of the Augsburg Confession.

But certain circumstances could justify breaking with the order taught in Article 14. When a genuine need arises because there is no pastor, or the pastor teaches false doctrine or serves the people inadequately, it is the duty and right of Christians to meet for edification and to exercise the pastor's work to the best of their ability, according to God's word and in a manner fitting to Christ. They do so, however, not by virtue of their universal priesthood, but as the assembly's emergency pastors who may depart from God's order for the sake of the need.[18]

Walther made his presentation the following day. He began with evidence from Scripture that the office of the Word belongs to the whole church, and that Christians are to use the Word not only for themselves, but sharing it with all those close to them, family, neighbors, and friends, seeking their salvation. "Woe to him who will not be a preacher; neither will he be a Christian, for a preacher and a Christian are one and the same."

Secondly, the professor made the case for the ordained ministry. Because most Christians are weak and frail in carrying out their duty of confessing and teaching the word, God has instituted the holy office of preacher or pastor. Certain persons are prepared, gifted, equipped, tested, and selected publicly to exercise this office in which they administer the Word and the Holy Sacraments and lead the assemblies for mutual edification with God's word. Ordinary Christians do not have these rights.

Finally, Walther addressed exceptional cases. Some lay participation is permissible when an emergency situation arises. Where
there is no ordained pastor, or the pastor teaches falsely, or
Christians are starving spiritually because they are inadequately
served the means of grace, it is not wrong for lay people to preach
God's Word and pray in a public meeting or to conduct public
baptism. When this happens, Walther insisted, echoing what the
Synod pastors had said, the lay people are not exercising their
spiritual priesthood or their common Christian right, but are administering the public office of priest or preacher for the sake of
the needs of the souls.[19]

The similarity between the delegates' discussion of lay activity
and Walther's exposition up to this point suggests that the St.
Louis professor consciously incorporated points from the previous day's discussion into his remarks. The special contribution
Walther made was to help the Norwegian Synod clarify the matter of need. In concluding his statement, he drew from the New
Testament an example of emergency pastors. These were the
members of the household of Stephanas who "devoted themselves to the service of the saints" (1 Corinthians 16:15). He also
quoted the following significant passage from the *Smalcald Articles*,
one of the Lutheran church's symbolical books: "Just as in a case
of necessity even a layman absolves, and becomes the minister
and pastor of another; as Augustine narrates the story of two
Christians in a ship, one of whom baptized the catechumen, who
after Baptism then absolved the baptizer."[20]

This "emergency principle" was strikingly similar to the
*Nødprincip* that several Norwegian immigrant pastors were familiar with from their mentoring under Gisle Johnson of the theology
faculty in Oslo. Perhaps both influential theologians, Johnson the
Norwegian and Walther the German American, drew their insight from the key statement in *The Smalcald Articles*.

The question of lay activity was brought to a resolution at the
Synod's annual meeting at Holden Lutheran church in June of

191

1862. While Walther was not present at this meeting, his paper given the previous year at Spring Prairie played a key role in providing a basis for agreement. It was read aloud at the Holden meeting and discussed by the assembly.[21]

The delegates worked their way through the three parts of Walther's paper, reinforcing and illustrating arguments with comments and quotations from Martin Luther. At the end, they set forth seven theses summing up Walther's statement on lay activity and adopted them. Regarding the crucial factor of need, the fifth thesis declared: "It is both a right and a duty in case of real need for anyone who can to exercise in proper Christian order the office of public ministry."[22] Walther's paper substantiated much of what Rasmussen and Muus had said earlier about the laity's ministry and satisfied the Synod pastors in defining the public ministry of the ordained. The idea of lay people acting in cases of demonstrated need was accepted by all. Reassured by what they heard that the Norwegian Synod did indeed recognize lay activity, Pastor Rasmussen and two colleagues joined the Synod.[23]

It must have been satisfying to Muus to have this important problem brought to a successful resolution at a meeting held in the Holden church, where he served as pastor. At this stage in his career, Muus was among those who expressed admiration for Walther and the Missouri Synod. In a report to the Norwegian journal *Norsk Kirketidende*, Muus had written most approvingly of "these old Missourians" who are not only drilled in the pure doctrine but who bring it to life so that they grasp things not only "on paper" but also in reality, "and the salvation of souls is their main concern."[24]

Not every controversy in which Muus and his colleagues were involved could be settled in such a relatively short time. When the doctrine of absolution was taken up for discussion at the Synod meeting in Luther Valley, Wisconsin, in the summer of 1861, no one could have suspected that the issue would be debated for forty-five years.

As with the topic of lay activity, Muus again would take a position out of step with the Norwegian Synod leadership's views. Absolution is a formal pastoral pronouncement of forgiveness to one who has made a confession of sins. The words of absolution are most commonly used in preparation for Holy Communion. After the person has made confession of sin, the pastor will place hands on the head of the penitent and speak such words as the following: "As a called and ordained minister of the Church of Christ, and by his authority, I declare to you the entire forgiveness of all your sins, in the name of the Father, the Son, and the Holy Spirit."[25]

In Muus's day and later, parishioners often heard the words of absolution in private confession before their pastor. More recently, absolution of a general and public kind has been incorporated into a brief preparatory service that precedes the service of Holy Communion. But whether spoken in private or in public, the words of absolution are never taken lightly. They reflect two profound realities, the graciousness of a God who can and will forgive sins, and the need that human beings have of that forgiveness. Moreover, the words of absolution carry out the specific function of assuring the penitent that he or she actually is forgiven.

As the Norwegian Synod was going about its business in the spring and summer of 1861, not everyone was equally concerned about the meaning of the doctrine of absolution. When the delegates gathered at Luther Valley from June 26 to July 2, they were much more exercised about two other matters curiously related to one another, slavery and establishing their own school. As Nelson and Fevold describe the situation, "For two days the laymen sat and listened to the pastors argue about absolution while they seethed inwardly over the slavery issue."[26]

The "seething" was related to the circumstance that the Synod had arranged to have its ministerial candidates trained in St. Louis at the Missouri Synod's Concordia College. In the spring and early summer of 1861, reports were circulating among Synod

193

members that the Concordia professors, including Laur. Larsen, were pro-slavery. If that were so, some members of the Synod were opposed to continuing the relationship with St. Louis. Thus a full discussion of slavery could not be avoided at the 1861 Synod meeting.

But first came the theological question of absolution. Professor Larsen introduced the topic by presenting eight theses on absolution prepared by Th. J. Brohm, a Missouri Synod pastor, and discussed by that synod at a meeting in October of 1860. Under the title of "The Missouri Synod's Discussion of Absolution," the Norwegian Synod's monthly journal of June and July 1861 published the theses and the Missouri Synod's commentary on them.[27]

Muus had been delegated to respond to Larsen's presentation. Muus had no comment on the first three theses, which equated absolution with the Gospel and asserted that the preachers of the Gospel or the whole Church are acting on behalf of the Triune God who is the one who forgives sins. But in the fourth thesis Muus found a phrase he could not accept, so he proceeded to offer a correction. Larsen had said, following the Missouri theses word for word, that absolution does not mean that the pastor acts as judge of the inner condition of the one confessing, nor that absolution is an empty wish that the sinner be forgiven. Rather, absolution consists "in a powerful impartation of forgiveness."[28]

Muus was troubled by the implication of the phrase "powerful impartation." It sounded as if forgiveness took place regardless of the attitude of the recipient of absolution; whether one believed or not, one still received the forgiveness of sins. Muus proposed the following substitution: "God *gives* and presents the forgiveness of sins in the Gospel or Absolution to all who hear the Word, and while indeed all in that sense receive it, nevertheless only the believers retain it." *Impartation* suggests that God gives the forgiveness of sins to unbelievers.[29]

Those who agreed that absolution is a "powerful impartation" affirmed that, indeed, forgiveness of sins is actually given to both believers and unbelievers. Absolution comes from God and is not dependent upon human responses. Just as a pardoned prisoner may despise the pardon and remain in jail, so the sinner who refuses to believe the gift of forgiveness nevertheless receives it, though he will not benefit from it.[30] Muus agreed, but maintained that one should not say that an unbeliever *has* the forgiveness of sin. Even if from God's side he receives it, if he does not keep it, he does not have it. With several others, Muus also held that absolution must be unconditional. There is no comfort in absolution if penitents are made to wonder whether they have sufficient remorse over their sins or whether it was earnest enough.

When discussion turned to the duty of the one hearing the confession, H. A. Preus declared it "a devilish idea" for the pastor to base absolution on a close questioning of the condition of the penitent's heart. Muus responded that in his view it was precisely the duty of the pastor to try to ascertain as far as possible the condition of the heart, not to judge, but to find out if the person's confession is from the heart or only from the mouth.[31]

This exchange sparked a heated and prolonged discussion. There was general agreement that a confession should be more than memorized words, and that the pastor with God's Word should help the penitent come to a true confession of sin and a living faith. That being the sentiment, pastors Muus and Fjeld, layman Erik Ellefsen, and a few others were unable to see why it was wrong to talk about trying the heart as far as possible. The reply was that only God knows the heart. It is blasphemy to try to do something that only God can do. That is what the pope and the Methodists do, putting themselves in God's place. In some cases, it was conceded, one can see from the false faith or ungodly life that a person has an unrepentant heart and is therefore a hypocrite. But one does not see the heart. Rather, God allows the unrepentant condition of the heart to be revealed. The main thing in preaching the Gospel and also in absolution is not only to demand remorse and faith, but much more to preach in such a way that the poor sinners can be awakened to repentance and faith.

195

Muus, supported by Pastor Fjeld, was not ready to give up his view on trying the hearts. Feeling that he had been misunderstood, he dictated for the minutes that it was his conviction "that it was a pastor's duty to try the condition of the heart, to the degree that a person is capable of doing so." He would do this, he explained, by testing the penitents' confession and life and thereby, as far as possible, he would try whether their confession was trustworthy. The majority of the pastors objected that "to try the heart" is something different from "to try the confession and life." They lectured Muus to be more precise in his language, rejecting his idea that one can determine whether a confession is sincere and proceeds from the heart. They warned Muus to withdraw his expressions or have them declared as containing false doctrine.[32]

The Synod then passed a resolution to that effect, declaring that in accordance with God's Word and the decision of the Lutheran Church it is false doctrine that a confessor as far as possible shall try the condition of the penitents' heart or try whether their confessions are trustworthy. The vote was 70 Yes and 6 No. Muus was now asked to withdraw his expressions since the Synod had declared them to contain false doctrine. Muus stated that he still was not persuaded otherwise. Therefore H. A. Preus proposed that the Synod should make the following declaration: "Since Pastor Muus has not withdrawn nor rejected those expressions, that one shall as far as possible try the hearts and try, whether the confession is trustworthy, which teaching the Synod has recognized to be against God's word, so the Synod will postpone the handling of this matter until later, in the hope that Pastor Muus by closer consideration and instruction later will come to acknowledge his error." The declaration was approved with six representatives opposed.

Turning again to the specific theses in the report on absolution, the Synod adopted the first four unanimously, with one exception. Pastor Muus and two other members of the Synod sought, without success, to have the words "powerful impartation" in the fourth thesis replaced by the word "given." Time did not permit further discussion of the topic, which had already taken up more than two days.[33]

Muus did not regard his part in the discussion as a rejection of the Synod's teaching on absolution. Nevertheless, it was obvious to all who were at the 1861 Synod meeting that he would state his views and hold to them despite pressure from the majority. As far as one can determine from the available correspondence, his comments on absolution did no lasting harm to the steady friendship between himself and Pastor Laur. Larsen. For example, Muus invited Larsen to preach at a place not far from Holden in April of 1862 and in May of that year he asked Larsen to do him a favor on his way to the Synod meeting at Holden.[34]

The topic of absolution was taken up by another group of Scandinavian-American Lutherans. Hearing how the Synod had debated the subject, the Scandinavian Augustanans, an offshoot of the Northern Illinois Synod, sided with Muus's position. This group met with Norwegian Synod leaders at Jefferson Prairie, Wisconsin, in 1864, where absolution again was discussed on the basis of Larsen's eight theses. The Augustanans, following Muus's reasoning, also objected to the phrase "powerful impartation" and stated that the gospel "offers the forgiveness of sins to all who hear it, but this forgiveness is given, imparted, and presented only to those who in faith receive it." The Synod position in effect reaffirmed "powerful impartation" in the following statement: "The preaching of the Gospel gives, presents, and imparts the forgiveness of sins to all to whom it is proclaimed, whether they believe or not (although it is not accepted by all)."[35]

There the issue remained for some time. In 1872 the Norwegian Synod dropped the controversial phrase, "powerful impartation." Not until 1906, when committees from the Norwegian Synod and two other Norwegian Lutheran bodies agreed on a set of five theses on absolution, was the question finally put to rest. Both sides seemed to retain the points they had contended for: absolution is genuine even when given to unbelievers, but it does not benefit without faith.[36]

"The vast majority of the Norwegian immigrants were of one mind in their aversion to slavery," write Nelson and Fevold.[37] An unambiguous stand against slavery was adopted in 1846 by Eielsen's Synod in the following resolution: "We, standing united, wholly repudiate the fearful sin of giving our approval to the slave traffic; rather shall we employ all possible diligence in promoting and supporting opposition to it, with a view to the freeing of the Negroes, for Jesus has said: 'Therefore all things whatsoever ye would that men should do to you, do ye even so to them; for this is the law and the prophets' (Matt. 7:12). They also are redeemed with the same blood and intended to inherit the same glory as other people. We counsel everyone to take this matter under a more careful consideration."[38]

Given this strong expression of anti-slavery by the earliest organization of Norwegian-American Lutheran immigrants, it is difficult if not impossible for modern readers to understand why there would be any controversy concerning slavery in the Norwegian Synod. Even more curious is the fact that the controversy, which began in 1861, actually gained momentum after the Civil War was over. The explanation, one is tempted to suggest, might be traced to an outbreak of *rabies theologorum* (the madness of the theologians), for in all Norwegian groups the laity, to a substantial extent, was opposed to slavery.

Muus shared the lay people's revulsion against the institution of slavery, but as the controversy unfolded, he could not break with the Synod leadership's fixed formula that, according to the Bible, slavery in itself is not a sin. In fact, he became a defender of this position over against C. L. Clausen, who struggled to free himself from it.

The disposition to tolerate slavery reached the minds of Norwegian Synod clergy through contacts with the Missouri Synod. As noted previously, the Norwegian Synod sent Laur. Larsen to teach at Concordia College in St. Louis with special responsibility for the Norwegian students who were studying for the ministry there. Larsen took up his duties in 1859. In 1860, A. C. Preus wrote to C. F. W. Walther of the St. Louis faculty about slavery. At the time, Preus believed that slavery was sinful, but Walther replied that it was a great misunderstanding to regard the institution of slavery as sinful. He wrote: "What God permits even to the Christian in the New Testament and does not command him to abolish, but even regulates, can in itself be no sin." But one should fight against the sinful abuses related to it. These views were advanced among members of the Norwegian Synod when they debated slavery.[39]

Soon after the firing on Fort Sumter on April 12, 1861, the St. Louis seminary closed down and the Norwegian students were sent home. In the Norwegian language newspaper *Emigranten* and among the congregations, questions were raised about the advisability of having Norwegian pastors trained in St. Louis, for the students were reporting that the faculty members there were pro-slavery and not supportive of the Union cause. If that was true, it seemed high time for the Norwegians to end the connection with the St. Louis school and set up their own institution of higher learning. While the pastors wished to continue the tie with St. Louis until a college could be permanently situated, the lay delegates favored a temporary school arrangement in one of the congregations. Thus the question of slavery gave urgency to the establishing of a Synod school, for which a site had already been suggested in Decorah, Iowa.[40]

As the discussion picked up steam, the lay people learned that many on the Concordia faculty were Democrats who supported states' rights, a political position opposite to the one held by the usually Republican and pro-Union Norwegians. What was also hard to accept was the contention by the Missourians and the Synod pastors who followed them—H. A. Preus, Laur. Larsen, Koren, and Ottesen—that the Bible was not anti-slavery. Once the debate on the slavery question was set in motion at the 1861

199

Synod meeting, Larsen and others defended the view, adopted from C. F. W. Walther, that "slavery in itself" was not sin.[41]

When asked to show from Scripture that slavery is not sin, Larsen cited l Timothy 6:1–2, which enjoins slaves to respect their masters, and Exodus 21: 1–7, with its instructions about freeing in the seventh year a slave whom one has bought or retaining him if he wishes to stay. Because the passage was central to the Synod's position on slavery, 1 Timothy 6:1–2 is quoted here: "Let all who are under the yoke of slavery regard their masters as worthy of all honor, so that the name of God and the teaching may not be blasphemed. Those who have believing masters must not be disrespectful to them on the ground that they are members of the church; rather they must serve them all the more, since those who benefit by their service are believers and beloved."

In Larsen's view, the apostle could not say that the masters in the First Timothy text were "believers and beloved" if it was a sin in itself to hold slaves. In the Old Testament God not only tolerated slavery but in some cases commanded it.[42]

Several pastors excused the lay delegates for not being able to grasp at once that slavery was a consequence of sin but not sin in itself, because they themselves had once believed, before looking at the matter more closely in the Word of God, that slavery in itself was a sin, especially when they learned about the many outrageous crimes that often went with it. Some delegates wanted to discuss slavery as a present reality, but were told that it was a historical or political question that did not belong in this meeting since it required historical proofs, knowledge of the laws in various states, and reliable information on the abuses of slavery that were claimed. All such abuses could be judged according to the Ten Commandments.[43]

Pastor John Fjeld, who had taken Muus's part in the absolution debate, flatly stated his opinion that slavery was a sin in itself. It strove against the whole spirit of the New Testament. But Muus concurred with the view that it was not in itself a sin to hold slaves. On the other hand, he believed that Christendom would lead to the abolition of such a ruinous institution, and that therefore to continue with slavery would be a sin. C. L. Clausen advanced a similar view. While slavery is not a sin in itself, he said, it is equally clear from God's word that it is one of the greatest temporal evils that every Christian would want removed and in love would seek to abolish. Later Clausen would take the lead in opposing the Synod view that slavery is not a sin.[44]

Layman Erik Ellefsen from Iowa, "the king of Big Canoe," was convinced that slavery had to be a sin. Perhaps the slaves in Paul's day were sold for debts or confined because of crimes. That one person can have unconditional property rights over another seemed to him to be against God's Word. Nor was I. Ingebritsen persuaded that slavery was not a sin. He thought that those on the other side were talking about an ideal slavery that did not exist in reality. The lay persons were not content to consider slavery in such abstract terms when it was clearly an evil that was dividing the country and compelling men to bear arms.[45]

Realizing that something had to be done to avoid a serious breach in the church, H. A. Preus and J. A. Ottesen drew up a resolution that they succeeded in getting all the pastors present to sign, including Muus and Clausen, both of whom had displayed sympathetic interest in the lay people's anti-slavery views. The resolution read as follows: "Although according to the Word of God, it is not in and by itself a sin to keep slaves, nevertheless it is in itself an evil and a punishment from God. We condemn all abuses and sins connected therewith, and furthermore, when official duties require it and when Christian love and wisdom demand it, we will work for its abolition."[46]

The strategy of ending the discussion of slavery with a unanimous declaration signed by all the pastors did not succeed. When the pastors' resolution was put to a vote by the lay delegates, it received twenty-eight votes in favor, ten votes against, and a significant twenty-eight abstentions, firmly revealing how far pastors and laity were separated on the matter of slavery.[47]

The lay people at the 1861 Synod meeting then formulated their own resolution that was placed on record although not put to a vote. It said, in part: "Slavery, viewed as an institution, can exist only under definite law, and since the laws upon which it is based stand in manifest conflict with the Word of God and Christian love, it is sin." The resolution concluded with the statement that slavery has been one of the country's greatest evils for church and state, and a pledge to work for its alleviation and abolition.[48]

After several years of heated debates at Synod meetings, at pastoral conferences, and in the Norwegian-language newspapers, the slavery controversy in the Norwegian Synod finally reached a settlement in Chicago in 1868 when the leading pastors of the Synod succeeded in getting the church body to approve the position first set out in the Pastors' Resolution of 1861. Thus the Norwegian Synod made official the teaching that according to the Word of God "it is not in and by itself a sin to keep slaves."[49]

When the controversy began in 1861, Muus and Clausen held similar views. At the time, they took a middle position, neither contesting Larsen's arguments nor totally endorsing the laity's conviction that slavery was an unqualified sin, although both spoke out against the evils of the institution. Both had signed the so-called Pastors' Resolution in 1861. Clausen soon regretted this step and in December of 1861 published a retraction, an action that pushed the slavery controversy to a new level of intensity.[50]

Curious enough to begin with, the controversy became even stranger after the Civil War was over. Having served a year as a chaplain in the war, C. L. Clausen had every reason to contend for the principle that slavery is a sin and out of harmony with love to one's neighbor. At pastoral conferences and in private, various Synod leaders pressured Clausen to admit that he was wrong. He would agree for a time, then return to his earlier position, opening himself to the charge of vacillation. In the midst of the Synod's efforts to deal with Clausen, the latter requested that Muus be one of the two Synod pastors appointed to confer with

*C. L. Clausen*
From E. Clifford Nelson and Eugene L. Fevold, *The Lutheran Church Among Norwegian-Americans*

him on the slavery question. The three-man conference agreed that there was no sin involved in the master-slave situation described in First Timothy 6:1, 2, but when Clausen returned home he had second thoughts and changed his mind. In the fall of 1864 Muus traveled to St. Ansgar, Iowa, to keep an appointment with Clausen, but the meeting was canceled because just as Muus arrived, Clausen was ready to board the train for Dubuque. There were other efforts to negotiate with Clausen, with unsatisfactory results.[51]

But in 1866 a new development took place. That year the Synod made public the correspondence it had been conducting covertly

203

since 1862 with the theology faculty in Oslo. On March 17, 1862, A. C. Preus, then president of the Synod, asked the faculty for its opinion on the 1861 Pastors' Resolution on slavery. The Norwegian faculty's response was equivocal, not the firm statement of support the Synod's leading pastors had hoped for. The exchange continued for the next few years, with only a limited number of Synod pastors having knowledge of it. Clausen was not one of them.[52] The belated publication of the Norwegian faculty's opinion in 1866 had the effect of re-opening the slavery controversy and renewing Clausen's determination to speak out against slavery as a sin since, in some respects, the Norwegian theologians seemed to give aid and comfort to Clausen's position. In 1867 both Clausen and H. A. Preus were in Norway where they had a conference with Gisle Johnson about slavery. The results of this meeting were inconclusive, but during the conversation Johnson offered the significant insight that the issue was one of history and not something that could be settled by Scripture.[53]

But this perspective, to recognize the role of historical factors and not restrict the debate to the citing and interpreting of Bible passages, did not appeal to Preus and his inner circle. They continued the drumbeat of "slavery is not a sin in and by itself" and repeated their distinction between slavery as an *evil* and slavery as a *sin* until eventually their view prevailed at the Chicago meeting of the Synod in 1868.[54]

Prior to the Chicago decision, Clausen and Muus were becoming alienated from one another. In a letter to H. A. Preus in October of 1866 Muus wrote that he was worried about a forthcoming pastoral conference and especially about Clausen: "he seems fallen beyond redemption."[55] It is not known whether Muus was kept informed about the secret communications with the Norwegian theology faculty. His increasing hostility toward Clausen is a matter of record, however. The two former friends sparred with one another in issues of *Emigranten* in 1866 and 1867. In December of 1866 Muus, taking the side of the Synod pastors, charged that Clausen's fight "against us" was not only about slavery, but against the principle that sacred Scripture is the only rule and guide for our faith and life. With unsparing severity, Muus went so far as to accuse Clausen of being a tool of the devil. Indeed, the heading of Muus's polemical piece in *Emigranten* was "Hestefoden." Anyone acquainted with Scandinavian folklore would know at once that this expression meant "the devil's hoof."[56]

Clausen forcefully countered Muus's attack in the January 14, 1867, issue of *Emigranten*, complaining that Muus had ascribed to him things he had never written. Not being able to overthrow Clausen's arguments, he charged, Muus had chosen the desperate course of accusing Clausen of denying that Scripture is the only rule and guide for faith and life. With Muus and the whole Lutheran Church, Clausen confessed the Bible to be the only guide and rule for faith and life, but added that he was not bound to Muus's interpretations of this or any other scripture passage, nor was he bound to prefer the translation that pleased Muus the most. If Muus wanted to brand Clausen as a devil and his teaching as devilish doctrine, he could do so, and defend it before God and his conscience, and before the Christian congregation in which he was a teacher. "It does not harm me or the cause for which I am fighting."[57]

Given the ongoing dispute, one might well regard an article by Muus in the February 1867 issue of *Emigranten* as another blow against Clausen. Titled "What is written?" the piece took up yet again 1 Timothy 6:1–2, a key passage discussed earlier in the slavery controversy. Perhaps to appear as if he were not interpreting, Muus simply drew up two lists of observations, what the passage says and what it does not say. The first list restated the content of the two verses. For example: that slaves should obey their masters and hold them in honor; if they do not, God's name and teaching will be profaned; it is not always contrary to the command of love that a Christian master have Christian slaves. What the passage does not say: that all people, or all Christians, have the right to have slaves, or that it is a sin to set slaves free, or that American slavery was good, or that slaves are not humans but monkeys.

By citing additional verses, 1 Timothy 6:3–5, Muus seemed to be admonishing Clausen. In part the verses say, "Whoever teaches otherwise and does not agree with the sound words of our Lord Jesus Christ and the teaching that is in accordance with godliness, is conceited, understanding nothing, and has a morbid craving for controversy and for disputes about words." To which Muus added the phrase, as if part of the citation: "Avoid such people!" After further quotations from Ephesians, Muus cited the apostle Paul's solemn warning in Galatians 1:8 that if anyone should proclaim "a gospel contrary to what we proclaimed to you, let that one be accursed!" To conclude his short Bible lesson Muus wrote: "This is what is written, and it will judge us and judge between us on the last day."[58]

Understandably, some readers of *Emigranten* were offended and wearied by the angry wrangling between the pastors. A contributor who signed himself as "A. O." expressed grief and astonishment that Pastor Muus, who had once been Clausen's good and trustworthy friend, could use such hateful language, referring to the earlier open attack on Clausen. The writer upbraided both pastors, who were called to be shepherds for Christ's church on earth, for attacking one another with scorn and insults. But with "Hestefoden" as the heading of his piece, it was clear that A. O. was aiming especially at Muus. Both clergy were criticized for making much of their loyalty to Scripture but, in defending their opinions, offending against the basic truths of Christianity. Without naming Muus, A. O. reproached those who had the gall to direct serious accusations against a colleague "who cannot believe the favorite teaching about slavery as a second gospel." To Muus's accusation that Clausen was really rejecting the Bible as the only rule and guide for faith and life, A. O had a pointed response. "True enough, the Bible is our faith's foundation," he conceded. "But that which is such a great abomination in Muus's eyes is, in reality, 'not to believe in slavery's divine institution,' and the person who dares to harbor any doubts about this, according to his view, preaches false doctrine."[59]

Officially, the slavery controversy ended in 1868 when the Norwegian Synod adopted ten theses amplifying the now-familiar idea that the forced servitude or slavery mentioned in the New Testament "is not in and by itself sinful." Yet one could rightly say that the last word on the subject was issued in 1869. At its meeting that year the Synod finally faced the fact of American slavery and granted that if one understands the term "in the less precise speech of daily life," recognizing how laws and regulations have been used to cover up the sins and ungodliness that accompany it, slavery in that sense was "a sin and an abomination." Nevertheless, the old Synod position was still reaffirmed and a statement included that masters did not sin in keeping slaves if they treated them "in love according to God's Word."[60]

After struggling in vain to introduce changes in the wording of the ten theses adopted in 1868, Clausen resigned from the Norwegian Synod in protest. The congregations he had served in Wisconsin and Iowa left with him, and there were others dissatisfied with the Synod's teaching on slavery. Congregations in Lee county, Illinois, where A. C. Preus had been pastor, broke with the Synod in 1863. The Big Canoe congregation in Iowa, of which Erik Ellefsen was a prominent member, resigned in 1868. Sixty families from J. A. Ottesen's congregation at Koshkonong also left the Synod.[61]

Students of the slavery controversy agree that Clausen was moved by admirable humanitarian and democratic instincts while the Synod leaders thought they were defending the authority of Scripture. Theodore C. Blegen characterized the positions of the contending parties in these words: "The central reality in the minds of the Synod leaders in the slavery controversy was the authority of the 'Word of God.' They fought for Lutheran orthodoxy as they conceived it, for a strict Biblical interpretation, for theological dogma. The central reality in the mind of Clausen was slavery in the United States and an unwillingness to have the church countenance it. He fought against contemporary slavery and for human freedom—a part of the same crusade that drew him to the Southern battlefields as an army chaplain."[62]

In retrospect, C. L. Clausen deserves credit for his efforts to insist on the sinfulness of slavery even though he was not a consistent debater. His fellow pastors faulted him for agreeing to a position and later changing his mind, but after 1861 he stayed with his position. The modern reader is moved to admiration for Clausen's conviction and his courage to stand virtually alone. He had sound instincts for justice and humanity, and a strong loyalty to the Holy Scripture.

From the perspective of a later time, Pastor Muus does not present an admirable figure in the slavery controversy of the 1860s. While personally convinced that slavery was terrible, and a sin to perpetuate, he stood with his pastoral colleagues in the Norwegian Synod on the issue. They chose not to allow the unspeakable horrors of American slavery to influence their arguments, being more absorbed in their role as stalwart champions of the Word of God. "For them," writes E. Clifford Nelson, "the question was the authority of the Bible which must be literalistically interpreted because its words were inspired and therefore inerrant."[63]

In the decade between his arrival at Holden in 1859 and the winding down of the slavery controversy in 1869, Muus received a vigorous initiation into the life of a pioneer immigrant pastor. The complex character of the man was becoming evident. He was unreservedly devoted to his calling to bring the Word of God to fellow Norwegians who had come to America, accepting as a matter of course the difficult conditions under which he worked. In spite of long and frequent absences from home, he ministered to the churches in the Holden area and tried to carry out his domestic roles as husband and father. In the wider circles of the Synod he had shown a capacity to find his own way on the issues of the day, not always agreeing with the views of the most influential pastors. As the exchange with Clausen revealed, Muus could be extremely harsh in dealing with those who disagreed with him, defending his vehemence as a necessary part of up-holding the Word of God and orthodox Lutheran teaching. At times Muus could seem incurably rigid, but a significant part of his contribution to church and society would come about be-cause, at crucial points, he dared to take issue with the unyielding orthodoxy of his peers and move in a new direction. Such would be the case twenty years later when the Norwegian Synod was in the throes of the election controversy.

# *Nine*

## *The School Question*

B. J. Muus, H. A. Preus, and other pastors in the Norwegian Synod distrusted the American common schools, and hoped instead to provide parochial schools for Norwegian immigrant children. Discussion of schools began before Muus arrived in America in 1859, but as it developed he became a visible and vocal participant. In 1870 Muus wrote: "I regard the common school as one that according to its principle must oppose the kingdom of God, and as an organization of poor quality inasmuch as the children in these schools learn much less than they can and ought."[1]

Muus here identifies two of the three main criticisms leveled against the common schools, that they were irreligious and that they were ineffective. The third charge was that they drew the Norwegian children away from their national, social, and intellectual roots, especially the Norwegian language.[2] The alternative, Muus and others argued, was for immigrant congregations to organize and operate their own schools.

Such in brief was the controversial "school question." It occupied Muus, Preus, and many other pastors of the Norwegian Synod, pastors of the Conference, and scores of Norwegian-American lay persons in Wisconsin, Minnesota, Illinois, and Iowa before and after the Civil War. In general, the laity were inclined to accept the common schools, while the clergy, especially those of the Norwegian Synod, favored parochial schools.[3]

The school question pertained basically to primary education, but Muus's interests led him before long to undertake two initiatives for teaching older children. One was the organization of an academy in the Holden parsonage in 1869. The second was the eventual founding, in 1874, of St. Olaf's School.

In the experience of several generations of Norwegian-American church people, parochial school was a period of religious instruction conducted during the summer months. But at the height of the school controversy from the late 1850s through the 1870s, advocates envisioned a more ambitious role for these schools. Instead of being limited to Bible, catechism, church history, and singing, they would also offer instruction in the English language and other useful subjects. The aim was that ultimately the parochial schools would replace, and not merely supplement, the American common schools as far as the Norwegian immigrants were concerned.[4]

In the earlier stages of immigration the school question was not an issue. In 1838, when B. J. Muus's uncle, the immigrant pathfinder Ole Rynning, was writing his *True Account of America*, two schools where children were learning English were already operating in the Fox River settlement in Illinois. Rynning explained to readers in Norway that the Americans set aside the sixteenth section of each township to be sold for school funds.[5] It was taken for granted that children of Norwegian immigrants should attend district schools and learn English in order to better themselves in their new surroundings.

That attitude persisted during the 1840s and 1850s as both schools established by churches and public schools became a familiar part of the Norwegian-American scene in the Upper Midwest. In a Wisconsin settlement, Thurine Oleson studied Norwegian and religion in the summer parochial school, and also attended the English school where she read English and studied geography, arithmetic, spelling, and writing.[6] The quality and regularity of the two kinds of schools varied from one community to the next. Sometimes the parochial school would move from house to house. In some places it actually offered more months of instruction than the common school. The public school system was still in its infancy, first adopted in Wisconsin in 1848 and stabilized in Illinois in 1850.[7]

A hint of the controversy to come appeared in 1848 when Hans A. Stub, a Lutheran pastor newly arrived from Norway, expressed dismay at the state of education among the immigrants and warned that too much dependence on the public schools would lure the Norwegians away from their ancestral Lutheran faith. Writing to Norway from the Muskego, Wisconsin, settlement in 1849, Stub reported: "Indifference on the part of many of the parents toward the Sunday school was soon discovered. They felt that the common or public school was enough. They seemed not to realize that the children did not get any religious instruction there."

So the pastor and a deacon went from house to house to explain that since religious instruction was not permitted in the public schools, it was the parents' responsibility to provide instruction in "the one thing needful." Was it right to train children for American citizenship without helping them claim their heavenly citizenship, the most important of all?[8]

As Pastor Stub's letter indicates, there was concern for children's education among Norwegian immigrant pastors even before the Norwegian Synod was formed in 1853. The pastors set rules for the qualifications of parochial-school teachers and agreed that the transition to the use of English should be gradual, not hasty. They criticized the American common schools for their poor discipline and their inability to foster the Christian nurture of the Norwegian children. Congregations were urged to establish their own schools and to build up good libraries.[9]

In June of 1858 a group of parochial-school teachers and pastors met at Coon Prairie, Wisconsin, to discuss the necessity of the Norwegian religious school and its relation to the English district school. The main speaker was the Reverend A. C. Preus, first

213

president of the Norwegian Synod and a leading spokesman for parochial schools. He reported an encouraging trend whereby the Norwegian religious schools were gaining more support among the immigrants. These schools, he believed, were necessary for the children, for family life, and for the church.[10]

The young could learn English by attending English schools part of the year, but he warned parents against using only the district schools and thereby neglecting the children's religious instruction. Nor would it do to send them to Sunday Schools operated by other denominations where the Bible was read in English. Besides the risk of exposure to heretical teaching there was the unnatural process of learning religion in a language other than the family's daily speech. Christianity is a matter of the heart, so one should learn religion "in the language of the heart: the mother tongue."

Norwegians should exert influence toward the hiring of good teachers in the district schools or secure Norwegian teachers who knew English. But the overriding concern was loyalty to the Christian faith. Preus anticipated the position that B. J. Muus and H. A. Preus would advance, that the parochial schools would be organized to teach not only religion but English and the other subjects usually taught in the district schools. In short, they would replace the English-language schools, and not merely supplement them. This had happened with German religious schools in the cities.[11]

Another meeting devoted to school matters took place in October of 1858 at Rock Prairie, Wisconsin. The assembly adopted the proceedings of the Coon Prairie meeting as its own view of the relation of the Norwegian religion school to the American district school. That meant an official endorsement of A. C. Preus's arguments for the necessity of the Norwegian religion schools, their expansion, and the ultimate replacement of the district schools.[12]

What had been a question discussed primarily within the Norwegian church community became a controversy when the

214

Synod's decisions regarding schools attracted the notice of a wider public. Theodore C. Blegen dates the beginning of the controversy to the Rock Prairie parochial school conference of 1858 and the challenge to its position issued by Rasmus Sorensen, a leader among Danish immigrants and a schoolteacher in Waupaca county, Wisconsin.[13]

Sorensen's provocative comments and A. C. Preus's reply were published in *Emigranten*, a Norwegian-language secular newspaper founded in 1852 that gave immigrants news and information to assist them in the transition to American life. Sorensen firmly stated the need to send immigrant children to American schools where they could learn English, "the language of our present fatherland." He deplored the influence of "the Norwegian preachers in this country" who spoke and worked against the district school system. They had gone further than Catholic priests in attacking the American district schools and declaring publicly that English is a foreign language. Sorensen was appalled that the Norwegian immigrants, once receptive to the district schools, had been persuaded to prefer the Norwegian religious schools.

What the Norwegian ministers ought to do, wrote Sorensen, is teach the confirmands and conduct services in the American language, and limit their use of Norwegian to the elderly and the latest newcomers from Norway. He foresaw religious and national war if each immigrant group stuck to its own language, established its own school systems, and hated and shunned the others "in language, in religion, in teaching, in education, in everything that should be common for all Americans." Sorensen predicted that the authority of the preachers could not hold the younger generation much longer.[14]

A. C. Preus responded that his own and his children's experience with American schools was that the teachers were too young, lacked knowledge, were unable to guide and discipline, and usually stayed only a term. Preus chided Sorensen for his personal "disregard for doctrinal matters." A Lutheran in Europe, Sorensen became an Episcopalian in America. "But we

Norwegians," proclaimed Preus to his Danish adversay, "cling fast to the teachings of our childhood," that is, Luther's Catechism and Pontoppidan's Explanation to the Small Catechism.

As a Lutheran pastor loyal to his church's doctrinal heritage, Preus was aghast at Sorensen's assumption that one could teach religion without a definite confession. "Has anyone ever heard of such a thing?" Religion taught without some pattern or creed is "tasteless stuff" that can have no healthy influence. It was not only the church's confessional stance that was important, but the teacher's personal convictions that would make religion come alive for the students.

Norwegians were not opposed to having their children learn English, as his own were doing. Yet to Norwegians English is indeed "a foreign language" because it is not the mother tongue. Again Preus stressed his principle that "the language which is the language of the home and of the family must be the language of the church and of the religious school." As to the Catholic priests, Preus believed that they wanted to control the public schools and use them to spread Catholicism. Of his own group Preus wrote: "We will not send our children to the American district schools until they are under the direction of competent teachers, so that we know that the schools are thorough in discipline and instruction."[15]

With the controversy breaking into the public press, eleven pastors of the Norwegian Synod met at Koshkonong, Wisconsin, in July of 1859 to make their position clear. They recognized the need for the immigrants to acquire a thorough knowledge of English for the sake of good citizenship and to be able to discriminate among religious writings. Hailing the worth of American religious freedom, they determined to bring their children up in the evangelical Lutheran faith. They added warnings against schools that would draw the children away from the faith, and against American Sunday Schools. Parents should investigate the quality of the district schools. Where they were in good condition, the pastors would recommend them to the congregations.[16]

After this declaration by Synod pastors in 1859 and until the end of the Civil War in 1865, there was a pause in the discussion concerning district and parochial schools. The year 1859 marked the coming of B. J. Muus from Norway to join the ranks of Norwegian Synod pastors and to accept a call to serve Holden and other settlements in Goodhue county, Minnesota. In due time he would be heard from in the controversy.

It was also the year that Laur. Larsen took up his duties as professor for the Norwegian students attending Concordia College in St. Louis, the theological seminary of the German Missouri Synod. In addition to the grounding they received in Lutheran doctrine, the Norwegian theology candidates gained an admiration for the Missouri Synod's system of parochial schools. The success of the Germans in this regard naturally spurred the Norwegians to promote such schools in their own circles.[17]

After the end of the Civil War, a report on religious schools was taken up at the meeting of the Norwegian Synod at Manitowoc, Wisconsin, in 1866. It had been prepared by a committee consisting of Pastor N. O. Brandt, Professor Friedrich Schmidt, and Larsen. According to Laurence M. Larson, the report and its adoption constituted "a definite educational policy." And in the view of Theodore C. Blegen, "it definitely steered the church in the direction of the Missouri Synod system of parochial schools, not to supplement, but to supplant the American public schools."[18]

The committee systematically made its case that it was *desirable* for the congregations to have their own Christian schools in order to bypass the common schools. Secondly, it was *possible* to reach the goal of establishing the kind of schools that would render unnecessary the use of the English-language schools. It would take money, but other groups such as the Germans had managed to do it. The new teachers' course begun at Luther College would aid the cause of finding teachers for the church's schools.[19]

The report lauded religious freedom, "one of the dearest benefits we enjoy under the present constitution." Naturally the state

217

could not permit instruction in Christianity in its schools, but it should realize that Christian training produces respectable citizens. Therefore it should allow congregations to care for the instructing of their children and not force them to attend the public schools. The Norwegians cheerfully accepted the state's right to tax citizens to support the public schools even if some did not make use of them.[20]

After ranging over many facets of the school issue and answering objections to the central case for congregational schools, the authors of the report finally and "briefly" summarized the entire exposition by setting forth twenty-seven theses. The most important of these recapitulated the view that in this country it is desirable and possible for Christians to establish such schools as will give instruction comparable to what is taught in the so-called common schools, making it unnecessary to use the latter. If adequate parochial schools could not be attained soon, congregations should seek to influence the district schools in selection of teachers and in determining when the schools would be in session.[21]

The following year, 1867, Synod president H. A. Preus took this message to Norway where he gave lectures on church conditions among the immigrants in America. The English-language schools are necessarily religionless, he explained, because of the many different confessions in America. Therefore congregations, not just the parents, must take steps to provide instruction in religion. "It is our endeavor," he said, "to arrange things with our congregational schools in such a way as to render the public, English schools superfluous on the part of members of our congregations." The congregational schools would have to add the English language, then arithmetic, geography, and history. Realizing that the Synod's opposition to the American school system had been criticized in Norway, Preus went into the issue more fully by citing all twenty-seven of the theses that had been discussed the year before at the annual meeting.[22]

Back in the American Midwest, the Norwegian Synod's firm position became the subject of passionate discussion in Norwegian-language newspapers. Knud Langeland, editor of *Skandinaven*, attacked the school theses of the Synod and invited lay people to consider how their children could better their futures by attending the common schools. Langeland appealed to the Scandinavians to choose their own educational path, and not follow the lead of the Missouri Synod.[23]

Another voice raised in favor of the common schools was that of Rasmus B. Anderson, then a young teacher in Wisconsin destined to gain notoriety among Norwegian Americans, as scholar and writer, for his outspoken and sometimes changing views of education, religion, and literature. Anderson and B. J. Muus crossed paths in a curious way in 1868 in connection with the annual meeting of the Synod in Chicago. Anderson was the delegate from East Koshkonong, although his pastor had tried unsuccessfully to block his election. At a dinner party in Chicago where both Anderson and Muus were guests, Muus was heard to say to the host, "It surprises me that an old congregation like East Koshkonong has so little appreciation of the proprieties as to send Rasmus Anderson as its representative."[24]

Yet the next day, on the floor of the convention, it was Muus who defended Anderson's right to speak when others wanted to deny him the privilege. Anderson wanted to amend the theses adopted at Manitowoc. He stated that the Synod should work with the common schools and seek to have Norwegian Lutheran teachers appointed in Norwegian communities. Perhaps the Norwegian language could be taught in some of the common schools, he suggested, and the Synod should aim to have Lutheran teachers appointed at certain American academies and colleges. Anderson's proposals were heard coolly by the delegates but not discussed.[25]

Anderson had another avenue for bringing about changes in education. His plan was to raise funds for Norwegian professorships at Wisconsin and other universities. He secured the collaboration of such prominent men as Knud Langeland, C. L. Clausen, who had recently left the Norwegian Synod, John A. Johnson, a businessman in Madison, and C. F. Solberg, another editor. A meeting announced for March 4, 1869, at the county courthouse in Madison, Wisconsin, drew approximately 300 persons, including a number of Synod pastors.[26]

At the Madison meeting the Scandinavian Lutheran Educational Society came into being. Its announced purpose was to promote "true enlightenment through the erection of Scandinavian Lutheran professorships at American higher schools." The Society aimed to promote "a broader type of education" by someday establishing a Scandinavian university, but for the present it was collecting funds for Scandinavian professorships in American schools. Such professorships would prepare public-school teachers competent in both English and Norwegian, provide an education for Scandinavian youth going into various civil positions, and encourage study of Scandinavian languages, history, and literature.[27] The Scandinavian Lutheran Educational Society did not last long, having only two more meetings before it disappeared. Nevertheless, it proved to be an important vehicle for widening the educational outlook of the Norwegian immigrants to include forms of education beyond the primary level.[28]

H. A. Preus was present at the March 4 meeting in Madison, taking issue with the plan to establish Scandinavian professorships. Preus led a group of about forty persons that met the next day in a Madison church to formulate their own church-centered ideas on promoting folk enlightenment. True enlightenment of the people can only be achieved when all the arts and sciences are understood in the light of scripture and faith, they asserted. The Preus faction could not work with the Scandinavian Lutheran Education Society to establish professorships in American schools because the latter are "either religionless or sectarian or even ruled by an outright unbelieving and anti-Christian spirit."[29] The splinter group also objected that there was no guarantee that such Scandinavian-Lutheran professors would be appointed or, if appointed, would provide a genuine Lutheran influence on students. Such reservations were fueled by the fact that the

Education Society admitted non-Lutherans and ex-Lutherans to its ranks. Turning to positive steps toward enlightenment, Preus and his adherents resolved to start with the improved instruction of children. Whether placing their own teachers in district schools or establishing their own parochial schools, they had to find teachers. Luther College had added another professor to teach English and had expanded its teacher training course to three years.

Next the Madison dissenters expressed the need to establish some "smaller high schools" (academies) in places accessible to youth in the areas of the larger and older Norwegian settlements, for example, in Koshkonong, Wisconsin, and Goodhue county, Minnesota. These schools would teach religion and the subjects taught in district schools. In addition, they would offer instruction in Norwegian, English, science, history, and so on. Students planning to attend Luther College would receive a good preparatory education in such academies.[30]

It was also noted at the meeting that there would be an increasing need for academies to serve those young people not intending to enter the direct service of the church as pastors and schoolteachers. That same year J. A. Ottesen and A. C. Preus called for church-established "middle schools" that would function between the parochial schools and Luther College. In effect, these would be high schools or academies. In the course of time, an astonishing number of academies were founded under Norwegian Lutheran auspices. One study lists seventy-five academies, the majority founded between 1870 and 1920, including a number that became seminaries or four-year colleges.[31]

B. J. Muus's part in the school controversy came into full view through three public engagements. The first was his founding of an academy in the Holden parish in 1869. The second was a vigorous, polemical newspaper exchange on the school question with Goodhue county Superintendent of Schools H. B. Wilson in 1870. The third was Muus's presentation of several theses on the

221

*Bernt Julius Muus*
Norwegian-American Historical Association Archives

common school at the annual meeting of the Norwegian Synod at Holden in 1874.

The decision by Muus to start an academy in Goodhue county was consistent with his advocacy of parochial schools and Christian education. It was also fully in keeping with the Madison suggestion for regional academies, although Muus was not present at that meeting. When Muus wrote to provide information about "my academy" to the editors of *Kirkelig Maanedstidende* in November of 1869, the school had already been in session for a term, probably from September to November. Muus spoke of the academy as something he had long considered, not as the result of any recent urging from the Synod. His statement about the school is important in the light of his later initiative with St. Olaf's School in Northfield. Muus wrote: "From the very beginning of my ministry, I was keenly conscious of the great benefits which would accrue from establishing a high school in which the youth of the congregations could acquire a better education than could be obtained in our parochial and common schools."[32]

The simple term "high school" is important. Most of the arguments about parochial versus common schools dealt with primary education. At this moment, in the fall of 1869, Muus has shifted his focus to the secondary level, having already invested thought, time, and his own money in a type of educational project that in time would leave the old common school battles behind. Nevertheless, a decade of wrangling about the common school still lay ahead, with Muus displaying his combative zeal in a heated exchange with the Goodhue county superintendent of schools, H. B. Wilson.

The dispute with Superintendent Wilson began when Wilson stated in his annual report that there was an element among the Scandinavians, "especially among the clergy," that was hostile to the common schools. Reading the report in *Nordisk Folkeblad*, a Minneapolis paper, Muus knew that he was the likely target of the superintendent's complaint. He responded by submitting an article titled "Schools and a Good School" to the La Crosse newspaper, *Fædrelandet og Emigranten*.

Since Wilson had praised the American school system, Muus wanted to examine it more closely. He takes up two claims about the place of religion in the common school. Some say there is no religion because, with so many different sects, religious freedom has to be secured for everyone. But is it possible to conduct school five days a week without conveying any kind of religious values? If stories are used to point a moral, what motives are given for

223

right behavior? If the motives are something other than seeking first the kingdom of God, then the children are being brought up as heathen. If on the other hand the school should urge children to act out of love of God and neighbor, that is teaching Christianity, which is forbidden.

The other claim takes a different direction. Defenders of the American school system will say, Yes, we do teach a kind of religion, but it is not the Christian religion. It is a general religion common to all people. In his reply to this claim, Muus draws a severe distinction: "The Christian religion stands precisely in direct opposition to the 'general' religion; if the general religion is true, then Christianity is false, and if Christianity is true, so the general religion is false." Again, consider the motives. The motives for the general religion that resides in everyone's nature are the use, advantage, benefit they can gain for themselves. The incentives are self-love and egoism. By contrast, the motive for Christian action is love for God, concern for what God wills that one should do for one's own and the neighbor's benefit. Therefore, whether the American common school teaches no religion or a general religion, it is clear that it is an institution that in principle must work against the kingdom of God. One can see some of the results in the behavior of young Americans, who act like wild animals.

Criticizing the instruction in the common school, Muus complained that for all the time and money expended, a pupil gets only a bit of reading, a little writing and arithmetic, some primitive geography, and one or another "novel" with the title, "United States History." The learning of English by Norwegian children is also disappointing. But Muus felt that it was not a sin for parents to send their children to the common school for the sake of learning English. The concluding thought and the main purpose of the article was that when the common school operates according to its basic principle, which is to work against the kingdom of God, it is a temptation for Christians.[33]

Superintendent Wilson read a translation of Muus's article and responded in the Goodhue county *Republican* with a piece titled

"Our Public Schools Versus Sectarian Schools in a Foreign Language." Of Muus's article Wilson wrote that "the reverend gentleman exhibits a spirit of the most narrow-minded bigotry and intolerance it has ever been my fortune to read." Muus opposed the interests of the Scandinavians by trying to perpetuate in this land "a foreign language, a foreign sentiment, and foreign institutions."

Wilson was incensed by Muus's negative comment on the behavior of American youth, challenging Muus to demonstrate that his church members and their children displayed better moral conduct than native-born Americans. When on business in Red Wing do they drink less whiskey? Are they more honest, less selfish? Do they give more for the support of the poor? Wilson was angered that "this foreign priest" regarded the struggles of the early American patriots as "only a romance." Further stung by Muus's insinuation that Norwegians would not send their children to school to become loafers, Wilson countered by characterizing Muus as "a man who has argued zealously in the sacred pulpit, to prove that the holding of human beings in slavery was no sin."

The superintendent refused to argue about church doctrine. He found it quite acceptable to teach "the cardinal principles of christianity as taught by our blessed Savior in the sermon on the Mount . . . the duty the child owes to God, his neighbor, his country and himself—the majesty of truth, the beauty of integrity, benevolence and all the christian graces." He held no animosity toward Muus and his church, he wrote. Foreigners should "lay aside their national prejudices and become American in all their feelings and practices." Before long, he predicted, the spirit of common-school instruction would spread and overcome all bigotry, intolerance, and superstition.[34]

In an unusual move, Muus answered Wilson's charges by submitting his response to the Goodhue county *Republican* in English, Most of his public writing was in Norwegian. In this case, Muus evinced a degree of self-consciousness in using English, but

225

handled the language quite well. Muus declared that he was not hostile to American institutions because he refused to praise them. He denied calling United States history itself a "romance"; his criticism had been directed at some of the textbooks.

The aim of his article, wrote Muus, had been to show that since there is no religion in the common school, one cannot expect to find Christian teaching there. The superintendent had said that the common schools "inculcate no religious or sectarian dogmas" but that "all the christian graces" may be taught. Muus admitted that he was unable "to catch the beauty of this argumentation," probably because he was "a foreign priest and aristocrat." He could not work up any enthusiasm for a Christianity in which there is no religion and a religion in which there is no Christianity.

For all that, Muus wished the common school all success. It could not teach the saving doctrines of Christianity, but it gave the children some education for this world. Christians, however, ought to have schools where the Word of God is taught as well as things useful to this world. To Wilson's hint that foreigners return to the Old World if they do not like American institutions, Muus replied that it was his understanding that foreigners are welcome to the United States where they are free to serve their God and work for themselves and the commonwealth. It would do little good if every foreigner would shed all peculiarities and copy the Americans in religion, ideas, and appearance. Enlarging this thought, Muus added: "In my opinion it is a benefit to this country that so many people of different nationalities are meeting. Their differences, and the new surroundings in which they live, stimulate their intellect, arouse their energy, and so benefit the community."[35]

In the same issue of the *Republican*, the editor sided with Wilson and accused Muus of denying his hostility to American institutions while opposing them at the same time. Muus continued the exchange by writing "Sectarianism the True Christianity," published in the *Republican* July 7, 1870. In his uncompromising way, he laid it down that any morality will be Christian or non-

Christian. "If it is by law prohibited to the school to teach Christianity, then the law compels the common school to resort to the heathen principle for man's work—namely, self-love." It must be one or the other.[36]

While arguing about the teaching of morals, Muus and his opponents clashed repeatedly over the terms "sectarian" and "sectarian influences." To Wilson and the *Republican*, it was a point of pride that the public schools could teach the "principles of Christianity" and at the same time avoid "religious, sectarian dogmas." For them and many others, "sectarian" was a bad word. For Muus, on the other hand, "sectarian" was a valid term; it denoted standing in a specific theological tradition and holding to clearly defined Christian teachings. "When 'all sectarian influences are carefully avoided,'" he had written, "I should like to know what is left of Christianity."[37]

The editor of the Goodhue county newspaper interpreted Muus's intransigence as "bigoted egotism," assuming that Muus thought his own church to be the only valid expression of Christianity. Certainly Muus was totally loyal to the Lutheran confession, but his aim was not the triumph of Lutheranism over all other groups. Rather, it was to distinguish clearly between sundry religious and moral ideas borrowed from Christianity on the one hand, and genuine, confessional Christianity on the other.

Muus employed a style of argument that was relentlessly logical, but also heavily didactic. Unfortunately, at times he could be "querulous and petty," as he attacked the common schools.[38] In drawing his stark contrasts, Muus infuriated his opponents by using such terms as "heathen" and "pagan." He can also be faulted for refusing to recognize that there could indeed be value in such Christian influences as were present in the common schools. Nor did he help his cause by attacking the public schools while admitting that he had little actual knowledge of them.

Throughout the dispute, Muus looked squarely at the fact that the common schools were state institutions and the Constitution forbade the teaching of religion. That being the case, he remained

227

convinced that the common school worked against the kingdom of God. The only kind of school he could endorse fully was one where the Word of God was central and uppermost.

The decade of the 1870s witnessed the last flurries between advocates and critics of the common school. But much was yet to be spoken and written on the topic. Halle Steensland defended the common school in an address to the Scandinavian Lutheran Educational Society in 1870. When Svein Nilsson succeeded Knud Langeland as editor of *Skandinaven* in 1872, the newspaper continued to support the American common school. In actual practice, children of Norwegian immigrants were patronizing the common schools in growing numbers and the aim of establishing parochial schools to supplant them was proving costly.[39]

At the meeting of the Norwegian Synod in 1873, President H. A. Preus set forth close to a hundred theses on the school issue. The lack of religion in the common schools ruled them out for Christians, but problems were being reported with parochial schools. For example, it was hard to find good teachers and pay them adequately. Pupils chose the common schools if they met at the same time as the religious schools. Nevertheless, Preus was undaunted in his zeal for organizing congregational schools, influencing selection of teachers in common schools, training teachers at Luther College, locating Lutheran academies at centers of Norwegian immigrant population, placing Lutheran teachers of Norwegian in American colleges and universities, and encouraging young people to enter the teaching profession. The Synod urged that Preus's proposals be studied.[40]

Pastor Muus made a third public stand on the school question in 1874 when the Norwegian Synod held its annual meeting at Holden church. There Muus presented several propositions on the common school, charging that it failed in the task of caring for the children's temporal and eternal welfare since it did not instruct them in the Word of God. In place of the Word it set forth useless resources that drew the children away from the only way of salvation. Under certain circumstances, he conceded, it would not be a sin to use the common school, but it was the duty of Christian parents to make every effort to provide Christian schools for their children.[41]

In the discussion of Muus's theses, some thought that it was not every school's task to be concerned about the children's eternal welfare, although it was agreed that every school is bound to influence the development of children, to imprint a certain character upon them. The main issue is what view of life, what principles are impressed upon the children. Is it this life and this world that are the goal, or is it principally the heavenly, spiritual, and eternal benefits? A school should be a helper to the parents in the upbringing of children. It is the parents' duty to see that children are brought up in the discipline and instruction of the Lord.

Differences of opinion arose on the parents' role over against the state. Muus and his supporters held that if the state should compel parents to send their children to schools that caused harm to the children's spiritual welfare, the parents should refuse to obey. Others pointed out that parents were under the law and must yield to the state unless they were required to act against the Word of God and conscience. In that case, they would have to take the consequences.[42]

Only three of Muus's theses were discussed by the Synod and no action was taken on them. In general, the assembly opposed the common school, but it became evident that some were not as alarmed by its reputed dangers as Muus was. It was said of Laur. Larsen, also an advocate of parochial schools, that he "could discover no peril in the subjects taught in the common school." And on the idea of parents disobeying the state, Muus and Preus did not persuade Schmidt and Koren, who pointed out the dilemma of choosing the laws one decides to accept.[43]

The school controversy was largely a phenomenon within the Norwegian Synod where the common school was criticized and parochial schools commended. The usually conservative Haugeans wanted their children educated in both English and Norwegian,

229

but not to the neglect of the district school. An acceptance of the common school also prevailed in another Norwegian Lutheran group. The Conference had among its leaders those who did not hesitate to recommend full use of the common school. In 1874, Professor Sven Oftedal of Augsburg Seminary wrote in *Skandinaven*: "I can only urge in the most serious terms that all Norwegian children be sent faithfully to the public school.[44] In 1878 Oftedal became a member of the Minneapolis Board of Education.

Georg Sverdrup, Oftedal's colleague at Augsburg, wrote an essay on the common school that employed the writings of Martin Luther to show the validity of keeping civil and religious institutions separate. Sverdrup was untroubled that the common school was called "religionless," but he deplored the fact that the designation had been used "to make the school into a scarecrow for unsuspecting people and to keep Norwegians away from it." Sverdrup praised the American principles that made the common school free of religious instruction, available for everyone without distinction of rank, and under the control and supervision of the people. Luther's teaching that all callings, secular as well as clerical, could be pursued with the blessing of God had a corollary in the American separation of church and state. The civic realm had its own legitimate existence. Civic instruction did not have to be placed under clerical or church control to be valid.[45]

Where Muus was convinced that the common school opposed the kingdom of God, Sverdrup described it as "the school for the rising generation of citizens in a self-governing people." It should be called a civic school, he wrote, not a pagan school. Let the parents send their children there with good conscience to receive civic instruction. Let the congregation assume its rightful responsibility for religious instruction "and let the state school continue to be without religious instruction as before." Sverdrup concluded "that it is neither necessary nor beneficial in our circumstances to have religious and civic instruction in the same school."[46]

Before the controversy died out at the end of the 1870s, the lively polemics continued in the Norwegian press. Rasmus B.

Anderson, the champion of Norwegian culture and language, also defended the common school as the cornerstone of the Constitution. He had no time for the parochial school enterprise, regarding the parish schools in the Norwegian settlements as "pitiful." In contributions to *Skandinaven* in 1876 and 1877 he attacked Muus and other Synod leaders for their inconsistency in promising to support the common schools while at the same time disparaging them. At about the same time Anderson placed these bellicose words on his letterhead: "Whoever directly or indirectly opposes the American common school is an enemy of education, of liberty, of progress. Opposition to the American common school is treason to our country."[47]

It could only have been a relief to many Norwegian Americans when the long-running debate became the target of satirical humor in *Skandinaven* in 1877. A series of letters in the Valdres dialect reported the disturbing influence of "*Skandinaven*, Professor Anderson, and the Yankee School." To meet the peril posed by these forces, a Valdres convention was held in Decorah. It denounced *Skandinaven* and of course unequivocally condemned the common school because "it puts ideas into the mind of the common man." The following resolution was passed unanimously by the Valdres meeting: "That we establish our own schools to prevent our children from learning anything in the common school."[48]

Three results of the controversy may be identified. First, despite all the attacks on the common school, Norwegian parents in fact sent their children to these public institutions. In one sense, history passed by the determined opponents of the common schools. Wrote Theodore Blegen, "The average Norwegian immigrant quietly accepted the public schools through all the years that the Synod ministers denounced them as 'heathen.'" Similarly, Frank Nelsen offered this conclusion: "By 1880, the majority of the Norwegians in America had made their decision. Not only was America to be the land of their choice, but its schools were to be their schools."[49]

231

Second, the Norwegian Synod did not succeed in establishing a comprehensive parochial school system on the scale of the German Lutherans in the Missouri Synod. The chief reason the immigrants rejected the idea of supplanting common schools with congregational schools, noted Blegen, "was a belief in the soundness of the democratic idea of primary education available, at public cost, to all." Nevertheless, religious schools meeting in the summer months became numerous and widespread and served as an important educational tool in Norwegian-American communities for generations. A report issued in 1909 showed that 1,715 out of 3,001 congregations had been conducting parochial schools.[50]

Third, even during the common school controversy, the idea of establishing high schools or academies was gaining ground. For Muus, it was more a matter of serving a different age group than a change of mind regarding educational goals. Like the parochial schools that were to supplant the common schools, the academies would center their program around the Bible and Christian teaching. The establishment of the Holden academy in 1869 was to be followed by a fresh effort in Northfield in 1874 when St. Olaf's School came into being as the result of Muus's vision and initiative.

## Ten

# The Founding of St. Olaf's School

With B. J. Muus as the leading spirit, St. Olaf's School was founded on November 6, 1874, when the Articles of Incorporation were signed in Northfield. Earlier that year, at the annual meeting of the Norwegian Synod held at Holden church June 12–21, Muus had taken two initiatives regarding education. First he presented his theses regarding the common school, and second he set in motion a proposal for the establishment of an academy in Northfield.

The interest in having church-sponsored academies was not a sudden turn in the Synod's educational thinking. It was quite in harmony with the promotion of parochial schools and the polemics against the common schools in which Muus had been involved. The continuity between the school issue and the drive for academies was evident in 1869. Synod leaders, meeting in Madison in March of that year immediately after the founding of the Scandinavian Lutheran Educational Society, took up the question, "How can we, in the best way, further a true folk-enlightenment among our countrymen?"[1]

Their first challenge was to improve the instruction of children, including establishing their own congregational schools where possible and finding capable teachers for them. Next, there was a growing need for high schools for young people not planning to become pastors or schoolteachers. The main purpose of the education available at "the Decorah school," that is, Luther College, was to prepare young people for direct service in the church. While many not dedicated to that end had also received a good education at Decorah, more should be done to achieve widespread popular enlightenment among the younger generation. Therefore smaller high schools or academies should be established near such larger and older settlements as Koshkonong in Wisconsin or Goodhue county in Minnesota.

These could start on a small scale and expand as interest grew. In view of the important calling women had as sisters, but especially as wives and mothers, one should give thought to providing opportunity for girls to receive more education than was generally their lot. But according to the report, this was not the time to decide whether the girls could be instructed at the same school as the boys. The proposed schools ought to have three teachers, and in addition to more solid instruction in religion and in the subjects taught in the district schools, should provide courses in Norwegian, English, science, history, and so on. "The spiritual uplift such schools would give our people is well-nigh incalculable. The parents would find that the money paid out for their children's, boys' and girls', education would be extremely well spent."[2]

The same idea, that of placing Lutheran academies in Norwegian centers, was part of the educational program H. A. Preus had set forth among his numerous theses at the Synod's 1873 annual meeting.[3] The next year Muus presented his educational theses before the Synod's gathering at Holden. The Synod assembly discussed a few of the theses but took no action on them. At the same meeting, Muus induced his Northfield friend Harald Thorson to make an offer of money and property for the establishment of a high school in Northfield.

The academy Muus had begun in his parsonage at Holden was perceived as "a high school in which the youth of the congrega-

234

*Pastor N. A. Quammen*
From Edna Hong, *Book of a Century*

tions could acquire a better education than could be obtained in our parochial and common schools."[4] Launched in 1869, the Holden academy lasted only a few years. Muus advertised it in the Synod's paper and kept it going by using his own money to hire teachers, but the time was not right, broader support did not materialize, and the rural location was not favorable. Yet Muus remained determined to establish an academy.

"Precisely now was the time to act, when the Synod was gathered [at Holden in 1874] and could give the enterprise a powerful shove forward." So stated the first Board of Trustees minutes for St. Olaf's School in reviewing the initial steps taken to establish

235

the Northfield institution.[5] At the annual meeting in Holden that June, educational aspirations were in the air.

The Synod accepted an offer from the congregation in Red Wing for property on which to build a normal school to train teachers for the congregational schools. Perhaps it would also approve an academy. Muus conferred privately with the Reverend N. A. Quammen, pastor of Christiania Church north of Northfield who also served the Norwegian Lutheran church in Northfield, and Harald Thorson, merchant and owner of a hardware store in Northfield. After they had spoken of the incalculable blessing such a school would be for the Norwegian people and especially for the surrounding area in which it would be located, Muus said to Thorson: "Why don't you come with an offer to get a school established in Northfield?" Thorson replied that he could certainly do so. Both he and Quammen felt confident that Northfield would do well by the cause.[6]

The next day Harald Thorson made the Synod an offer of five acres of land worth $1,500 and $500 in cash if an academy would be established in Northfield. Thorson believed that considerably more money could be raised to buy land and buildings and take care of teachers' salaries. The Synod would appoint teachers and supervise the school. The Synod's response was pious but penurious. On a motion by J. A. Ottesen, it thanked Thorson for his generous offer and "with joy and thanksgiving to God" expressed the wish that such an academy might be founded in Northfield.[7] Nothing was promised regarding financial support.

Northfield was a suitable choice because it had a railroad connection, but the same was true of Red Wing. Moreover, both towns had Norwegian Lutheran congregations founded with Pastor Muus's direct involvement, and Red Wing probably had a larger population of Norwegians. According to Anna E. Mohn, wife of the first principal of St. Olaf's School, Northfield seems to have been Muus's first choice.[8] In the summer of 1874, Red Wing was already the prospective site of a normal school, so another town could be considered for an academy. Very likely Muus's

*Harald Thorson*
Norwegian-American Historical Association Archives

friendship with Quammen and Thorson through the Northfield congregation influenced his decision.

Having the Synod's general approval of an academy was of some encouragement, but since the church body had provided no material assistance, Muus shifted his hopes to church people in the area. He and Thorson met with a group of pastors and lay people in the Northfield vicinity, but received encouragement only from Quammen. At this point Muus realized that it was up to him, backed by Thorson and Quammen, to take the necessary

237

*Division Street, Northfield, ca. 1874*
Courtesy Northfield Historical Society

steps to establish the projected academy and to assume responsibility for its success or failure.[9]

The tide was turned when the people of Northfield responded with enthusiasm to the news that the Norwegian Lutherans were thinking about placing a school in Northfield. In his capacity as secretary of the Board of Trustees, Thorson recorded the favorable attitude on the part of the citizens, noting in the minutes that they "considered the worldly profit the city would receive from such a school."[10] As a merchant himself, Thorson would not be indifferent to that benefit. In a remarkable display of interest and good will, Northfield people gathered in Lockwood's Hall on October 1, 1874, to hear about the school. The assembly elected A. O. Whipple chairman and Harald Thorson secretary. Whipple called on Muus and Quammen to state their plans, and a number of Northfield residents spoke, "all expressing their interest in having the institution located here." One of them was C. A. Wheaton, editor of the *Rice County Journal*, in which a report of the meeting was published. A committee consisting of Thorson, G. M. Phillips, and A. O. Whipple was appointed "to see what material aid the people of Northfield will afford," and a second meeting was announced for October 15. Editor Wheaton shared his own enthusiasm with his readers: "This is an important enterprise to our town, and should and we trust will, receive liberal encouragment. H. Thoresen will set a noble example as he proposes to give to this object in the outset two thousand Dollars!"[11]

Important as the Northfield academy was for Muus, it was not the only educational project on his mind. In a letter to his friend and colleague Laur. Larsen, president of Luther College, written on October 9, 1874, right between the two important meetings in Northfield, Muus touched on four separate and quite different schools. One was Luther College itself, for which Muus raised money and recruited students year after year. The second was the academy at Holden, which he referred to as a "preparatory institution for Decorah" with four pupils at present.

The third he called "Northfield Academy," with the news that it would begin in January with Th. N. Mohn as teacher, and that a meeting would be held in Northfield on October 15th "to see about making it permanent." The fourth educational effort was a hoped-for teachers' seminary, or normal school, in Red Wing. Congregations in Red Wing and Hoff had raised $6,000 for the seminary and Muus himself had sent in that year about $2,500.[12] Thus Muus and the Synod were dealing with education on more than one front in the fall of 1874. It is worth noting that all of these had to do with education on the secondary level and above.

In Northfield, the announced meeting was held October 15, 1874, in Wheaton's Hall. In publishing his account of the second meeting, the editor referred to the group as "the friends of the new project for establishing a Norwegian College." The committee reported that $5,400 had been raised and gave its view that the

239

figure could easily reach $6,000 or more. The editor's account had the same tone of friendly rapport between "our Norwegian friends" and "our own people." After Muus and Quammen had spoken, several townspeople added encouraging words about the school project and the advantages of this locality. J. T. Ames then offered the following resolution: "That we extend to our Norwegian brethren a cordial invitation to locate their College at Northfield and that we pledge to them our hearty sympathy and support."[13]

The resolution was "unanimously and heartily adopted." Mr. H. Scriver drew a round of applause when he foresaw good support for the new school based on his earlier experiences with the beginnings of Carleton College. "It was an excellent meeting in every respect," wrote Wheaton. Before it adjourned, those present learned that "our Norwegian brethren" had made an offer to the Board of Education to buy lots 4, 5, 6, and 7 in Block 24 and the two buildings on them soon to be vacated by the public schools. "They want this property for present use till they get more elaborate structures on larger grounds," explained Wheaton.[14]

The location of the property in question was close to downtown Northfield, on the southwest corner of Union and Third Streets, now the site of the First United Church of Christ (Congregational) of Northfield. The larger of the two former public school buildings was two stories in height, with four large classrooms and two smaller rooms. The smaller of the two buildings had one rather large classroom. "Both buildings had once been white," wrote I. F. Grose, a student at the School, "but now presented a dingy, grayish look."[15]

The success of the October meetings, the money raised and pledged, and the hearty interest of Northfield townspeople gave Muus confidence to take the next steps in making the school a reality. The Board purchased the five acres with the buildings from the Northfield School Board for $2,500. Next Muus was eager to form an organization and get the school functioning as soon as possible.

240

*Thorbjørn Nelson Mohn*
St. Olaf College Archives

On the advice of Northfield lawyer O. F. Perkins, Muus formed a close corporation. The signing of the Articles of Incorporation took place on November 6, 1874, making that date the official beginning of St. Olaf's School, celebrated yearly as Foundation Day or Founders' Day. Members of the first Board of Trustees signed the document. They were B. J. Muus, president, Harald Thorson, secretary, K. P. Haugen, O. Osmundson, and O. K. Finseth. Because Muus was president of the Board of Trustees, he has sometimes been regarded, understandably but mistakenly, as the first president of the institution.[16] That honor and title belonged to the Reverend Thorbjørn Nelson Mohn, a pastor in St. Paul, Minnesota, whom Muus had secured earlier in the fall to head the new school.

241

As a boy of about nine years, Mohn had come from Norway with his parents in 1853, settling first in Wisconsin, then moving to a farm in Dodge county, Minnesota. After graduating from Luther College in 1870 and Concordia Seminary in 1873, Mohn had served a congregation in Chicago before moving to St. Paul. He arrived in Northfield to take up his work in December. His official title was "Principal," changed to "President" in 1889 when St. Olaf's School became St. Olaf College. In actual practice, however, he was usually known and referred to as Professor Mohn.

The name of the School chosen by Muus honored King Olav Haraldsson, the patron saint of Norway. King Olav died in battle July 29, 1030, at Stiklestad, a site not far from Snåsa, Norway, where Bernt Julius Muus was born. The great Nidaros cathedral at Trondheim was built over the place where King Olav had been buried. Olav became a Christian and was baptized during a Viking expedition. The battle of Stiklestad in which he lost his life has been interpreted as part of the struggle to bring Christianity to the Norwegian people. Muus also adopted as the motto of the school the battle cry sounded, as legend would have it, at Stiklestad, "Fram, Fram, Kristmenn, Krossmenn, Kongsmenn." The seal of the institution, bearing Olav's coat of arms, would carry the modified form "Fram, Fram, Cristmenn, Crossmenn," meaning "Forward, Forward, Men of Christ, Men of the Cross."

The first paragraphs of the Articles of Incorporation, quoted below, give the name and location of the School, its educational and religious purpose, and the intention to turn it over to the Norwegian Evangelical Lutheran Church in America, that is, the Norwegian Synod, which "with joy and thanksgiving" had expressed its wish that such an academy be founded. "This certifies that we the undersigned have associated ourselves together for the purpose of establishing an institution of learning in the village of Northfield, Rice County, Minnesota, under the name and style of 'St. Olaf's School' in its corporate capacity.

"The general purpose of the corporation is for the advancement in education of pupils, from fifteen years of age and upwards, as

242

a college: to preserve the pupils in the true Christian faith, as taught by the Evangelical Lutheran Church and nothing taught in contravention with the Symbolum Apostolicum, Nicenum & Athanasianum; the Unaltered Confession delivered to the Emperor Charles the Fifth at Augsburg in Germany in the year of our Lord 1530 and the small Catechism of Luther.

"Our purpose is to give this school in the charge of the Synod for the Norwegian Evangelical Lutheran Church of America or that part thereof that is in the State of Minnesota. If said Synod or said part of it shall accept the school, it shall have the power to elect Directors or Board of Trustees for the school and conduct the same in the way they may deem it most expedient for the school provided that the true Evangelical Lutheran creed above named shall be faithfully taught therein."[17]

The Articles are consonant with the views of Muus as administrator, educator, and churchman. He knew the importance of proper legal language, often assisting his parishioners with their legal problems. Here he had an opportunity to shape a school that placed learning in close relationship to Christian faith. And as a loyal Norwegian Synod pastor he made sure that the Articles of Incorporation stated the Board's desire to place the school under the wing of his church body, the Norwegian Synod.

The statement of purpose in the Articles pinpoints two key elements: first, "advancement in education of pupils, from fifteen years of age and upwards," and second, "to preserve the pupils in the true Christian faith." Implied in the first element, and stated elsewhere, is that the education is to be useful for all walks of life, not just the ministry and teaching. Muus described it as "an education for the practical affairs of life."[18] The age of the pupils indicates a "higher" education beyond the common and parochial schools. As to the second element, to "preserve" the young people in the Christian faith suggests a nurturing rather than a converting function.

The three paragraphs cited say nothing about co-education, yet the pamphlet containing the addresses given at the dedication,

January 8, 1875, includes the explicit statement: "The School's purpose is 1) to give the Christian confirmed youth of both sexes a higher education for the practical life than the schools at home are capable of giving; 2) to exercise care for the pupils' moral conduct." In a report to the Synod, Muus wrote that the school was for "confirmed young people of both sexes."[19] Establishing a co-educational school was unprecedented among Norwegian Lutherans of that time.

The name "St. Olaf's School" was appropriate for an institution recognized at its inception as an academy or high school, but the Articles also speak of the education of pupils "as a college." Two interpretations of the word "college" in the Articles are possible: the school began as an academy but one day would become a college, or St. Olaf's School was planned as a high school or academy, and nothing more. The former is the more familiar view in St. Olaf historiography. It assumes that the founders intended that one day the institution would be a four-year college, offering courses leading to the bachelor's degree. But realizing that it would take time to attain that goal, they modestly chose to begin with the name "School."[20] And indeed, the time arrived when the school did in fact become a college in the usual sense of that term.

A less familiar way of understanding the term in the Articles of Incorporation is to take "college" as simply a synonym for academy or high school, at the same time signifying, according to an older use of the word, a residential school. Support for this point of view comes from Carl A. Mellby, a highly respected professor of history who had personal ties to Muus and the other early builders of St. Olaf. He discussed their ideals in his book, *Saint Olaf College through Fifty Years 1874–1924*, where he also sketched the educational needs of Norwegian Lutheran youth who were not aspiring to the ministry, and the limited opportunities available to them. Many were of an age that going to public school with children did not meet their needs. Only the larger cities had high schools, and of course they did not offer religious instruction. Wrote Mellby: "It was to meet a situation such as this, that St. Olaf's school was planned. It was not primarily to prepare for a college course or one of the learned professions nor was there at the time any intention of eventually expanding it into a college. It was rather to be a popular grammar and high school, with courses and methods devised to meet immediate and practical needs."[21]

It is known that "at the time" Muus himself always insisted on the term, "St. Olaf's School." Th. Eggen, another well-informed churchman who had personal memories of Muus, wrote that St. Olaf was originally meant to be only an academy that would satisfy a need in the closest Norwegian settlements and serve as a "feeder" for Luther College. Later developments in the church led to the school being expanded into a college.[22]

Additional evidence would be required to overthrow the first view, held by most, that the founders looked to the day when the academy would become a college in the modern sense of the word. Nevertheless, there is strength in the views of Mellby and Eggen. The talk in the Synod prior to 1874 had been about the desirability of establishing "academies." The Synod already had a degree-granting institution, Luther College. Moreover, when St. Olaf, more than a decade later, actually became a college, it seemed to come about because of unforeseen developments, as Eggen suggests, not through the orderly unfolding of an original plan. Thus the case for the "academy" view merits consideration.

The second paragraph of the Articles of Incorporation reveals Muus's vision of a school totally within the orbit of Lutheran teaching and influence. In his role as critic of the common schools Muus had contended more than once, to the exasperation of his opponents, that it was nonsense to claim allegiance to "Christian principles" and at the same time to disavow any "sectarian" influence. For him Christianity could only be apprehended in terms of specific teachings about God, humans, sin, and salvation, and such teachings were to be found in the creeds of the church. And since he was baptized, confirmed, and ordained as a pastor in the Norwegian Lutheran Church, he was committed to its creedal statements.

245

The third paragraph, viewed in retrospect, sheds unexpected light on the early history of the Northfield institution. At the outset, the founders sought support from the Norwegian Synod, without success. And they continued to hope that the Synod would adopt the school. The reality, however, was that St. Olaf, first as academy and later as college, was constrained to struggle through most of its first quarter–century as an independent institution, not really a church-related school. It was not until 1899, after painful church turmoils, that St. Olaf College could be defined in the full sense as a college of the church.

But it was "St. Olaf's School" that Muus advertised in the December 10, 1874, issue of *Fædrelandet og Emigranten*. The announcement offers the following information: "St. Olaf's School, an evangelical Lutheran high school in Northfield, Minnesota. Purpose: 1) To give confirmed youth a higher education for practical life than the local schools can do; 2) To direct the moral conduct of the students. Subjects taught in the lowest class: Religion, English, Norwegian, History, Geography, Penmanship, Singing. Tuition for half a year (from January 8, 1875, to July 1) $15.00; room in the school building, $10.00; board, whatever it will cost. Pupils furnish their own bed-clothes, towels, light, and laundry. Write to T. Mohn, in care of H. Thorson, Northfield, Minnesota.

B. J. Muus, President Board of Trustees"[23]

St. Olaf's School was dedicated to the Triune God on January 8, 1875, with Pastor Muus presiding and giving the dedicatory address in Norwegian. In the afternoon, Professor Mohn presented an address in English. At the evening session H. G. Stub preached a sermon on 1 Corinthians 3:11, "For no other foundation can any one lay than that which is laid, which is Jesus Christ." N. A. Quammen closed the meeting with a prayer for the school, the teachers, and the students.

The dedicatory address by Muus was the main feature of the day. He began, "Dear brothers and sisters in the faith," and

246

greeted his listeners with the ancient biblical words, "God's Peace!" Considering the future of the school he said, "Generation succeeding generation will perhaps receive their education in this school that today begins its work in a very humble manner. Here perhaps will be planted many a seed that later will bear rich fruit." He chose to say "perhaps" because the beginning was modest. Everything would depend on God's blessing and the support of countrymen and fellow believers. As Muus set out to make clear the significance of such an educational institution, he deplored the fact that his abilities were small for doing justice to the task and that he had lacked sufficient time to prepare a suitable address. Citing the commandments to love one's neighbor and to serve others, he stressed how children need to be served, and instructed, giving examples from family life. There is a social dimension to all learning. Just as the church is a body whose members help and support one another, so in a sense humanity is also a body that shares discoveries and experiences from one generation to the next. A person is not limited to one's own experience. "The more one can appropriate of the whole human race's experience, the more fitted one becomes to carry out one's work."

Similarly, the individual Christian gets help from others in searching the Holy Scriptures. What the church has experienced helps the Christian to understand what is revealed in Scripture, be made aware of perplexities, avoid errors, and penetrate into the deeper truths. Taking what some would regard as an elitist view, Muus employed the analogy of the "frame" of a building to demonstrate that a higher education is for the future leaders. Those special people who possess the Spirit's power constitute the frame of the house. So it is in church, state, natural science, literature, and all other fields. In democratic America as well it is not the great masses nor the great worldly powers that decide how things will go. "It is the individual prominent spirits who give the age its direction." Likewise in small circles, in the settlement, in the congregation, some few persons give the surroundings their character and direction.

Common instruction should be taken as far as possible, but Muus here stresses the need for institutions that offer instruction on a higher level for those who can use the gifts that the great masses cannot appropriate. Yet the development of special talents is for the sake of society, the "house" that needs such a frame in order to be held together.

This is nothing new, some will say. People have realized this before and have established higher schools. Why not use them? "Why should we be assembled here in this much-used old schoolhouse instead of in the new palaces around us?" asked Muus. The answer was his ardent commitment to education based on Christ, the firm foundation, "the only cornerstone which can support a house, the only one which can assure blessings for time and eternity." The world is a decaying mass, he said, that needs the salt of God's revealed word to save it from corruption.[24] Great gifts and abilities may be misused, in the state and in the church. On the other hand, a few gifted persons who fear God and love their neighbor, indeed, even one such person, may preserve a nation from corruption. This school is established to make our children instruments in God's hands, through the power of God's Word, to give God honor and to further the temporal and eternal welfare of their fellow human beings.

Muus then spoke directly to Principal Mohn, admonishing him to lead the students "to a true fear of God and to thorough knowledge." He urged the students to be diligent in appropriating the gifts offered by the teachers. "Let it be your great goal as far as possible to make yourselves capable of serving God and your fellowmen in that position where God might place you!" Coming to the end of his address, Muus dedicated the school in these words:

"Hereby let St. Olaf's School be dedicated to the service of the Triune God! May He give it thriving and growth. May He be its shield and defense, may He let it be a blessing to us and the coming generations! May He also bless our coming in and going out! Amen in Jesus' Name."[25]

The fact that Principal Mohn used English in his speech was a clear signal that English would be the language of St. Olaf's School, even though much use of Norwegian was inevitable for many years. In a report to the Synod Muus wrote, "Naturally we have tried to underscore the importance of the English language and to use it in the instruction. As the language of our country, it is of the greatest practical use to the student."[26] Principal Mohn, twelve years younger than Muus but also born in Norway, had an affinity for things American to a greater degree than was the case with Muus. He arrived in America at the age of nine and had his formal education in this country. William Benson wrote of St. Olaf's young principal: "Mohn proved to be intensely American in thought and purpose from the beginning. Though Norse in understanding, spirit, and temper, he was predominantly the product of his American environment." Before entering college Mohn had taught in the common schools near his home.[27]

Addressing the group assembled on dedication day, Mohn spoke of education and religion in terms of their benefits to the whole of society and the nation. Christian faith enables one to overcome egotism as a motive for action. "This religion the Norwegians ought to retain in their hearts," he said, "cherish in their schools, and bring, with their other treasures, to the common altar of our adopted nation."[28]

Classes at the newly founded school began on January 9, 1875. At first, Mohn was the sole teacher but soon Lars S. Reque, a graduate of Luther College, joined him. Miss Ella Fiske, preceptress for the girls and music teacher, also joined the faculty that first term. Thirty-six students were enrolled at the start of the term. That number grew to a total of 50, 13 girls and 37 boys. English, geography, mathematics, penmanship, and music were taught in English. Religion, history, and Norwegian were taught in Norwegian. New courses added the second year were Latin, German, United States history, and algebra.[29]

St. Olaf's School moved to a site west of Northfield, later called Manitou Heights, in the fall of 1878. Through the initiative of

*Students at St. Olaf's School, 1875*
St. Olaf College Archives

Harald Thorson, twenty acres of land on the wooded hill had
been purchased in 1876, but there was a serious shortage of funds
that fall. There had been a financial panic in 1873 followed by a
few years of grasshopper plagues. The number of Board members had been increased to fifteen, among them N. A. Quammen.
He had already raised respectable sums among his congregations, but thought that he might be able to collect another $2,500
in subscriptions. Muus had been actively soliciting money in
Goodhue county and Mohn had visited several congregations.

Nevertheless, the prospects for bringing in sufficient money
were not bright. Within the Board there was serious talk about
closing the school in the fall of 1876. But Muus, with support from
Thorson, Mohn, and Quammen, moved that they proceed with
the building. With additional affirmative votes from Haugen,
Finseth, Osmundson, and Westermoe, the motion passed, the opponents abstaining. The courageous decision to continue was

250

confirmed, fortunately, by an excellent yield of wheat in Goodhue county in 1877, the year construction was underway. Supporters from that area contributed the largest amount toward the new building.[30]

The cornerstone of the Main building, later known as Old Main, was laid on July 4, 1877, with Muus and H. A. Preus, president of the Norwegian Synod, as the leading participants. It was a festive occasion with a thousand people attending, many of them coming by train from the annual meeting of the church. President Preus gave the main address, based on Psalm 111:10, "The fear of the Lord is the beginning of wisdom." Muus had written a formal document in Latin, "In Nomine Jesu," which he read, translated into Norwegian for the listeners, and placed in the metal canister that went into the cornerstone. The first paragraph states that the cornerstone was laid by Herman Amberg Preus, president of the Synod of the Norwegian Evangelical Lutheran Church in America, on July 4, 1877. The second paragraph records the founding of the school and its purpose, as follows: "St. Olaf's School was founded on the 6th of Nov., 1874, in order to offer the Norwegian Evangelical Lutheran youth of both sexes, who may desire a more advanced education than that offered in the home schools, a better opportunity to educate themselves for life here and for life to come."[31]

The third and fourth paragraphs express the founders' prayer that teachers and students will be guided by the Holy Scriptures in doctrine and life, and that their successors will preserve the glorious treasure of the symbolical books of the Lutheran Church. The last part of the document names the officers of the school, the teachers, and members of the Board of Trustees. It closes with the words: "May the triune God, in whose name this cornerstone is laid, be the firm foundation of this school to all eternity! Amen."[32]

After Muus had read and translated this document, the crowd moved to the building site for the laying of the cornerstone, on which had been carved a Celtic cross and the date 1877. Members of the Board of Trustees put the cornerstone in place and Preus tapped it three times with a hammer, "invoking God's blessings on the building and on the work for which it was being erected."[33] During the first years of St. Olaf's School's existence Muus made many trips by horse and buggy to Northfield from his rural Holden parish. As founder of the school, president of the Board of Trustees, and chief fund-raiser, he was the central figure in each successive ceremonial occasion as well as at meetings of the Board. Also to be noted is the presence of Synod President Preus at the cornerstone laying and the dedication of the Main. For the latter occasion President James Strong of Carleton College and President Laur. Larsen of Luther College were also present.[34]

The day chosen for the dedication of the first building to occupy the permanent campus was November 6, 1878, the fourth anniversary of the founding. The service began with the reading of the sixth chapter of Deuteronomy and the offering of a prayer by Preus. This particular biblical text was read regularly by Muus at Board meetings and often cited by him in his addresses, including the one given on this important occasion. The chapter emphasizes the duty of the present generation to heed the words of the Lord and teach them to its children and grandchildren. In his address Muus read parts of Deuteronomy 6 and drew the parallel between the deliverance of Israel under Moses from thralldom in Egypt and the church being delivered by God's Son from the devil's bondage. Applicable to the school was the motif of telling the coming generations of God's power to deliver. To quote Muus directly: "This school is established and this house is built for one thing only, to help us fulfill the blessed duty that the Lord has laid upon us, to show our children and grandchildren the Lord's mighty arm, which delivers from Satan's thralldom, which leads his people securely through this evil world's roaring sea, and which forces 'the last enemy' to become a servant to lead them into the promised land."[35]

The children of God have always been in the forefront in building civilization, declared Muus. Wherever the Gospel of Christ has penetrated, it has raised the level of culture. But while God's

252

children know the value of worldly art and knowledge, they do not make idols of them. In the spirit of Moses they consider the ignominy of Christ greater wealth than the treasures of Egypt. What is all-important is to love God with one's whole heart. Norwegians in America have worked hard, have been blessed by God, and want to educate their children. Christian youth with talents need further training if they are to fulfill their duty of making a contribution to the welfare of this country. There is no lack of higher schools, but either they ban the Word of God or mix the Christian religion with human fancies. Lacking God's Word, such schools impress only worldly concerns upon the pupils and make the love of self the motive for doing one's work.

Just as previously he had attacked the common schools, now, in his dedication address, Muus discussed the inadequacies of higher schools in this country. Christians could not make use of schools that claimed to be religionless but actually endorsed the values of this world. Neither could they send their children to schools that claimed to follow "Christian principles" but dissociated themselves from any "Christian sect." Also to be avoided were schools that were "Christian" to a degree but where Christianity was mixed with human lies and fabrications.

Fathers and mothers of young people in their most dangerous years, between fifteen and twenty, sending them out into a world filled with temptations, would be asking: who would look after them, lead them, raise them up when they fall, remind them of the commandments? Such reflections, said Muus, had led to the establishing of this school. It will offer such advantages as instruction in the English language, thoroughness, discipline, and so forth, but the one and only reason it was built, emphasized Muus, was "that we wanted to be obedient to God's word, and that in the fear of the Lord we love our children."

Before Muus reached the end of his speech, he was interrupted by a messenger who had ridden in from Holden to summon Muus to the deathbed of his son, Jens. Controlling his emotions, Muus managed to conclude, ending his address with a prayer of dedication: "So we present this building, which you have given us to build, to you, our God. Receive our offering and let it be a blessing for us and the coming generations!"[36] Before hurrying off to Holden, Muus also had a word with the principal. Taking Mohn aside, Muus charged him to look after the school. According to Mrs. Mohn, Muus said, "Now I have done what I can for the school; after this time all responsibility for its success must rest upon you."[37]

In succeeding years, Muus left Principal Mohn free to use his judgment in leading the school forward but remained in close touch with its progress. Muus continued to serve as president or chairman of the Board of Trustees until 1889 and helped the school in many ways, especially in gathering funds for its support among the generous farmers in Holden and neighboring parishes. The founder also came to the St. Olaf campus for special observances such as Founders' Day, and frequently was invited to give the main address on such occasions.

One has to be impressed that Muus founded St. Olaf's School as one task among many in his work as a busy rural pastor. He continued with his duties as pastor of Holden Lutheran Church and was in frequent touch with other congregations in Goodhue county and elsewhere that he had either founded or served in his earlier years in Minnesota. He was active in synodical meetings, pastoral conferences, and other church activities, most of which required extensive traveling. Soon he would be elected president of the Minnesota District of the Norwegian Synod, a position he held from 1876 to 1883.

The achievement of establishing "an evangelical Lutheran high school" in Northfield must also be measured against the lack of assured financial backing, the personal risks taken by Muus, Mohn, and the Board members, the difficulties of travel and communication, and the boldness of opening a school for both sexes that offered a general education. One must also appreciate the determination, energy, planning, and concentration of effort Muus had to summon on the repeated trips from Holden to Northfield

*The Main, St. Olaf College*
Courtesy Northfield Historical Society

to get the school launched and to see it through the difficult early years.

The building of the Main was a heartening sign that the small academy would survive and continue its mission. Within a decade after the dedication of the Main, St. Olaf's School and its leaders, Muus and Mohn, would be caught up in a bitter church dispute. One result was that the status of the School was changed from academy to college.

# Eleven

## Family Trials

When Pastor B. J. Muus reached the Holden parsonage after dedicating the Main at St. Olaf's School, his son, Jens Ingebrigt Rynning, was already dead, a victim of typhus. Jens was the third of the six children born to Bernt Julius and Oline Muus. The oldest was the only daughter, Birgitte Magdalena, named for Muus's mother and born November 24, 1860, a little over a year after the parents arrived in Minnesota from Norway. The second child was Nils, born January 7, 1863. Then came Jens, whose birthdate was January 12, 1866.

The other three boys were born in the decade of the 1870s. Paul Johan Elster was born March 22, 1872. Petter Herman arrived December 14, 1874, at the time preparations were underway in Northfield to open St. Olaf's School the following month. The youngest of the Muus children was Harald Steen, born July 2, 1878, four months before the dedication of the Main building at St. Olaf and the death of Jens.

As the children were born, Muus noted their arrival, sometimes with a touch of playful humor, in his correspondence with Laur. Larsen, president of Luther College. Also in letters to H. A. Preus, president of the Norwegian Synod, Muus conveyed occasional news about his family. After Nils was born, Muus wrote in an

257

offhand way to Preus: "If it is of any interest to you, I can report that my wife gave birth to a son. All is well." Larsen received a more colorful version, learning that the Muuses "had a big boy who eagerly makes music at both opportune and inopportune times. My wife is healthy and brisk and all is well." After Paul was born, his father passed along the comment: "Little Paul cries a little and demands much food. For the rest, all is well."[1]

The untimely death of Jens at age 12 was one of the trials the Muus family was to suffer as the years went by. Another was when Birgitte gave birth to a son out of wedlock in 1881.[2] The event heaped more distress on a family that was already the object of shocked public attention because of a lawsuit brought by Mrs. Muus against her husband.

The most serious of the family trials was the rift that developed between husband and wife, with painful repercussions for the whole family and for the Holden community. Mrs. Muus brought suit against her husband to recover the inheritance she had received from her father, and at the same time brought charges of cruelty and neglect. In time, the courts awarded her the full inheritance, but only after Oline sued for divorce and obtained a legal separation.

Pastor and Mrs. Muus spent their first Minnesota winter in the farm home of Knut P. Haugen, who later became one of the incorporators of St. Olaf's School and a member of the first Board of Trustees. By March of 1860 the first floor of the 18-by-26-foot parsonage was ready for occupancy. It was a log house, so poorly constructed that in the winter snow would blow through the cracks. Muus hired a reliable man to look after the twelve acres of farmland that belonged to the parsonage property. Counting all the land occupied by the church, the graveyard, and the parsonage, the Holden congregation owned a total of 100 acres.[3]

In 1867, by the time there were three children in the family, the parsonage was enlarged considerably and a basement put under the entire house. The additional space was to provide not only for

*Birgitte Muus Klüver*
St. Olaf College Archives

the growing family and servants, but also for meetings of the confirmation classes, a parochial school, and the academy that Pastor
Muus launched in 1869. The large house also accommodated
teachers hired for the academy or for the Muuses' own children.

Common backgrounds and similar responsibilities created
bonds of friendship among the Norwegian Synod pastors and
their wives. Cordial greetings flowed in letters from Pastor and
Mrs. Muus to the Laur. Larsen and H. A. Preus families and others. After a few years in which Muus addressed Larsen and Preus

259

with the formal "De" and "Dem," in about 1863 he began using the more familiar words for the personal pronoun "you," namely "du" and "deg," indicating close friendship.

Muus frequently used the expression, "We live well." But times of illness were also reported. Mrs. Muus had suffered repeated attacks of summer diarrhea in the fall of 1863, wrote Muus, but seemed to be improving. "Otherwise, we live as usual." The children had been sick for a time, he wrote in January of 1864, but had recovered.[4] A pensive note of isolation was sounded in Muus's letter to Larsen in December of 1864. "We live as usual, yet even more excluded from the world than usual since we seldom get any mail." He closed with a greeting for the season: "God give you and yours a happy Christmas."[5]

The family's health was good, according to letters from 1865 and 1866. "My family has been uncommonly healthy this winter," wrote Muus in the spring of 1865. "We are living as well as we can." When Muus was in Norway in 1870, Mrs. Muus kept Larsen informed of local happenings and sent greetings from her husband. On the way from Chicago to Quebec, she related, he had fallen into the water from a dock "and thus got an unexpected bath."[6]

In March of 1871 Muus informed Larsen that Mrs. Muus had been very ill but had improved. She sent her greetings. A period of recurring illness seemed to extend from 1872 through 1874, affecting Mrs. Muus and a young man being cared for at the parsonage.[7] Mrs. Muus later traced her illnesses to the lack of adequate heat and other comforts in the parsonage.

In matters of health, Oline Muus was possessed of some medical skill, which made her an active care giver in the community. Her parents had sent along a home medicine chest that she used to good effect. They also sent with her some medical instruments. From a Norwegian brother-in-law, a doctor, she had learned how to do bloodletting and to assist in medical emergencies. Reportedly she practiced bloodletting also among the Indian families she visited.[8] Although she seldom asked anything for these services, people paid her in money and gifts.[9]

Another of Oline Muus's activities in the Holden area drew upon her knowledge of music. She was said to be "highly gifted, well educated, an accomplished pianist."[10] She gave music and singing lessons. In 1874 she organized and directed a church choir called the "Kolibri [Hummingbird] Sangforening." Its four-part singing, a novelty in the community, was well received in the church. One woman said, "It sounds like an organ." One year her choir sent a box of clothing to needy students from Holden who were at Luther College. Mrs. Muus was the choir's only director. It disbanded about the time she brought suit against her husband.[11]

When Muus wrote to Larsen and others that "we live well," he meant that he and his family had the basic necessities of life, certainly not luxuries. Muus believed that the pastor and his family should share the same temporal conditions as the parishioners.[12] For him, it was good to have a home to return to after being away on synod business or visiting distant settlements, and it was also satisfying that Mrs. Muus recognized the importance of his missionary labors. From Mrs. Muus's standpoint, however, the frugality her husband insisted upon was excessive, causing needless privation in the household when they could well afford better. When she had an opportunity to give her version of life in the Holden parsonage, she described a situation she had endured ever since their arrival in Minnesota. While their acquaintances knew that Pastor Muus favored a simple mode of life for himself and his family, they did not realize the extent of his wife's discontent until the newspapers revealed that she had brought suit against her husband in Goodhue County District Court in December of 1879.[13]

Oline Muus's father, Johan Kristian Pind, died in Norway in 1863, leaving her an inheritance that amounted to $3,700. After the estate was settled in 1869, Pastor Muus received the first installment, a sum of $2,600, and invested it with his own funds. A second installment, the remaining $1,100, arrived in 1874. Norwegian law at the time stipulated that any personal property a married woman received became the property of her husband, who could hold it and dispose of it as he wished. Since Bernt and Oline Muus were both Norwegian citizens, he believed that he was acting according to his rights.[14]

For a few years, Oline Muus's inheritance and her husband's control of it were matters known only within the Muus household. In June of 1879, she asked him for an accounting of the money he had received from her father's estate. Apparently he refused to provide it. In December of 1879, she brought suit in Goodhue County District Court to recover the amount of her inheritance. Arguing her need of the money, she cited the austere living conditions in the home. She had been allowed only fifteen dollars per month to cover all household expenses, an amount that remained the same despite the growth of the family and the keeping of servants to work the farm. She supplemented this meager allowance by teaching voice, embroidering, sewing, knitting, gathering herbs for medicine, and selling hops.[15]

After she broke her leg in the spring of 1877 she was no longer able to earn extra money. Unfortunately, she broke it again the following year, before it was fully mended. This distressing accident became the subject of much dispute as her allegations became more widely known. To Mrs. Muus and her sympathizers, Pastor Muus's supposedly callous attitude in the face of his wife's accident and pain epitomized what she called his cruel and inhuman treatment of her.

In her suit, Mrs. Muus claimed that after her leg was broken her health deteriorated and the primitive conditions in the parsonage made matters worse. Her room was cold, without a carpet or a stove. She pleaded for these things, and for warmer clothes, but was refused even though a physician had told her husband in November of 1879 that they were necessary. Similarly, Mrs. Muus claimed that her husband refused to provide the necessary clothing for the children and treated them cruelly. Such conditions, straddling a line "between cruelty and austerity," Kathryn Ericson has observed, could be "bearable to someone propelled by great purpose and vision, but beyond endurance for those accompanying the visionary." When Mrs. Muus could bear no more, she asked the court to order her husband to release the inheritance money to her.[16]

Muus replied through W. C. Williston, his lawyer, that the money was his by virtue of Norwegian law. He had received it "in his own right and as his sole property," and not in trust for his wife or as her property. He denied his wife's claim that he had concealed the fact that he had received the money. He was not able to furnish details about where and how the money was invested since he regarded it as his own property and invested it with other of his own monies. Muus also maintained that until within the past two years, his wife had never shown any interest in the inheritance money or said that she wanted it as her separate property. He added that they were both citizens of the kingdoms of Sweden and Norway and not citizens of the United States of America. Significantly, Bernt denied "each and every allegation" charging him with "any cruel or inhuman treatment" of his wife or any member of the family. He also denied the alleged neglect and refusal to provide necessary things for their comfort and support. He argued that the action against him could not be sustained since it did not commence within six years of the distribution of the inheritance money.[17]

Through her lawyer, Andreas Ueland of Minneapolis, Mrs. Muus replied to Pastor Muus's statements on February 15, 1880. She contended that under Norwegian law a husband had no right to any property to which his wife became entitled until it actually came into his possession. The inheritance was never "adjudged or decreed" by any court to Pastor Muus, but to Mrs. Muus and to nobody else. She also denied all of his claims.[18]

The eventual decision by District Judge F. M. Crosby was based on Minnesota law, since the Muuses had lived in the state for twenty years. Under Minnesota law, what a married woman inherited was her separate property. Muus was ordered to pay his wife the sum of $1,118.05 with seven percent interest from

September 20, 1874, when he had received the second installment of the inheritance. The statute of limitations barred the judge from awarding her the amount of the first installment, received by Muus in 1869, more than six years before the beginning of the case. Both parties appealed to the Minnesota Supreme Court, but the original decision was affirmed in May of 1882.[19]

Word of the lawsuit appeared in January of 1880 in St. Paul's *Pioneer Press*, which had received the information from Ueland, Mrs. Muus's lawyer. At about the same time it was also published in *Budstikken*, a Norwegian-language newspaper in Minneapolis established in 1872 that had a reputation for being somewhat anti-clerical. Other Norwegian-language publications that followed the story were *Norden* and *Skandinaven*. *Budstikken* issued a pamphlet of some twenty-five tightly printed pages under the heading, in large Gothic type, "Mrs. Oline Muus contra Pastor B. J. Muus." This collection reported developments through March 30, 1880, including reports on the meetings held at Holden church regarding Mrs. Muus's lawsuit, editorial comments, and items from other newspapers and from contributors. Such Goodhue county newspapers as *The Republican*, *The Advance*, and *The Red Wing Argus* quickly seized the story and devoted columns to it month after month.[20]

Newspaper accounts tended to be sympathetic toward Mrs. Muus, both by the amount of space given to her suit and by comments critical of her husband. "He has not been laboring for the Lord for nothing all these years," noted *The Republican*, citing Mrs. Muus's estimate of the pastor's average income as $1,500 per year. *The Advance* prefaced a review of the case by recalling caustically that "our great and Reverend B. J. Muus" was known for his opposition to the common schools. Muus is now in the courts, wrote the editor, "for a course of inhuman treatment toward the wife of his bosom—combined with a cool appropriation to himself of her inherited fortune, while he starved her and the children she had borne him, on fifteen dollars a month."[21]

264

Some took Muus's side and defended him in print. The editor of *The Republican* hoped that the minister would be able to disprove the charges against him. A neighbor and friend of Muus deplored how the privacy of the Muus family had been exposed, and called Muus "a kind-hearted man." The writer granted that Muus was frugal, but said there was no lack of what was necessary for a healthy and comfortable life. The Muus house was known for "great hospitality." G. R. Norsving found Mrs. Muus's accusations hard to believe in light of his personal knowledge of how the pastor provided for his family's needs, but was sympathetic regarding Mrs. Muus's accidents and poor health.[22]

Readers of *The Republican* were reminded that a person is to be considered innocent until proven guilty. The editors of *Budstikken* defended going public with a private matter with a familiar argument. "Because of the right of the public to know, we see in this case the undeniable right it has to know about the private lives of its teachers and leaders as soon as these in one way or another come into public scrutiny."[23] Some of those most eager to know were members of the Holden congregation of which Muus was pastor.

A remarkable feature of the interest in Mrs. Muus's lawsuit was that it became the topic of a series of meetings at Holden church in 1880 and 1881. An estimated 1,000 people attended a meeting called by Pastor Muus for February 18, 1880, for the purpose of deciding whether or not the congregation wanted him to continue as its spiritual leader. The turnout prompted *The Red Wing Argus* to observe: "It would be desirable that people would crowd the churches thus at prayer meetings or at the regular services." With only one dissenting vote, the congregation decided that Pastor Muus should remain in his position until the case had been resolved in district court.[24]

"The interest in the matrimonial relations at the parsonage continues unabated." wrote a correspondent for *The Republican* as word spread that meetings were to be held in Holden church March 10 and 11, 1880. Approximately 800 people attended the

March 10th meeting, called by Muus for the purpose of placing his wife under church discipline. He contended that Mrs. Muus had questioned the degree to which a wife was required to obey her husband. The biblical text referred to during the discussions was Ephesians 5:24: "Just as the church is subject to Christ, so also wives ought to be, in everything, to their husbands." In Norwegian Bibles, "in everything" was rendered *i alle ting* (in all things). Receiving less attention in the discussions was the verse following: "Husbands, love your wives, just as Christ loved the church and gave himself up for her." (Ephesians 5:25)

Action on the discipline was delayed when the assembly, under the chairmanship of Pastor M. O. Bøckman, moved to hear the reading of a "statement of defense" submitted by Mrs. Muus, who stipulated that she would leave the meeting if the statement was not read. This document, addressed "to the Holden congregation," elaborated in greater detail the complaint first brought against Pastor Muus in district court the previous December. She gave the reason for her suit: "I have brought action against my husband in order to secure from him the inheritance from my father." She asked the congregation to consider what she had endured for twenty years before turning to the law for help. Early in the statement she firmly rejected the principle of a woman's total subservience to her husband. She wrote: "I feel no heavy reproach in placing myself in opposition to the Synod's teaching concerning a wife's blind and unconditional obedience to her husband; I can never accept this teaching, and I will not be a hypocrite. If God had created woman to be her husband's slave in every manner, He would not have given her the ability to act and think for herself."[25]

With Mrs. Muus present in the church as her lengthy statement was read, one can well visualize the people present watching her facial expressions and those of her husband as the many grievances were set forth. Clothing had to be stored in the granary. Only Pastor Muus had a dresser. A large box served as dining-room table. There was no clock. Their son Paul, six and one-half years old and in poor health, had to walk four miles to school and back in worn-out boots. The steady diet of bread, butter, and pork did not agree with Mrs. Muus. She had to sleep in a tiny, unheated, damp room, with water dripping on her bed, which was responsible for her chronic illness.

Mrs. Muus regretted that the original complaint's use of such words as "inhuman treatment" might have suggested "slaps and beatings, which I have never been subjected to." But words could hurt too, as well as the absence of words in her husband's cold, indifferent manner. The parsonage was literally cold as well. Mrs. Muus had asked for a rug for the living room and a stove in her bedroom, but had been refused. Her husband insisted that in order to save wood, only one room in addition to the kitchen should have a stove, although the parsonage had sixteen or seventeen usable rooms.

Perhaps the most dramatic accusation was related to the accident in 1877 when Mrs. Muus broke her leg. A remark made by Pastor Muus on that occasion achieved lasting notoriety in Holden lore. After being brought home, Mrs. Muus asked that a doctor be summoned at once. It turned out that her regular physician, Dr. Christian Grønvold, was not at home, but she knew that there were good doctors in Cannon Falls and Zumbrota. She said that she would never forget how her husband answered her. He did not want to send his hired man and the horse out into the night to fetch a doctor, so "I should butter myself with patience until the doctor came."[26]

The phrase caught the imagination of Marcus Thrane, Norwegian reformer and labor leader who emigrated to America where he became a photographer, editor, playwright, and composer. Thrane wrote a satirical three-act operetta entitled, "Holden, eller Smør Dig med Taalmodighet" (Holden, or, Anoint Yourself with Patience). The operetta, performed in Chicago in June of 1880, portrayed an authoritarian pastor, identified only as "Bernt," who demanded blind, unquestioning obedience from his wife. Very likely Thrane had read about the Muus case in *Skandinaven*, published in Chicago. Thrane also ridiculed Muus and other pastors in mock biblical language in another satire, *Den Gamle Wisconsin Bibelen* (The Old Wisconsin Bible), first published in 1881.[27]

In her statement of defense read before the Holden congregation, Mrs. Muus affirmed that finally her situation became intolerable. She told her husband that he would have to let her have the money she needed or she would consult an attorney. Then she made contact with Attorney Andreas Ueland to claim her inheritance under United States law. Muus soon went to Red Wing to ask a lawyer whether the inheritance was his according to Norwegian law, or hers.[28]

When the reading of Mrs. Muus's statement was completed, Chairman Bøckman returned to the matter of church discipline, starting with his own discourse on marriage. He reiterated the teaching that wives should be subject to their husbands "in everything," adding that one could call the wife a slave, but not in the bad sense of the word. "Obedience for her should be a dear duty." Pastor L. M. Biørn, appointed to speak for Mrs. Muus, interpreted "in everything" as a relative, not an absolute concept, and was challenged by Muus. Meeting again on March 11th, the congregation decided to seek advisory help from the outside. A motion to convene a later meeting also called for the presence of H. A. Preus, president of the Synod, and two district presidents, U. V. Koren of Iowa and J. B. Frich of Wisconsin.[29]

With these three clergymen on hand, the Holden congregation met again on May 13 and 14, 1880. After hearing from several persons regarding Mrs. Muus's charge that her husband had treated her in a heartless way when she broke her leg, the assembly concluded, in a 57 to 1 vote, that the complaint had not been proved. Witnesses established that Pastor Muus's conduct on the occasion had been considerate and blameless. On the second day, there was further labored discussion of the broken leg incident and related details. Koren, sensing the futility of the entire congregation acting as an investigating body, suggested the formation of a committee by the congregation. Elected were pastors Biørn, Bøckman,

*Ulrik Vilhelm Koren*
From Gerhard Belgum dissertation, "The Old Norwegian
Synod in America 1853–1890"

and Th. A. Hansen, plus three persons chosen by Muus, three by
Mrs. Muus, and six by the congregation as a whole. Pastor Biørn
was chosen as chairman.[30] This committee met for three days in
early June but accomplished relatively little, in large part because
Mrs. Muus refused to meet with the committee until her case was
settled in court; she also declined to call or identify her witnesses.
Moreover, Mrs. Muus gave the committee another statement in
which she issued accusations not only against her husband but
also against the congregation and the synod. Pastor Muus told
the committee that he was not obligated to prove the falsehood of
what the other party had failed to prove as true.[31]

269

Inevitably, the Muus troubles came before the June 1880 meeting of the Minnesota District of the Norwegian Synod, of which Pastor Muus was president. A committee was appointed to determine what position the Synod should take regarding the complaint against Muus. The decision was to take no action affecting Muus's position as president of the district, since the complaints had not been proved and, in fact, one charge had been found to be untrue.[32]

The next set of meetings at Holden church took place in July with President Preus as chairman. Mrs. Muus was reprimanded for bringing false charges against her husband, the congregation, and the Synod. Muus was asked to account for his "extraordinary conduct" in not speaking to his wife for two or three years except when absolutely necessary. He replied that when the time for speaking was past, one might try to win the spouse by God-fearing conduct. He had not accused his wife, and would rather not do so, but he reminded the congregation that during the handling of the matter she had shown herself to be mendacious and malicious. Since there was no motion that Muus should step down temporarily as pastor until the court case was settled, the matter was dropped. Likewise, the congregation postponed a decision on Mrs. Muus's discipline until after the court had ruled.[33]

Where the leadership of the Norwegian Synod was generally supportive of Pastor Muus, opinion from the Norwegian-Danish Conference was on the side of Mrs. Muus. An article in the Conference paper, *Lutheraneren*, expressed sympathy with Mrs. Muus, "whose life seems to be like a crushed reed under the weight of her domestic unhappiness." In the writer's view, the Norwegian Synod had not handled the case in a manner befitting the church of Jesus Christ. An attempt should be made to ascertain Pastor Muus's guilt in the matter. To the question whether Muus truly can serve the congregation for its edification, "we must answer No."[34]

Publicity regarding the Muus case took new turns in 1881. The actual trial of Muus vs. Muus took place in the Red Wing courtroom on January 5, 1881, attracting a large crowd of spectators. A key question was whether the laws of Norway or the laws of Minnesota should apply to the disposition of Mrs. Muus's inheritance. A reporter found the case interesting for the lawyers, "but it did not afford much amusement to the spectators." Not until November would the decision of Judge F. M. Crosby be made known.[35]

Two famous writers had their say about the Muus case in 1881. Norway's renowned man of letters, Bjørnstjerne Bjørnson, was on a lecture tour in America during the winter of 1880–1881. Not only was he apprised of the Muus case, but he met with Mrs. Muus in Red Wing and hoped to speak with Mr. Muus as well. There is no evidence that he saw him but his meeting with Mrs. Muus was memorable.

Bjørnson had left his earlier Christian views and had adopted the stance of an unbeliever. Convinced that the Norwegian Synod pastors were hopeless bigots, his sympathies were entirely with Mrs. Muus. Writing to his wife, Karoline, in March of 1881, Bjørnson described the meeting with Mrs. Muus. He found her lively and still attractive with her black hair, but other impressions were unflattering. Characterizing her as "a real mountain troll" he exclaimed: "God almighty, how he must have struggled with that female." In Bjørnson's view she was "all worldliness, indifference, defiance, intelligence, craving for fun, and in her way just as strong as he is." At first she seemed pious and quiet, he wrote, but when Bjørnson "made fun of the Bible and Muus and holiness, she laughed uproariously and was full of gaiety at once." Bjørnson meant to reach Pastor Muus. "I think most of the fault lies with him, there is no doubt about that; now it is important to separate them from one another, and that's what I want to talk seriously about with him."[36]

That same year Kristofer Janson, Norwegian-American Unitarian minister and well-known writer, published five lectures on conditions in America. He devoted several pages to the Muus case in his fifth lecture, being fully supportive of Mrs. Muus and unsparing in his castigation of Pastor Muus and the Norwegian Synod. What had happened in Goodhue county revealed that the Norwegian people there were spiritually under age, blind slaves under the pastors' prosaic, literalistic rule. Janson hailed with approval the protest of Professor Georg Sverdrup who wrote in *Lutheraneren*: "The case is of such a nature that it lays sorrow on every Christian heart among us and casts a blush of shame over the face of every man among our people."[37]

As if the family had not suffered enough, on August 27, 1881, Birgitte Muus, the only daughter, gave birth to her son out of wedlock. The boy was baptized September 18, 1881, and called Sverre Muus. The father was Johannes Olsen Kongsvik. He and Birgitte took out a wedding license but no marriage was recorded. Sverre was brought up in the Muus household.[38]

During these stressful years, since 1876, Muus had held the office of president of the Minnesota District of the Norwegian Synod. In September of 1881, Synod president H. A. Preus forwarded to Muus with his own endorsement the District's advice that Muus resign as district president "on account of the very grievous offenses in your household." Preus asked Muus to weigh the matter and make the decision that would be to God's glory and the welfare of the church.[39] Muus did not resign, but he was defeated when he sought re-election in 1883.

On October 12, 1881, Oline Muus was called before the Holden congregation for church discipline on the same charge as before, that she had denied the scriptural word that wives should be subject to their husbands "in all things." Invited to give her own understanding of the passage, she conceded that for the sake of peace in the house, a wife might obey her husband even in some, but by no means all, unreasonable demands. Husbands and wives should respect one another's views. If a wife is not allowed to think and act according to her conscience, she becomes her husband's slave.

Several agreed with Mrs. Muus's statement, but Pastor Muus declared it ambiguous, insisting that a wife is to obey her husband in everything that is not sin. Muus wanted to have the congregation press the point, but the assembly was not disposed to excommunicate Mrs. Muus. A solution of sorts was found by having chairman P. Langemo ask Mrs. Muus a series of questions. She agreed that it was a sin to ascribe to the Synod the doctrine that the wife was a slave when she was not certain that the Synod so taught. Under the chairman's coaching she asked the congregation for forgiveness. The congregation forgave her, Pastor Muus and the members were satisfied, and the meeting was over.[40] Later that fall she withdrew from membership in Holden Lutheran Church.

Serious unrest continued in the Muus home. It was reported that Mrs. Muus threatened violent harm to the three youngest children if Birgitte should marry a certain man, presumably Johannes Olsen Kongsvik, the father of Sverre. At that time Paul was nine, Petter (often called Peter) was seven, and Harald three. About the middle of November, Birgitte recalled, her father arranged to have Petter and Harald taken to live with the Hans Westermo family. Approximately a week later, Oline Muus moved away.[41]

The long-awaited decision of the court of the First Judicial District was made public on November 28, 1881. Oline Muus, the plaintiff, was to recover from the defendant, Bernt J. Muus, the sum of $1,704.04. This amount was the part of Mrs. Muus's inheritance that was not subject to the statute of limitations. On the same day, Oline Muus appealed the decision to the Supreme Court of the State of Minnesota.[42]

In late December of 1881 and again in January and February of 1882, the Holden congregation held meetings to decide whether or not Bernt J. Muus should continue as its pastor. In early February, "at the end of a long and tedious discussion," the congregation voted 73 to 37 in favor of having him stay. The vote indicates that Pastor Muus's support was not as strong as it had been at an earlier stage. The minority sent a letter to the Minnesota

273

*Four Muus children. Harald, Birgitte, Paul, Petter*
Photo from Don McRae album

District of the Synod expressing its view that Muus should step aside temporarily from his pastoral office.[43]

Reports in local newspapers that Mrs. Muus had moved to Minneapolis also carried the news that she intended to sue for divorce.[44] Beginning with a complaint heard in Hennepin County District Court in late December of 1881, followed by a lawsuit in January of 1882, Oline Muus filed for dissolution of her marriage, asking that she "be forever freed and divorced from the obligations thereof," but if that were not granted, that she "be forever separated from the bed and board of the defendant." The motion for divorce failed, as did the request for temporary alimony. The case that went forward was for legal separation, and that was the ultimate outcome. Thus two court actions were pending, Mrs.

Muus's appeal regarding the inheritance, and the new development when she sued for separation.[45]

In March of 1882, Muus also appealed the district court's decision regarding the inheritance, arguing through his lawyer that the court was wrong in finding that any part was exempt from the statute of limitations. But on May 16, 1882, the Supreme Court affirmed the district court's original decision, whereupon Muus satisfied the judgment by paying Mrs. Muus the sum of $1,701.04.[46]

For the separation case, depositions for both plaintiff and defendant were taken from a number of witnesses in the Holden area in December of 1882. Witnesses appeared before John Naeseth, justice of the peace for Goodhue county. On behalf of the defendant, Ole J. Solberg testified that when Mrs. Muus broke her leg, Pastor Muus gave directions to a hired man who was ready with a horse and sent him off to find Dr. Grønvold. Ole Sampson related that when Mrs. Muus was packed and ready to move away, Muus would not let her take her possessions until he examined them. He objected that a Bible and a muff belonged to Birgitte, but Mrs. Muus explained that their daughter had given her the articles and Birgitte herself confirmed this.[47]

Birgitte testified that the management of the house passed to a servant girl and then to herself when her mother no longer wanted to be in charge. Her mother seemed fond of the two children who were taken away to live with another family; they asked for their mother the day they were taken away. Regarding her mother's reaction on that occasion, Birgitte said, "Mother seemed to feel bad about her children for about a half a day, after that she did not seem to feel bad." Maren Ramstad, a servant girl, testified that relations between the pastor and his wife were rather cold. He rarely spoke to Mrs. Muus. Miss Ramstad did not remember Mr. Muus speaking a kind word to his wife, but neither did she ever hear him abuse her. Asked whether Mrs. Muus was pleasant toward him and more anxious than he to be friendly, Maren replied, "I thought not."[48]

Søren Monsen, who lived in the house as a private tutor, found

Mrs. Muus to be a capable manager and housekeeper. She took the removal of the two children from the home very hard. Two members of Holden Church recalled hearing Muus explain that a man's wife and children were his slaves. Knut Haugen testified that during discussions of church discipline for Mrs. Muus, Muus had said that the congregation had to be glad to be rid of such a person. Haugen was struck by the pastor's harsh words about his wife, that she was "sinful, ungodly, and malicious." Knut Haugen, it may be recalled, was the farmer the Muuses stayed with their first winter in the Holden community.[49]

On the whole, the depositions depict a family existence in the parsonage that could appear relatively peaceful on the surface, but seethed with strain and tensions. Pastor Muus seemed cold, controlling, but not abusive. Mrs. Muus's behavior covered a spectrum from ordinary functions as housewife and mother, to resigned indifference regarding household management, to sorrow, rage, and acceptance regarding removal of the two children, and finally to a calm decision to move out.

Oline Muus's separation case against Bernt J. Muus was brought before a court without a jury in Hennepin county on January 3, 1883. On January 20 Judge A. H. Young of Hennepin County District Court announced the court's judgment. It found "that plaintiff is entitled to be forever separated from the bed and board of the defendant on the ground that defendant's conduct towards plaintiff has been such as to render it unsafe and improper for plaintiff to continue to live and cohabit with him."

Other provisions were that the defendant pay the plaintiff $2,575.20, money received by him from the estate of his wife's father, and the further payment of $150.00 per year for a period of ten years. Bernt also had to pay $100.00 for plaintiff's legal fees, and $161.93 for plaintiff's disbursements for witness fees. The defendant received care and custody of the minor children.[50]

The language of the judgment makes clear that the settlement was a separation, not a divorce. It is true that Mrs. Muus sued for a limited divorce with alimony, as her attorney, Andreas Ueland, noted in his autobiography.[51] The actual outcome, however, was a separation that had the virtual effect of a divorce. This view is supported by the final part of Judge Young's decree of January 20, 1883, stating that Oline Muus had no claim on Bernt Muus's property once the sum of $2,575.20 was paid. With respect to the defendant's present and future real and personal estate, the decree states that the defendant is to "have, hold and possess the same and have a right to sell convey and dispose of the same in all respects as fully and completely as he would have were the relation of husband and wife between said parties absolutely dissolved."[52]

Earlier in January, Judge Young wrote the following about the Muus marriage: "The evidence clearly shows, that for many years the conduct of both parties in their home has been such as tended to estrange them from each other, and in respect to which neither party has been free from blame; and that this conduct has been of such duration, that the parties have long since ceased to love each other as husband and wife."[53]

Oline Muus herself was close to the mark in analyzing the relationship with her husband in the statement read to the Holden congregation on March 10, 1880: "Differences in character, viewpoints, and disposition are difficult to deal with in a marriage." Wrote G. R. Norsving even as he tried to defend Muus against his wife's accusations, "Pastor Muus is known from church controversies to be a stubborn and uncooperative individual, and he is always true to himself."[54] From all appearances, Oline and Bernt Muus simply were not suited for one another as marriage partners.

One cannot escape the impression that a nascent but powerful feminism was at work in Oline Muus's words and actions. Living in the relative isolation of the Goodhue county parsonage, she may not have been informed of the women's movement in America nor of the feminist ideology in Norway that found expression, for example, in Henrik Ibsen's famous play, "A Doll's House," published in 1879. Nevertheless, in an intuitive and outspoken way

277

Oline Muus was on a similar wave length. In the spring of 1880, pressed by the Holden congregation and the president of the Norwegian Synod to make an appearance for purposes of church discipline, she sent Synod president Preus a bristling commentary on why she could not be obedient to her husband "in all things." She fired off several sentences in an angry cadence that began with, "When my husband orders me to . . ." and concluded defiantly with, ". . . I am not obligated to obey such a command." For example: "When my husband orders me to go out and clean out the stable, which has happened more than once, I feel absolutely no obligation to obey such an order." Addressing herself directly to "you pastors and presidents," she wrote: "Test yourselves and ask your wives, and you will see that we are right. Do not come with commands and orders to us wives that you yourselves, in our place, would not lift a finger to carry out."[55]

After Mrs. Muus moved to Minneapolis, she had the opportunity to come into personal contact with a noted Norwegian reformer and leader in the women's movement, Aasta Hansteen. During a Minnesota speaking tour in 1882, Hansteen, who was well informed about the inheritance case, visited Mrs. Muus at her place of residence in Minneapolis. Mrs. Muus made a trip to Boston in the spring of 1882, raising the intriguing possibility that she could have met leaders in the American women's movement there.[56]

The emotional and spiritual toll exacted by the troubles in the Muus family cannot be measured. The lives of the Muus children underwent painful disruption, to say the least. Certainly the Holden congregation paid a price in loss of members and public criticism. On the positive side, according to L. M. Biørn, the congregation displayed a patience, composure, and steadiness during the many meetings that awakened general surprise and admiration.[57]

As far as Pastor and Mrs. Muus were concerned, both found the necessary strength to go on with their lives. Following the separation, Muus continued with his local and synodical pastoral duties. Oline Muus was in Minneapolis for a few years teaching piano. She moved to Columbia, South Dakota, in 1889, and in 1896 to Fruithurst, Alabama, where she lived out the rest of her days.

# Twelve

## The Divided Family

Most of what is now known about Bernt Julius Muus, his wife Oline Muus, and their children is from public documents. Occasional items of personal interest appear in correspondence between Muus and fellow pastors, and a limited number of letters written by Mrs. Muus survive. But personal letters, diaries, memoirs, and family reminiscences that would enable one to gain a closer acquaintance with the family have not been available.

Despite the absence of source material that would give a fuller picture of the personalities involved, the events recounted in the previous chapter revealed certain traits of Bernt and Oline Muus in their strained relationship. One must realize that the family lived under the pressure of multiple stresses of unusual severity, any one of which would have inflicted major psychological damage on any family group. Within the five-year span from 1878 to 1883, a young child died, the wife brought suit against the husband, there was frequent illness in the home, the wife broke her leg, the only daughter gave birth to an illegitimate child, the congregation held meetings about the family's situation, the husband was under pressure locally and in the Synod, a separation took place, and the family suffered a permanent division.

This impression of nearly unrelieved domestic misery leads one

to view Bernt and Oline Muus solely as characters in a dark trag-
edy, forgetting that they were very able and interesting people.
Oline Muus was gifted in many ways, in music, medicine, and
handwork. When Bjørnson met her in Red Wing, he found her
pretty, intelligent, full of fun, and strong in her own way. From his
account of the meeting, Bjørnson also observed traits in her that
must have made her difficult to live with.

Bjørnson hoped to speak with Pastor Muus as well, but there is
no record of their meeting. In the letter to his wife describing his
encounter with Mrs. Muus, Bjørnson offered a revealing comment about Birgitte and her father. He wrote that Mrs. Muus
"had a sweet daughter, cleanly and particular like her father, who
wants to talk with me but was away."[1] Bjørnson seems to have
known that Muus was neat and fastidious in dress, even if they
did not meet. But Muus was not vain about his appearance. He
was once seen at a Synod conference dressed in homespun. When
leading a church service Muus, like other Synod pastors, sought
to cultivate dignity and propriety in worship. He celebrated Holy
Communion with full clerical vestments and candles on the altar.[2]
The Holden ministerial books show meticulous care in keeping
records of pastoral acts. Similarly, in his correspondence with
President Larsen, he was exact to the penny in reporting amounts
of money collected and sent to Luther College.

The image of Muus that emerged from the court cases tended to
be that of a grim, controlling husband and father who imposed
strict, inviolable rules on his household. But L. M. Biørn, a neighboring pastor who at times took issue with Muus, had known a
different, less forbidding man. Wrote Biørn, "Pastor Muus was an
attractive man, well-proportioned, in robust health, who suffered
hardship like a horse without a word of complaint, making few
demands for life's comforts." Muus was uncommonly generous
and anything but stingy, Biørn continued. "He was hospitable
and courteous to all his visitors. In his happier days he could be
cheerful and witty; later he became taciturn and somber."[3]

The purpose of the present chapter is to report how the Muus family fared after the separation. Observations will be made about the separation beyond the facts stated earlier. Questions about the Muus marriage that have become part of Holden history cannot be answered with certainty. Inasmuch as Oline Muus outlived her husband by twenty-two years, her moves and activities after she left the Holden community are of interest, as are the fates of the Muus children. Finally, the account reports an attempt to bring about a reconciliation between Pastor and Mrs. Muus.

As the Muus case has been discussed over the years, the consensus emerging is that there were faults on both sides. Toward the end of the separation case Judge A. H. Young wrote that "neither party has been free from blame." Mrs. Muus stated the same view in a 1912 letter: "That the greatest fault and guilt was on my side is true enough," she wrote, "but that my husband was not without blame is also true. As in all cases like this, sin and fault are on both sides."[4] It is permissible to add, however, that the culpability of the two principals has been viewed differently according to the constituency involved.

In the wider public, Oline Muus is the one whose story receives the most sympathetic hearing. She is viewed as the oppressed wife, the victim of an insensitive clerical husband whose conduct was guided by literal adherence to the biblical teaching that wives should be subject to their husbands in all things. That viewpoint was first established on December 26, 1879, when she brought suit in district court to recover her inheritance. It was reinforced and dramatized on March 10, 1880, when her statement of defense was read at a meeting of the Holden congregation. That statement received wide publicity and won her a great deal of support.

Because Mrs. Muus eventually received the inheritance money and won a separation from her husband, it is natural to assume that her charges against him were valid. What is not generally known, however, is that Mrs. Muus sought later to dissociate herself from some of the complaints in the legal suit. Moreover, many of her charges were never substantiated and, in particular, the allegation that her husband had refused to send for a physician after she broke her leg was found to be untrue. Discussions at the congregation's meetings of May 13 and 14, 1880, brought to light discrepancies between the original charges and what witnesses recalled.[5]

Even though factors can be found that soften the picture of Pastor Muus as a tyrannical figure, the impression lingers among the general public that Oline Muus was the victim in an unhappy marriage. But in one particular circle, the mention of Mrs. Muus did not elicit sympathetic interest. In her book *The Old Main*, Edel Ytterboe Ayers, daughter of St. Olaf professor Halvor Ytterboe, tells of attending a supper party among old St. Olaf families, probably during the 1930s. Since Mrs. Ayers lived in Alabama and had visited Fruithurst, Alabama, she thought it would be of historical interest to her fellow guests to hear something about the place where Mrs. Muus had lived and died. Recalled Mrs. Ayers: "I started to say something about Mrs. Muus. As soon as I mentioned her name out loud, I was met by a dead and forceful silence. Friends looked at me as though I had said something unspeakably vulgar and out of place. I realized that the subject was fresh in the minds of the 'Old Guard' and that it was still an unmentionable subject in their minds and hearts."[6]

Mrs. Ayers was stunned by the reaction. Reflecting on the incident, she stated that she had her reservations whenever she saw pictures of St. Olaf representatives laying wreaths at the grave of the Reverend Bernt J. Muus in Trondheim. "My thoughts turn with compassion to Mrs. Muus, who lived the greater part of her life so far away from her children, her family and friends."[7]

In comparing B. J. Muus's later reputation with that of his wife, the situation is roughly reversed. Subject to criticism in larger public and secular circles, Muus has been honored by his Holden congregation, by St. Olaf College, which he founded, and by church historians. As an example of a virulent portrayal of Bernt Julius Muus, one thinks of Marcus Thrane's farcical play,

284

"Holden," in which Muus is caricatured as an angry, dictatorial minister who terrorizes his wife and children, fleeces his congregation, and seeks the company of other women. Muus was also the object of Thrane's satirical humor in *The Wisconsin Bible*. In a recent popular novel, Pastor Muus is not portrayed as harshly. In *Julia's Children* he appears as a doctrinally proper Synod minister known for his refusal to bury unbelievers in the sacred soil of the Holden cemetery.[8]

At St. Olaf College, Pastor Muus's role as founder is remembered with appreciation in college histories and anniversary speeches. Fittingly, a bronze bust of the founder has been placed in the Old Main. Students keep the nose shiny, touching it for good luck on their way to exams. As the structure Muus was instrumental in having built, and the only building on the campus in use during his time, the historic Old Main is uniquely linked with his memory. For many members of the College constituency, it seems odd that the founder of the institution is not honored with a building bearing his name. That the name Muus looks and sounds like both the Norwegian word for "mouse" and the English word "moose" and thus might prompt a bit of obvious humor is hardly reason enough to deny the founder a deserved honor. It is more likely that earlier leaders of the College were embarrassed by the fact that the founder was one whose domestic life was so unsettled that his wife left him.

Returning to the separation and its aftermath, how did the painful events affect the participants themselves? During the emotionally stressful spring of 1880, the usually self-contained Pastor Muus broke down during a church service. "A couple of Sundays ago," reported *Budstikken*, "he surprised the church folk when, overwhelmed by grief and anxiety, he could not preach his sermon, or even read one, so the precentor (*klokker*) had to take over the reading." A moment's silence followed, with sobbing and weeping, before he regained control over his feelings. Then he announced that he had been accused before a court of law and that a congregational meeting would be held February 18 at which

*Bronze bust of B. J. Muus dedicated. Paul Granlund, sculptor, great-grandsons Bernt Julius and Herman Muus, St. Olaf President Harlan F. Foss. Boe Chapel, November 6, 1984*
St. Olaf College News Bureau photo

the congregation itself must decide if it wanted him to remain as pastor among them.[9]

At the end of a letter to Laur. Larsen in September of 1881, Muus alluded briefly to his personal situation. It was not the most pleasant, and there was little hope that it would get better. With ironic humor and an eye to the current controversy over the doctrine of election he wrote: "That which helps me now when everything seems to be giving way is that I am neither a Missourian nor a Calvinist." In a more serious vein he added: "I also know that I have a Savior who supports me and who will deliver me out of my difficulty if I trust in him."[10]

Oline Muus also found comfort in God during the separation ordeal and long afterward. In her statement to the congregation on March 10, 1880, she said: "When I consider my own situation, which has caused me to lose many friends, I find a deep need to seek my God earnestly and truly. I trust in Him and I know I will receive from Him the comfort and strength I so sorely need."

More than thirty years later, writing from Alabama, Mrs. Muus looked back on her sufferings. "All the punishment and hardship I have undergone and continue to experience is perhaps well deserved and for my betterment. God punishes us to bring us to a realization of guilt, to repentance, and to a better life. When this goal is reached, we have taken the discipline in the right manner."[11]

In the same letter, Mrs. Muus commented on the situation between her deceased husband and herself. The main difficulty, at least in the beginning, was this: "We did not understand each other, mostly I believe because of our entirely different understanding of life which in turn grew out of our different characters and our very different upbringing."

She had only kind feelings toward the Holden congregation. She understood that the Synod would defend one of its bishops, and that she would be "trampled upon." The congregation should not be criticized because it respected and loved her husband. It was natural that it would be on his side, having no knowledge of the situation between the two of them. "Those who told the worst lies about me were people outside our congregation." During the twenty years at Holden, the congregation showed her hospitality and friendliness, and bestowed gifts upon her. They still remembered her with friendly letters and gifts.[12]

In the oral tradition regarding the Muuses, there has long been a question whether another set of factors lay beneath the surface of events related to their separation. The fact that a wife should bring suit against her husband, a pastor in the church, was obviously seen as a scandal in 1880. But was there perhaps a scandal behind the scandal? No, according to Andreas Ueland, Mrs. Muus's attorney. Summarizing the case in his autobiography, Ueland wrote:"There was no moral delinquency involved on either side, yet the suit made a great sensation because of the character and standing of the parties and the clash between old and modern ideas of the marital relation."[13]

Then what were the lies that were told about Mrs. Muus? An undercurrent of speculation has persisted that she may have been guilty of infidelity. In addition to being intrinsically embarrassing, the subject is an elusive one. While there is no decisive evidence of "moral delinquency," questions remain. Those who could have put them to rest have long since passed on. The written records only point to the fact that Mrs. Muus herself was aware that such speculation existed.

One context in which the possibility of a hidden scandal came to light was a letter exchange between Mrs. Muus and Synod president H. A. Preus in the spring of 1880. She expressed her indignation at how she had been treated by her husband and by other pastors in the Norwegian Synod. In a scathing letter she declared that she felt no obligation to obey certain orders from her husband. In no uncertain terms she informed Preus that if the Synod wanted to expel her for that reason, she was ready at any time, preferably as soon as possible.[14]

There were other letters to Preus that spring, written in pain and anger. Part of the exchange concerned Oline Muus's requested appearance at a forthcoming meeting of the congregation. Preus urged her to attend in order to prove the charges she had made public against her husband. Another topic was Mrs. Muus's distress at rumors that were circulating about her. On the basis of some anonymous letters, she actually accused Preus and his colleagues of "spreading false, defamatory accusations against me of the worst kind." In reply, Preus asked for more information and proof that he had spoken ill of her. If he had sinned against her he would gladly ask for her forgiveness.[15]

More anonymous letters arrived, some from Norway. In her next letter to Preus Mrs. Muus toned down her accusation against him and specified the content of the rumors. "I have not as yet obtained full certainty that you were the one who had brought these ugly reports about me to Norway," she wrote. But she was determined to find out who it was. If it was Preus, he had committed a great sin against her. His Christian duty was to turn to her first to investigate the matter. "You as a pastor presumably know that it is a significant thing to be accused of unfaithfulness to one's husband." In tracing the rumors to their source, she was about to identify the instigator as someone in her own vicinity and would expose him publicly if he was unable to produce distinct and clear proof of his accusations.[16]

As both Pastor Preus and Mrs. Muus were aware, the rumors were related to the fact that she had brought suit against her husband. For her part, she could not rid herself of the feeling that Synod pastors and Preus in particular were behind the spreading of the rumors. Another letter from Norway, received in May of 1880, seemed to renew her belief that he was somehow responsible for evil reports about her. In her fury she faced him with a very blunt question: "Have you written to a theologian in Christiania that now there have arisen such malicious rumors about me that they will explain why I have brought suit against my husband?" She demanded a straight Yes or No answer. Should he refuse, there would be unpleasant consequences for him and for the entire Norwegian Synod. If he was an honest and upright Christian, he would not only openly admit his guilt but would also write immediately to those persons in Norway and tell them that they had engaged in untruth. Otherwise she demanded that he produce sworn witnesses to what he had told about her. If Preus responded the letter is not available.[17]

Mrs. Muus also spoke about the accusations in the complaint filed in Hennepin County District Court on December 26, 1881. She alleged that, in addition to taking away from her the management of the household, her husband had alienated the children's affection for her by telling them that their mother was "a heathen, a liar, a wicked woman, and on the road to hell," and therefore one whom the children should not obey. At the meetings held in the church her husband falsely accused her of lying and deceit in the presence of her friends and acquaintances. Referring specifically to the meetings of May 13 and 14, 1880, Mrs. Muus complained that the defendant, in the presence of more than 500 people, had said "in a sneering and contemptuous manner that there were certain reasons why he had not for years spoken to or come near" her, and that "there might be certain things between plaintiff and defendant which for their own sake as well as for the sake of their children and descendants should not be revealed to the world." Mrs. Muus was informed and believed that by these words he intended to have the congregation believe "that plaintiff was an unchaste woman and guilty of adultery." Ever since that time, she said, there have been and are public rumors circulating to that effect.[18]

The factual part of Mrs. Muus's recollection of the May meetings is confirmed by the published record of them. Muus indeed did speak about "certain things" that ought not to come before the world. He alluded to the fact that for the past two or three years he had not spoken to Mrs. Muus more than was absolutely necessary, and also stated that he could not approach his wife "for certain reasons that perhaps might come to light later."[19] That her husband thereby was obliquely accusing her of adultery was how she understood his comments.

In her letters to Preus, Mrs. Muus was not sure whether it was Preus himself or some local party who was responsible for spreading malicious stories about her. In her legal complaint, she clearly accused her husband of speaking about her in such a way as to encourage the damaging public rumors. Such material is far from proving any wrongdoing on the part of Mrs. Muus; it only provides documentation for the fact that she knew such rumors were circulating about her.

A fascination with the domestic situation of Pastor and Mrs. Muus prior to their separation has become a permanent part of Holden history. More often the speculation about possible marital misconduct is directed toward Mrs. Muus, but the reputation of Pastor Muus in that regard has also suffered, and in a public form. In his satirical drama "Holden," Marcus Thrane portrayed "Bernt" as trying to conduct romances with Kate, the saloon-keeper's daughter, and with a Mrs. Olsen. And apart from farcical fiction, Pastor Muus has not been entirely immune from gossip.

Some might take the view that gossip against the pastor and his wife could have its roots in the resentment of uneducated rural people toward persons of higher education and social standing. Indeed, in the complaint filed in Hennepin County District Court in December of 1881, Oline Muus had referred in so many words to their "high social standing at the time of their marriage" and her desire, in the light of her husband's "wealth and high standing," to be treated by him "in a way becoming a lady in her station of life." But even though she used those words, there is no indication that she put on airs or saw herself as superior to those around her. Similarly, while Pastor Muus was authoritarian, he seemed to have won the loyalty of his parishioners by his selfless labors and down-to-earth ways.

Looking back at the Holden community over a century later, one can view the situation that prevailed in the light of objective historical interest without harming reputations. Even if there is no convincing evidence of scandal, one can report as a matter of history that certain opinions were expressed to that effect and ask why members of the community voiced them. Invariably, such historical curiosity encounters the name of Dr. Christian Grønvold, Mrs. Muus's physician and a friend whom she may have known in Norway. It has not been proved that there was an illicit relationship between Mrs. Muus and the highly respected doctor, but certain items of common knowledge support the belief that a friendship existed between them.

She was a pretty woman whose husband was frequently away from home. He was a capable, energetic professional man who lived a short distance down the road. Both were interested in medicine; both were active in promoting music in the community. It was only to be expected that a woman not entirely comfortable in the role of pastor's wife, harried with the tasks of raising six children and running a large household, would enjoy conversations with an educated, cultured man with whom she shared many interests. Very likely they had comparable memories of social and cultural experiences in Norway's capital city. As

291

Andreas Ueland wrote, with her musical gifts and knowledge of Norwegian literature, Mrs. Muus "aspired to many things outside the parsonage."[20]

Just Christian Grønvold was born in Norway in 1833. He graduated from the University in Oslo with highest honors in mathematics and natural science. He came to America in 1865 and studied medicine at Humboldt Medical School in St. Louis, graduating in 1869, the year he came to Goodhue county. For a time in 1870, Grønvold actually lived in the Muus household, being listed in the census as a "farm laborer."

As a physician he soon built up a thriving practice in Wanamingo, also gaining a name in wider medical circles for his research in leprosy. He served on the Minnesota State Board of Health and met regularly with fellow members of the Goodhue County Medical Society, of which he was a charter member. Grønvold was known as a generous, public-spirited man and an excellent physician. As a lover of good music and of Scandinavian folk tunes, he organized a musical group of over a hundred members called "The Norway Singing Society and Brass Band."[21]

In 1873 Dr. Grønvold built a house on the site where Holden congregation was first organized in 1856. The property is located about a thousand feet west of the Holden parsonage. The following year Grønvold married Eli Brandt of Decorah, Iowa, a niece of the Reverend Nils Brandt, pioneer pastor then teaching at Luther College. They had eleven children.

Dr. Grønvold was asked to provide medical assistance in the Holden neighborhood where he lived as well as in other places. When Mrs. Muus broke her leg in the spring of 1877, and later complained that Pastor Muus had refused to send for the doctor, it was her husband's recollection that he himself had walked over to Dr. Grønvold's house, where he learned that the doctor had gone to treat someone in the Swedish settlement. In reviewing the episode and noting that a doctor from Cannon Falls or Red Wing could not get there before Grønvold was expected to return, Pastor Muus said this: "The proper, steady treatment must be counted on from Dr. Grønvold. Mrs. Muus has received more physician's care than is surely anyone's lot here in the country, indeed, more than is commonly rendered in the cities, perhaps more than if she had been in a hospital; for Dr. Grønvold was with her several times a day when it was needed."[22]

Stories are told of the droll, sparring verbal exchanges between Pastor Muus and Dr. Grønvold when they happened to meet. The doctor was not a churchman, although his children were all baptized at the Holden church. Once when the doctor let loose with some profanity in Muus's hearing, the pastor corrected him. Dr. Grønvold replied, "I swear but you pray, but we don't mean anything by it, either of us." On another occasion the two happened to be in Borlaug's store and post office at the little corner village known as Norway. Pastor Muus was buying a broom and Grønvold wanted to know what he planned to do with it. Muus said he might use it for sweeping away the sins of some of the neighbors. To this Grønvold commented, "Ah, is that so? Do the sins sit so loose then?"[23]

Whether there was ever anything improper between Mrs. Muus and Dr. Grønvold may never be known. Some acquainted with the story find it highly improbable. It is a matter of record, however, that when Dr. Grønvold died, in September of 1895, Pastor Muus refused to allow him to be buried in the Holden cemetery. As a result, Grønvold and his wife were laid to rest in the cemetery of Aspelund Church, the nearby congregation of the Hauge Synod. The reason given by Muus, it was said at the time, was that Dr. Grønvold was not an actual member of the Holden Church.[24]

After Mrs. Muus moved to Alabama, she submitted letters and articles to the Norwegian language publication *Amerika*. In two such letters, she reviewed her life and wrote of her relationship with Pastor Muus and confessed her failings. Especially candid was a letter that appeared in *Amerika* on February 23, 1906, twenty-five years after she left Holden. Looking back on her youth, she described herself as a spoiled child, the youngest in her family, whose parents gave her everything she wanted. As an adult she discovered that her upbringing made it "much more difficult for me to overcome my sinful desires and my naturally corrupted heart." She concluded that it would lighten her burden if she could marry a man of faith and devotion to God even if her love for him was not as strong as young people would prefer. Continuing, she wrote: "According to my parents' desire and will, at a little over 18 years of age I was engaged to Pastor Muus, at that time a theological candidate, and after two and one-half years we were married on July 12, 1859 by Pastor Landmark in Fett Church. There was a raging storm that day, so we scarcely managed to get across the Glommen River to the church. A bad omen."

Regarding Pastor Muus she wrote: "My husband was endowed with an iron will, a man of conviction. If he thought something was right, he stood firm with his principle, even if heaven and earth collapsed." He did not treat her as an equal, but as a naughty child who needed to be disciplined. When she finally realized that such was his attitude, it was like an iron hand on her breast. Had she been of the right stuff, she could have borne with patience the times of distress. "But my faith, steadfastness, and devotion to God were not great enough; I sinned and fell into temptation time after time. Yet I know that God has forgiven me, as I hope my husband also had done before he died. In any case I asked him for forgiveness several times."[25]

Knowing that Mrs. Muus felt that her reputation was under a cloud, and that an honest person of Christian faith values the importance of confession and forgiveness, one might read the admissions above as applying to marital offenses. On the other hand, one can easily take such admissions of sin and guilt as referring to any number of human failings having nothing to do with unfaithfulness in marriage. Such was the case in her statement that was read to the congregation in March of 1880. "While I have listed above the sins and weaknesses of my husband, I do not wish to pretend that I myself do not have many sins on my conscience. It is especially my thoughtlessness and my quick tem-

*Bernt Julius Muus*
Photo from Don McRae album

per that get the better of me and cause grief and misunderstanding. I know there are many things I need to ask forgiveness for, but one thing I do know and that is that I have tried to the best of my ability to maintain a good relationship by enduring as long as possible what I in reality found to be an intolerable situation."[26]

Despite all accusations, questions, and rumors, the three characters in the Holden drama mentioned above reached the end of their lives as respected citizens who contributed their talents to noble causes in their communities. Dr. Grønvold is remembered as "a great power for good," a man who "gave his influence, time, and money freely, for he was generous and liberal hearted to a

295

fault."[27] Pastor Muus was severely wounded by the separation, and by the theological strife that engulfed the church in the 1880s, but he remained devoted to his pastoral tasks until his health and strength were exhausted. Mrs. Muus proved to be a resilient woman of courage who did not let her unhappy years in Holden prevent her from building a new and satisfying life for herself.

When Oline Muus left the Holden parsonage in late November of 1881, she took up residence in Minneapolis, having received money for the move from professors Georg Sverdrup and Sven Oftedal of Augsburg Seminary. The professors also supported her until she began receiving money from her inheritance. From late 1881 to 1888, she lived in the neighborhood of Augsburg Seminary, earning some income from giving piano lessons. On a Sunday evening in 1884, she was present at a Norwegian Women's Society bazaar as piano accompanist for violinist Jacob Seeman. Kristofer Janson, controversial Norwegian-American Unitarian minister, was the speaker at the program. During her Minneapolis years, Mrs. Muus became acquainted with Janson's wife, Drude, and with the latter's close friend, Valborg Hovind Stub, wife of Synod professor Hans Gerhard Stub.[28]

For reasons unknown, Oline Muus found her way in about 1889 to the town of Columbia, Brown county, South Dakota, where she operated a coffee shop. For a time Columbia was under consideration for county seat, but Aberdeen was chosen instead. Responding to questions from acquaintances, Mrs. Muus described conditions in and around Columbia to readers of *Decorah–Posten*. Columbia had been a promising town, but the high hopes of its residents were disappointed when commercial interests shifted to Aberdeen. Commenting on church life, Oline had praise for the well-regarded, anti-Missourian pastor Sven Ulsaker who, she said, "is not one of these new-style churchly game-cocks" but preaches the word of God in quietness and tries to live by it, which is preferable to "useless strife about different concepts and orthodoxy's various learned expressions."[29]

On the advice of her doctor who recommended the warmer southern climate for her asthma and arthritis, Oline Muus moved to Fruithurst, Alabama, in the fall of 1896. No doubt she had heard of the migration of Scandinavians from northern states to Texas, Mississippi, and three colonies in Alabama: Thorsby, Silverhill, and Fruithurst.[30]

An advertisement appearing in *Decorah–Posten* June 9, 1896, claimed that there were more than 500 Scandinavians in Fruithurst, a town that boasted good water, good climate, and a $50,000 hotel. One could buy a ten-acre vineyard for $400 on easy terms. Two acres were already planted. Within two years, once the vines began to bear fruit, one could earn at least $150 per acre per year. Signing the ad was a Swede, J. A. Westerlund, an agent for the Alabama Fruit Growers and Winery Association, who also served as mayor of Fruithurst. A later ad in *Decorah–Posten* offered excursions from Minneapolis to Fruithurst for $12.85.[31] For a time Fruithurst, "The Vineyard City," enjoyed prosperity as a little southern paradise, with broad streets, substantial homes, a profusion of roses, thriving businesses, three newspapers, grape harvest celebrations at the imposing Fruithurst Inn, and the exporting of a variety of choice wines. The decline of Fruithurst's wine industry was because "there was no good market for the wine, so profits were held to a bare minimum." Prohibition had little to do with the downturn since there was only one winery left by 1919.[32]

Arriving in October of 1896, Mrs. Muus participated in Fruithurst's best years, which seemed to be from the last half of the 1890s until approximately 1910. She was proprietress of "Mrs. Muus' Hotel," as her letterhead identified it. Remaining in the town after the wineries were closed, she was active in church affairs, offering the dining room of the former hotel, which remained her home, for worship services of Scandinavian Lutherans. One of her hobbies was embroidery. She had a reputation in Fruithurst as a kind, pleasant, and gifted lady whose house and gardens were always neat and attractive.

297

Despite the permanent limp she suffered from the accident years before, Mrs. Muus diligently took care of her house, and the yard that she called her "park"; she also cultivated an additional piece of land she was able to buy with money from a relative. In all, she owned more than two acres where she raised strawberries to sell, she wrote to Laur. Larsen. With her piano teaching and the $12.00 she received each month beginning in 1902, she was able to stay out of debt.[33]

To a marked extent, Oline Muus kept in touch with the midwestern Norwegian community she had left behind through a vigorous correspondence. In private letters, contributions to Norwegian-language newspapers, and even a regular "Grandmother's Column" in the publication *Amerika*, Oline Muus communicated her experiences, feelings, and opinions. Nor did she hesitate to reflect on her failed marriage to Pastor Muus. Her autobiographical letter to *Amerika* of February 23, 1906, offered additional thoughts on her marriage. During the first years, her husband's forbidding way of treating her made her stubborn and angry, but later she became more lethargic and indifferent, letting things take their course. "I was like a passive instrument, a machine that is wound up and goes without wit and will until it stops." It will be recalled that her daughter said in a deposition that first Maren Ramstad then she herself took care of the housework "because my mother did not want the management of the house."[34]

Oline Muus wrote that she had suffered alone during those years in the Holden parsonage. Nevertheless, the Lord had looked after her, providing more than she had ever dreamed of. She had a beautiful home in the lovely South, good health, all she needed to live on, and best of all, God's grace, peace, and blessing to body and soul. She wanted the readers to know that she had never wanted the divorce, as she called it, but left her husband so that the home would be more peaceful for him and the children. It was his desire that she should leave, as he made very clear to her and others. She wrote this short life history to convince both friends and foes: (1) that she had never regretted the step she took twenty-five years earlier; (2) that since that time she had never suffered want in body or soul; (3) that now she was living as well as she could wish in this world.[35]

As far as she knew in 1906, her children were all well. She longed to see them on occasion but never did. She prayed that God would hold his hand over them wherever they went. The next year Mrs. Muus received a visit from her daughter, now Birgitte Klüver. Birgitte had married Lorentz D. Klüver, a well-known Trondheim merchant, in 1887. They had three children, a daughter and two sons. Birgitte and her husband were divorced in 1908.[36] Birgitte recalled arriving in Fruithurst on Christmas Eve, 1907. "The fragrance of the magnolia trees met me like a friendly greeting." She woke up on Christmas morning to the singing of birds, the sun shining, and the smell of violets streaming in through the doors and windows. "Then my dear mother served me with a breakfast tray on my bed—the lovely aroma of coffee, an egg, and sandwiches—what better could a sick body and a wounded heart ask for?" One surmises that divorce proceedings were then in progress.

Birgitte stayed with her mother for a number of years. She reported that the local people made much of visiting the sick, and soon asked Birgitte to come with them and help. If she could do nothing else she should pray over their sick friends. When she went out to milk the cows she was always accompanied by a crowd who tagged along to watch. Apparently Birgitte returned to Norway in 1918. On her mother's death in 1922 she inherited the Fruithurst property. In Norway she resided in Oslo, serving as a member of the board of Nordmanns Forbundet until her death on August 18, 1935.[37]

One of the sons of Birgitte and Lorentz Klüver, J. W. Klüver, visited his grandmother in Fruithurst in 1915. The other son, the painter Bernt Klüver, who was regarded by Edvard Munch as the most gifted young artist in Norway, was honored at a dinner at St. Olaf College in November of 1932 and a number of his paintings were displayed. He had an exhibit at the Minneapolis Art Institute in 1933.[38]

Most of the children of Bernt and Oline Muus spent some time at St. Olaf's School. Birgitte attended from 1876 to 1878. There is no record that Nils, the oldest son, enrolled at St. Olaf, nor that Paul Johan attended. Jens, the boy who died young, spent one year at the school. The two youngest sons, Petter Herman and Harald Steen, lived at the home of F. A. Schmidt in Northfield while attending St. Olaf. Their father felt that they needed a mother's care. Harald was in and out of the Academy between 1889 and 1895. Petter completed both the Academy and the College, receiving the B. A. in 1896. Sverre Muus, son of Birgitte, attended the Academy for several terms between 1891 and 1896.[39]

Interesting details about the young Muus boys at St. Olaf are found in letters Pastor Muus wrote to H. T. Ytterboe between 1889 and 1892. Petter left Mrs. Schmidt's house and moved into the College building. Muus asked Ytterboe to explain why Harald was not being advanced to the next class. Was he too lazy? Petter wasn't making progress in other subjects because he wasn't learning English. Harald wanted to move up to the College because the other boys at Schmidt's talked and laughed all the time when he was trying to study. Pastor Muus gave his permission if it was all right with Ytterboe. Harald came home at Pentecost without his father's permission, but he said Professor Ytterboe had approved. Part of the money for the trip he earned by catching pocket gophers and selling them for ten cents each. Muus regularly sent checks to Ytterboe to pay for his sons' expenses and to give them their monthly pocket money.[40]

Nils, the oldest son, lived as a young man in Kenyon, then attended Luther College in Decorah, Iowa. In 1886 he married Josephine Sortedal, daughter of Holden township farmers. They farmed for a time west of Fertile, in Polk county, Minnesota. From 1891 he served as Clerk of Court for Polk county. Later they lived in Crookston, Neilsville, and Littlefork. Nils began banking activity in the latter two places. After they moved to Floodwood in

300

*Nils and Birgitte Muus, ca. 1880. Oldest children of Bernt and Oline Muus*
St. Olaf College Archives

1921 he was a civic leader and president of the First State Bank of Floodwood and an active member of Trinity Lutheran Church. Nils died August 2, 1932. Both he and his wife were buried in the cemetery at Holden. They had ten children. One of them, Herman Ingebrigt Muus, was a Lutheran pastor who served parishes in St. James and Fergus Falls, Minnesota.[41]

Jens Ingebrigt Rynning Muus died when he was twelve years old, a victim of typhus. As noted in an earlier chapter, his death occurred at Holden on November 6, 1878, while his father was dedicating the Main building at St. Olaf's School.

301

*Petter Herman Muus*
Photo from Don McRae album

The third son, Paul Johan Elster Muus, was only 18 when he died of consumption in 1890. In her statement to the Holden congregation in 1880, Oline Muus had asserted that "our little son Paul," then six and one-half years old and sickly, had been ordered by his father to walk to school every day, a total distance of four miles, in boots that were worn out.[42]

After graduating from St. Olaf College, Petter Herman Muus studied for a short time at the theological seminary of the United Norwegian Lutheran Church, but because of throat problems shifted to the study of medicine at Hamline University. Having received the M. D. degree in 1901, he practiced medicine in Kensington and Albert Lea, Minnesota. He died August 16, 1913, and was buried in Albert Lea.

302

The youngest child of Bernt and Oline Muus was Harald Steen Muus. He married Bertha Ellestad, daughter of Pastor N. J. Ellestad, in 1900. They lived in Kenyon, Minnesota, for a time before they moved to Petaluma, California. In California, where his occupation was that of a rancher, Harald was known as Harold Moose. He and his wife had two children. Harald died May 23, 1954.[43]

Sverre Muus, Birgitte's son, was brought up in the Muus household as another child in the family. In addition to the time spent at St. Olaf's School, Sverre later entered Luther College. Letters from Pastor Muus to Luther's president, Laur. Larsen, indicate that in the spring of 1898 Sverre was having difficulty with sums of money Pastor Muus had sent him. Some "riffraff" in Decorah had tricked him out of $10, he wrote, and two days later someone had stolen $19 from him at the school. Next Pastor Muus received word that Sverre had been expelled from Luther and was looking for work in Decorah.[44] A year later, Muus wrote to Larsen about the unpaid bills Sverre had left behind in Decorah. In May of 1899 Sverre was working in a hotel in Oregon. He had left a wife and daughter in Montana. Coming to Minneapolis, he worked as a cook and also served thirty days in the workhouse. Eventually, Sverre Muus appeared in Probate Court in Goodhue county where he was examined by two doctors who declared him to be "of unsound mind." By order of the Judge of Probate Court he was committed to the State Hospital at Rochester, Minnesota, on June 27, 1923.[45]

Apart from having the companionship of Birgitte in Fruithurst for a decade or so, Oline Muus knew little about her children. In a letter written to the Norwegian man of letters Bjørnstjerne Bjørnson in 1899, she complained that when she left Holden the two oldest children, Birgitte and Nils, sided with their father. She also asserted that the two had been "sent" to Norway to spread rumors about her and to convince her siblings that Mrs. Muus was at fault and Pastor Muus completely innocent.[46]

Oline Muus had no further direct contact with her husband, but

*Oline Muus in her later years*
Courtesy Minnesota Historical Society

in 1899 Pastor L. M. Biørn made an effort to bring about a reconciliation between the separated spouses. The information is from
the same letter Mrs. Muus wrote to Bjørnson in July of 1899. From
Biørn she learned that her husband had suffered two strokes, was
paralyzed on his left side, and thought he was dying. When Biørn
had visited Pastor Muus, the latter "had indicated a wish to extend a hand of reconciliation to me and admitted that there were
faults on both sides, that we needed God's forgiveness as well as
our mutual forgiveness."

Pastor Biørn wanted Mrs. Muus to return to Minnesota to care
for her husband. Unfortunately, she did not have the $50 that the

journey would cost, but she wrote at once that she would be very pleased to achieve a reconciliation. A later letter from Biørn stated that Pastor Muus was better and no longer needed her help. Oline Muus explained to Bjørnson: "I then wrote to my husband and told him that it was sinful of him to thus cast me aside, asked him to think about it and to try to forgive me and to forget the big and small transgressions I had committed against him. But I received no reply."[47]

As the years passed, Oline Muus remained vitally engaged in such favorite activities as reading, writing, and embroidering, even after she had to be in a wheelchair or bedfast the last five years of her life. Under the latter circumstances she managed to complete two beautiful embroidery pieces depicting birds on white silk. These were sent as anniversary gifts to Dr. Hans G. Stub and his wife.

Despite her rheumatism and other hardships, Oline Muus had a reputation in Fruithurst for optimism and cheerfulness. "She was a very pleasant person, always interested in things that happened at school and in the community," recalled a woman who as a child delivered milk to Mrs. Muus's house. Mrs. Muus was known for her enthusiasm for Norwegian culture, news of Norwegian immigrants, and church affairs. During the last weeks of her life she recited from memory long passages of scripture and some of her favorite hymns.[48]

Oline Muus received Holy Communion for the last time on August 6, 1922. On Sunday, September 3rd, a Norwegian worship service again was held in her home, and the pastor prayed at her bedside in the presence of members of the congregation. Mrs. Muus died shortly after 1:00 a.m. on September 4, 1922. She was eighty-three years of age. The funeral sermon was preached in Norwegian and English by Wilhelm Pettersen, then serving as a mission pastor for the Augustana Synod in Thorsby and Fruithurst, Alabama. Pettersen, a recognized poet in Norwegian-American literary circles, had known Mrs. Muus since his student days in Minneapolis. His daughter, Leona Pettersen, played

Chopin's "Funeral March." Pastor Pettersen also conducted the burial service at a cemetery outside Fruithurst.[49]

The marker on Oline Muus's grave is in the shape of a large flower vase on a pedestal. The only information carved on the marker is her name, "Olene Muse." "Olene" is simply a misspelling. "Muse" was the name by which she was known in Fruithurst. But she always signed her letters "Oline Muus."

As the narrative returns to Bernt Julius Muus in the next two chapters, he will be seen in his role as pastor and church leader, taking an important part in a controversy that has been called "the most bitter episode in the history of theological warfare among the Norwegians."[50] The final chapter reports on events in Muus's last decade, his illness and return to Norway in 1899, and his death in Trondheim in May of 1900.

# Thirteen

## Church Leader and Dissenter

Bernt Julius Muus's leadership qualities were evident long before he held elective office in his church body, the Synod for the Norwegian Evangelical Lutheran Church. As one of the first Lutheran pastors to settle and work among Norwegian immigrants in Minnesota, he assumed responsibilities of such scope and devoted such prodigious energy to them that he was marked from the outset as one expected to lead. He founded and nurtured congregations close to his Holden base and far beyond it. In the area of church-sponsored education he spoke out strongly on behalf of the parochial school cause, and also boldly fashioned a new kind of academy in Northfield without material help from the Synod.

The dissenting side of Pastor Muus was also visible early on. It will be recalled that in the 1860s Muus showed a degree of nonconformity in defending lay activity in the church, and that he challenged Synod leaders, including his good friend Laur. Larsen, on the doctrine of absolution. A more drastic break between Muus and his Norwegian Synod colleagues took place in the 1880s when Muus emerged as a leader of the opposition with respect to the doctrine of election.

The present chapter meets Muus again in his favorite role as

307

parish pastor in the Holden region, but now with the addition of new tasks and travels as president of the Minnesota District of the Norwegian Synod. When the Synod implemented a new constitution and created three districts in 1876, Muus was chosen to lead the Minnesota District. He served in that position until 1883. Previously he was a member of the Synodical Church Council, from 1861 to 1863 and again from 1873 to 1884. Beginning in 1871, he served as secretary of the Synod for two years.[1]

The developments to be reported below cover a decade or more, from Muus's installation as district president to the results of the so-called Election Controversy in the latter part of the 1880s. Among other results, the controversy brought about a change in the status of St. Olaf's School, the academy Muus started in Northfield in 1874. In 1889, fifteen years after its founding, the school became St. Olaf College.

Even while Pastor Muus's personal and family life was in upheaval as the decade of the 1880s began, there were changes taking place on other fronts. After a lull in the early 1870s, immigration from Norway to America surged again in 1880 and reached its highest number in 1882. More than 4,000 Norwegians were living in Goodhue county in 1870, and the numbers increased each decade, bringing new families into the churches.[2]

Realizing from the beginning that he would need help with his several congregations, Muus had repeatedly pressed the Synod and the Church in Norway for additional pastors to share his duties in southern Minnesota. In 1875 he had the satisfaction of installing M. O. Bøckman, a young candidate in theology from Oslo, as an assistant in the congregations related to Holden, especially Gol and Moland. In 1878 a third pastor, Th. Aug. Hansen, came from Norway to work with Muus and Bøckman, with particular responsibility for Urland and Vang. Hegre was then established as a new congregation.[3]

After Bøckman's arrival and installation, the *Holden Ministerial Book* with its journal of clerical activities indicates how Muus and

Bøckman divided the work between them. On September 26, 1875, for example, the Eighteenth Sunday after Trinity, Muus was at Gol and Bøckman at Urland. Other congregations served regularly by the two pastors were Dale, Holden, Lands, Minneola, and Vang, and Muus had pastoral trips to such other places as Red Wing, Wanamingo, and Northfield, where he attended meetings of the St. Olaf Board of Trustees.

The installation of Th. Aug. Hansen was held in Dale church on September 22, 1878. Thereafter the journal entries show Hansen taking his share of the pastoral duties. On the Twenty-Second Sunday after Trinity, November 17, 1878, Muus was in charge at Holden, Bøckman was at Vang, and Hansen was at Moland. One notes from the journal that "Thanksgiving Day" is entered in English. On that holiday in 1878, Muus held a service at Urland.[4]

Pastor Muus traveled extensively during his first decade in Minnesota, making fall and spring journeys to more distant settlements that were without regular pastoral service. In the 1870s and 1880s, he continued to have church-related business that required travel. Some but not all of his trips were required by his duties as president of the Minnesota District, although journal entries after 1876 seldom make clear whether a given journey was on district business or not. In that era, when there were no synodical or district offices, Synod leaders still functioned as local pastors and their week-to-week routines continued much as before.

Using the 1877 calendar year as an illustration, by far the majority of entries record regular pastoral activities at Holden and the daughter congregations. Trips by Muus beyond that community were to Red Wing in April, to Northfield in May and again for a trustees meeting at St. Olaf's School in June, to a Synod meeting at Norway Lake in Kandiyohi county June 26 to July 3, and to Northfield again July 4 for the laying of the cornerstone for the Main at St. Olaf's School. Muus attended a pastors' conference in Eau Claire, Wisconsin, in the middle of October. Another meeting at St. Olaf's School in Northfield November 7 completed his travels for 1877.[5]

As district president, Muus still took part in many of the same pastors' conferences, synod meetings, ordinations, and church dedications that he had usually attended as a parish pastor. Journal entries that record "visitations," however, point to his ecclesiastical duties as district president or bishop. Such an episcopal visitation was a four-day trip in October of 1879; another took place November 17–28 of that year. On these travels he visited congregations in Chippewa, Renville, Blue Earth, Brown, and Nicollet counties. Of Muus's visitations someone wrote, "Few bishops have won the favor of the pastors and congregations to a higher degree than he."[6] Naturally a district president served as chairman at district meetings and addressed the gatherings. A fuller idea of the duties and multiple concerns Muus had as a district president may be gained from one of his reports to his district. These district meetings, usually attended by the president and other leaders of the Norwegian Synod, were also in an important sense *Synod* meetings since the entire Synod met only every third year. In fact, the official report of a district meeting was actually called the report of a "Synod meeting."

The annual meeting of the Minnesota District of the Norwegian Synod was held June 16–23, 1880, in the Le Sueur River church in Waseca county, a church Muus himself had organized in 1861. At the beginning of his report Muus reminded his listeners that in light of the assaults of the devil, the world, and our flesh, it is a miracle that the church body continues to exist. God's grace upholds the church against the enemy of souls. The same strife goes on between light and darkness, truth and lies, love of God and love of the world. God's Holy Spirit continues to work among the children of men.

One of the well-known enemies is the vice of drunkenness. Muus said that intoxicating drinks belong to God's good creation, but deplored their misuse. He recommended voluntary abstinence as an act of Christian freedom for the sake of oneself and others. To combat drunkenness and other vices required the preaching of God's word and hence more pastors. More support was needed for teachers' salaries. The president encouraged devotions in the homes and lay witnessing, and hoped for improvement in the Christian schools in the congregations. St. Olaf's School had dedicated a new building in 1879, by which he meant Ladies' Hall. At Luther College enrollment had decreased since 1876. Luther Seminary in Madison had acquired a new teacher in Johannes Ylvisaker but still needed another faculty member. Little progress had been made toward establishing a common seminary for training of evangelical Lutheran pastors.[7]

In the latter part of the report Muus spoke of the money received for the mission among Negroes, inner mission work, emigrant missions in New York and Baltimore, and plans of the Bible committee to print a New Testament. He recounted the church visitations he and fellow pastors had made during the year, the names of the six men he had ordained, the pastors entering or leaving the Minnesota district, and a few statistics on congregations, worship services, pastors, and schoolteachers.[8]

The 1880 Minnesota District meeting was especially significant for Muus and the Norwegian Synod for two reasons. First, Muus's role as presiding officer was challenged. Even before Muus delivered his report and presidential address, someone asked "to what extent it was proper or wise" that Muus take the chair because of the "unpleasant situation" he had been drawn into and the writings recently directed against him. The assembly discussed the matter at some length and had a committee bring a report. Since the accusations against Muus had not been proved, the Synod decided by a 45 to 38 vote to make no change, for the time being, in Muus's function as district president. The close vote showed that Muus's support was tenuous.[9]

The second reason the 1880 district meeting was significant was that Muus used the occasion to deliver, without prior notice, a discourse on a theological matter that had blossomed into a controversy. In the middle of his report, he gave his views on an issue that had caused unrest in the church, namely, the controversy

311

regarding election or predestination. This surprise introduction of a thorny topic gave the delegates another reason to take sides for and against the district president.

The fact that he addressed this topic seemed to catch everyone by surprise. The committee elected to respond to the president's address was clearly unhappy that Muus had done so, and expressed itself in the following resolution: "Since the doctrine of the election of grace (*Naadevalget*) had not been appointed and thus not prepared for treatment at this Synod meeting, the Synod regards the method by which the district president handles and develops this matter at its present stage to be dubious; it goes without saying that the president's presentation of this doctrinal question is his own responsibility, which is noted here in order to prevent possible misunderstanding."[10]

What was the doctrine of election and what did Muus say about it that was so disturbing? In general, election or predestination means that God from eternity chooses who will be saved. One important biblical text on election is Romans 8:29–30, which states: "For those whom he [God] foreknew he also predestined to be conformed to the image of his Son, in order that he might be the firstborn within a large family. And those whom he predestined he also called; and those whom he called he also justified; and those whom he justified he also glorified."

What did Muus say about election at the district convention in 1880 that troubled many of his colleagues? In a word, he offered a view of election that was not acceptable to those who favored an interpretation taught by C. F. W. Walther and the Missouri Synod. Muus and many other Norwegian Lutherans in his day learned their definition of election from Erik Pontoppidan, a Danish theologian and Bishop of Bergen in the eighteenth century who gave posterity an explanation of Luther's Small Catechism. To the question, "What is Election?" Pontoppidan answered: "God has appointed all those to eternal life who He from eternity has foreseen would accept the offered grace, believe in Christ, and remain constant in this faith unto the end."[11]

*Friedrich A. Schmidt*
From E. Clifford Nelson and Eugene L. Fevold,
*The Lutheran Church Among Norwegian–Americans*

At the beginning of his speech Muus noted that the controversy over election had actually originated within "the German-
speaking part of our church," referring to the fact that Friedrich A.
Schmidt, a German-born member of the Norwegian Synod, recently had taken issue with Walther's interpretation of election.
In fact, Muus had heard Schmidt and Walther debate election at
a Synodical Conference meeting in Columbus, Ohio, in July of
1879. On his return he said, "It was a pleasure to hear a debate between two who are so well informed on a subject." When asked
which of the two he agreed with, Muus replied, "I am not ready
to say. The matter is a difficult one." Within a year Muus had decided to support Schmidt, a friend for whom he had high regard.[12]

At an appropriate point in his address Muus cited Romans

313

8:29–30 and interpreted it by virtually paraphrasing Pontoppidan's definition of election. Said Muus, "God from eternity has appointed some individual persons to eternal life, namely, those who from eternity he has seen will receive the offered grace, believe in Christ, and be found in this faith at the end of their life."

Only God knows the future, Muus continued. It is presumptuous to brood over what we do not know. We do not build the hope of eternal salvation on something that no one knows about except God. What we may believe is a clear, unambiguous, firm, and unwavering way of salvation that has been revealed to us. We know that the Son of God and Son of Man has redeemed us; and we know that the one who believes and is baptized will be saved, but whoever does not believe will be condemned. The almighty and gracious God has both the power and the will to save us and see us through to our final salvation, but it is also true that we could slip away from our baptismal covenant. We will be saved only if we remain in the faith in Jesus Christ to the end. To say this is not to build our hope for future salvation on our own works. The Lord is the one who must begin and complete every good work in us. Unfortunately, because of our flesh, we have both the power and the will to resist the operation of God's grace. Therefore, we are admonished to work out our salvation with fear and trembling insofar as we are able with God's assistance.[13]

After hearing Muus's statements on election, the assembly expressed uneasiness about having the president's views made public because the topic was such a difficult one and its discussion had not been anticipated. Synod president Preus and others wanted to confine the subject to pastoral conferences. A few felt that Muus was justified in airing the topic, pointing out that the Missourian view had been published in the church paper. Printing Muus's statement could stimulate thinking. The majority of delegates at the meeting appealed to Muus to omit his comments on election from the official printed record, but he refused. In the end, his remarks were printed, but so was the committee's statement that the views Muus had presented were his alone.[14]

By speaking out on election at the district meeting of 1880, Muus was entering into a controversy that had begun earlier. The origins of the dispute went back to 1878 when Professor Ole Asperheim of the Norwegian Synod's theological seminary in Madison, Wisconsin, issued criticisms of theological tendencies in the Missouri Synod. At first Asperheim was opposed by his colleague, F. A. Schmidt, but soon Schmidt became alarmed at the Missourian teaching on election as spelled out by C. F. W. Walther the year before. Among other things, Walther said: "God has even from eternity chosen a certain number of persons unto salvation; He has determined that these shall and must be saved, and besides them none others."[15] Schmidt saw in Walther's thinking something perilously close to the determinism associated with the reformer John Calvin. Lutherans generally did not consider the doctrine of election as a main article of faith. With Luther, they regarded it as a source of comfort for believers, an assurance of God's saving love. They were careful to avoid Calvin's idea of double predestination, that God chooses some to be saved and some to be damned.

Professor Schmidt made public his disagreements with Walther on election in a periodical he began in 1880 called *Altes und Neues* (Old and New) and in a pamphlet titled *Naadevalg-Striden* (The Election Controversy), published in 1881. These actions singled out Schmidt as the spokesman for the anti-Missourian stand on election, but according to U. V. Koren "the *enfant terrible* was Muus." The able Pastor Koren led the response from the other side, making it known that any attack on Walther and the Missourian view was an attack on him.[16]

Walther's view of election drew heavily upon Article XI of *The Formula of Concord*, a Lutheran doctrinal summary not officially included among the confessional writings subscribed to by the Church of Norway and the Norwegian Synod. Within the *Formula*'s longer treatment of Article XI, "Of God's Eternal Election," one finds this explanatory statement: "The eternal election of God, however, not only foresees and foreknows the salvation of the elect, but is also, from the gracious will and pleasure of God in Christ Jesus, a cause which procures, works, helps, and promotes our salvation and what pertains thereto; and upon this [divine predestination] our salvation is so founded that the gates of hell cannot prevail against it."[17]

The interpretation of the Missourians placed heavy emphasis on the sovereignty of God's grace in the salvation of human beings. Election was the cause of salvation, unrelated to anything in the human situation. The principle of salvation by grace alone made them especially eager to fend off any suggestion that the human being contributed anything toward or cooperated in his or her salvation. To God alone must go all the glory when a human being is saved and brought to eternal life.

Schmidt, Muus, and others in the Norwegian Synod, who came to be known as the "Anti-Missourians," did not quarrel with the venerable Lutheran doctrine of salvation by grace and the corresponding rejection of human merit or works as grounds for salvation. Where they differed with Walther and the Missourians was a concern that election would be perceived as the "cause" of salvation without due attention to the role of faith in the process. Granted, faith too is a gift from God, but it is engendered in the interaction between God and the human person. The loving God, willing and able to save everyone, approaches a person with the word of the Gospel and the wooing of the Holy Spirit. One person responds in repentance and faith, and is saved; another fails to respond. Therefore the Anti-Missourians felt that Pontoppidan had it right: "He elected those who He foresaw would believe in Christ through the power of His Word and Spirit."[18]

Sometimes the expression "two forms" was used in distinguishing the two different understandings of election. The "first form," advocated by Walther, the Missouri Synod, and many influential pastors in the Norwegian Synod, was derived from Article XI of *The Formula of Concord*. The following definition sums up the "first form" position: "Election is that act of God from eternity, who before the foundations of the world were laid, solely because of God's grace and mercy, and the holy merits of Christ, resolved to call, justify and glorify those who finally would be saved."[19] Election was unrelated to anything God might foresee in the human being, including faith. Walther and his supporters accused the other side of synergism, the notion that human beings cooperate in their salvation.

The "second form," espoused by Schmidt, Muus, and many others in the Norwegian Synod, has been traced to the formulation of Aegidius Hunnius, Lutheran theologian of the sixteenth century, who wrote: "Election is that act of God from eternity which before the foundation of the world was laid determined to glorify all those who He foresaw would come to faith in Christ until the end." The difference is the idea that God appoints persons to salvation "in view of foreseen faith," *intuitu fidei* in Latin, the phrase Hunnius contributed to discussions of election.[20] The same key idea was present in the Pontoppidan definition of election familiar to Muus's generation. In fact, the majority of Norwegian-American Lutherans of that era had been nurtured by Pontoppidan and the "second form" of election. God elects those who he foresees will believe and remain faithful until the end. The Anti-Missourians accused their opponents of bringing a Calvinizing element into Lutheranism and of playing down the factors of repentance and faith.

The controversy regarding election was bound to affect the understanding of conversion. The Missourians warned against human cooperation, or synergism. God alone saves. Election is the cause of salvation. The Anti-Missourians insisted that one could not ignore the differences in human attitudes toward the offered grace of God. Some rejected and some accepted. In giving God all the glory one did not need to view the human person as a

317

passive entity. Certainly a person participated when conversion took place.

Muus insisted on repentance and faith in the process of salvation in a number of articles during the rest of the decade. He resisted the suggestion of being irresistibly converted that he sensed in Missourian teaching. He asked, "Are *all* men whom God calls through the Word able to convert themselves (*omvende sig*), or are *only* those able to convert themselves whom God compels?" The Missourians, he charged in an 1884 article, taught that God had chosen certain persons for "an infallible attainment of eternal blessedness" without taking into account their future situation in time. He contended in another published piece that it is clear from God's Word that a person's salvation depends on repenting and believing in Christ, and further, that a person can do so when God is at work to that end by his Spirit and grace.[21]

In his insistence that human beings should and could respond to God's offer, Muus sometimes cited Revelation 3:20, "Listen, I am standing at the door, knocking; if you hear my voice and open the door,I will come in to you and eat with you, and you with me." He also quoted the account in the book of Acts where Peter and the apostles were asked by their Jewish listeners, "Brothers, what should we do?" Peter's reply was, "Repent, and be baptized every one of you in the name of Jesus Christ." Peter did not say, suggested Muus artfully, "Listen, my friends. You can do absolutely nothing for your conversion and salvation. It is only the modern Pelagian and synergistic teachers who lead you to believe that you can and must do something to be saved."[22]

Muus felt that the other side did not allow sufficiently for the operative power of the Word of God in conversion. A slogan for the Missourians, wrote Muus, is this: "No one can be converted before he is converted." That is, they failed to see that through the Word God gave the unregenerate person the strength to receive the Gospel. True, by nature a person has no ability to contribute toward conversion, nor does God force anyone to be converted. When a person is converted it is not against that person's will, but a choice of the will is made possible by God who imparts new abilities by the Holy Spirit through the Word.[23]

Long after the controversy of the 1880s, the Norwegian Lutherans in America resolved their differences over the doctrine of election. They did so, not by one side defeating the other, but by agreeing to incorporate both points of view, both "forms," in an agreement signed in Madison, Wisconsin, in 1912. A paragraph from the Madison Agreement sheds light on the issue that was debated so furiously in the decade of the 1880s: "We have agreed to reject all errors which seek to explain away the mystery of election (*Formula of Concord*, Part II, Article XI) either in a synergizing or a Calvinizing manner, in other words, every doctrine which either on the one hand would deprive God of His glory as only Savior or on the other hand would weaken man's sense of responsibility in relation to the acceptance or rejection of grace."[24]

Such an eventual reconciliation seemed unattainable during the heated arguments that continued through most of the 1880s. A few of the steps that led to a damaging split in the Norwegian Synod may be noted. F. A. Schmidt began a bi-weekly paper called *Luthersk Vidnesbyrd* (Lutheran Witness) that presented the Anti-Missourian cause to the church public. P. A. Rasmussen, another Anti-Missourian, thought the time had come for the Norwegian Synod to break its ties with the Synodical Conference. Hastening that break was an incident at the 1882 convention of the Synodical Conference in Chicago when Schmidt was denied his rightful seat on the grounds that he could not be recognized as a "brother in Christ," but as an "enemy." The only one who voted against the motion to deny Schmidt his seat was B. J. Muus.[25]

The movement to separate the Norwegian Synod from the Synodical Conference gained force and even the support of such strong Synod leaders as H. A. Preus and U. V. Koren. In 1883 the actual break took place. The same year, because of the ongoing struggle regarding election, Preus and his son and assistant, C. K.

319

Preus, were actually deposed from one of their congregations in southern Wisconsin.[26]

Muus also felt the sting of the fray in 1883 when he was defeated in his bid for re-election as president of the Minnesota District. The loss was bitter enough since his rival, Bjug A. Harstad, was a Missourian, but also because the vote was extremely close. The meeting took place in Zumbrota, Minnesota. "The two parties in the Synod stood sharply opposed to one another, girded for battle and sword in hand," wrote editor and novelist Peer Strømme, who was present at the meeting. The test would come at the election for district president. Under peaceful circumstances, the incumbent's re-election would have been a foregone conclusion since, in Strømme's admiring judgment, Muus "was a head taller than all the people." A delegate from Red Wing who would have voted for Muus was barred because of some irregularities in his election. Ole Fingarsen from Rock Dell told the assembly that he would have voted for Muus but did not dare for fear of being disciplined by Pastor J. A. Thorsen. On the third ballot, Harstad won by a vote of 57 to 53.[27]

For a time afterward, Muus refused to recognize Harstad's election as legal. Harstad, who served from 1884 to 1892, assumed office in the latter part of 1884. As of June 1 of that year, Muus as president of the Minnesota District sent a report to the president of the Synod with no mention of a successor. Among other matters, he referred to confusion among pastors because of "Calvinistic ideas of election and conversion." In a noticeably icy tone, Muus commented on an ordination: "A deplorable insult against our faith and order was caused this current year because Pastor H. A. Preus ordained a theological candidate as pastor whom the district's president did not wish to ordain." The candidate whom Muus had refused to ordain was Otto Ottesen, son of Pastor J. A. Ottesen. Young Ottesen did not satisfy Muus when questioned about conversion.[28]

The controversy moved closer to the critical point at a pastoral conference in Decorah, Iowa, in November of 1884 when Synod

320

pastors of the Missourian viewpoint issued "An Accounting" (*En Redegjørelse*) of their position on grace, conversion, election, and assurance. The Anti-Missourian pastors refused to sign the document, met separately, and produced their own "Confession." At the same time, they took the significant step of establishing an independent fund outside Synod control to help support Anti-Missourian church-school professors whose incomes might be in jeopardy because of their theological views. B. J. Muus was the one who authorized payments from the fund. His leadership in this regard drew from Laur. Larsen the impatient question, "Must Muus positively be a president within the Synod, whether he is chosen to that office by the Synod or not?"[29]

As events now moved rapidly toward an open schism in the Norwegian Synod, theological differences had a far-reaching impact on educational matters. Forty of the pastors who had signed the Anti-Missourian "Confession" in Decorah met the following year in Red Wing, Minnesota. Two of their decisions involved financial support for Anti-Missourian theological professors. Incidentally, Synod president H. A. Preus wrote to Muus asking for a list of the pastors and professors who voted for the Red Wing resolutions, but Muus declined to supply it.[30]

Uppermost in the minds of the leaders of the Anti-Missourian group, including B. J. Muus, F. A. Schmidt, M. O. Bøckman, and Thorbjørn Nelson Mohn, was the education of pastors. Schmidt faced an uncertain future as one of three professors at the Synod's Luther Seminary in Madison, Wisconsin. For theological reasons, it was desirable for the Anti-Missourians to establish their own seminary. Muus was the key figure in putting into effect a decision to use the facilities of St. Olaf's School in Northfield as the location of the Anti-Missourian seminary. In the fall of 1886 the new institution, called "Lutheran Pastors' School" (Lutherske Presteskole), began classes with F. A. Schmidt and M. O. Bøckman as the professors. Located on the second floor of the Main building at St. Olaf, the seminary continued in operation until 1890, when the United Norwegian Lutheran Church was formed.[31]

*St. Olaf Board of Trustees July 13, 1886*
Felland collection, St. Olaf College Archives

Part of the agreement in establishing the seminary was that the Anti-Missourian group would pay St. Olaf's School $1,200 a year to introduce college-level work, beginning with a first-year class in the fall of 1886. It was no longer fitting to send pre-theological candidates to the Synod's school, Luther College. The plan was put into operation. In the spring of 1889, the Board of Trustees moved to change the name of St. Olaf's School to St. Olaf College and to give Principal Thorbjørn Nelson Mohn the title of president.[32] The first students to receive the B. A. degree from St. Olaf College graduated in the spring of 1890.

Obviously establishing a theological seminary was regarded as an act of defiance by the Norwegian Synod. At the general Synod meeting held in Stoughton, Wisconsin, in the summer of 1887, resolutions were passed denouncing the founding of the seminary in Northfield. 1. "The Synod can not but consider the erection of the new theological school at Northfield (a) as an act of opposition to break down the Synod's schools which have been established in accordance with its constitution; (b) as a breach of the Synod's constitution . . . ; (c) as an act which is in itself divisive . . . . 2. Therefore the Synod can not tolerate in its members that such activities be continued and must earnestly admonish those who have taken part in them to admit their error and withdraw from them."

Speaking for the opposition was not Muus, but Mohn, principal of St. Olaf's School, which had become "the focal point of interest for Anti-Missourian activity." On the floor of the convention he delivered the following statement: "Since the Synod has stated that it can not tolerate the Lutheran seminary at Northfield and its work, and since the work of the seminary is for us a matter of conscience and is an undertaking pleasing to God, and since we must obey God rather than men, we declare that we can not close the Lutheran seminary in Northfield so long as the Missouri teaching in regard to predestination and conversion is conducted at the Synod schools."[33]

Mohn's protest was signed by thirty pastors and twenty-seven lay representatives. The split with the Norwegian Synod became a reality at a later meeting when the Anti-Missourians, with Mohn presiding, decided formally to withdraw from the Synod. By 1888, about one-third of the pastors and congregations had left the Norwegian Synod. Instead of organizing a new synod, the group formed itself into the Anti-Missourian Brotherhood, with L. M. Biørn as president. Besides raising funds to sustain the seminary at St. Olaf and promoting the college program, the Brotherhood soon joined the Conference for the Norwegian-Danish Evangelical Lutheran Church in America and the Norwegian Augustana Synod to form, in 1890, the United Norwegian Lutheran Church in America.[34]

When the fateful schism in the Norwegian Synod took place in 1887, Pastor Muus was not among those who left. In this respect, too, he was a dissenter. He had led the fight against the Synod's teachings on election and conversion, and he had used his influence, including his strategic position as chairman of the St. Olaf Board of Trustees, to found a theological seminary at the school in Northfield. But he himself chose not to withdraw from the Synod. At a meeting of Anti-Missourians held at St. Olaf's School in June of 1887, he urged those who had broken with the Synod to return to its fold.[35]

Characteristically, Muus remained in the Norwegian Synod out of principle even when his congregation left in 1887 to join the United Church in 1890. It was his duty to stay, to fight for the truth and oppose false doctrine. His colleagues objected that it was no use to remain when one was cut off from the opportunity to help. But Muus replied that love of God and neighbor compelled him to stay in the Synod. "What is required of us is that each one be found faithful at that post where God has placed him." When all was said and done, Muus was a stubbornly loyal churchman. A decade later, he left the Norwegian Synod only because he was asked to leave.[36]

It was as a churchman that Muus became a champion of the Anti-Missourian cause, struggling against what he perceived as serious departures from Lutheran teaching regarding election and conversion. He was not always judicious in how he argued for human participation in salvation, at times giving his adversaries openings to accuse him of synergism and Roman Catholic leanings. But despite such slips, he upheld the Lutheran teaching that human beings are saved by grace alone. In harmony with that honored doctrine, Muus contended, is the experience that the Word of God addressed to human beings gives them power to accept God's grace and to be saved.[37]

# Fourteen

## Final Years

The immediate results of the theological controversy of the 1880s were the split in the Norwegian Synod, the withdrawal of approximately one-third of the pastors and congregations, the establishing of a theological seminary at St. Olaf's School in Northfield, Minnesota, and a movement to unite non-Synod Norwegian Lutherans in the new United Norwegian Lutheran Church in America. In the new situation that unfolded, B. J. Muus's part in the controversy had continuing relevance.

As the Anti-Missourian leader he became, Muus argued for human free will in opposition to what he perceived as the Missourian belief in conversion by coercion (*tvangsomvendelse*). Invoking the catechism as well as other sources, he insisted that it was authentically Lutheran to hold and to teach that God the Holy Spirit, through the word of the Gospel, freed the human will from its bondage and gave the person power to repent and believe in Christ. Even if not free in the absolute sense, surely the will must be engaged in the all-important transaction between God and the sinner that results in salvation.[1]

Pastor Muus's views resonated with the needs of ordinary people. Unlike most of his Synod colleagues, Muus had been touched by the Haugean movement and by the later awakening led by Gisle Johnson. During the course of his ministry, Muus had won the confidence of lay people by serving them in an unassuming manner and sharing their lot. It was said of him, "He was like another farmer."[2]

His good relations with the laity were in harmony with a theology that gave dignity to the human personality, recognizing the role of the individual's response to the divine initiative. Sharing his views were Thorbjørn Nelson Mohn, president of St. Olaf College, and a considerable circle of Anti-Missourian pastors and lay people drawn to the college and the Lutheran seminary established on the campus.

According to an astute essay by Leigh Jordahl, the election controversy brought into being a new constituency in the Norwegian Lutheran community of the Midwest. It made St. Olaf the rallying point for a broad churchmanship "influenced by and oriented toward the American democratic ideology." And this new churchmanship, observed Jordahl, reflected "the grass roots faith of the Norwegian immigrants."[3] By intuition and experience, both Muus and Mohn were attuned to the grass roots faith of the immigrants. When compared to such Synod leaders as Preus, Koren, Ottesen, and Larsen, Muus stood out, noted Jordahl, as "the man most sensitive to the American environment and the emerging *temperament* of the constituency." This view of Muus is both interesting and unexpected, given his persistent "Norwegianness" in other matters. For example, he knew English quite well but rarely used it in his sermons and public addresses.

In any case, Muus's affirmation of the human will as a factor in conversion was an idea in harmony with the American environment and one that had considerable appeal. In personal bearing he was more the democrat than the aristocrat, despite his university training and ministerial office. Muus's pietistic leanings aided his understanding of ordinary people, a need intensified by frontier conditions.

Thorbjørn Nelson Mohn has been characterized as "intensely American in thought and purpose from the beginning." Though

*B. J. Muus and Th. N. Mohn front and center. Twentieth anniversary of St. Olaf College, 1894*
Felland Collection, St. Olaf College Archives

Norwegian-born, he had received his entire education in this country, having suffered the poverty and hardships of pioneer life in Wisconsin and Minnesota. Before entering Luther College, he had taught in the public common schools. Mohn once described St. Olaf College as "an institution founded by Norsemen for the purpose of turning Norwegians into Americans."[4]

In reflecting on St. Olaf as the rallying point for the broad churchmanship of which Leigh Jordahl wrote, one recalls that the original vision forged by Muus and Mohn was that of a school offering a general education to young people of both sexes. Even though a theological seminary was in operation on the campus from 1886 to 1890, and even though students were encouraged to prepare for the ministry, St. Olaf College continued to educate students to enter many different kinds of occupations as American citizens. Martin Luther's idea of vocation, that Christians could serve God and their neighbors in any secular occupation, was at the heart of St. Olaf's founding vision. In an address at the college

327

in 1894, Muus said: "The question of what you are going to be is one that all of you have considered. In one sense it is immaterial what position you enter. God wants to have His servants in *all* occupations; it does not matter so much what position one goes into but that one serves God in this position."[5]

It was difficult to realize the fruits of such ideals in the decade of the 1890s because St. Olaf College was soon plunged into a struggle for its very existence. As expected, B. J. Muus did his share and more to keep the college alive when the financial support from the newly organized United Church came to an abrupt end. But Muus was not the central figure as the college worked through the crisis. President Mohn and Professor H. T. Ytterboe came to the rescue while Muus was less visible.

At least two factors tended to keep Muus in the background. First, he gave up his position as president of the Board of Trustees of the College in June of 1889. He had informed the Board the previous year that he would not accept election as president or member of the Board, and he stood by his decision. He may have felt that after fifteen years on the Board and the change to college status it was an appropriate time to step aside. Elected in his place was Professor M. O. Bøckman.[6] Second, Muus was not a member of the United Church that in 1890 voted to make St. Olaf its college. When pastors and congregations, including Muus's own, left the Norwegian Synod in 1887 and the years immediately following, Muus stayed with the Synod. It was indeed a strange position, to be in the Norwegian Synod with the body, but in the United Church with the heart.[7]

The United Church came into existence when three predominantly Norwegian Lutheran groups merged in 1890. They were the Norwegian Augustana Synod, the Conference for the Norwegian Evangelical Lutheran Church, and the Anti-Missourian Brotherhood. Hauge's Synod was interested in the prospective union at first, but withdrew from the merger plans in 1889.[8] When the new church was organized in June of 1890, it resolved that Augsburg should be its theological seminary and St. Olaf in Northfield should be its college.

This agreement was soon thrown into confusion when the Augsburg board of trustees refused to transfer ownership of Augsburg Seminary to the new church. Professors Sven Oftedal and Georg Sverdrup, the main Augsburg leaders, wanted to maintain control of the institution and preserve its preparatory and collegiate units, which they regarded as threatened by the United Church's choice of St. Olaf College. They frankly distrusted St. Olaf, regarding it as "a secular educational institution whose traditions and ideals were not in harmony with the kind of preliminary training needed for the study of theology."[9]

The painful result of three years of dispute, rightly called "The Augsburg Controversy," was that the United Church in 1893 annulled the resolutions that had made St. Olaf its college. With this important source of support cut off, the Northfield institution was forced into six years of uphill financial struggle. But the college survived, with Ytterboe leading the way in heroic fund raising, Mohn sacrificing his full energies to keep the institution alive, and Muus upholding the effort even as he expressed his critical opinion about the Augsburg faction's relationship to the transfer question. After a time, the Augsburg group went its own way to form the Lutheran Free Church in 1897. In 1899 the United Church again adopted St. Olaf as its college and pledged to support it.[10]

Writing to H. T. Ytterboe in May of 1893, Muus noted with approval that Ytterboe was at work raising money for St. Olaf. With a touch of grim humor, Muus added that someone has to gather money, otherwise St. Olaf also will go to the dogs or to the Catholics. Three years later Muus received an encouraging financial report from Ytterboe and responded with praise to God that it had gone so well. He continued: "And I also want to thank you for your persevering labors. God reward you for them! The schools, the schools, that is the future."[11]

Pastor Muus was invited to give the Founders' Day address at

329

St. Olaf on November 6, 1893, one of the bleakest years in the institution's experience because of the United Church's decision to drop St. Olaf as its college. In the address Muus analyzed what it meant to be a Norwegian evangelical Lutheran institution of higher learning. Good schools are necessary to provide society with the wise, informed leadership it needs. But for knowledge to be used in the right way, the Word of God must be present to teach us to walk as free persons in the world and to conquer death. Looking ahead at St. Olaf's future, he granted that prospects were not bright. But there was still the strength of life in the school. "Let us therefore not bother ourselves too much with how *many* enemies or how *many* friends we have. That is only to waste valuable time. It is better to look forward to the goal and with fresh courage to heed the command: 'Fram, Fram, Christmenn, Crossmenn!'"[12]

A year later, when St. Olaf celebrated its 20th anniversary, Muus again gave the Founders' Day speech. His starting point was that human beings belong to the animal kingdom, but since God has created us with immortal souls we do not want to be regarded *only* as animals. Above all, we want to belong to *God's* kingdom. There are enough schools that instruct in what pertains to this world, but they lack the most important thing for those who are called to eternal life. "Therefore *this* school is established, in order that the young people, while they are being prepared to step forth independently on life's battleground, here shall have all the help they need to be enabled in the coming days to carry out their battle in the ranks of God's children, for the extension of God's kingdom and its strengthening within them and around them."

Speaking of the importance of serving God, whatever one's chosen line of work, Muus cited the need for Christian editors, politicians, physicians, judges, but, above all, pastors and teachers. Do not forget the goal, he admonished, which is not to be educated to be the foremost among the animals, but to be *human beings*, that is, people who are called to be members of *God's* king-

330

dom, co-workers for the growth of God's kingdom, workers not only for time, but also for eternity.

Looking back at St. Olaf's beginning, Muus said that it was built in weakness. We had no money and found little sympathy for such a work. Nearly everyone was against us. But we set out depending on the almighty God who created heaven and earth. We believed that the institution was necessary in order that His work could be carried out among us. Up to this point He has helped us. We hope that also in the future, despite all the dark prospects, He will help us carry out His work.[13]

B. J. Muus as educator still remained the pastor. Much as his active mind thrived on scholarly discourse, he did not advance specific theories of education or discuss all the intellectual currents of the day. His theological studies in Norway and the demands of pastoral tasks in America led him to found an institution centered on the Bible and Lutheran teaching. Yet, even as he promoted the ministry and teaching, his genius was in valuing education for society's needs beyond church callings, and in inspiring others to share that vision. St. Olaf College would contribute to the wider society through its young men and women prepared in a variety of subjects to serve God and humanity in many different fields. At every opportunity, Muus enunciated his conviction that teaching and learning that glorifies God will be of both temporal and eternal benefit to future generations.

During his last years of pastoral ministry in Goodhue county, Muus was serving Holden and Dale congregations. Over his strenuous objections, these two congregations joined in the formation of the United Church in 1890. At the crucial Stoughton meeting of the Norwegian Synod in 1887, when many Anti-Missourian pastors broke with the Synod rather than agree to close down the rival seminary located in Northfield, Pastor Muus did not join them. Yet Muus had been at the center of the action in placing the new seminary on the St. Olaf campus. Muus felt that, inasmuch as the Missourian view of election was false, it was his duty to remain in the Synod and fight against it. For example,

Muus engaged in regular correspondence with Pastor U. V. Koren during the late 1880s and early 1890s. The two theological combatants cordially but tirelessly defended their respective positions on election and conversion, citing Scripture and the fathers.[14]

It is not surprising that Muus did not exert leadership in the organization and early life of the new United Church. He kept up with developments in the United Church to some extent since its action would affect his congregations. He attended their annual meetings, but according to N. J. Ellestad, who succeeded Muus as pastor at Holden, never asked for the floor during discussions.[15]

As to Muus's relations with the Norwegian Synod, there were two dynamics at work. One was Muus's initiatives to continue conversations with Synod pastors regarding disputed doctrines, including election and conversion. He wrote to President Preus to get his cooperation in setting up a colloquium between Missourians in the Norwegian Synod and Anti-Missourians.[16]

In 1893 Muus called a meeting of "opposition congregations" in an unnamed settlement at which he delivered a lecture, "Drive the Spirit of Dissension Out!" Dissension was against God's will and harmful to the Christians, he argued. Christians could love one another and work together even if they did not agree on every point. Christian unity means being united by faith in Christ, and in love to him to learn from him and in love to the brothers to learn with them until all come to unity of faith and knowledge of the Son of God.[17] Another attempt by Muus to restore unity in the Norwegian church took the form of organizing free conferences for discussion of church teachings. He sent invitations to members of the Norwegian Synod, Hauge's Synod, and the United Church for such a conference in Lanesboro, Minnesota, from September 15 to 22, 1897. The invitation attracted 28 from the Synod, 11 from Hauge's Synod, and 71 from the United Church. The assembly debated Muus's thesis that defined conversion as follows: "that a person turns away from sin, seeks salvation and believes that Christ has redeemed [him/her] who was lost and condemned to eternal death." Muus defended his thesis,

332

Amund Mikkelsen represented the Synod view, and O. S. Meland of Hauge's Synod sided with Muus.[18]

The second dynamic in Pastor Muus's relationship to the Norwegian Synod during the later years of his ministry was the Synod's growing annoyance at Muus's gadfly role. It seemed to be the case, as Muus himself was to say, that he was the "black sheep" in the Norwegian Synod. He wrote provocative articles in the church papers that irritated Synod members. He refused to retract his strictures against the Synod's teaching or to change his own views, despite repeated appeals from Synod leaders. He was charged with showing contempt for the Synod, neglecting meetings, or coming late and leaving early.

These were among the complaints voiced against Muus by the president of the Minnesota District, Pastor Knut K. Bjørgo, at its meeting in La Crosse in 1896. In Bjørgo's opinion, by his conduct Pastor Muus in effect had already left the Synod. The district meeting passed a resolution to have a committee negotiate with Muus and bring a report to the next Synod meeting. Muus and the committee met in Robbinsdale in 1897, but with no clear result. These steps were preliminary to Muus's expulsion from the Minnesota District and the Norwegian Synod at the 1898 meeting of the Minnesota District held in the Sheyenne congregation's church, Cass county, North Dakota, south of Fargo.[19]

The district meeting in Cass county took place June 15–21, 1898. The committee that had been investigating "Pastor Muus's case" placed four paragraphs of complaints against Muus as the basis for its recommedation that "he be regarded as one who himself has severed his churchly connection with us." Muus was charged with rejecting what God's Word taught on preparatory grace, Christian assurance, and prayer. He had defended doctrines in conflict with God's Word and the Lutheran Church's confession regarding conversion, assurance, and prayer. He had retained his false doctrines despite repeated negotiations and public and private appeals. In many ways Muus had broken with the Synod, had trespassed against its constitution and resolutions, including

333

his work with the Anti-Missourian Brotherhood, and for several years had not participated in the work of the Synod. And still he had not recognized the sinfulness in all of this and made amends.[20]

Muus was given the opportunity to respond to the committee's statements and did so briefly, stating his desire to bring an end to the matter. In the give and take between himself and various Synod members, including Koren and Larsen, Muus restated his views. The German Missouri Synod had adopted a Calvinist doctrine of election that had been rejected unanimously by the Lutheran Church after the time of the Book of Concord, he maintained. When the Norwegian Synod turned to the Missouri teaching, Muus decided to oppose it. The Synod spokesmen had committed a great sin against God and people by adopting that doctrine of election. Regarding conversion, he believed that an ungodly person must convert him/herself to God in order to be saved. God does not turn anyone around by force, but works on the will so that the person wants to be moved from the condition of sin to the condition of grace.[21]

Larsen denied that the Synod had changed its view on election, that it taught an absolute election, that they were Calvinists, that they taught that a person is converted by force. "We have never taught anything but that which is in the Book of Concord," said Larsen. Koren declared that the Synod teaching was that of the Formula of Concord, citing two sentences that Muus agreed with, but Koren said he was equivocating. The assembly decided to have the committee's report read point by point and have Muus reply. During the procedure, each of Muus's replies was challenged by one or more of the Synod pastors.

An important moment was reached when a Pastor Monson asked Muus to explain why he himself stayed in the Norwegian Synod when his congregations no longer belonged to it. Without hesitation Muus replied: "In order to complete my ministry." If the leaders in the Norwegian Synod chose to abandon the old Lutheran doctrine, he like Joshua would serve the Lord. The church is like a hospital. Those with spiritual gifts should use them to heal the weak. "The Norwegian Synod is a continuation of our fathers' church. . . . One should not forsake his own assembly; but one should remain with that which is given us historically, even if in some respects it is in error." The command of love calls for helping those who are going astray.[22]

Muus's Synod adversaries were not moved by any of his statements. Pastor Ole P. Vangsnes accused Muus of being the single person most responsible for the split in the Norwegian Synod. It was time to adopt the committee's recommendation. Koren agreed that things had gone on too long before they showed Muus "this last deed of love." Now it was time to show in practice that members of the Norwegian Synod will not tolerate false teaching. Two laymen spoke up. A Mr. Qui said he had known Muus as long as anyone present. "He has been my pastor; he is a man who fears no one." Whether what was proposed was right or wrong, he could not say, but he could not vote for the motion. A Mr. Walby said he did not have sufficient acquaintance with the case to vote for or against.

The vote was called for. As noted above, the proposal stated that Muus "should be regarded as one who himself has severed his churchly connection with us." The tally was 139 for, 2 against, and 11 abstaining. When the results were announced, Muus took the floor to ask, "The meaning then is that I no longer belong to the Minnesota District?" Then he proceeded to offer his hearty thanks to the Norwegian Synod for the bygone years of cooperation. It had been his lot to work toward the goal of bringing souls to God. "And I must say that the help I received in former days from the Norwegian Synod has been invaluable." It was his desire that members of the Synod would receive more light and love to achieve even more to God's glory and the salvation of souls, especially among the Norwegians, that their temporal and eternal welfare might be advanced. "God bless you!"

In reading the published report of the meeting, one senses that the atmosphere changed when U. V. Koren took the floor. He had been asked "to speak a friendly word to Muus to take with him."

335

He made it clear that the action of the Minnesota District was also taken on behalf of the Norwegian Synod. Koren still insisted that it was "a deed of love." The only proper explanation was that they wanted to help "dear Pastor Muus."

Muus knew that Koren was sincerely fond of him and had tried to show it after disagreements arose. "We have not forgotten and will not forget what the Norwegian Synod in its time has owed him." Koren assured Muus that it was not only the older ones who were fond of him, but he had won respect and love also from the young generations. "Therefore, on behalf of the entire Synod, I want to say to Pastor Muus that it is with bleeding hearts that we are separated from him." The Synod sent its best wishes and prayers with him and wished Muus every blessing. Concluding with "Farvel da Muus!" (Farewell, Muus, farewell!), Koren extended his hand to say goodbye.[23]

The severity of this blow to Muus was incalculable. L. M. Biørn wrote: "Muus grieved more over this treatment than many imagined who saw him calmly smoking his pipe outside of the church where the judgment over him had fallen."[24]

According to Th. Eggen, another fellow pastor, with the exception of the dark period in his family life, this was certainly the most tragic moment in his whole life. Yet Muus's words of farewell were characteristic of the man: no hate, no bitterness. Muus had the capacity to separate the substance of a matter from the persons involved. Those whom he had fought against and who had pronounced this hard judgment over him had been and remained his friends. His final words had to do with what Muus regarded as most important, the kingdom of God and the salvation of souls, not his own person or his feelings.[25]

In physical appearance Bernt Julius Muus was a relatively small man and rather thin but, as described by L. M. Biørn, handsome, well-proportioned, and in good health. S. O. Simundson reported that one first noticed the triangular-shaped head and especially the high forehead. Rasmus Anderson recalled that Muus had "a deep bass voice." Toward the end of his days, however, when his voice was broken, it was difficult to hear him. He was not known for eloquence as a speaker. In his preaching he was logical, clear, and easy to follow. His effectiveness was affirmed by M. O. Bøckman, who said, "I have never heard anyone who could preach the Gospel like Muus could. It was so sweet to sit beneath his pulpit and hear him preach Jesus Christ."[26]

As Muus's contemporaries put into writing their impressions of the man, they showed in various ways what a strong and compelling personality he was. They told of a man who felt so unworthy to be a pastor that he tried to leave theology for engineering. He chose not to seek a call in Norway and gave thought to missionary work in Africa before coming to America. Yet this self-effacing man became a leader of such stature that old and young listened when he spoke. He discovered the self-confidence that enabled him to found a school that became a leading college, to assume the respected office of bishop, and to lead the fray in theological disputes.

Muus took part in the Synod's work and theology by writing numerous articles for *Kirkelig Maanedstidende* and other papers. As Pastor Bøckman noted, Muus was too burdened with practical duties to carry out an extensive authorship. Neverthless, he wrote a few books, including a popular Lutheran Almanac, a reissue and translation of Volrath Vogt's *Bible History*, a polemical pamphlet against Professor August Weenaas, a set of sermons to five congregations, and a collection of confirmation sermons from the 1880s. A trip to Norway in 1894 enabled Muus to add more material to the family history, *Nils Muus's aet*, which he first published in 1890. In 1895 he published a book on conversion, a topic he had debated vigorously during the election controversy.

Candor required his admiring friends to face the harsh, combative side of B. J. Muus. N. J. Ellestad related that Muus expressed himself tersely and powerfully, capturing everyone's attention. When he fought as a champion of the Norwegian Synod in battles against other church groups, he wielded a verbal sledgehammer, arousing opposition to himself and to the Synod. Once he was convinced that a given standpoint was supported by the Word of God, he was unsparing of those who did not see the issue in the same light. He thought he was doing his Christian duty, but some adversaries thought he was motivated by hatred. In time, however, wrote Ellestad, those who were once his opponents came to regard Muus as a thoroughly honest man, a genuine Viking of the old authentic type, a man who despite all his failings always meant well.[27] After Muus's working days were over, these words about him appeared in *Decorah–Posten*: "Muus was a character, peculiar in his makeup, contentious, unbending, apparently hard as flint, but one from whom flashed warm sparks that kindled the hearts. One does not find such a man in every bush."[28]

Pastor L. M. Biørn also knew the prickly side of Muus's personality, how he used sharp words when something offended him, though never in hate or revenge. A more polite treatment of his churchly opponents would have been desirable. Muus was a straightforward man, not always tactful. Once while presiding at a district meeting at Lands church, Biørn asked Muus if he had a comment on the sermon they had just heard. Muus replied by saying, "It seems to me that there has been enough talk. If I should say anything by way of edification it would rather be that we adjourn." Biørn found the remark uncalled for and said as much, whereupon Muus took his hat and coat and left.[29]

Muus cultivated the plain and humble virtues. He worked hard, accepted long hours, endured tedious travel, and faced all the hardships a rough, unfinished society posed for a clergyman. He asked little for himself by way of comfort, goods, or wealth. He was frugal, possibly too much so if even some of his wife's complaints about austerity in the parsonage were accurate. Sharing the hard lot of fellow immigrants was important to him. Apart from his wife's inheritance and his income as a minister, Muus was a rich man from a prosperous family, but he did not use his wealth for his own advantage or pleasure. He told his younger colleague Bøckman, "A pastor should live by the Gospel, not from the inheritance from his father."[30]

Muus's ability to raise money for worthy causes was legendary. He persuaded church people to give generously to Luther College, to St. Olaf College, to the building and maintenance of churches, to foreign and inner missions, and other goals. On one occasion he was observed raising funds for a church building. "Put Asle down for $100, Erik for $100, and Ole for $100." Muus ignored their protests and went down the list. The men chuckled quietly and paid.[31]

Muus himself was generous in giving. When it was his turn to collect money among his fellow pastors, they knew that they had to pay up. But when he finished, he would say, "How much is required from me?" When an amount was named, he said, "Good and well," and promptly paid. Muus quietly helped students continue their education. One whom he helped financially, enabling him to attend Luther College, was John Nathan Kildahl, who became the second president of St. Olaf College. Another pastor who had received money for his education from Muus later tried to pay it back. But Muus brushed him aside with the comment, "You take that and help some needy student you may meet to get an education."[32]

The demands of work and the absence of self-indulgence did not rob Muus of a few of life's pleasures. He enjoyed smoking a long pipe, using Bull Durham tobacco. His daughter Birgitte recalled that on their many buggy rides when she was taking him to or from the station, or to visit the sick, he asked her to handle the reins while he smoked his pipe. She also remembered rides on moonlight nights when he would describe the courses of the heavenly bodies and tell her the names of constellations and stars. Had he not become a minister of the Gospel, he would say, he would have become an astronomer.[33]

Birgitte also wrote of her father's love of nature. The two of them took interest in flowers, shrubs, trees, animals, and other living things. When S. O. Simundson as a student intern came

*John Nathan Kildahl*
St. Olaf College Archives

over from Gol to call on Muus, he was prevailed on to stay for dinner. Afterward, Muus took him outside to show him around the yard where he stood and patted one of his favorite trees.[34]

Muus was concerned about the dangers of alcohol, but he was not a prohibitionist. In one speech he recognized intoxicating drink as belonging to God's good creation, but recommended a voluntary abstinence from alcohol for the sake of one's neighbor. Another statement attributed to Muus was on the side of moderate use. "God has given us intoxicating liquor in order that we may use it to our own welfare, when we need it and we feel that

340

it benefits us, and nobody has a right to forbid the moderate use of it."[35]

On one occasion, Muus showed his strong disapproval of drinking at an outdoor wedding reception. The bride's father had invited him, and Muus promised to come if there would not be drinking. The father so promised, and after the church ceremony Muus drove his buggy to the reception. Before getting out, he looked around and saw wine and liquor being served. Immediately he grabbed the reins, slapped them against the horses, and drove away, calling out as he left, "Oh, it's the same old swinishness."[36]

That Muus could appreciate the comic elements in human existence was evident in various situations. Driving across the countryside with S. O. Simundson to a pastor's conference, Muus regaled the younger man with stories. They passed the home of a man who had been disciplined for being drunk. His excuse had been, related Muus, that somehow he had eaten some frozen alcohol, and when it thawed it made him drunk.

"It was never boring in Pastor Muus's company," declared an article in *Decorah–Posten* in relation to his humor and stories. Riding along in a cart driven by Gunnulf Lien, Muus was reminded of an incident on the emigrant ship leaving Norway. A lively chap climbed the tallest mast and looked about. When he came down the captain asked him, "Did you see anything of Norway?" "No, I didn't see Norway, but I could see the houses in Bergen."[37]

Muus was not much of a singer, but encouraged the use of a simple instrument called a *salmodikon* (or monochord) for use in learning hymns. One day after services in Urland church he announced that he had some of these instruments to sell. With a smile he observed: "You know that there will be beautiful singing in heaven, but if you don't learn to sing here, you will not have great happiness when you get there."[38]

His humor was not always droll and kindly. It could also be sardonic and blunt, as when he responded to an article that appeared

341

in the Synod's *Evangelisk Lutherske Kirketidende* with a series in *Norden* entitled "Rubbish i Synodens Organ." To take a different setting, Muus was having a meal in a hotel when a traveling man noticed him bow his head to say grace. Making fun of the minister, the man asked, "Does everybody say grace before they eat where you come from?" Muus replied, "No, the pigs don't."[39]

There was playful humor with an edge when Muus expressed to Ytterboe his worry that St. Olaf might become a "humbug" institution. He sensed a trend in colleges not to teach the students any facts but "to develop their judgment." Old-fashioned rote learning and memorizing were ridiculed. Muus believed that youth is the time to learn facts, "to cram, if you will," to store in the memory what later can be used in exercising judgment.

In a remarkably disarming statement, coming from the founder of the institution, Muus continued: "I emphasized when I worked for that school that Christianity is *honest*, it avoids all humbug. An *honest* school will insure that the pupils learn what they 'learn,' whether they learn little or much."[40]

After Ytterboe replied, Muus wrote to thank him for his letter and also to thank him for not becoming angry because Muus wrote what he thought. As to the topic itself, naturally the teachers would have the final say, he wrote. This sentiment was fully in keeping with Muus's policy of leaving St. Olaf in the hands of Mohn and the rest of the faculty. "A good house governs itself," he said once when asked if he had any advice for running the college.

When the work of Bernt Julius Muus is summed up, there are three major contributions to church and society for which this flinty pioneer pastor should be honored. In chronological order, the first is his labor as local and missionary pastor. The second is the founding of St. Olaf's School. The third is his role in the election controversy that, for all its disruptiveness, created new possibilities for the Norwegian Lutheran community. It also led to St. Olaf becoming a four-year college, a development in harmony with Muus's belief that the schools are the future.

342

In all three instances, Muus devoted his efforts to building a future for the Norwegian people in America. Uppermost in his pastoral heart was the mandate of implanting the Word of God in his people so that it could benefit them and the generations to come. To accomplish that goal meant more than zealous circuit riding; it meant creating and maintaining institutions.

For that reason Muus established congregations, supported Luther College, promoted parochial schools, created an academy in his parsonage, founded St. Olaf's School, helped establish an Anti-Missourian seminary, and presided over the transition of St. Olaf to a college. Muus had the vision to see things in the long-range perspective and the practical sense to understand that sound institutions are necessary for the future welfare of the children and grandchildren.

Pastor Muus was among the several clergymen who attended a pastoral conference at St. Olaf College February 21–23, 1899, meeting in the office of President Mohn. On the evening of February 22nd, Mohn invited the pastors to attend a student program observing the birthday of George Washington. He also asked Muus to speak at the close of the program, held in the chapel room in the southwest corner of the second floor of the Main building.

The program included a piano solo, Weber's "Invitation to the Dance," an essay on the "Childhood and Youth of Washington," read by Ray Mohn, a violin solo by Andrew Onstad, a talk on "The Home Life of Washington," a vocal solo, "One Spring Morning," and an oration on "The Public Services of Washington."[41] At the conclusion, President Mohn introduced Muus, inviting the founder of the college to speak. S. O. Simundson, a young pastor who was present on the occasion, recalled the scene. "I can see Rev. Muus as he arose from his place to the left of the platform— stooped over as he came up to the speaker's desk—straightened up, looked the student body over and began: *"Nos Morituri Te Salutamus, Caesar"* (We who are about to die salute you, Caesar.)

343

With these words the gladiators went in and saluted the statue of Caesar before they went to a combat that meant death to them."

Continuing, Pastor Muus said that these were the words he wanted to leave with the students. "My sun is descending," he said, "your sun is ascending; my work is nearly done, you are just to begin yours. As you take up your work, you will also go forth to a battle that will lead you to death. But remember that all your work must be done for the purpose of honoring, not an earthly king or potentate, but the King of kings. Strive in your life to glorify Him, His name, then it matters not even if it is to death—it will lead to honor and glory through Him."

Simundson reported that Muus was so moved emotionally that he had to stop several times during the brief five-minute speech. He seemed to have a premonition that his time was short. It was his last visit to the college he had founded. The next month, on March 14th, Muus had his first stroke, leaving him partially paralyzed. He rallied and was able to fulfill his ardent desire to preach to his congregation on Easter Sunday. He had another light stroke in the middle of April. On May 3, 1899, he resigned his pastorate.[42]

On May 8, 1899, Muus wrote to Laur. Larsen at Luther College, asking him to inquire about the bills he had received from Decorah merchants for goods that Sverre Muus had purchased on credit. After listing the charges, he noted: "I have laid down my position because I cannot do any more—paralyzed in the left side and powerless. Otherwise have no pain. God be praised!"[43]

Incidents from Muus's last summer at Holden have been recorded by S. O. Simundson, who at the time was serving Gol Church and took over many of Muus's pastoral duties. Simundson later became the pastor at Holden. In the summer of 1899 he visited the ailing Muus in his bedroom at the parsonage and administered Holy Communion to him. Expecting to die soon, Muus instructed Simundson about his funeral and stipulated that the text should be the one used at his ordination, 2 Corinthians 12:8–10: "'My grace is sufficient for you, for my power is made

*S. O. Simundson*
Photo from Don McRae Album

perfect in weakness.' So I will boast all the more gladly of my weaknesses, so that the power of Christ may dwell in me."

"Preach to the living," he ordered Simundson. "I hate these speeches praising the dead!" Simundson should read a sketch of Muus's life. Muus had asked Ole Hylland to make a simple coffin. "I want to lie in the northwest corner of the cemetery with my children." As it happened, Pastor Muus was not buried in the Holden cemetery. His daughter Birgitte Muus Klüver came from Norway to take Pastor Muus to live with her and her husband, Lorentz Klüver, in Trondheim.

Departure from the Kenyon train station took place on July 21,

345

1899. Muus was driven up and down the streets of Kenyon for a time before being brought to the depot. Pastor Simundson found a chair for him as they waited for the train to arrive. There were hundreds of people to see him off. Muus was unable to say good-bye to so many, but he did exchange farewells with an old friend of forty years, Per Langemo. When the train arrived, Simundson and another person assisted Muus aboard. The porter led the old pastor to his place, and the train pulled out.[44]

A few messages passed between Minnesota and Norway during Muus's last months. Speaking at the Twenty-Fifth Anniversary of St. Olaf College, Professor Carl Weswig said of Muus: "The rumor has come across the sea that he yearns for the scene of his active labor. He longs to see the college he began once more. This day he is praying that God may continue to bless this institution." When Muus learned of the death of Thorbjørn Nelson Mohn in November, he sent his sympathy to Mrs. Mohn, saluting his colleague as "one of the most faithful co-workers I have ever had."[45]

For a time during the winter in Trondheim Muus had enjoyed good health, eating and sleeping well, and even putting on weight.[46] His daughter hoped that he would recover his strength so as to enjoy pleasant times in the warmth of summer. But Bernt Julius Muus died at his daughter's home on Ascension Day, May 24, 1900. Birgitte wrote to the Reverend J. N. Kildahl, the new president of St. Olaf College, about her father's passing. "He had an uncommonly beautiful death on Ascension Day at sunset. The sun sent its last lovely rays over his face when he drew his last breath—no sighing, and not the slightest sign of pain."

The day before he had been completely lucid and spoke much with Birgitte and her husband, but then he became incoherent and patted them on the shoulder in taking leave from them. Added Birgitte: "Beautiful is his memory. May we all one day meet again in a better land where there is no divorce." Pastor Muus was buried in the churchyard of the Trondheim Cathedral.

Sending the report of Muus's death to the church paper *Lutheraneren*, Kildahl concluded with these words. "Here in the

*B. J. Muus monument, Trondheim*
St. Olaf College Archives

shelter of the Cathedral's walls rest the earthly remains of the noble champion of the Lord and father in Christ. Blessed be his memory!"[47]

St. Olaf College students and alumni by the hundreds have visited the grave of Bernt Julius Muus in Trondheim. Beginning with the St. Olaf Band in 1906 and the St. Olaf Choir in 1913, music organizations from the College touring in Norway regularly have laid wreaths on the grave. The monument is a round pillar placed on a rectangular base. In observance of the College's centennial in 1974, the words "Founder of St. Olaf College" were inscribed on the side of the base that faces the Cathedral.

# Notes

## Chapter One

[1] Bernt Julius Muus and Alfred Muus, *Niels Muus's æt: Muus-slegten i Snaasa, 1642–1942* (Trondheim, 1942), 7.

[2] Parish Register of Snåsa for 1832, in National Archives, Trondheim, Norway; letter from Eilert Bjørkvik, Archivist, National Archives in Trondheim, to Joseph M. Shaw, March 10, 1994.

[3] Hans Skar, *Snaasens kulturhistorie til aaret 1907* (Oslo, 1907), 74; Bernt Julius Muus, *Jens Rynnings æt*, 1894, 2.

[4] *Niels Muus's æt*, 7, 10, 26, 37; N. J. Ellestad, "Pastor Bernt Julius Muus, Et Minde," in *Lutheraneren*, 6 (29 August 1900), 584; L. M. Biørn, "A Commemorative Word about Pastor Muus," in *Festskrift: Jubelfest holdt i Holden menighed 1906*, Biørn, ed. (Minneapolis, 1908), 7.

[5] On the front side of the grave marker is the name, BERNT JULIUS MUUS, date of birth, 15 March 1832, date of death, 24 May 1900, the words, "FOUNDER OF ST. OLAF COLLEGE," and below that in slightly smaller letters, "IN OBSERVANCE OF THE COLLEGE CENTENNIAL, 1974."

[6] *Niels Muus's æt*, 22.

[7] Rolf Falch-Muus, "Mester Niels til Snaasen," reprint from *Nord-Trondelag historielags aarbok for 1958* (Steinkjer, 1959), 3.

[8] Falch-Muus, "Mester Niels," 5.

[9] Falch-Muus, "Mester Niels," 9, 11.

[10] Falch-Muus, "Mester Niels," 6.

[11] *Niels Muus's æt*, 7.

[12] Falch-Muus, "Mester Niels," 12.

[13] *Niels Muus's æt*, 11.

[14] Falch-Muus, "Mester Niels," 13; Skar, *Det gamle Snaasen* (Oslo, 1906), 30–31; *Niels Muus's æt*, 11, notes 3 and 4.

[15] *Niels Muus's æt*, 11, 15–16; Kaare Granøyen Rogstad, *Fest-skrift til Snåsa ved kyrkja sitt 100 aars og 750 (?) jubileum* (Snåsa, 1970), 57.

[16] Falch-Muus, "Mester Niels," 13. Skar, *Det gamle Snaasen*, 31, mentions a place named "Muusro."

[17] Jørn Sandnes, *Snåsaboka: Bygdehistorien fram til aar 1800* (Snåsa, 1956), 1:307.

[18] *Niels Muus's æt*, 23. In Norwegian the word for "mouse" is *mus*, which for a time was spelled *muus*. There would be occasions also in the life of B. J. Muus when puns would be made on the name.

[19] Falch-Muus, "Mester Niels," 22; *Niels Muus's æt*, 21–22; Sandnes, *Snåsaboka*, 1:309.

[20] Sandnes, *Snåsaboka*, 1:309.

[21] *Niels Muus's æt*, 7.

[22] Rogstad, *Fest-skrift til Snåsa kyrkja*, 67–68.

[23] Sandnes, *Snåsaboka: Bygdehistorien etter år 1800* (Snåsa, 1960), 2:62.

[24] Sandnes, *Snåsaboka*, 2:63.

[25] Letter by Jens Rynning dated September 4, 1839, published in *Morgenbladet*, October 10, 1839, in Norwegian-American Historical Association Archives, Northfield, Minnesota (hereafter referred to as NAHA).

[26] J. Rynning, *Morgenbladet*.

[27] J. Rynning, *Morgenbladet*; Theodore C. Blegen, "Historical Introduction" to *Ole Rynning's True Account of America*, trans. and ed. by Blegen (Minneapolis, 1926), 19–20.

[28] Odd S. Lovoll, *The Promise of America: A History of the Norwegian-American People* (Minneapolis, 1984), 34.

[29] For an English translation of the full title page of this book see Blegen, ed., *Ole Rynning's True Account of America*, 61. The Norwegian title of Ole Rynning's book is *Sandfærdig beretning om Amerika, til oplysning og nytte for bonde og menigmand*. The volume prepared by Blegen has the complete Norwegian text of the book as well as the translation.

[30] Knut Gjerset, *History of the Norwegian People* (New York, 1915), 2:470–471.

[31] Reidar Dittmann, "'Stor arv . . .' Bernt Julius Muus, kulturimmigrant," a lecture at the Bernt Julius Muus-Jubilee in Snåsa 1982, in *Sol-Sang*, Snåsa congregation paper, 42 (Fall, 1982), 24.

[32] Karen Larsen, *A History of Norway* (Princeton, 1948), 405–406, 419.

[33] Quoted in Blegen, "Historical Introduction," 14–15.

[34] Dittmann, "'Stor arv . . .'," 24.

[35] B. J. Muus, quoted in Rasmus B. Anderson, *The First Chapter of Norwegian Immigration (1821–1840), Its Causes and Results* (Madison, Wisconsin, 1906), 204–205.

[36] Rogstad, *Fest-skrift til Snåsa . . . kyrkja*, 69.

[37] Blegen, "Historical Introduction," 18.

[38] Anderson, *First Chapter of Norwegian Immigration*, 205.

[39] Quoted in Blegen, "Historical Introduction," 18; letter from Joralf Gjerstad to Joseph M. Shaw, November 18, 1993.

[40] *Niels Muus's æt*, 68–69.

[41] Sandnes, *Snåsaboka*, 2:150.

[42] *Niels Muus's æt*, 70.

[43] *Niels Muus's æt*, 71.

[44] *Niels Muus's æt*, 7.

[45] Letters from B. J. Muus to Ingebrigt Muus, April 7, June 2, October 26, 1854, in St. Olaf College Archives.

[46] Letters from B. J. Muus to Ingebrigt Muus.

[47] Falch-Muus, "Mester Niels," 5–6.

[48] Biørn, *Holden Festskrift*, 8, 13, 41.

[49] B. J. Muus Dedicatory Address, in I. F. Grose, "Fifty Memorable Years at St. Olaf," reprinted from the *Northfield News*, 1925. See also "St. Olaf's School," dedication pamphlet (Decorah, Iowa, 1875), 4.

[50] Foreword, *Niels Muus's æt*, 7.

[51] Ingrid Semmingsen, *Veien Mot Vest: Utvandringen fra Norge til Amerika 1825–1865* (Oslo, 1941), 79.

[52] Rogstad, *Fest-skrift til Snåsa . . . kyrkja*, 68; Skar, *Det gamle Snaasen*, 53.

[53] Ellestad, "Pastor Bernt Julius Muus: Et Minde," 584; cf. William C. Benson, *High on Manitou: A History of St. Olaf College 1874–1949* (Northfield, 1949), 7, where it is stated that young Muus "remained under private tutelage" in the home of his mother's parents until 1842.

[54] Biørn, "A Commemorative Word about Pastor Muus," 8.

[55] Cf. letters from B. J. Muus to Ingebrigt Muus, April 7 and June 2, 1854.

[56] Thorleif Sather, "B. J. Muus—mannen som grunnla St. Olaf College," 16. Photocopy of an article by Sather, Stavanger, from an unnamed journal in Norway.

[57] Letter from B. J. Muus to Martinus Muus (?), November 26, 1870, in St. Olaf Archives.

[58] *Niels Muus's æt*, 8.

[59] Sandnes, "Fra hedensk hov til kristen kirke paa Vinje," in *Sol-Sang*, 30 (1970), 5.

[60] *Niels Muus's æt*, 112–113; English translation of the inscription by Anne Groton, Professor of Classics, St. Olaf College.

[61] *Niels Muus's æt*, 9, 112, 115.

[62] C. M. Weswig, "John Nathan Kildahl (1857–1920), En biografisk skisse," in R. Malmin, ed., *Dr. John Nathan Kildahl: En Mindebok* (2nd ed., Minneapolis, 1921), 45.

[63] *Niels Muus's æt*, 73; conversation with Jørn Sandnes, June 8, 1989.

[64] Letter from B. J. Muus to cousin Nils Muus, November 14, 1894.

## Chapter Two

[1] Skar, *Snaasens kulturhistorie*, 99.

[2] Semmingsen, *Veien mot vest*, 79.

[3] Larsen, *A History of Norway*, 451.

[4] Gjerset, *History of the Norwegian People*, 2:554.

[5] "Characterliste for Discipel af Trondhjems Lærde Skole Bernt Muus ved halvaars-examen 1844," December 29, 1844, in St. Olaf Archives.

[6] Einar Molland, *Norges kirkehistorie i det 19. aarhundre* (Oslo, 1979),1:256.

[7] Gjerset, *History of the Norwegian People*, 2:497.

[8] The quotation is among the invaluable notes on B. J. Muus compiled by Eugene L. Fevold, Professor Emeritus at Luther Seminary, St. Paul, Minnesota, and generously made available to me. Early in his career Dr. Fevold did extensive research on the life and work of B. J. Muus. In this instance Fevold indicates that the statement is from a piece signed "Th. B." but the publication source is not certain, perhaps *Decorah-Posten*, as Fevold notes with a question mark.

[9] *Vaar Frue kirkebok*, in regional archives, Trondheim.

[10] "Senatus Universitatis Regiae Fredericianae," B. J. Muus Papers, in St. Olaf Archives.

[11] E. Clifford Nelson and Eugene L. Fevold, *The Lutheran Church Among Norwegian-Americans: A History of the Evangelical Lutheran Church* (Minneapolis, 1960) 1:98, n. 5. There was a higher mark, *laudabilis prae ceteris*, "praiseworthy beyond others."

[12] O. N. Nelson (ed.), *History of the Scandinavians and Successful Scandinavians in the United States* (Minneapolis, 1900) 1:446. Cf. J. C. Jensson, *American Lutheran Biographies* (Milwaukee, 1890), 545.

[13] *Niels Muus's æt*, 7.

[14] Blegen, Historical Introduction to *Ole Rynning's True Account of America*, 15–16.

[15] Blegen, Historical Introduction, 5; Skar, *Det gamle Snaasen* (Oslo, 1906), 39–40; Semmingsen, *Veien mot vest*, 79.

[16] Larsen, *History of Norway*, 394–395.

[17] Larsen, *History of Norway*, 397–404, 415–416.

[18] Larsen, *History of Norway*, 405, 407, 411, 419, 433, 451.

[19] Larsen, *History of Norway*, 421; Gjerset, *History of the Norwegian People*, 2:470–471; Theodore Jorgenson, *Henrik Ibsen: A Study in Art and Personality* (Northfield, 1945), 28.

[20] Gjerset, *History of the Norwegian People*, 2:510–513.

[21] Larsen, *History of Norway*, 439.

[22] Larsen, *History of Norway*, 438–444.

[23] Gjerset, *History of the Norwegian People*, 2:518–520.

[24] Larsen, *History of Norway*, 446.

[25] Larsen, *History of Norway*, 432. The data gathered by Eilert Sundt and his wife is still regarded as a valuable source of information on social conditions in Norway from 1800 to 1870.

[26] Letter from B. J. Muus to Ingebrigt Muus, 7 April 1854.

[27] Letter from B. J. Muus to Ingebrigt Muus, 2 June 1854.

[28] Letter from B. J. Muus to Ingebrigt Muus, 26 October 1854.

[29] Molland, *Church Life in Norway 1800–1950*, tr. Harris Kaasa (Minneapolis, 1957), 3.

[30] Molland, *Church Life*, 28.

[31] Molland, *Norges kirkehistorie i det 19. aarhundre*, 110.

[32] By "churchly view" is meant an interpretation of the church, the creed, and the sacraments that would ascribe to the Apostles' Creed spoken at baptism an authority Lutherans believed should belong solely to Scripture. According to

Lutheran teaching, the Creed had a derived authority. "It had its authority because its content was taken from Scripture and agreed with Scripture," writes Molland in *Norges kirkehistorie*, 121.

[33] Molland, *Norges kirkehistorie*, 159–160.

[34] H. Fred Swansen, *The Founder of St. Ansgar: The Life Story of Claus Laurits Clausen* (Blair, Nebraska, 1949), 24–25; Nelson and Fevold, *The Lutheran Church Among Norwegian-Americans* 1:85.

[35] Letter from B. J. Muus to Laur. Larsen, 5 April 1859, in St. Olaf Archives.

[36] Molland, *Church Life*, 32–33; Larsen, *History of Norway*, 450.

[37] Molland, "Det teologiske fakultets historie 1811–1961," in *Norsk teologisk tidsskrift*, 4 (1962), 280; Molland, *Church Life*, 40.

[38] Molland, *Norges kirkehistorie*, 281–282; Molland, "Det teologiske fakultets historie," 284–285.

[39] Molland, "Det teologiske fakultets historie," 281; Molland, *Church Life*, 35.

[40] Molland, *Church Life*, 40; cf. Molland, "Det teologiske fakultets historie," 281.

[41] Molland, *Church Life*, 35–36; Molland, *Norges kirkehistorie*, 198.

[42] Molland, *Norges kirkehistorie*, 198.

[43] Molland, *Norges kirkehistorie*, 198; Molland, *Church Life*, 37.

[44] Molland, *Norges kirkehistorie*, 198–199.

[45] Molland, "Det teologiske fakultets historie," 282–283.

[46] Notes on Gisle Johnson's lectures, Muus Papers, in NAHA archives.

[47] S. O. Simundson, "Rev. B. J. Muus as I learned to know him," address given at St. Olaf College, 1931, in St. Olaf Archives.

[48] Letter from B. J. Muus to Laur. Larsen, 5 April 1859, in St. Olaf Archives.

[49] Benson, *High on Manitou*, 8; cf. Ellestad, "Pastor Bernt Julius Muus," 584.

[50] Molland, "Det teologiske fakultets historie," 281.

[51] Molland, "Det teologiske fakultets historie," 282.

[52] Molland, "Det teologiske fakultets historie," 285, 287; Molland, *Norges kirkehistorie*, 196, 281.

[53] Molland, "Det teologiske fakultets historie," 286; cf. Molland, *Norges kirkehistorie*, 196.

[54] Molland, "Det teologiske fakultets historie," 286; Molland, *Church Life*, 44.

[55] Quoted in Molland, "Det teologiske fakultets historie," 286–287.

[56] Letter from B. J. Muus to Ingebrigt Muus, 26 October 1854.

[57] *Niels Muus's æt*, 72.

[58] Christiania Borgerskole handbook, 1828, 1, in State Archives, Oslo.

[59] *Norsk kirketidende*, No. 27, July 3, 1859. In the July 3, 1859, issue of the paper appeared the notice: "From and with this number the undersigned Muus has resigned as publisher of 'Norsk Kirketidende,' which until further notice will be published by the undersigned Bernhoft alone. B. Muus. Th. C. Bernhoft." Bernhoft continued as editor until 1863.

[60] *Norsk kirketidende*, No. 1, January 6, 1856.

[61] J. B. Halvorsen, ed., *Norsk forfatter-lexikon 1814–1880* (Oslo, 1896), 4:213.

[62] Mrs. Alfred Gatty, *Parables from Nature* (3rd ed., London, 1856); B. J. Muus, *Parabler fra Naturen* (Oslo, 1857).

[63] "Characterliste for Bernt Muus ved halvaars-examen 1844."

## Chapter Three

[1] Letter from Bernt Julius Muus to King Oscar, May 10, 1859, in Norwegian State Archives, Olso.

[2] Letter from B. J. Muus to A. C. Preus, July 5, 1859, in Luther College Archives, Decorah, Iowa. Letters: Bishop J. L. Arup to Church Department, June 22, 1859; Church Department to Christiania Bishop, June 27, 1859, in Norwegian State Archives, Olso.

[3] Letter from B. J. Muus to A. C. Preus. Translation of Latin phrases in the letter graciously supplied by Anne Groton, Professor of Classics, St. Olaf College.

[4] Letter from B. J. Muus to A. C. Preus.

[5] Letter from Church Department to Christiania Bishop.

[6] Larsen, *Laur. Larsen: Pioneer College President* (Northfield, Minnesota, 1936), 35.

[7] Simundson, "Rev. B. J. Muus as I learned to know him."

[8] Letter from B. J. Muus to Otto Lundh, May 20, 1857, in University Library, Oslo.

[9] "Fra Mrs. Oline Muus," in *Amerika*, February 23, 1906.

[10] Letter from B. J. Muus to Otto Lundh, May 4, 1885, in University Library, Oslo.

[11] Letter from B. J. Muus to Laur. Larsen, April 5, 1859, in St. Olaf Archives.

[12] Jan E. Horgen, ed., *Bygde-Historie for Fet* (Fetsund, 1985), 2, 222.

[13] "Fra Mrs. Oline Muus."

[14] Letter from B. J. Muus to A. C. Preus.

[15] Larsen, *Laur. Larsen*, 115.

[16] Larsen, *Laur. Larsen*, 116–125, 135; David T. Nelson, *Luther College 1861–1961* (Decorah, Iowa, 1961), 53.

[17] Letter from B. J. Muus to Laur. Larsen.

[18] *Norsk Kirketidende*, 1 (May 18, 1856).

[19] *Norsk Kirketidende*, 4 (February 6, 1859).

[20] *Norsk Kirketidende*, 3 (September 26, 1858); 4 (October 10, 1858).

[21] *Norsk Kirketidende*, 5 (June 10, 1860).

[22] Biørn, Address at Holden 50th Anniversary, in Biørn (ed.), *Festskrift: Jubelfest holdt i Holden menigheds 1906*, 40.

[23] Blegen, *Norwegian Migration to America: The American Transition* (Northfield, 1940), 13.

[24] Halle Steensland, "Recollections from My Journey to America and My First Years in America," trans. by Odd S. Lovoll, in *Norwegian-American Studies*, 33 (Northfield, Minnesota, 1992), 236.

[25] Marie Voxland, ed., "*Holden Through One Hundred Years 1856–1956*," 14.

[26] *Holden Through One Hundred Years*, 13; cf. B. J. Muus, "Kort Oversigt over Holden Menigheds ydre Historie i de første 25 Aar," in *Festskrift: Holden Menigheds Jubelfest 1906*, 69.

[27] *Holden Through One Hundred Years*, 13.

[28] Muus, "Kort Oversigt," 70.

[29] Muus, "Kort Oversigt," 71.

[30] Larsen, *Laur. Larsen*, 34–35.

[31] Larsen, *Laur. Larsen*, 76–77.

[32] Letter from B. J. Muus to Laur. Larsen.

[33] P. O. Floan, "Reminiscences from the Pioneer days in Goodhue County, Minnesota," Unpublished typescript, 1941, 12. This document and other materials written by Floan were made available to me by the late Don McRae, Northfield, Minnesota, a grandson of Peter O. Floan.

[34] *Niels Muus's æt*, 8.

[35] Larsen, *Laur. Larsen,* 31; Nelson, *Luther College,* 40.

[36] Simundson address, 1931.

[37] Ellestad, "Pastor Bernt Julius Muus: Et Minde," 584.

[38] Th. Eggen, "Erindringer om pastor Muus," in *Symra,* 6 (Decorah, 1910) 56–57; Simundson address.

[39] Molland, "Det teologiske fakultets historie 1811–1961," 283.

[40] Letter from B. J. Muus to Laur. Larsen. H. P. S. Schreuder founded the Norwegian Lutheran Mission in South Africa in 1843 under the auspices of the Norwegian Missionary Society. See Nelson and Fevold, *Lutheran Church Among Norwegian-Americans,* 1:98, 285; Ellestad, "Pastor Bernt Julius Muus," 584.

[41] Letter from B. J. Muus to Laur. Larsen.

[42] Letter from B. J. Muus to Laur. Larsen. See also Letter from B. J. Muus to A. C. Preus.

[43] Kristiania Politikammer, Passprotokoll no. 7, 1857–1861, in National Archives, Oslo. I am grateful to Andres A. Svalestuen, senior archivist at Norway's National Archives, for his persistence in determining the date of Pastor and Mrs. Muus's departure for America.

[44] In *Norwegian Migration to America, The American Transition,* 14, 22, Blegen reports that a large number of Norwegian ships were bringing emigrants to Quebec in the 1850s. In 1859, the year Pastor and Mrs. Muus arrived in North America, presumably at Quebec, seventy-seven Norwegian vessels were seen in Quebec.

[45] *Kirkelig Maanedstidende,* 1 (January, 1860), 7, 10.

## Chapter Four

[1] Franklin Curtiss-Wedge, ed., *History of Goodhue County Minnesota* (Chicago, 1909), 733–734.

[2] Curtiss-Wedge, *History of Goodhue County,* 1.

[3] Theodore L. Nydahl, "The Early Norwegian Settlement of Goodhue County, Minnesota" (M. A. Thesis, University of Minnesota, 1929), 4; C. A. Rasmussen, *A History of Goodhue County Minnesota* (n.p., 1935), 1.

[4] Rasmussen, *History of Goodhue County,* 1–2.

[5] Nydahl, "Early Norwegian Settlement of Goodhue County," 4.

[6] P. O. Floan, "A Family History," 13.

[7] Blegen, *Minnesota: A History of the State* (Minneapolis, 1963), 310.

[8] Nydahl, "Early Norwegian Settlement of Goodhue County," 44–45.

[9] Blegen, *Minnesota: A History of the State,* 168–169.

[10] William E. Lass, *Minnesota: A Bicentennial History* (New York, 1977), 88–89.

[11] Blegen, *Minnesota: A History of the State,* 174.

[12] William Watts Folwell, *A History of Minnesota,* 1 (St. Paul, 1956), 354.

[13] Lass, *Minnesota: A Bicentennial History,* 88–89.

[14] Blegen, *Minnesota: A History of the State*, 174.

[15] Odd S. Lovoll, *A Century of Urban Life* (Northfield, 1988), 5. See also Lovoll, *The Promise of America* (Minneapolis, 1984), 16–28, and Carlton C. Qualley, *Norwegian Settlement in the United States* (Northfield, 1938), 4–6.

[16] Semmingsen, "Norwegian Emigration To America During the Nineteenth Century," in *Norwegian-American Studies and Records*, 11 (Northfield, 1940), 68. See also Lovoll, *The Promise of America*, 14.

[17] Lovoll, *Promise of America*, 9–10. For details of the Sloopers and their historical voyage see Blegen, *Norwegian Migration to America, 1825–1860* (Northfield, 1931), Chapter 2.

[18] Qualey, *Norwegian Settlement in the United States*, 5–7. See also Elin Strøm and Wenche Hervig, *Norwegians to America* (Oslo, 1984), 55.

[19] Einar Haugen, "Norwegian Migration to America," in *Norwegian-American Studies and Records* 18 (1954), 13. On p. 11 Haugen charts the five acts with low and high periods of immigration as follows:

Act I   Low Migration 1836/48: 10,500; High 1849/62:  57,920
Act II  Low Migration 1863/65:  9,400; High 1866/73: 109,469
Act III Low Migration 1874/78: 20,878; High 1879/93: 262,273
Act IV  Low Migration 1894/99: 34,179; High 1900/14: 224,541
Act V   Low Migration 1915/22: 30,277; High 1923/30:  52,655

[20] *Norwegians to America*, 38.

[21] Karl E. Erickson, "The Emigrant Journey in the Fifties," ed. by Albert O. Barton, *Norwegian-American Studies & Records*, 8 (Northfield, Minnesota, 1934), 81.

[22] Lovoll, *Promise of America*, 12.

[23] *Holden Through One Hundred Years 1856–1956*, 14.

[24] Nydahl, "Early Norwegian Settlement of Goodhue County," 30–32.

[25] Nydahl, "Early Norwegian Settlement," 10–12.

[26] Semmingsen, *Norway to America*, tr. Einar Haugen (Minneapolis, 1978), 70.

[27] Leola Nelson Bergmann, *Americans from Norway* (Philadelphia, 1950), 90.

[28] Nydahl, "Early Norwegian Settlement," 2; Hjalmar Rued Holand, *De Norske Settlementers Historie* (Ephraim, Wisconsin, 1909), 337.

[29] *Holden Through One Hundred Years*, 12.

[30] Nydahl, "Early Norwegian Settlement," 26–27; Holand, *De Norske Settlementers Historie*, 484–485; Holand, *Norwegians in America: The Last Migration*, trans. by Helmer M. Blegen, ed. by Evelyn Ostraat Wierenga (Sioux Falls, South Dakota, 1978), 145.

[31] *Holden Through One Hundred Years*, 12; cf. Holand, *Norske Settlementers Historie*, 486.

[32] Lovoll, *Promise of America*, 39.

[33] Martin Ulvestad, *Nordmændene i Amerika, deres Historie og Rekord* (Minneapolis, Minnesota, 1907), 93.

[34] Ulvestad, *Nordmændene i Amerika*, 93.

[35] Nydahl, "Social and Economic Aspects of Pioneering as Illustrated in Goodhue County, Minnesota," in *Norwegian-American Studies and Records*, 5 (Northfield, 1930), 58; G. K. Norsving, "Noget om indvandringen til Vang i Goodhue County," in *Samband*, 35 (March, 1911), 154.

[36] Nydahl, "Aspects of Pioneering," 58–59; Ulvestad, *Nordmændene i Amerika*, 93.

[37] Nydahl, "Aspects of Pioneering," 50.

[38] Holand, *De Norske Settlementers Historie*, 485

[39] Holand, *Norwegians in America*, 145–146.

[40] This and the following five paragraphs are based on Holand, *De Norske Settlementers Historie*, 487–490. The "law of the club" was a not-uncommon phenomenon among immigrants and was not limited to Norwegians.

[41] Holand, *Norwegians in America*, 147–148. Holand's account was likely somewhat embroidered.

[42] *Holden Ministerial Book* I: 248. The Reverend Michael J. Lockerby, pastor of the Holden and Dale churches, graciously allowed me to examine two important record books containing data on ministerial acts in the Holden parish from before and during the pastorate of B. J. Muus.

[43] *Holden Ministerial Book* I: 504, 505, 519.

[44] Holand, *Norwegians in America*, 148–149.

[45] Holand, *De Norske Settlementers Historie*, 493–494.

[46] Floan, "Reminiscences," 9.

[47] Holand, *Norwegians in America*, 150.

[48] Rasmussen, *History of Goodhue County*, 303; Curtiss-Wedge, *History of Goodhue County*, 481–482.

[49] Curtiss-Wedge, *History of Goodhue County*, 480.

[50] *Kirkelig Maanedstidende*, 15 (15 January 1870), 17–26.

[51] Holand, *Norwegians in America*, 150.

[52] Nydahl, "Aspects of Pioneering," 50, and "Early Norwegian Settlement," 13.

[53] Merrill E. Jarchow, *The Earth Brought Forth: A History of Minnesota Agriculture to 1885* (St. Paul, Minnesota, 1949), 48.

[54] Nydahl, "Aspects of Pioneering," 54.

[55] Rasmussen, *History of Goodhue County*, 59.

[56] P. M. Langemo, Speech at Holden Fiftieth Anniversary, in *Festskrift, Holden Menigheds Jubelfest 1906*, 50.

[57] Jarchow, *The Earth Brought Forth*, 165, 175.

[58] Rasmussen, *History of Goodhue County*, 52.

[59] Nydahl, "Early Norwegian Settlement," 46–48; Nydahl, "Aspects of Pioneering," 55–56; Langemo, speech, 49–50.

[60] Jarchow, *The Earth Brought Forth*, 191, 194, 196.

[61] Langemo, speech, 48.

[62] Norsving, "Noget om indvandringen til Vang i Goodhue County," 153.

[63] Nydahl, "Aspects of Pioneering," 51; Langemo, speech, 48.

[64] Blegen, *Norwegian Migration to America: The American Transition*, 40.

[65] Bergmann, *Americans from Norway*, 134; "Mrs. Oline Muus Contra Pastor B. J. Muus," in *Budstikken*, March 30, 1880.

[66] Norsving, "Noget om indvandringen," 156.

[67] Norsving, "Noget om indvandringen," 154; Floan, "Reminiscences," 4.

[68] Langemo, speech, 50–51; *Holden Through One Hundred Years*, 68.

[69] Ellen G. and H. S. Hilleboe, "*For the sake of their children*," 102. Manuscript in NAHA Archives.

[70] Nydahl, "Aspects of Pioneering," 52.

[71] Norsving, "Noget om indvandringen," 154.

[72] Floan, "Reminiscences," 12.

[73] Floan, "Reminiscences," 13.

[74] Langemo, speech, 48–49.

[75] Floan, "Reminiscences," 12; J. W. Hancock, *Goodhue County, Minnesota, Past and Present* (Red Wing, Minnesota, 1893), 168.

[76] Rasmussen, *History of Goodhue County*, 98–99. For more on J. W. Hancock see Curtiss-Wedge, *History of Goodhue County*, 138–139.

[77] Floan, "Reminiscences," 13.

[78] Nydahl, "Aspects of Pioneering," 59.

[79] Langemo, speech, 51.

## Chapter Five

[1] Nelson and Fevold, *The Lutheran Church Among Norwegian-Americans*, I: 75–76.

[2] Nelson and Fevold, *Lutheran Church Among Norwegian-Americans*, 81.

[3] Nelson and Fevold, *Lutheran Church Among Norwegian-Americans*, 129.

[4] Nelson and Fevold, *Lutheran Church Among Norwegian-Americans*, 126. Cf. S. S. Gjerde and P. Ljostveit (eds), *The Hauge Movement in America* (Minneapolis, 1941), 155.

[5] "Past. Muus død," obituary by Th. B. in *Decorah–Posten*, n.d. Since B. J. Muus died in Trondheim, Norway, May 24, 1900, the obituary would have appeared in late May or early June of 1900.

[6] Nelson and Fevold, *Lutheran Church Among Norwegian-Americans*, 151, 156.

[7] *Evangelisk Luthersk Kirketidende*, 27 (29 June 1898), 504.

[8] Biørn, ed., *Festskrift: Holden Menigheds Jubelfest 1906*, 12.

[9] Voxland, *Holden Through One Hundred Years 1856–1956*, 12.

[10] Voxland, *Holden Through One Hundred Years*, 13.

[11] Jensson, *American Lutheran Biographies*, I: 107–108; O. M. Norlie, *Norsk lutherske prester i America 1843–1913* (Minneapolis, 1914), 98.

[12] Nelson and Fevold, *Lutheran Church Among Norwegian-Americans*, 162; Norlie, *Norsk lutherske prester*, 98.

[13] Nydahl, "The Early Norwegian Settlement of Goodhue County," 26.

[14] Voxland, *Holden Through One Hundred Years*, 13.

[15] Voxland, *Holden Through One Hundred Years; Holden Ministerial Book* I: 3–6.

[16] Information in this and the following paragraph comes from Voxland, *Holden Through One Hundred Years*, 13–14.

[17] Kristiania Politikammer, *Passprotokoll* no. 7, 1857–1861, in National Archives, Oslo.

[18] Lovoll, *The Promise of America*, 21.

[19] David T. Nelson (ed.), *The Diary of Elisabeth Koren* (Northfield, Minnesota, 1955), xiii; Halle Steensland, "Recollections from My Journey to America and My First Years in America," trans. by Odd S. Lovoll, in *Norwegian-American Studies*, 33 (Northfield, 1992), 238; H. Cock-Jensen, "An Emigrant Voyage in the Fifties," *Norwegian-American Studies and Records*, I (1926), 128, 133.

[20] *Diary of Elisabeth Koren*, 41.

[21] *Diary of Elisabeth Koren*, 25.

[22] *Diary of Elisabeth Koren*, 6, note 1.

[23] Cock-Jensen, "An Emigrant Voyage," 127; Erickson, "The Emigrant Journey in the Fifties," 76, 89–90.

[24] Cock-Jensen, "An Emigrant Voyage," 129–130; Erickson, "Emigrant Journey," 75, 86.

[25] Cock-Jensen, "An Emigrant Voyage," 128; Erickson, "Emigrant Journey," 77–79; *Diary of Elisabeth Koren*, 17, 35, 44.

[26] Semmingsen, *Norway to America*, 61.

[27] Semmingsen, *Norway to America*, 56–57; Lovoll, *Promise of America*, 18.

[28] Semmingsen, *Veien Mot Vest*, 140–142; *Norwegians to America*, 49; Semmingsen, *Norway to America*, 52; Steensland, "Erindringer," 85–86; cf. also Erickson, "Emigrant Journey," 68.

[29] Voxland, *Holden Through One Hundred Years*, 14–15.

[30] Letter from B. J. Muus to Adolph C. Preus, July 5, 1859.

[31] Melvin Voxland, *Voxland Viking Saga*, 1980, 26–27; conversation with Erling Jorstad regarding Tosten and Oline Aabye, Jorstad's great-grandparents.

[32] A. A. Rowberg (ed.), *The Aker Saga, 1797–1914* (Northfield, Minnesota, 1914), 8–9, 19; *Holden Ministerial Book* I (1855–1871), Baptisms, 8. Marie Aaker was born January 30, 1860, and baptized April 1, 1860.

[33] *The Aker Saga*, 9, gives the date as August 13, 1862.

[34] *Holden Ministerial Book*, I, Membership, 240; S. O. Simundson address, "Rev. B. J. Muus as I Learned to Know Him," 1931, 9.

[35] B. J. Muus, "Kort Oversigt," 71.

[36] *Holden Ministerial Book*, I, "Geistligt Dagregister," 504.

[37] Letter from B. J. Muus to Laur. Larsen, March 12, 1860, in Luther College Archives; *Holden Ministerial Book*, I, 505.

[38] *Holden Through One Hundred Years*, 14.

[39] This unusual source, a 4" x 4" block of wood, was made available for examination by the Reverend Michael J. Lockerby, pastor of Holden and Dale churches.

[40] *Holden Festskrift*, 72.

[41] *Holden Through One Hundred Years*, 16.

[42] *Holden Ministerial Book*, I, 504.

[43] Larsen, *Laur. Larsen, Pioneer College President*, 2, 98.

[44] Letter from B. J. Muus to Laur. Larsen, February 6, 1860, in Luther College Archives.

[45] B. J. Muus and Alfred Muus, *Niels Muus's æt*.

[46] B. J. Muus, "Kort Oversigt," 69–76.

[47] B. J. Muus, "Kort Oversigt," 72–73.

[48] Letter from B. J. Muus to Laur. Larsen, March 12, 1860.

[49] Letter from B. J. Muus to Laur. Larsen, June 5, 1860, in Luther College Archives.

[50] Larsen, *Laur. Larsen*, 125.

[51] Letter from B. J. Muus to Laur. Larsen, January 10, 1861, in Luther College Archives.

359

[52] Nelson and Fevold, *Lutheran Church Among Norwegian-Americans*, 28, 31, 37, 154.

[53] Letter from B. J. Muus to Laur. Larsen, April 15, 1861, in Luther College Archives.

[54] Letter from B. J. Muus to Church Council, November 27, 1861, in Luther College Archives.

[55] Letter from B. J. Muus to Church Council, February 24, 1862, in Luther College Archives.

[56] Letter from B. J. Muus to Laur. Larsen, April 12, 1862, in Luther College Archives.

[57] The Half-Breed Tract, sometimes called the Wabasha Reservation, was designated as such at a conference in 1830 held at Prairie du Chien. Traders related to the Sioux by marriage were allowed to occupy a tract of land along the Mississippi, on the west side of Lake Pepin, a rectangle fifteen miles wide starting at a point below Red Wing and extending thirty-two miles down the river. This stretch of excellent farmland took in most of Wabasha county and about one-fifth of Goodhue county. It was made available to white settlers in 1854 when Minnesota delegate Henry M. Rice introduced a bill in Congress providing for certificates to be issued to the half-breeds, which they could exchange for other land. See Folwell, *History of Minnesota*, I: 321–324; Nydahl, "The Early Norwegian Settlement of Goodhue County," 7–9.

[58] Letter from B. J. Muus to Herman A. Preus, January 15, 1863, in Luther College Archives.

[59] Letter from B. J. Muus to Laur. Larsen, February 6, 1863, in Luther College Archives.

[60] Letter from B. J. Muus to Herman A. Preus, August 15, 1864, in Luther College Archives.

[61] Letter from B. J. Muus to Laur. Larsen, December 8, 1864, in Luther College Archives.

[62] Letter from B. J. Muus to Laur. Larsen, April 20, 1865, in Luther College Archives.

[63] Letter from B. J. Muus to Herman A. Preus, December 4, 1865, in Luther College Archives.

[64] Letter from B. J. Muus to Herman A. Preus, October 5, 1866, in Luther College Archives; *Holden Ministerial Book*, I, 527.

[65] Letter from B. J. Muus to Herman A. Preus, October 5, 1866.

[66] Letter from B. J. Muus to Laur. Larsen, April 20, 1865. Cf. also letters dated February 23, 1865, February 9, 1866, August 11, 1867, all in Luther College Archives.

[67] Letter from B. J. Muus to Laur. Larsen, April 16, 1867, in Luther College Archives.

[68] Letter from B. J. Muus to Laur. Larsen, December 2, 1867, in Luther College Archives.

[69] Letter from B. J. Muus to Herman A. Preus, May 22, 1868, in Luther College Archives.

[70] Letter from B. J. Muus to Herman A. Preus, June 19, 1868, in Luther College Archives.

[71] *Holden Festskrift*, 72–73; Letter from B. J. Muus to Laur. Larsen, November 16, 1868, in Luther College Archives; *Kirkelig Maanedstidende*, 13 (15 December 1858), 371.

[72] Letter from B. J. Muus to Laur. Larsen, November 21, 1868, in Luther College Archives.

[73] Letter from B. J. Muus to Laur. Larsen, December 7, 1868, in Luther College Archives.

[74] B. J. Muus, "Hon. Knut K. Finseth," in *Kirkelig Maanedstidende*, 15 (15 January 1870), 21–23.

[75] *Kirkelig Mannedstidende*, 14 (1 December 1869), 383. The notice Muus published about the academy is translated and quoted in full in Grose, "The Beginnings of St. Olaf College," in *Norwegian-American Studies and Records*, 5 (1930), 113.

[76] Letter from B.J. Muus to Herman A. Preus, December 9 ,1869, in Luther College Archives.

## Chapter Six

[1] Larsen, *Laur. Larsen,*, 62.

[2] B. J. Muus, "Kort Oversigt," 72.

[3] B. J. Muus to Herman A. Preus, May 16, 1871, in Luther College Archives, Decorah, Iowa.

[4] *Kirkelig Maanedstidende*, 5 (January, 1860), 10.

[5] *Holden Ministerial Book* I, "Geistligt Dagregister 1859," 504. *Ministerial Bog for Holden Menighed* is the title of the two record books in which Muus and other Holden pastors listed baptisms, confirmations, marriages, burials, membership lists, and a daily record of pastoral services. The last-named section is the "Geistligt Dagregister," i.e., clergy daily journal. This journal is also valuable for information about Muus's travels to mission stations beyond the Holden area. Subsequent references will be to *Holden Ministerial Book* I, which pertains to the period 1855 to 1872. *Holden Ministerial Book* II covers ministerial activities from 1872 to 1899.

[6] Harold Severson, *We Give You Kenyon: A Bicentennial History of a Minnesota Community* (Kenyon, Minnesota, 1976), 223.

[7] B. J. Muus, "Kort Oversigt," 72.

[8] B. J. Muus to Laur. Larsen, November 16, 1868.

[9] *Kirkelig Maanedstidende*, 13 (15 December 1868), 372–373.

[10] B. J. Muus, "Kort Oversigt," 75.

[11] O. I. Flaten, "Valdris Settlement i Goodhue County, Minn.," in *Valdris Helsing* 7 (May, 1905), 88–89; B. J. Muus, "Kort Oversigt," 72.

[12] *Kirkelig Maanedstidende*, 13 (15 December 1868), 371, 375; Curt Schneider, *Vang Lutheran Church Anniversary Book*, 1987, 18, 21. Pastor Schneider prepared this book for Vang Lutheran Church's 125th Anniversary in 1987.

[13] B. J. Muus, "Kort Oversigt," 71; Schneider, *Vang Book*, 21.

[14] *Holden Ministerial Book* I, 518.

[15] *Kirkelig Maanedstidende*, 13 (15 December 1868), 374; Schneider, *Vang book*, 21.

[16] B. J. Muus, "Kort oversigt," 72; Voxland, *Holden Through One Hundred Years 1856–1956*, 16.

[17] Schneider, *Vang Book*, 18–19.

[18] Schneider, *Vang Book*, 18–21.

[19] Schneider, *Vang Book*, 32; Norlie, *Norsk lutherske prester i Amerika 1843–1913*, 152, 188, 281; Benson, *High on Manitou*, 335.

[20] Rasmussen, *A History of Goodhue County Minnesota*, 170–171.

[21] *Evangelisk Luthersk Kirketidende* (23 October 1874), 681.

[22] Norlie, *Norsk Lutherske Menigheter i Amerika 1843–1916*, 1 (Minneapolis, 1918), 460, and *Norsk lutherske prester*, 171, 195.

[23] Norlie, *Norsk Lutherske Menigheter*, 460.

[24] G. B. Odegaard, *A History of the Southern Minnesota District, Evangelical Lutheran Church 1854–1959*, n.d., 27.

[25] Schneider, *Vang Book*, 21.

[26] Norlie, *Norsk Lutherske Menigheter*, 460.

[27] *Holden Ministerial Book* I, 504.

[28] *Kirkelig Maanedstidende*, 13 (1 November 1868), 331.

[29] Voxland, *Holden 100*, 14; *Kirkelig Maanedstidende*, 13 (1 November 1868), 331.

[30] *Holden Ministerial Book* I, 504.

[31] B. J. Muus, "Kort oversigt," 72; *Kirkelig Maanedstidende*, 13 (1 November 1868), 331.

[32] Norlie, *Norsk Lutherske Menigheter*, 471.

[33] Kay Hope, "Valley Grove History from 1957–1973," written for Nerstrand Bicentennial, 1976, addendum to G. M. Bruce, "A Brief History of Valley Grove Lutheran Church" (Northfield, 1976).

[34] Joseph M. Shaw, *History of St. Olaf College 1874–1974* (Northfield, Minnesota, 1974), 39–40, 51.

[35] Severson, *We Give You Kenyon*, 226.

[36] B. J. Muus, "Kort oversigt," 72.

[37] *Holden Ministerial Book* I, 528–529.

[38] Severson, *We Give You Kenyon*, 226.

[39] *Minutes of Dale Lutheran Church*, 1 (8 January 1874), 1.

[40] *Evangelisk Luthersk Kirketidende* (1878), 105; B. J. Muus, "Kort oversigt," 73; Norlie, *Norsk lutherske prester*, 152; Severson, *We Give You Kenyon*, 226.

[41] Norlie, *Norsk lutherske prester*, 106.

[42] Severson, *We Give You Kenyon*, 226.

[43] *Evangelisk Luthersk Kirketidende*, 31 July 1874, 490.

[44] Shaw, *History of St. Olaf College*, 38; Grose, *Fifty Memorable Years at St. Olaf*, 25.

[45] B. J. Muus, "Kort oversigt," 73.

[46] *Evangelisk Luthersk Kirketidende*, 31 July 1874, 491.

[47] "Gol Lutheran celebrates 125 years," in *The Lutheran* (June 14, 1989), 31.

[48] Severson, *We Give You Kenyon*, 221.

[49] Voxland, *Holden 100*, 16; "Gol Lutheran celebrates," 31; Severson, *We Give You Kenyon*, 223; Norlie, *Norsk Lutherske Menigheter*, 525.

[50] "History of Moland Lutheran Church, 1880–1960," Eightieth Anniversary booklet, 1–5.

[51] Simundson, "Rev. B. J. Muus as I Learned to Know Him."

[52] "History of Moland Lutheran Church 1880–1960," Eightieth Anniversary booklet, 1, 3; "Moland Church 1880–1980," Centennial booklet, n.p.

[53] "History of Moland, 1880–1960," 2; "Moland Church 1880–1980."

[54] "History of Moland, 1880–1960," 3; Severson, *We Give You Kenyon*, 228.

[55] "Moland Church 1880–1980," n.p.

[56] B. J. Muus, "Kort oversigt," 72.

[57] B. J. Muus, "Kort oversigt," 74.

[58] Betty Bailey, *Lands Congregation, 1867–1992*, 125th Anniversary of Lands Lutheran Church (Zumbrota, Minnesota, 1992), 12.

[59] *Holden Ministerial Book* I, 504; Bailey, *Lands Congregation*, 9–10; Voxland, *Holden 100*, 12.

[60] *Holden Ministerial Book* I, 507, 510–512, 514, 518, 521.

[61] B. J. Muus to Herman A. Preus, January 22, 1868, September 14, 1868, in Luther College Archives, Decorah, Iowa; *Kirkelig Maanedstidende*, 13 (15 December 1868), 371.

[62] Bailey, *Lands Congregation*, 11–12.

[63] Information in this and the next paragraph comes from Bailey, *Lands Congregation*, 12–13.

[64] Bailey, *Lands Congregation*, 14, 20–21, 23, 25.

[65] Carl M. Gunderson, ed., *A History of Crow River Lutheran Church, 1861–1961*, 8.

[66] Rasmussen, *History of Goodhue County*, 171.

[67] Bailey, *Lands Congregation*, 83; *Holden Ministerial Book* I, "Geistligt Dagregister 1867," 530.

[68] Bailey, *Lands Congregation*, 12–13.

[69] Bailey, *Lands Congregation*, 83; B. J. Muus, "Kort Oversigt," 73.

[70] Bailey, *Lands Congregation*, 84; Norlie, *Norsk Lutherske Menigheter*, 465.

[71] *Holden Ministerial Book* I, 504.

[72] B. J. Muus to Laur. Larsen, February 8, 1860, in Luther College Archives, Decorah, Iowa.

[73] *Holden Ministerial Book* I, 513; B. J. Muus to Laur. Larsen, March 1, 1866, in Luther College Archives, Decorah, Iowa.

[74] Bailey, *Lands Congregation*, 84; *Holden Ministerial Book* I, 530, 531.

[75] Bailey, *Lands Congregation*, 84.

[76] Bailey, *Lands Congregation*, 84–85; B. J. Muus, "Kort Oversigt," 73; Norlie, *Norsk lutherske prester*, 291, and *Norsk lutherske menigheter*, 465.

[77] Bailey, *Land Congregation*, 85.

[78] Gertrude Richardson, Mary Ann Ferrin, Harold Harrison, and Myrtle Christiansen, *United Lutheran Church History, 1858–1958* (Red Wing, 1983), n.p.

[79] *Holden Ministerial Book* I, 504, 506, 607, 510–511.

[80] *Kirkelig Maanedstidende*, 12 (January 1867), 21.

[81] *Kirkelig Maanedstidende*, 12 (January 1867), 20–22.

[82] *Kirkelig Maanedstidende* 13 (15 December 1868), 372.

[83] *Kirkelig Maanedstidende* 13 (15 December 1868), 371–373.

[84] B. J. Muus, "Kort Oversigt," 73.

[85] Severson, *We Give You Kenyon*, 227; B. J. Muus, "Kort Oversigt," 74.

[86] Norlie, *Norsk lutherske menigheter*, 467; Severson, *We Give You Kenyon*, 227.

[87] Severson, *We Give You Kenyon*, 227.

[88] B. J. Muus, "Kort oversigt," 75.

## Chapter Seven

[1] Herman Amberg Preus, *Vivacious Daughter: Seven Lectures on the Religious Situation Among Norwegians in America*, translated and edited with an introduction by Todd Nichol (Northfield, Minnesota, 1990), 10, 42.

[2] Laur. Larsen, "Beretning om min reise til Norge," in *Kirkelig Maanedstidende*, 6 (1861), 69. See also Fevold, "Spanning the Great River," in *Norsemen Found a Church*, J. C. K. Preus, T. F. Gullixson, and E. C. Reinertson, eds. (Minneapolis, 1953), 149.

[3] Fevold, "Spanning the Great River," 149; Voxland, *Holden Through One Hundred Years 1856–1956*, 19; Norlie, *Norsk lutherske prester i Amerika*, 23.

[4] Norlie, *Norsk lutherske prester*, 104.

[5] Preus, *Vivacious Daughter*, 10.

[6] B. J. Muus, "Kort Oversigt," 75–76.

[7] *Holden Ministerial Book* I, "Geistligt Dagregister," 506, 524.

[8] Olav Lee, "The History of St. John's Church," in *St. John's Norwegian Lutheran Church, Northfield, Minn., A Record of the first Fifty Years 1869–1919* (Northfield, Minnesota, 1920), 1; Edna Hong, *The Book of a Century: The Centennial History of St. John's Lutheran Church, Northfield, Minnesota* (Northfield, 1969), 9.

[9] Lee, "History of St. John's Church," 2, 8.

[10] Lee, "History of St. John's Church," 5, 8; *Holden Ministerial Book* II, "Geistligt Dagregister 1881," 688.

[11] Lee, "History of St. John's Church," 45; Fevold, "Spanning the Great River," 152; Hong, *Book of a Century*, 16; B. R. Biørn, "St. John's and St. Olaf," unpublished article (Northfield, 1949); Shaw, "125 Years of Collaboration," in *Celebration*, 125th Anniversary Book, St. John's Lutheran Church, ed. by Frederick H. Gonnerman (Northfield, 1994), 14–19.

[12] *Kirkelig Maanedstidende*, 12 (15 February 1867), 54.

[13] Theodor Ellingson Strand, "The Norwegian Fox Lake Settlement. Memories and traits from the colonist days in Minnesota," typed manuscript (Tacoma, Washington, 1931), 2, 5, in St. Olaf College Archives; Lillian S. Teisberg, *Our Journey of Faith: The History of First English Lutheran Church 1861–1991* (Faribault, Minnesota, 1992), 128; *Holden Ministerial Book* I, 521; B. J. Muus, "Christiania og anekterede Menigheder i Minnesota," in *Kirkelig Maanedstidende*, 12 (15 February 1867), 52.

[14] Strand, "Norwegian Fox Lake Settlement," 5; Agnes Hanson to Joseph M. Shaw, March 29, 1994; Affidavit of Compliance, Fox Lake Lutheran Cemetery Association, January 14, 1993; Teisberg, *Journey of Faith*, 127–128.

[15] Teisberg, *Journey of Faith*, 33; Karen Larsen, *Laur. Larsen*, 81, cited in Teisberg, *Journey of Faith*, 8.

[16] *Holden Ministerial Book* I, 522–523; Norlie, *Norsk lutherske menigheter i Amerika,* 472; Teisberg, *Journey of Faith,* 33, 35, 44.

[17] A. Gerald Dyste, "The Twin Churches of Christiania, Minnesota, from 1854 to 1864: A Study of the Causes of Immigrant Church Conflicts," in *Norwegian-American Studies,* 33 (Northfield, Minnesota, 1992), 91; Norlie, *Norsk Lutherske Menigheter,* 476–477.

[18] B. J. Muus, "Christiania og anekterede Menigheder," 51; Dyste, "Twin Churches of Christiania," 73–98.

[19] B. J. Muus, "Christiania og anekterede Menigheder," 52; Norlie, *Norsk Lutherske Menigheter,* 476.

[20] Muus was not unalterably opposed to revivals. When Ole Paulson visited Goodhue county Muus welcomed him and gave him permission to hold revival meetings and sell books in the Holden area. See Ole Paulson, *Memoirs: Reminiscences of a Pioneer Pastor in America, 1850–1885,* trans. by Torstein O. Kvamme (Minneapolis, 1907), 53.

[21] *Centennial: Christiania Lutheran Church, 1857–1957* (Farmington, Minnesota, 1957); Dyste, "Twin Churches," 85, 88.

[22] *Holden Ministerial Book* I, 527. Dyste ("Twin Churches," 84) depicts Muus as aggressively competing for members to join the Synod congregation, claiming that he "visited Dakota county twelve times in 1860, undoubtedly to meet with the emerging opposition faction within the Christiania congregation." Dyste's source, *"Holden Through One Hundred Years 1856–1956,"* 15, actually states that between the beginning of Advent in 1860 and the same Sunday a year later, Muus held twelve "Services" in Dakota county. It was customary for missionary pastors to hold more than one service per visit to a given community. Muus's clergy journal discloses a two-day visit to a settlement "north of Northfield" June 7 and 8, 1960, but it is not clear that the place was necessarily Christiania. The journal records three visits to Dakota county in 1861: March 14–15, June 17–19, October 3–4. See *Holden Ministerial Book* I, 506, 509, 510. These were regular pastoral visits undertaken because Muus had been called to serve at Christiania. He was far too busy with his many congregations and preaching places to spend extra time competing for adherents at Christiania.

[23] *Christiania Lutheran Church, 125 Years 1857–1982* (Lakeville, Minnesota, 1982), 6–7.

[24] *Kirkelig Maanedstidende,* 12 (15 February 1867), 52.

[25] "Historical Highlights 1858–1983," North Waseca Lutheran Church 125th Anniversary History Booklet (1983).

[26] *Holden Ministerial Book* I, 506–507; North Waseca "Historical Highlights."

[27] C. A. Mellby, *St. Olaf College Through Fifty Years 1874–1924* (Northfield, Minnesota, 1925), 82.

[28] *Who's Who Among Pastors in all the Norwegian Lutheran Synods of America 1843–1927,* 3rd ed. of *Norsk lutherske prester i Amerika,* trans. and rev. by Rasmus Malmin, O. M. Norlie, and O. A. Tingelstad (Minneapolis, 1928), 168; Norlie, *Norsk Lutherske Menigheter,* 514–515; *A History of the Le Sueur River Lutheran Church,* 1861–1961 (New Richland, Minnesota, 1961), 8.

[29] *History of Le Sueur River Lutheran Church,* 9; *Holden Ministerial Book* I, 513, 516.

[30] *History of Le Sueur River Lutheran Church*, 9, 11.

[31] *History of Le Sueur River Lutheran Church*, 11; *Holden Ministerial Book* I, 522.

[32] "Jackson Lake Church Notes 75th Anniversary," in *Blue Earth County Enterprise*, October 1, 1937; Norlie, *Norsk Lutherske Menigheter*, 515.

[33] *Who's Who Among Pastors*, 168; "Jackson Lake Church Notes 75th Anniversary"; *Evangelisk luthersk kirketidende*, 6 (October 24, 1879), 683. *Evangelisk luthersk kirketidende* was the weekly publication of the Norwegian Synod that succeeded the monthly and bi-monthly *Kirkelig Maanedstidende* in 1874.

[34] "Early Missionary Inspired Church Organization," in *Blue Earth County Enterprise*, October 1, 1937.

[35] *Linden Lutheran Church, One Hundred Twenty-Fifth Anniversary Book* (Hanska, Minnesota, 1984), 3–4. The Linden 125th anniversary history includes two tantalizing items about "Rev. Frederickson," as it spells the name: that he was a fur trader who had the nickname "Skinnbrok presten" (literally, Leather Pants Pastor, or the expression could convey that he was a rustic, a rough-and-ready man), and that toward the end of 1859 he was defrocked for unknown reasons. In *Norsk Lutherske Menigheter i America*, 597, 514, 515, A. E. Friedrichsen is listed as one of the first pastors at Jackson Lake, Delavan, and Rosendale.

[36] *Linden Lutheran Church*, 4; B. J. Muus to Laur. Larsen, May 14, 1861, in Luther College Archives; *Holden Ministerial Book* I, 509, 513.

[37] "History of the Rosendale Congregation 1859–1959," 100th Anniversary booklet; *Holden Ministerial Book* I, 509, 513, 516.

[38] "Norseland Norwegian Evangelical Lutheran Church," typescript early records, trans. by Milton E. Tweit (St. Peter, Minnesota, 1994), 1–2. My thanks to Kathryn Ericson for making a copy of this document available to me.

[39] "Norseland Church," 3–4; *St. Peter Herald*, June 9, 1933.

[40] *Holden Ministerial Book* I, 506–516; "Norseland Church," 5–6.

[41] *Kirkelig Maanedstidende*, 9 (November, 1864), 336–337.

[42] Holand, *De Norske Settlementers Historie*, 479; *Holden Ministerial Book* I, 506, 507, 509, 510, 516; Norlie, *Norsk Lutherske Menigheter*, 479; *Kirkelig Maanedstidende*, 14 (August 1, 1869), 252.

[43] "Norseland Church," 5.

[44] "Norseland Church," 6; *Holden Ministerial Book* I, 506, 509, 510, 513, 516; *St. Peter Herald*, June 9, 1933.

[45] "Norseland Church," 5, 6, 8; *Holden Ministerial Book* I, 506–516.

[46] *Kirkelig Maanedstidende*, 4 (March & April, 1859), 46, 53; *Holden Ministerial Book* I, 506–516.

[47] "Norseland Church," 3, 7, 10; *Holden Ministerial Book* I, 516.

[48] Muus, "Kort Oversigt," 73; Norlie, *Norsk Lutherske Menigheter*, 511.

[49] Norlie, *Ness Jubelskrift, 1911: Ness norsk luthersk menighed, Meeker County, Minn.* (Minneapolis, 1911), 30–31.

[50] *Ness Jubelskrift, 1911*, 6.

[51] *History of Ness church, 1861–1948* (Litchfield, Minnesota, 1948), 2.

[52] Norlie, *Norsk lutherske menigheter*, 519; *Ness Jubelskrift, 1911*, 36; *History of Ness church, 1861–1948*, 5; Charles R. Ness, Jr., "Reminiscing with Mother Ness," in program, "Minnesota State Monument Centennial, Ness Church and Cemetery,"

Litchfield, Minnesota, September 10, 1978, in ELCA Region 3 Archives, Luther Seminary, St. Paul, Minnesota.

[53] Norlie, *Norsk lutherske menigheter*, 520.

[54] Norlie, *Norsk lutherske menigheter*, 503.

[55] Blegen, "Immigrant Women and the American Frontier," in *Norwegian-American Studies and Records*, 5 (Northfield, Minnesota, 1930), 26, n. 5; *Crow River Norsk Ev.-Luth. Kirke, Femtiaarsfest, 1861–1911* (Kandiyohi and Stearns counties, Minn, 1911).

[56] Carl M. Gunderson, ed., *A History of Crow River Lutheran Church, 1861–1961* (Belgrade, Minnesota, 1961), 8; Einar Odden, "Whiskey-George from Gausdal founded a community in Minnesota," in *The New London Times*, October 11, 1979.

[57] *History of Crow River Church*, 7–8.

[58] *Holden Ministerial Book* I, 507, 509, 511, 513.

[59] *History of Crow River Church*, 10.

[60] The *History of Crow River Church* mentions "several" visits by Muus. Muus's clergy journal, however, confirms only the October 23, 1864, services at St. Francis River, and the October 26, 1864, ministry at the Monongalia or Crow River congregation. See "Geistligt Dagregister," 1864, *Holden Ministerial Book* I, 521.

[61] *History of Crow River Church*, 15.

[62] *Keeping the Faith. . . Sharing the Faith, History of First Lutheran Church of Norway Lake, 1862–1962* (New London, Minnesota, 1962), 8–9; *Holden Ministerial Book* I, 513.

[63] *Keeping the Faith*, 12–14.

[64] Norlie, *Norsk lutherske menigheter*, 497, 650.

[65] *Keeping the Faith*, 38–39.

[66] *History of Crow River Church*, 10; *Holden Ministerial Book* I, 521.

[67] *Holden Ministerial Book* I, 536; Minutes, Our Savior's Lutheran Church, July 21, 1873, December 30, 1873, March 22, 1874; *Evangelisk luthersk kirketidende*, 1 (April 17, 1874), 252–253.

[68] Muus, "Kort oversigt," 75. I am indebted to Professor Todd Nichol of Luther Seminary for information on Immanuel Lutheran Church. Nichol to Shaw, 9 July 1994. For data on the early history of Immanuel and Our Savior's churches, see Norlie, *Norsk Lutherske Menigheter*, 547.

[69] *Holden Ministerial Book* I, 511.

[70] *Kirkelig Maanedstidende*, 16 (January 1, 1871), 13..

[71] *Our Second Century in Christ 1868–1968, Centennial Book of Christ Lutheran Church on Capitol Hill* (St. Paul, Minnesota, 1968), n.p.

[72] Laur. Larsen, "Skandinavisk-lutherske Menigheder," in *Kirkelig Maanedstidende*, 4 (March & April, 1859), 48–49.

[73] Larsen, "Skandinavisk-lutherske Menigheder," 51–53.

[74] *Holden Ministerial Book* I, 509, 513, 521, 536, 538.

[75] *Our Second Century in Christ.*

[76] *One Hundredth Anniversary, The Rush River Lutheran Parish 1855–1955* (River Falls, Wisconsin, 1955), n.p. in ELCA Region 3 Archives.

[77] Karen Larsen, *Laur. Larsen*, 65; Norlie, *Norsk Lutherske Menigheter*, 211–213; *Holden Ministerial Book* I, 506, 511.

[78] B. J. Muus to Laur. Larsen, May 16, 1860, in Luther College Archives.

[79] B. J. Muus to Laur. Larsen, April 15, 1861; *Holden Ministerial Book* I, 506, 508, 511, 514.

[80] *One Hundred Years of Bearing the Light 1858–1958*, Little Elk Creek Lutheran Church, Menomonie, Wisconsin, 1958, in ELCA Region 3 Archives; *Holden Ministerial Book* I, 514; Karen Larsen, *Laur. Larsen*, 67.

## Chapter Eight

[1] Norlie *et al.*, *Norsk lutherske prester i Amerika*, 23.

[2] *Norsk Kirketidende*, 34 (25 August 1861).

[3] *Aftenbladet*, 29 October 1870; Lovoll, *The Promise of America*, 98.

[4] B. J. Muus to Laur. Larsen, May 6, 1862, in Luther College Archives, Decorah, Iowa; Floan, "Reminiscences from the Pioneer Days in Goodhue County," 7.

[5] *Kirkelig Maanedstidende*, 7 (15 August 1862), 246; Norlie, *Norsk lutherske prester*, 98.

[6] Gerhard Lee Belgum, "The Old Norwegian Synod in America, 1853–1890" (Ph. D. dissertation, Yale University, 1957), 343.

[7] Belgum, "The Old Norwegian Synod," 346, citing *Kirkelig Maanedstidende*, 4 (1859), May, 67; June, 118; October, 145.

[8] J. Magnus Rohne, *Norwegian American Lutheranism Up To 1872* (New York, 1926), 162, 169. The text of Article XIV is found in the Preface to the Christian Book of Concord, *Augsburg Confession*, Article XIV: Of Ecclesiastical Order, in *Triglot Concordia: The Symbolical Books of the Ev. Lutheran Church* (St. Louis, Missouri, 1921), 49.

[9] J. A. Bergh, *Den norsk lutherske kirkes historie i Amerika* (Minneapolis, 1914), 109; Rohne, *Norwegian American Lutheranism*, 168.

[10] Rohne, *Norwegian American Lutheranism*, 169; Belgum, "The Old Norwegian Synod," 346, quoting C. F. W. Walther's letter to J. A. Ottesen: "Luther teaches that the keys or office belongs originally and immediately to the whole Church, that is, all believers. God has, however, provided that the public office is to be occupied only by specially called men, who are capable of teaching, and who now in a special sense serve in their office in the Name of and on behalf of Christ."

[11] Bergh, *Norsk lutherske kirkes historie*, 112.

[12] Rohne, *Norwegian American Lutheranism*, 169; Bergh, *Norsk lutherske kirkes historie*, 113.

[13] Bergh, *Norsk lutherske kirkes historie*, 113–114.

[14] Bergh, *Norsk lutherske kirkes historie*, 115; Rohne, *Norwegian American Lutheranism*, 170; Nelson and Fevold, *The Lutheran Church Among Norwegian-Americans*, 166.

[15] Bergh, *Norsk lutherske kirkes historie*, 115–116.

[16] Nelson and Fevold, *Lutheran Church Among Norwegian-Americans*, 167; Rohne, *Norwegian American Lutheranism*, 174.

[17] *Kirkelig Maanedstidende*, 6 (September 1861), 266; *Norsk Kirketidende*, 34 (25 August 1861), 266.

[18] *Kirkelig Maanedstidende*, 6 (November 1861), 333–337.

[19] *Kirkelig Maanedstidende*, 6:338–342.

[20] *The Smalcald Articles*, "Of the Power and Jurisdiction of Bishops," Tractate 67 (Latin text), *Triglot Concordia*, 523.

[21] *Kirkelig Maanedstidende*, 7 (1 August 1862), 214, 220.

[22] *Kirkelig Maanedstidende*, 7:228; Rohne, *Norwegian American Lutheranism*, 178.

[23] Rohne, *Norwegian American Lutheranism*, 179; Nelson and Fevold, *Lutheran Church Among Norwegian-Americans*, 168.

[24] *Norsk Kirketidende*, 34 (25 August 1861).

[25] *Lutheran Book of Worship* (Minneapolis, 1978), 56.

[26] Nelson and Fevold, *Lutheran Church Among Norwegian-Americans*, 174; *Kirkelig Maanedstidende*, 6 (August 1861), 258.

[27] *Kirkelig Maanedstidende*, 6 (June 1861), 166–174; July, 193–201.

[28] *Kirkelig Maanedstidende*, 6 (August 1861), 237, 244; Rohne, *Norwegian American Lutheranism*, 227.

[29] *Kirkelig Maanedstidende*, 6:244; Rohne, *Norwegian American Lutheranism*, 229; Nelson and Fevold, *Lutheran Church Among Norwegian-Americans*, 243.

[30] *Kirkelig Maanedstidende*, 6:244; Rohne, *Norwegian American Lutheranism*, 229.

[31] *Kirkelig Maanedstidende*, 6:245, 249–250.

[32] *Kirkelig Maanedstidende*, 6:250–252.

[33] *Kirkelig Maanedstidende*, 6:253; Rohne, *Norwegian American Lutheranism*, 230.

[34] B. J. Muus to Laur. Larsen, April 12, 1862; May 6, 1862.

[35] Rohne, *Norwegian American Lutheranism*, 232; Nelson and Fevold, *Lutheran Church Among Norwegian-Americans*, 243.

[36] Rohne, *Norwegian American Lutheranism*, 232–233.

[37] Nelson and Fevold, *Lutheran Church Among Norwegian-Americans*, 169.

[38] Bergh, *Norsk lutherske kirkes historie*, 30; Blegen, *Norwegian Migration to America: The American Transition*, 419.

[39] C. F. W. Walther to A. C. Preus, January 8, 1860, quoted in Blegen, *Norwegian Migration . . . American Transition*, 421.

[40] Nelson and Fevold, *Lutheran Church Among Norwegian-Americans*, 172–174.

[41] Nelson and Fevold, *Lutheran Church Among Norwegian-Americans*, 174.

[42] *Kirkelig Maanedstidende*, 6 (September 1861), 258; Rohne, *Norwegian American Lutheranism*, 204.

[43] *Kirkelig Maanedstidende*, 6:260.

[44] *Kirkelig Maanedstidende*, 6:261; Rohne, *Norwegian American Lutheranism*, 205; Blegen, *Norwegian Migration . . . American Transition*, 426.

[45] *Kirkelig Maanedstidende*, 6:261; Nelson and Fevold, *Lutheran Church Among Norwegian-Americans*, 174–175; Blegen, *Norwegian Migration . . . American Transition*, 426.

[46] *Kirkelig Maanedstidende*, 6:261–262; Nelson and Fevold, *Lutheran Church Among Norwegian-Americans*, 175.

[47] Rohne, *Norwegian American Lutheranism*, 207.

[48] *Kirkelig Maanedstidende*, 6:262; Blegen, *Norwegian Migration . . . American Transition*, 428.

[49] Blegen, *Norwegian Migration . . . American Transition*, 446.

[50] Rohne, *Norwegian American Lutheranism*, 209; Nelson and Fevold, *Lutheran Church Among Norwegian-Americans*, 175–176.

[51] Rohne, *Norwegian American Lutheranism*, 210, 212, 213; B. J. Muus to Laur. Larsen, November 13, 1868, in Luther College Archives, Decorah, Iowa; *Holden Ministerial Book* I, 520 (September 7–12, 1864).

[52] Blegen, *Norwegian Migration . . . American Transition*, 439–441; Rohne, *Norwegian American Lutheranism*, 214, 230.

[53] Blegen, *Norwegian Migration . . . American Transition*, 444; Nelson and Fevold, *Lutheran Church Among Norwegian-Americans*, 177.

[54] Rohne, *Norwegian American Lutheranism*, 210.

[55] B. J. Muus to H. A. Preus, October 5, 1866.

[56] *Emigranten*, December 10, 1866.

[57] *Emigranten*, January 14, 1867.

[58] *Emigranten*, February 18, 1867.

[59] *Emigranten*, February 18, 1867.

[60] Rohne, *Norwegian American Lutheranism*, 219; Blegen, *Norwegian Migration . . . American Transition*, 450.

[61] Blegen, *Norwegian Migration . . . American Transition*, 447; Nelson and Fevold, *Lutheran Church Among Norwegian-Americans*, 179.

[62] Blegen, *Norwegian Migration . . . American Transition*, 450.

[63] Nelson and Fevold, *Lutheran Church Among Norwegian-Americans*, 179.

## Chapter Nine

[1] B. J. Muus, "Skole og god Skole," in *Fædrelandet og Emigranten*, March 10, 1870.

[2] Laurence M. Larson, "Skandinaven, Professor Anderson, and the Yankee School," in *The Changing West And Other Essays* (Northfield, Minnesota, 1937), 118–119.

[3] Frank C. Nelsen, "The School Controversy Among Norwegian Immigrants," in *Norwegian-American Studies*, 26 (Northfield, Minnesota, 1974), 218.

[4] "Beretning om Skolelærermødet," Coon Prairie, Wisconsin, 28 June 1858, in *Kirkelig Maanedstidende*, 3 (September, 1858), 139; Blegen, "The Immigrant and the Common School," Ch. 8, in *Norwegian Migration to America: The American Transition*, 249.

[5] Blegen, "Immigrant and Common School," 241.

[6] Lydia Bredesen Sundby, "Holding High the Torch," in *Norsemen Found a Church*, edited by J. C. K. Preus, T. F. Gullixson, and E. C. Reinertson (Minneapolis, 1953), 305.

[7] Blegen, "Immigrant and Common School, " 244–245; Larson, "Skandinaven, Professor Anderson, Yankee School," 118; Arthur C. Paulson and Kenneth Bjork, trans. and eds., "A School and Language Controversy in 1858: A Documentary Study," in *Norwegian-American Studies and Records*, 10 (Northfield, Minnesota, 1938), 78.

[8] Sundby, "Holding High the Torch," 301.

[9] Rohne, *Norwegian American Lutheranism*, 122; Blegen, "Immigrant and Common School," 246.

[10] "Beretning om Skolelærermødet," 137–139.

[11] "Beretning om Skolelærermødet," 139.

[12] "Uddrag af Forhandlingerne ved Skolelærermødet," in *Kirkelig Maanedstidende*, 4 (March & April 1859), 40; Blegen, "Immigrant and Common School," 249.

[13] Blegen, "Immigrant and Common School," 249.

[14] Paulson and Bjork, "A School and Language Controversy," 82–86, 90–93.

[15] Paulson and Bjork, "A School and Language Controversy," 97–99.

[16] "Erklæring om vore Skole- og Sprogforhold," in *Kirkelig Maanedstidende*, 4 (October 1859), 156. A good summary of this declaration is found in Blegen, "Immigrant and Common School," 252–253.

[17] Larson, "Skandinaven, Professor Anderson, Yankee School," 121. See Walter H. Beck, *Lutheran Elementary Schools in the United States* (2nd ed., St. Louis, Missouri, 1965) for a history of the development of the Missouri Synod's parochial schools.

[18] Larson, "Skandinaven, Professor Anderson, Yankee School," 122; Blegen, "Immigrant and Common School," 254.

[19] "Indstilling til Synoden om vore Menighedsskoler," in *Kirkelig Maanedstidende*, 11 (June 1866), 210, 214.

[20] *Kirkelig Maanedstidende*, 11 (May 1866), 146.

[21] *Kirkelig Maanedstidende*, 11 (June 1866), 220–222.

[22] Preus, "Lecture II: Congregational Polity," in *Vivacious Daughter*, 63, 65–67.

[23] Larson, "Skandinaven, Professor Anderson, Yankee School," 123–125; Blegen, "Immigrant and Common School," 257.

[24] Rasmus B. Anderson, *Life Story of Rasmus B. Anderson* (Madison, Wisconsin, 1915), 99.

[25] Anderson, *Life Story*, 99; Larson, "Skandinaven, Professor Anderson, Yankee School," 127–128; Blegen, "Immigrant and Common School," 257–258.

[26] Lloyd Hustvedt, *Rasmus Bjørn Anderson: Pioneer Scholar* (Northfield, Minnesota, 1966), 66; Blegen, "Immigrant and Common School," 258.

[27] Hustvedt, *Rasmus Bjørn Anderson*, 70–71; Blegen, "Immigrant and Common School," 259.

[28] Nelsen, "The School Controversy among Norwegian Immigrants," 213, n13; Blegen, "Immigrant and Common School," 260.

[29] "Beretning om et Møde til Fremmelse af Folke-Oplysning blandt Skandinaverne i America," published pamphlet (Decorah, Iowa, 1869), 8. See also *Kirkelig Maanedstidende*, 14 (15 March 1869), 118.

[30] "Beretning om . . . Folk-Oplysning blandt Skandinaverne," 12–13.

[31] Larson, "Skandinaven, Professor Anderson, Yankee School," 129; B. H. Narveson, "The Norwegian Lutheran Academies," in *Norwegian-American Studies and Records*, 14 (Northfield, Minnesota, 1944), 217–221.

[32] Cited and translated by Grose in "The Beginnings of St. Olaf College," 113.

[33] Muus, "Skole og god Skole."

[34] H. B. Wilson, "Our Public Schools Versus Sectarian Schools in a Foreign Language," in *The Republican*, May 5, 1870.

[35] *The Republican*, June 2, 1870.

[36] B. J. Muus, "Sectarianism the True Christianity," in *The Republican*, July 7, 1870.

[37] Muus, "Sectarianism the True Christianity."

[38] Nelsen, "The School Controversy," 213, n14.

[39] Blegen, "Immigrant and Common School," 262, 267.

[40] Blegen, "Immigrant and Common School," 268–269.

[41] *Synodal Beretning om det femtende ordentlige Synodemøde* (La Crosse, Wisconsin, 1874), 61–62.

[42] *Synodal Beretning, 1874*, 65–66; Larson, *"Skandinaven*, Professor Anderson, Yankee School," 135.

[43] Larson, "Skandinaven, Professor Anderson, Yankee School," 135; Blegen, "Immigrant and Common School," 270.

[44] Rohne, *Norwegian American Lutheranism Up To 1872*, 109. The statement by Oftedal is cited in Larson, "Skandinaven, Professor Anderson, Yankee School," 138.

[45] Georg Sverdrup, "The Common School," in James S. Hamre, "Georg Sverdrup's Concept of the Role and Calling of the Norwegian-American Lutherans: An Annotated Translation of Selected Writings" (Ph. D. dissertation, University of Iowa, 1967), 111, 125.

[46] Sverdrup, "Common School," 108, 128, 130.

[47] Larson, "Skandinaven, Professor Anderson, Yankee School," 141–142.

[48] Larson, "Skandinaven, Professor Anderson, Yankee School," 145.

[49] Blegen, "Immigrant and Common School," 274; Nelsen, "The School Controversy," 219.

[50] Blegen, "Immigrant and Common School," 274–276.

## Chapter Ten

[1] "Beretning om et Møde til Fremmelse af Folke-Oplysning blandt Skandinaverne i Amerika," 11. The report also appears in *Kirkelig Maanedstidende*, 14 (1 April 1869); see 122.

[2] "Folke-Oplysning blandt Skandinaverne," 13.

[3] Blegen, "The Immigrant and the Common School," Ch. 8 in *Norwegian Migration to America: The American Transition*, 269.

[4] Grose, "The Beginnings of St. Olaf College," 113.

[5] *Minutes of Board of Trustees Meetings*, St. Olaf College, Book No. 1 (1874–1911; 1920–1923) (Northfield, Minnesota, 1874), 2.

[6] *Minutes of Board of Trustees Meetings*, 2; N. C. Brun, "Norsk-amerikanske skoler, II. St. Olaf College, Et kort omrids af dets opkomst og vækst," in *Symra*, 6 (Decorah, Iowa, 1910), 84.

[7] *Beretning om det femtende ordentlige Synodemøde af Synoden for den norsk-evang.-luth.Kirke i Amerika* (La Crosse, Wisconsin, 1874), 96; Brun, "St. Olaf College," 84.

[8] Anna E. Mohn, "Reminiscences," in *Manitou Messenger*, 19 (1906), 170.

[9] Grose, "The Beginnings of St. Olaf College," 117.

[10] *Minutes of Board of Trustees*, 2.

[11] *Rice County Journal*, October 7, 1874, cited in *Minutes of Board of Trustees*, 2–3.

[12] Muus to Laur. Larsen, October 9, 1874, in Luther College Archives, Decorah, Iowa.

[13] *Rice County Journal,* October 21, 1874. John T. Ames was the older son of Captain Jesse Ames. The younger was Adelbert Ames. Jesse Ames and sons were owners of the Ames Mill, later owned solely by John T. Ames, who served as mayor of Northfield.

[14] *Rice County Journal,* October 21, 1874; Grose, "The Beginnings of St. Olaf College," 117; *Minutes of Northfield School Board,* October 16, 1874, in St. Olaf College Archives.

[15] Grose, "Reminiscences," in *Manitou Messenger,* 18 (November, 1904), 146.

[16] In a Latin document titled "In Nomine Jesus," written by Pastor Muus to be placed in the cornerstone of the Main, the words "Praeses Scholae" appear before his name. These words indeed have been translated as "President of the School," signifying Pastor Muus's role as chief officer and guardian of the School, but in actual operation of the institution Thorbjørn Nelson Mohn was clearly the person in charge, first as principal and later as president.

[17] *Minutes of Board of Trustees,* 5–6. See also Shaw, *History of St. Olaf College 1874–1974,* 42.

[18] "Report of the Reverend Bernt Julius Muus concerning St. Olaf school to the Norwegian Synod, June 18, 1875," typescript, 1, in St. Olaf College Archives.

[19] "St. Olaf's School, en evangelisk luthersk Høiskole i Northfield, Minn.," Dedication Pamphlet (Decorah, Iowa, 1875), inside front cover; Muus, "Report to the Norwegian Synod," 1.

[20] William C. Benson, *High on Manitou: A History of St. Olaf College* (Northfield, Minnesota, 1949), 22; Anna E. Mohn, "Reminiscences," 171; Brun, "St. Olaf College," 86; Shaw, *History of St. Olaf College 1874–1974,* 15, 21–22, 43.

[21] Mellby, *Saint Olaf College Through Fifty Years 1874–1924,* 19.

[22] Benson, *High on Manitou,* 22; Eggen, "Erindringer om pastor Muus," 60.

[23] Trans. and cited by Grose in "The Beginnings of St. Olaf College," 118.

[24] "St. Olaf's School," Dedication Pamphlet, 4–6.

[25] "St. Olaf's School," 7–8; Shaw, *History of St. Olaf College,* 47–48.

[26] Muus, "Report to the Norwegian Synod," 2.

[27] Benson, *High on Manitou,* 24–27.

[28] "St. Olaf's School," 10; Shaw, *History of St. Olaf College,* 48.

[29] Shaw, *History of St. Olaf College,* 49.

[30] *Minutes of the Board of Trustees Meetings,* 26 October 1876, 14; Anna E. Mohn, "Reminiscences," 208.

[31] B. J. Muus, "In Nomine Jesu," hand-written document, 1887, original in St. Olaf College Archives. Latin text in *Quarter Centennial 1874–1899 Souvenir of St. Olaf College,* edited by J. A. Aasgaard (Northfield, 1900), n.p.

[32] Portions of "In Nomine Jesu" in translation are in Joseph M. Shaw, *Dear Old Hill: The Story of Manitou Heights, the Campus of St. Olaf College* (Northfield, Minnesota, 1992), 25.

[33] O. G. Felland, "History of St. Olaf College," in *Quarter Centennial Souvenir of St. Olaf College.*

[34] *Quarter Centennial Souvenir of St. Olaf College.*

[35] B. J. Muus, Dedication Address, November 6, 1878, in *Evangelisk Luthersk Kirketidende*, 5 (November 22, 1878), 735.

[36] Shaw, *History of St. Olaf College*, 54; *Evangelisk Luthersk Kirketidende*, 5 (November 22, 1878), 741.

[37] Anna E. Mohn, "De første aar ved St. Olaf College," in *Samband*, 103 (November, 1916), 27.

## Chapter Eleven

[1] B. J. Muus to H. A. Preus, January 15, 1863; B. J. Muus to Laur. Larsen, February 6, 1863, April 24, 1872, in Luther College Archives.

[2] Birgitte's son was born August 27, 1881, and baptized September 18, 1881. He was named Sverre Muus and brought up in the Muus household. The father was Johannes Olsen Kongsvik. He and Birgitte obtained a wedding license, but did not marry. *Holden Ministerial Book* II, "Døbte" (Baptized), 1881, 73. Marriage record No. 281. State of Minnesota, District Court for the County of Goodhue, Red Wing, August 10, 1881.

[3] B. J. Muus to Laur. Larsen, March 12, 1860. "Holden Church Called 'Cradle of St. Olaf,'" in *Goodhue County Historical News*, June, 1967.

[4] B. J. Muus to Laur. Larsen, September 18, 1863, in Luther College Archives. B. J. Muus to Laur. Larsen, January 15, 1864, in St. Olaf College Archives.

[5] B. J. Muus to Laur. Larsen, December 8, 1864.

[6] B. J. Muus to Laur. Larsen, April 20, 1865; Oline Muus to Laur. Larsen, August 23, 1870, September 19, 1870, in Luther College Archives.

[7] B. J. Muus to Laur. Larsen, December 6, 1872, December 13, 1872, March 15, 1873, February 12, 1874, September 16, 1874, November 22, 1874, in Luther College Archives.

[8] Conversation with Ella Valborg Rolvaag Tweet, June 3, 1998. Mrs. Tweet recalled meeting Birgitte Muus Klüver in Norway, being shown a box in which Mrs. Muus kept medical instruments, and hearing Birgitte tell of her mother's visits to Indians.

[9] "Mrs. Oline Muus contra Pastor B. J. Muus." *Budstikken* pamphlet. It contained reports of congregational meetings held in connection with Mrs. Muus's lawsuit, as well as editorials and statements from other newspapers and contributors, up to and including March 30, 1880. An especially valuable article on the Muus lawsuit is Kathryn Ericson, "Triple Jeopardy: The Muus vs. Muus Case in Three Forums," in *Minnesota History*, 50 (Winter, 1987), 302. Ericson's article was the first to bring the Muus vs. Muus case before the general public.

[10] Andreas Ueland, *Recollections of an Immigrant* (New York, 1929), 41.

[11] Oline Muus to Laur. Larsen, December 4, 1877, in Luther College Archives. Floan, "Reminiscences of the Early History of Singing in Holden congregation," unpublished typescript (St. Paul, Minnesota, 1938).

[12] Marcus O. Bøckman, "Bernt Julius Ingebretsen Muus," n.d., 3, from Knut Gjerset papers in NAHA Archives.

[13] *Budstikken* pamphlet.

[14] Ericson, "Triple Jeopardy," 303; Charles O. Richardson, "Landmark Cases In Goodhue County: Muus v. Muus," in *Goodhue County Historical News*, February, 1981, 3.

[15] Oline Muus vs. Bernt J. Muus, Supreme Court, State of Minnesota, Appellant's Case and Brief, Complaint, December 26, 1879, 4; *Budstikken* pamphlet, 16; Ericson, "Triple Jeopardy," 302.

[16] Ericson, "Triple Jeopardy," 303; Muus vs. Muus, Appellant's Case and Brief, Complaint, December 26, 1879, 5.

[17] Muus vs. Muus, Appellant's Case and Brief, Defendant's Answer, January, 1880, 6–13.

[18] Muus vs. Muus, Appellant's Case and Brief, Plaintiff's Reply, February 15, 1880, 13–15.

[19] Muus vs. Muus, Decision, September 8, 1881, 15–19; Ericson, "Triple Jeopardy," 303.

[20] Ericson, "Triple Jeopardy," 304; *Budstikken* pamphlet.

[21] *The Republican*, January 29, February 5, 1880; *The Advance*, January 28, 1880.

[22] *The Republican*, February 5, 1880; *Norden*, March 10, 1880. See also *Budstikken* pamphlet.

[23] *The Republican*, January 29, February 5, 1880; *Budstikken* pamphlet, 2.

[24] *Red Wing Argus*, February 26, 1880; *The Advance*, February 25, 1880; Ericson, "Triple Jeopardy," 304.

[25] *Budstikken* pamphlet, 14.

[26] *Budstikken* pamphlet, 16.

[27] Terje I. Leiren, *Marcus Thrane: A Norwegian Radical in America* (Northfield, Minnesota, 1987), 121–127; Marcus Thrane, "Holden," photocopy of typed manuscript in University Library, Oslo, Norway. There is an English translation of "Holden" by Henriette C. K. Naeseth in the Marcus Thrane papers, NAHA archives. See references to Muus in Marcus Thrane, *Den Gamle Wisconsin Bibelen* (Chicago, 1938), chapters 4–8. An English version, *The Wisconsin Bible*, was translated and edited by Linsie Caroline Krook and F. Hilding Krook, New Ulm, Minnesota, 1955.

[28] *Budstikken* pamphlet, 16–17.

[29] *Budstikken* pamphlet, 19, 22; *Norden*, April 7, 1880.

[30] *Norden*, June 2, 1880; *The Republican*, June 3, 1880.

[31] L. M. Biørn to H. A. Preus, June 12, 1880, in Luther College Archives. See also H. A. Preus, U. Koren, J. B. Frich, "Redegjørelse fra Holden Menighed, Minn.," in *Beretning om det Tredie ordentlige Synodemøde for Det østlige Distrikt af Synoden for den norske evang.luth. Kirke i Amerika*, held in Wiota, Wisconsin, June 3–9, 1880 (Decorah, Iowa, 1880), 774.

[32] "Anklage mod Pastor Muus," in *Beretning om det Tredie ordentlige Synodemøde af Minnesota Distrikt af Synoden for den norske evang.luth. Kirke i Amerika*, held in Le Sueur River church, June 16–23, 1880 (Decorah, Iowa, 1880), 63–64; *Evangelisk Lutherske Kirketidende*, 1880, 438.

[33] Preus et al., "Redegjørelse fra Holden Menighed," 775–776.

[34] *Lutheraneren*, December, 1880, 408, 412–413.

[35] *Red Wing Argus*, January 13, 1881.

[36] Bjørnstjerne Bjørnson to Karoline Bjørnson, March 3 (?), 1881, in *Land of the Free: Bjørnstjerne Bjørnson's America Letters, 1880–1881*, edited and translated by Eva Lund Haugen and Einar Haugen (Northfield, Minnesota, 1978), 228.

[37] Kristofer Janson, *Amerikanske Forholde: Fem Foredrag* (Copenhagen, 1881), 157.

[38] *Holden Ministerial Book* II, "Døbte," 1881, 73.

[39] H. A. Preus to B. J. Muus, September 16, 1881, in Luther College Archives.

[40] *Norden*, November 9, 1881.

[41] Oline Muus vs. Bernt J. Muus, State of Minnesota, Hennepin County District Court, Finding by Judge A. H. Young, January 10, 1883; *Norden*, January 24, 1883; Birgitte Muus deposition before Justice of the Peace John K. Naeseth, December 19, 1882.

[42] Oline Muus vs. Bernt J. Muus, State of Minnesota, Supreme Court, Appellant's Case and Brief, March 11, 1882, File No. 3250, 24–25.

[43] *Red Wing Argus*, February 16, 1882; *Beretning*, Minnesota District, 1882, 95096.

[44] *Red Wing Argus*, January 5, 1882; *The Republican*, January 7, 1882.

[45] Oline Muus vs. Bernt J. Muus, State of Minnesota, County of Hennepin District Court, Complaint of Plaintiff, December 26, 1881.

[46] State of Minnesota, Supreme Court, File Nos. 3250 and 3189, March 13, 1882; May 16, 1882.

[47] State of Minnesota, County of Hennepin District Court, Oline Muus vs. Bernt J. Muus: Depositions before John K. Naeseth, Justice of the Peace, Goodhue county, by Ole J. Solberg and Ole Sampson, December 20, 1882.

[48] Depositions before John Naeseth by Birgitte Muus and Maren Ramstad, December 19, 1882.

[49] Depositions before John Naeseth by Halvor Enertson, Ole Halvorson, Søren Monsen, and Knut Haugen, December 20, 1882.

[50] State of Minnesota, County of Hennepin District Court, Oline Muus, Plaintiff, against Bernt J. Muus, Defendant, January 20, 1883.

[51] Ueland, *Recollections*, 42.

[52] State of Minnesota, County of Hennepin District Court, Oline Muus, Plaintiff, vs. Bernt J. Muus, Defendant, January 20, 1883.

[53] State of Minnesota, County of Hennepin District Court, Oline Muus vs. Bernt J. Muus, January 10, 1883.

[54] *Budstikken* pamphlet, 10, 18.

[55] Oline Muus to H. A. Preus, May 4, 1880, in Luther College Archives.

[56] Ericson, "Triple Jeopardy," 308; Janet E. Rasmussen, "'The Best Place on Earth for Women': The American Experience of Aasta Hansteen," in *Norwegian-American Studies*, 31 (Northfield, Minnesota, 1986), 253; *The Republican*, May 7, 1882.

[57] L.M. Biørn, "Tribute to Pastor Muus," in *Festskrift: Holden Menigheds Jubelfest 1906* (Minneapolis, 1908), 11–12.

## Chapter Twelve

[1] Bjørnstjerne Bjørnson to Karoline Bjørnson, March 3 (?), 1881, *Land of the Free*, 228.

[2] N. [Nils Olson?] Giere, quoted in Hilleboe, *For the sake of their children*; M. O. Bøckman, "Pastor Muus," in *Jul i Vesterheimen* (1914), n.p.

[3] Biørn, "Tribute to Pastor Muus," 8–9.

[4] Oline Muus vs. Bernt J. Muus, State of Minnesota, Hennepin County District Court, January 10, 1883; "Brev fra fru Oline Muus," in *Amerika*, April 5, 1912.

[5] *The Advance*, March 3, 1880; *Norden*, June 2, 1880; *The Republican*, June 3, 1880.

[6] Edel Ytterboe Ayers, *The Old Main* (Anniston, Alabama, 1969), 17.

[7] Ayers, *The Old Main*, 17.

[8] Thrane, "Holden," Act II, Scene 6; Margaret Chrislock Gilseth, *Julia's Children: A Norwegian Immigrant Family in Minnesota* (St. Charles, Minnesota, 1987), 56, 95.

[9] *Budstikken* pamphlet, March 30, 1880, 4–5.

[10] B. J. Muus to Laur. Larsen, September 23, 1881, in Luther College Archives, Decorah, Iowa.

[11] *Budstikken* pamphlet, March 30, 1880, 18; "Brev fra fru Oline Muus."

[12] *Amerika*, April 5, 1912.

[13] Ueland, *Recollections Of An Immigrant*, 42.

[14] Oline Muus to H. A. Preus, May 4, 1880, in Luther College Archives.

[15] Oline Muus to H. A. Preus, April 15, 1880; H. A. Preus to Oline Muus, April 19 and 26, 1880, in Luther College Archives.

[16] Oline Muus to H. A. Preus, ca. April 23, 1880, in Luther College Archives.

[17] Oline Muus to H. A. Preus, May 6, 1880, in Luther College Archives.

[18] Oline Muus Plaintiff against Bernt J. Muus Defendant, State of Minnesota, District Court, County of Hennepin, December 26, 1881. The May 13 and 14, 1880, meetings are reported in *Budstikken*, May 18, and 25, 1880. See also the Goodhue County *Republican*, June 3, 1880.

[19] *Budstikken*, May 18, 1880.

[20] Ueland, *Recollections*, 41.

[21] Curtiss-Wedge, ed., *History of Goodhue County Minnesota*, 326; Rasmussen, *A History of Goodhue County, Minnesota*, 267.

[22] "Menighedsmødet den 14de Mai," in *Budstikken*, May 25, 1880. See also *Norden*, June 2, 1880.

[23] *The Kenyon News*, March 6, 1930.

[24] *Kenyon Leader*, September 26, 1895.

[25] "Fra Mrs. Oline Muus," in *Amerika*, February 23, 1906.

[26] *Amerika*, February 23, 1906.

[27] Rasmussen, *History of Goodhue County*, 267.

[28] "Brev fra fru Oline Muus," April 5, 1912; Nina Draxten, *Kristofer Janson in America* (Boston, 1976), 118, 158–160; Kathryn Ericson, "Triple Jeopardy," 307–308.

[29] *Decorah Posten*, March 13, 1889.

[30] Wilhelm Pettersen, "Fra Alabama," in *Skandinaven*, August 22, 1922.

[31] Lilly Setterdahl, "Scandinavians in Alabama: Migration from the Midwest," in *American Friends of the Emigrant Institute of Sweden, Inc., Memories Preserved*, 2 (East Moline, Illinois, 1992), 77.

[32] Virginia Voss Pope, *Fruithurst: Alabama's Vineyard Village* (2nd ed., Albertville, Alabama, 1975), 28, 34; *Skandinaven*, August 25, 1922.

[33] Oline Muus to Laur. Larsen, March 12, 1905, in Luther College Archives. See also "Brev fra fru Oline Muus," April 5, 1912.

[34] State of Minnesota, County of Hennepin District Court, Oline Muus Plaintiff against Bernt J. Muus Defendant, Deposition of Birgitte Muus before Justice of the Peace John Naeseth, Goodhue county, December 19, 1882.

[35] "Fra Mrs. Oline Muus," February 23, 1906.

[36] Bernt Julius Muus and Alfred Muus, *Niels Muus's æt*, 78.

[37] Wilhelm Pettersen, "Fra Alabama," in *Skandinaven*, August 25, 1922; *Niels Muus's æt*, 77–78.

[38] *Minneapolis Tidende*, January 26, 1933.

[39] Paul G. Schmidt, *My Years at St. Olaf* (Northfield, 1967), 15; St. Olaf Registrar Record, St. Olaf College Archives, Northfield, Minnesota.

[40] B. J. Muus to H. T. Ytterboe, October 3, 1889; March 31, April 10, 26, May 5, October 4, 1890; February 2, June 2, 1891, in Muus Papers, NAHA Archives.

[41] *Niels Muus's æt*, 78–79; Conversation with Bernt Julius Muus, son of Herman Ingebrigt Muus, December 29, 1998.

[42] *Budstikken* pamphlet, March 30, 1880, 16.

[43] State of California, County of Sonoma, "Certificate of Death." Certified Copy issued December 22, 1998.

[44] B. J. Muus to Laur. Larsen, April 21, May 13, 1898, in Luther College Archives.

[45] B. J. Muus to Laur. Larsen, May 8, 1899, in Luther College Archives; File #6662 State of Minnesota, County of Goodhue, "Report of Probate Judge and County Attorney," June 27, 1923. A copy of this report is in the NAHA Archives.

[46] Oline Muus to Bjørnstjerne Bjørnson, July 30, 1899. Photocopy of letter received by Joseph M. Shaw from University Library, Oslo, Norway.

[47] Oline Muus to Bjørnson, July 30, 1899.

[48] Clara Strickland to Erling Kindem, ca. 1979, in Muus Papers, St. Olaf College Archives. See also Ericson, "Triple Jeopardy," 308.

[49] *Who's Who Among Pastors in all the Norwegian Lutheran Synods of America 1843–1927*, 461–462; Orm Øverland, *The Western Home: A Literary History of Norwegian America* (Northfield, Minnesota, 1996), 228–229; Wilhelm Pettersen, "Mrs. Oline Muus død," in *Decorah Posten*, September 11, 1922, in Oline Muus Papers, NAHA Archives.

[50] Nelson and Fevold, *The Lutheran Church Among Norwegian-Americans*, 253.

## Chapter Thirteen

[1] Nelson and Fevold, *The Lutheran Church Among Norwegian-Americans*, 182; Norlie, *et al, Who's Who Among Pastors In All The Norwegian Lutheran Synods of America*, 394.

[2] Lovoll, *Promise of America*, 23, 26; Nydahl, "The Early Norwegian Settlement of Goodhue County, Minnesota," 14.

[3] B. J. Muus, "Kort Oversigt," 73; *Beretning om det Tredie ordentlige Synodemøde af Minnesota Distrikt*, 1880 (Decorah, Iowa, 1880), 17. See also *Holden Through One Hundred Years 1856–1956*, 17.

[4] *Holden Ministerial Book* II, "Geistligt Dagregister," entry for November 28, 1878, 683.

⁵ *Holden Ministerial Book* II, 1877, 677–680.

⁶ *Holden Ministerial Book* II, 1879, 685; "Formandens Synodetale og Indbe-retning," *Beretning ... Minnesota Distrikt*, 1880, 15; "Past. Muus død," obituary in *Decorah-Posten*.

⁷ "Formandens Synodetale og Indberetning," 1880, 7–11.

⁸ "Formandens Synodetale og Indberetning," 1880, 15–17.

⁹ "Anklage mod Pastor Muus," in *Beretning ... Minnesota Distrikt*, 1880, 65.

¹⁰ "Kommitteindstilling angaaende Formandens Synodetale og Indberetning," in *Beretning ... Minnesota Distrikt*, 1880, 18.

¹¹ Cited in Nelson and Fevold, *Lutheran Church among Norwegian-Americans*, 256–257.

¹² The Synodical Conference, organized in 1872, brought together for discussions of church and theological topics representatives of four conservative Lutheran bodies, the Ohio, Missouri, Wisconsin, and Norwegian synods. Nelson and Fevold, *Lutheran Church among Norwegian-Americans*, 182–183. "Formandens Synodetale og Indberetning," 1880, 12; "Past. Muus død."

¹³ "Formandens Synodetale og Indberetning," 1880, 11–14.

¹⁴ "Kommitteindstilling angaaende Formandens Synodetale og Indberetning," 1880, 20–22.

¹⁵ Cited in Nelson and Fevold, *Lutheran Church among Norwegian-Americans*, 259. See also Bergh, *Den norsk lutherske Kirkes Historie i Amerika*, 267.

¹⁶ Belgum, "The Old Norwegian Synod," 395; Nelson and Fevold, *Lutheran Church among Norwegian-Americans*, 258, 260.

¹⁷ *The Formula of Concord*, Thorough Declaration, Article XI, "Of God's Eternal Election," in *Triglot Concordia*, 1065.

¹⁸ Nelson and Fevold, *Lutheran Church among Norwegian-Americans*, 257.

¹⁹ Belgum, "The Old Norwegian Synod," 385.

²⁰ "Nogle Vidnesbyrd af Aegidius Hunnius," in *Lutherske Vidnesbyrd*, I (March 1, 1882), 70; Belgum, "The Old Norwegian Synod," 385–386; Nelson and Fevold, *Lutheran Church among Norwegian-Americans*, 257.

²¹ Fevold, "The History of Norwegian-American Lutheranism, 1870–1890" (Ph. D. dissertation, University of Chicago, 1951), 348–349; B. J. Muus, "Differents mellem Lutheranere og norske Missouriere," in *Lutherske Vidnesbyrd*, 3 (October 1, 1884), 456; "B. J. Muus, Eph. 1:1–4," in *Norden*, December 16, 1884; B. J. Muus, "Rubbish i Synodens Organ, II," in *Norden*, January 27, 1885.

²² B. J. Muus, "Diskussionsmøde i Vestre Norway Lake," in *Norden*, April 1, 1885.

²³ B. J. Muus, "Rubbish i Synodens Organ, III," in *Norden*, April 15, 1885; Fevold, "History of Norwegian-American Lutheranism," 348.

²⁴ *The Union Documents of the Evangelical Lutheran Church* (Minneapolis, 1949), 39.

²⁵ "Referat om vor Udstødelse fra Synodalkonferencens Møde," in *Lutherske Vidnesbyrd*, 1 (December 1, 1882), 354–355; Fevold, "History of Norwegian-American Lutheranism," 338.

²⁶ Nelson and Fevold, *Lutheran Church among Norwegian-Americans*, 264–265; Bergh, *Den norsk lutherske kirkes historie i Amerika*, 268–270.

²⁷ Peer Strømme, *Erindringer* (Minneapolis, 1923), 193–194; Fevold, "History of Norwegian-American Lutheranism," 345.

²⁸ B. J. Muus to President of the Norwegian Synod, June 1, 1884, in Luther College Archives. See B. J. Muus, "Fra Minneapolis," in *Lutherske Vidnesbyrd*, 3 (February 10, 1884), 67–69.

²⁹ Nelson and Fevold, *Lutheran Church among Norwegian-Americans*, 266–267; B. J. Muus, "Luthersk Hjælpecasse," in *Lutherske Vidnesbyrd*, 3 (December 1, 1884), 550–555; Fevold, "History of Norwegian-American Lutheranism," 357.

³⁰ Nelson and Fevold, *Lutheran Church among Norwegian-Americans*, 266–267; H. A. Preus to B. J. Muus, November 15, 1885; B. J. Muus to H. A. Preus, November 29, 1885, in Luther College Archives.

³¹ B. J. Muus, "Luthersk Præsteskole og College," in *Lutherske Vidnesbyrd*, 5 (August 1, 1886), 365; "Mødet i Northfield," *Lutherske Vidnesbyrd*, 6 (July 10, 1887), 358–361.

³² St. Olaf College, *Minutes of Board of Trustees Meetings*, Book No. 1, 54–55, June 20, 1889.

³³ Benson, *High on Manitou*, 55–56; Bergh, *Den norsk lutherske kirkes historie i Amerika*, 270–271.

³⁴ Nelson, *The Lutheran Church Among Norwegian-Americans* (Minneapolis, 1960), II, 23–26; Belgum, "The Old Norwegian Synod," 415.

³⁵ Benson, *High on Manitou*, 57.

³⁶ L. M. Biørn, Tribute to Muus, in *Festskrift*, 12; B. J. Muus, "Luthersk Præsteskole og College," 364.

³⁷ Fevold, "History of Norwegian-American Lutheranism," 363–364.

## Chapter Fourteen

¹ B. J. Muus, "Diskussionsmøde i Vestre Norway Lake," in *Norden*, April 18, 1885.

² "Past. Muus død," *Decorah Posten*, June, 1990, in NAHA Archives.

³ Leigh D. Jordahl, "Centennial Article: F. A. Schmidt," in *Luther Theological Seminary Review*, 8 (November, 1969), 26.

⁴ Benson, *High on Manitou*, 24–25, 27; Th. N. Mohn to F. N. Sanborn, November 28, 1888, in NAHA Archives.

⁵ *The Manitou Messenger*, 8 (November, 1894), 119.

⁶ St. Olaf College, *Minutes of Board of Trustees Meetings*, Book No. 1, June 20, 1889. See Benson, *High on Manitou*, 59.

⁷ Eggen, "Erindringer om pastor Muus," 58.

⁸ Nelson, *The Lutheran Church Among Norwegian-Americans*, 19–20.

⁹ Benson, *High on Manitou*, 76.

¹⁰ Ellestad, "Pastor Bernt Julius Muus: Et Minde," 585; Nelson, *The Lutheran Church Among Norwegian-Americans*, 79–81; Benson, *High on Manitou*, 93.

¹¹ Muus to H. T. Ytterboe, May 7, 1893, May 17, 1896, in St. Olaf College Archives.

¹² *The Manitou Messenger*, 7 (December, 1893), 134.

¹³ *The Manitou Messenger*, 8 (November, 1894), 116–120.

¹⁴ Examples are Muus to U. V. Koren, May 13, 1890, January 23, 1891; Koren to Muus, February 18, 1891, March 9, 1891, in Luther College Archives.

¹⁵ Ellestad, "Pastor Bernt Julius Muus," 585.

[16] Muus to Preus, March 14, 1888, August 13, 1888, in Luther College Archives.

[17] Muus, "Driv Splittelsens Aand ud!" Published Lecture (Minneapolis, 1893), 3, 6–7.

[18] Bergh, *Den norsk lutherske Kirkes Historie i Amerika*, 417–430.

[19] *Beretning, Minnesota Distrikt*, 1896, 116–118.

[20] "Past. Muus's Sag," *Beretning, Minnesota Distrikt*, 1898, 130–131.

[21] "Past. Muus's Sag," 1898, 133–134.

[22] "Past. Muus's Sag," 1898, 137–138.

[23] "Past. Muus's Sag," 1898, 141.

[24] Biørn, "Tribute to Pastor Muus," in *Festskrift*, 12.

[25] Eggen, "Erindringer om pastor Muus," 59.

[26] Biørn, "Tribute to Pastor Muus," 8, 10; Simundson, "Rev. B. J. Muus As I Learned To Know Him."

[27] Ellestad, *Pastor Bernt Julius Muus*, 585.

[28] "Past. Muus død," *Decorah Posten*, June, 1900.

[29] Biørn, "Tribute to Pastor Muus," 10; Boral R. Biørn, "A Biography of Ludvig M. Biørn," Unpublished typescript (Mesa, Arizona, 1989), 75.

[30] Bøckman, "Pastor Muus."

[31] Biørn, "Tribute to Pastor Muus," 8.

[32] Biørn, "Tribute to Pastor Muus," 8; Simundson address, "Rev. B. J. Muus."

[33] Birgitte Muus Klüver to I. F. Grose, cited in I. F. Grose, "The Beginnings of St. Olaf College," *Norwegian-American Studies and Records*, 5 (Northfield, 1930), 115–116.

[34] Simundson address.

[35] Cited in Nydahl, "The Early Norwegian Settlement of Goodhue County, Minnesota," Nydahl's source is Colbein Jacobsen. "Pastor Muus og Afholds-sagen," in *Nordstjernen*, 3 (August 6, 1897), 13.

[36] Eggen, "Erindringer," 63.

[37] Simundson address; "Den første Skolemester i Goodhue County," *Decorah Posten*, August 2, 1940.

[38] P. O. Floan, "Reminiscences of the Early History of Singing in Holden Congregation, Goodhue County, Minnesota," Unpublished typescript, St. Paul, Minnesota, 1938.

[39] *Norden*, January-April, 1885; Simundson address.

[40] Muus to Ytterboe, April 10, 1890, in St. Olaf College Archives.

[41] *The Manitou Messenger*, 13 (March, 1899), 52–53.

[42] Simundson address.

[43] Muus to Larsen, May 8, 1899, in Luther College Archives.

[44] Simundson address.

[45] *The Manitou Messenger*, 13 (November, 1899), 141; Muus letter to Mrs. Th. N. Mohn cited in Benson, *High on Manitou*, 108.

[46] *Kenyon Leader*, May 31, 1900. Information received by Harald Muus from his sister, Birgitte Klüver.

[47] J. N. Kildahl, "Lidt om Pastor Muus's Endeligt," in *Lutheraneren*, 6 (August 29, 1900), 586–587.

# Index